Capital-in-Crisis, Trade Unionism and the Question of Revolutionary Agency

Capital-in-Crisis, Trade Unionism and the Question of Revolutionary Agency

Shaun May

PETER LANG
Oxford • Bern • Berlin • Bruxelles • New York • Wien

Bibliographic information published by Die Deutsche Nationalbibliothek.
Die Deutsche Nationalbibliothek lists this publication in the Deutsche
Nationalbibliografie; detailed bibliographic data is available on the Internet
at http://dnb.d-nb.de.

A catalogue record for this book is available from the British Library.

Library of Congress Control Number: 2018933752

Cover design by Peter Lang Ltd.

ISBN 978-1-78874-115-6 (print) • ISBN 978-1-78874-116-3 (ePDF)
ISBN 978-1-78874-117-0 (ePub) • ISBN 978-1-78874-118-7 (mobi)

© Peter Lang AG 2018

Published by Peter Lang Ltd, International Academic Publishers,
52 St Giles, Oxford, OX1 3LU, United Kingdom
oxford@peterlang.com, www.peterlang.com

Shaun May has asserted his right under the Copyright, Designs and
Patents Act, 1988, to be identified as Author of this Work.

All rights reserved.
All parts of this publication are protected by copyright.
Any utilisation outside the strict limits of the copyright law, without
the permission of the publisher, is forbidden and liable to prosecution.
This applies in particular to reproductions, translations, microfilming,
and storage and processing in electronic retrieval systems.

This publication has been peer reviewed.

Rise, like lions after slumber
In unvanquishable number!
Shake your chains to earth like dew
Which in sleep had fallen on you:
Ye are many – they are few!

— SHELLEY
The Masque of Anarchy

O gentlemen, the time of life is short!
To spend that shortness basely were too long,
If life did ride upon a dial's point,
Still ending at the arrival of an hour.
An if we live, we live to tread on kings;
If die, brave death, when princes die with us!
Now, for our consciences, the arms are fair,
When the intent of bearing them is just.

— SHAKESPEARE
Henry IV, Part I, Act 5, Scene 2

Contents

Preface to the First Edition — xi

Preface to the Second Edition — xvii

CHAPTER 1
Introduction: 'Practical Critical Activity' and the Conception of Revolutionary Agency — 1

PART I Globalizing Capital-in-Crisis — 13

CHAPTER 2
The Altered Character of Capital's Crisis — 15

CHAPTER 3
A Century of Lenin's *Imperialism* — 39

CHAPTER 4
On Changes in the Proletariat with Capitalist Globalization and the Need for a Critique of Marx's Conception of the Proletariat — 55

CHAPTER 5
The Impact of Capital-in-Crisis on Nature — 71

CHAPTER 6
The Trajectory of Trade Unionism under Capital's Unfolding Structural Crisis — 93

CHAPTER 7

Capital's Offensive against Social Provision   117

PART II   Impasse and Outmodedness:
The Twilight of the Trade Unions   137

CHAPTER 8

The Organization of the Proletariat under Cyclical and Structural Forms of Capital's Crisis   139

CHAPTER 9

Labour's Growing Crisis of Organization   163

PART III   Breaking Out of the 'Bottleneck' of Historically Limited, Self-Subsistent Trade Union Organization   191

CHAPTER 10

'Socialist Pluralism' and the Conception of the 'Social Union'   193

CHAPTER 11

From Trade Unions Towards the Formation of 'Social Unions'?   217
  [i] The Struggle for Democracy within the Trade Unions   217
  [ii] The Case of UNITE's 'Community Membership' Initiative   224
  [iii] Transitional Proposals and a 'SUM' within and outside Trade Unionism?   228
  [iv] The Social Union as the Revolutionary Democracy of the Class Movement of the Proletariat   235

CHAPTER 12

The Social Union as Revolutionary Agency against the Capital Order   245

[i]	The Universality of Capital's Structural Crisis Drives the Conflict between the 'Social Unions' and 'Capital in Power'	245
[ii]	Long Term Objectives: From Free-Market to Market-Free Zones	255
[iii]	On Means and Ends in the Revolutionary Strategy of Agency	260
[iv]	By Peaceful Means if Possible	266
[v]	Restructuring the 'Social Metabolism' beyond Capital	273
[vi]	Restructuring and the Economic Parameters of the Capital Order	275
[vii]	Restructuring and the State Power of Capital	283
[viii]	Necessary Mutability of the Forms of Revolutionary Agency	289

PART IV The Question of Revolutionary Agency in the Twentieth Century   299

CHAPTER 13

Lenin and the Question of Revolutionary Agency   301

[i]	Lenin's Ahistorical 'Appeal to the Model Character of the Russian Revolution'	301
[ii]	From the Temporally Conditioned Strategy of Lenin's *What is to be Done?* in 1901 to the Ideologically Posited Internationalized Statutes of the *Comintern* in 1920	310
[iii]	The 'Intelligentsia', the 'Origin Myth' of Socialism and 'Consciousness from the Outside'	319

CHAPTER 14

Trotsky's *Transitional Programme*, the 'Bolshevist-Leninist' Approach to Trade Unionism and the Demise of the Sectarian Politics of the 'Revolutionary Left'   331

CHAPTER 15

A Critique of 'Vanguardism' and the 'Party-Form'   351

Appendices 373

APPENDIX I
Marx's Realms: Capital, Natural Necessity, True Realm of Freedom 375
1. Hegel, Marx and 'Freedom and Necessity' 375
2. Realm of Global Capital 380
3. A Note on Human Individuality in the Epoch of Capital 392
4. Moving Against and Beyond Capital: Realm of Natural Necessity and True Realm of Freedom 396

APPENDIX II
The Broadcasting and Print Media: In the Ideological Service of Capital and its State Power 419

APPENDIX III
Whatever Happened to the 'National Liberation Struggle'? 423

Bibliography 429

Index 439

Preface to the First Edition

The birth of this work on revolutionary agency has been long and somewhat difficult; the outcome of many years of reading, observation, political activity and experience, struggles, conflicts and lessons drawn since my youth. However, there are two fundamental strands woven together in its inception and development: the emergence and unfolding of capital's structural crisis since the 1970s and the impact of this crisis on the traditional forms of organization of the proletariat, specifically trade unionism.

This latter has been clearly manifest in the downwards trajectory which trade unionism has taken since the early 1980s up to the present day and is continuing to take. An attempt to understand the relationship between capital's crisis and this trajectory has led me on to a consideration of the question of revolutionary agency as capital's crisis must inevitably widen and deepen in consequence of its endogenously structural character.

My own activities – as a trade unionist and socialist down the decades – and experiences, observations and studies in the course of this, have served as a source of conceptions in regard to the character of trade unionism in different periods of its historic development. However, the major theoretical influences, specifically on the question of capital's crisis, in the writing of the book have been Marx, of course, and the work of István Mészáros to which I am deeply indebted on a theoretical level. Moreover, without my lifelong, and at times somewhat tortuous studies of Hegel, I could not have approached the elaboration of the content of the work with what I consider to be the requisite degree of intellectual discipline and method furnished by dialectics. Marx, of course, always acknowledged his intellectual debt to Hegel. And 200 years after the publication of the *Science of Logic*, many thinkers are still working with the altered legacies of that mighty thinker.

Without a study – over the past twenty years – of the work of Mészáros, this work would not have been possible. Specifically, his groundbreaking work *Beyond Capital* has been fundamentally influential in this regard. In the course of developing my argument, I have drawn heavily on his writings and for that he has my acknowledgements and gratitude.

The most essential, theoretically grounding and animating category in the book is that of 'structural crisis' which has been developed by Mészáros in his work over the decades. This constitutes the foundation for addressing the question of revolutionary agency. But we must not ignore the simple truth that the conception of 'structural crisis' is to be *found implicit* in Marx and especially in his work in Volume 3 of *Capital* and in the *Grundrisse*.

The great theoretical and political service which Mészáros has done for the class movement of the proletariat is to make this structural character of capital's crisis *explicit*, to bring it out and develop it for the conditions of the existence and rule of capital in the twenty-first century. Theoretically implicit in Marx, it starts to become actualized in the final quarter of the twentieth century and it is Mészáros who acts as the agent for its theoretical and political articulation. He works to provide us with an understanding of it as it starts to unfold in the last four decades.

This 'structural crisis' stands as a qualitatively different and higher form of capital's crisis. The old 'boom and bust', 'conjunctural' phase of cyclical crises is over. The significance and ramifications of this for the old, traditional, 'defensive' forms of organization of the proletariat are profound. It must mean a growing crisis for these previously established forms, more suited to the old 'pre-structural' conditions. It points the way to a fork in the road of human history for these organizations. Either transform or perish.

Accordingly, a major intention of the writing of this book has been to try to provide a provisional theoretical and political framework within which the question of revolutionary agency can be addressed, can be examined, evaluated, questioned, disputed, developed and even rejected. It is not the author's design or intention – conscious or otherwise – to present a *pronunciamento*. All conceptions developed in the text are provisional and disputable in the spirit of dialectics, anti-doctrinairism and anti-positivism. Ultimately, it is the 'real movement', the unfolding life-process and practically articulated experiences and consciousness of the proletarian class movement as a whole in struggle against capital and its state power which determines the degree of 'historical adequacy' of any conceptions of 'revolutionary agency'. The truth and relative adequacies and limitations of such conceptions are demonstrated (and reaffirmed or negated) in real life, in practice, not on the page, as the ultimate 'criterion of truth' (Lenin). The book is, therefore, a political and, unavoidably, a polemical document which, of course, does not discount its use and application by the academic community.

The author sincerely hopes that the work may also be deployed in this respect, despite its somewhat 'popular' format, and, indeed, attract the attention of progressive academics and students in higher education. The book is levelled, primarily and specifically, at a trade unionist readership but hopefully may invite the interest of those 'on the left' in general and broadly the 'anti-capitalist movement'. However, I have endeavoured, unashamedly, to present a text where the terminology, simplicity and directness of 'written word' makes it accessible to as wide a readership as possible without compromising the actual content.

The work attempts to address the question of revolutionary agency in the twenty-first century – based on the work of both Marx and Mészáros – within the locus of the old, 'defensive' 'universal historic form' of proletarian organization; namely, located within the trade union form itself.

Trade unionism remains a movement with many millions of members across the world and still the dominant form of organization of the class movement of the proletariat globally, despite its decline over the last four decades. The concept of 'structural crisis' is developed in its relation to the current tendencies of development of trade unionism and how this relates to the potential for the whole labour movement to move forward to new, historically more 'adequate and concrete' forms of agency for the age of capital's structural crisis.

The conception of the 'Social Union' form – as eclipsing the trade union form – emerges, dialectically, out of the antecedent development in the text. This prior content seeks to address many questions being posed about the trajectory of trade unionism as the epoch of capital's structural crisis develops and intensifies globally and, specifically, the social needs of the proletariat as a whole class (not simply its employed, workplace-based section) with the unfolding of the coming century.

A major, and I think significant, weakness in Mészáros has been the absence of a coherent, concentrated and concrete formulation of the question of 'revolutionary agency'. I attempt to locate this question of agency on the theoretical basis of his conception of 'structural crisis' but, necessarily, within the 'gravity and orbit' of the temporally existent and major organizational form of the class movement of the proletariat i.e. within trade unionism and its attendant forms of consciousness.

The evolving relationship between this deepening structural crisis of the capital order and the traditional organizations of the proletariat – founded under different 'conjunctural' and 'defensive' conditions – is analysed in the text. This analysis proceeds to implicate the conception of 'outmodedness' within trade unionism itself which was created and developed under past, dead conditions and is now confronted with the qualitatively different conditions of the structural crisis of the capital order globally. This relation (interaction, dialectics) between the new conditions and the old forms of workplace-based organization then raises the question of new forms of agency necessary to mobilize against and go beyond the capital order.

By way of an introduction, the first chapter of the book is pre-occupied with method of approach to the whole question of revolutionary agency. Here I draw on the work of Marx and Engels in the 1840s and especially the *Theses on Feuerbach*. Part I of the text focuses on 'globalizing capital' as a crisis-process. The altered character of capital's crisis is then compared to its crises in previous periods and the epoch of 'globalizing capital' is analyzed against the backdrop of Lenin's early twentieth-century conception of 'Imperialism'.

This takes the discourse on to the ways in which the emergence of capitalist globalization has altered the social and occupational composition and character of the proletariat globally which calls for a critique of Marx's conception of the proletariat in order to inform the question of revolutionary agency. After a chapter on the impact of capital-in-crisis on nature, the analysis seeks to grapple with the immediate and direct social manifestations of this crisis in terms of its impact on trade unionism itself and on social provision ('public services') under capital's offensive arising out of this structural crisis. I try to grapple with the way this qualitatively higher form of capital's crisis has altered the approach of trade unionism to capital itself and its state power, giving illustrations from both Britain and the United States.

Part II of the book takes a more detailed and involved look at the relationship between the structural crisis of capital, its emergence and development over the last four decades, and the path which trade unionism has taken. And how the way the proletariat has responded in its relationship with capital under the determinately different 'cyclical' and 'structural' forms of capital's crisis. This passes over into a consideration of labour's growing crisis of organization which must necessarily arise out of the widening, deepening and intensification of the character of capital's 'structural crisis'. We arrive at the conception of the traditional organizations of the proletariat in the 'bottleneck of history' and self-subsistent, conservative, hierarchically structured trade unionism as a historically outmoded form of proletarian organization.

Part III of the text: breaking out of this 'bottleneck of history'. The introductory chapter here is to move into an understanding of the idea of 'socialist pluralism' found in Mészáros and deploy this to derive the 'preliminary notion' and perspective of the 'Social Union' as a higher form of unionism vis-à-vis trade unionism. The conception of 'dialectical negation and return' is important here. The 'fractal' relationship between trade union and social union.

The discourse then evolves into the realm of considering the potential movement from trade unions towards social unions, the struggle for democracy within the trade unions, an example in Britain of a prefigurative attempt to expand trade unionism beyond its workplace boundaries, transitional proposals to move beyond trade unionism and how the 'Social Union' could constitute itself as the revolutionary democracy of the class movement of the proletariat. Finally, in this third section, the 'Social Union' as the initial instrument (form of revolutionary agency) for the proletariat to mobilize against the capital order and its state powers and global agencies is examined in its different yet interconnected aspects.

Part IV is wholly concerned with a detailed historical consideration of the question of revolutionary agency in the twentieth century. Chapter 13 investigates Lenin's conceptions and the limits of those conceptions today under conditions of structural crisis. Chapters 14 and 15 consider and critique the work of Trotsky's Fourth International, its sectarianism, vanguardism and its formulaic approach to trade unionism. The final chapter also contains a critique of the 'Party form'.

Finally, I have added three appendices which I think are relevant to the major body of the text. 'Marx's Realms' which gives a broad conception of the epoch of capital and the basic characteristics of that which will replace it once capital is transcended in the course of the 'transitional period'. This appendix has been included to further inform the reader of what is simultaneously being 'fought for' and 'fought against'. Appendix II focuses on the role of capital's media in the age of its structural crisis and the final appendix is a retrospective on the 'national liberation struggle'.

I would like to thank the staff at Peter Lang for making the publication of this work possible, especially Lucy Melville, Jasmin Allousch and Emma Clarke. The advice offered by Craig Phelan (School of Economics, Politics and History, Kingston University London and Editor for the Peter Lang series 'Trade Unions: Past, Present and Future') regarding the internal structuring of text was invaluable and served in the presentation of a more publishable manuscript. I would also like to take this opportunity to thank the Brynmor Jones Library at the University of Hull for giving me access to its probably unrivalled collection of socialist literature in the course of my studies down the years.

Finally, I am indebted to the many socialists and trade unionists with whom I have had discussions on the question of revolutionary agency over the past twenty years and before. A 'little piece' of each of them is to be found in the pages of this book. The final word, of course, must go to Marx. In reading this book, my recommendation is, as always, 'doubt everything'.

Shaun May, Hull, October 2016

Preface to the Second Edition

The second edition now stands independently of the Peter Lang series (Trade Unions: Past, Present and Future) as a separately published text. The detail and discourse of the content have been expanded with a more developed argument and discussion of its themes and theses. Furthermore, additional quoted material has been introduced into the main body of the text and into the notes sections in order to give a fuller, more elaborated explanation and referencing of content. In the first edition, this material was merely cited within the notes sections or cited internally within the body of the text. It has now been inserted for the convenience of the reader who does not have to refer to the specific references unless they simply remain cited as previously in the first edition. This is intended to serve to improve the detailed continuity and 'flow' of the discourse. Otherwise, on the whole, the content and major animating themes of the work remain essentially the same as in the first Peter Lang edition.

Shaun May, Hull, November 2017
On the Centennial of the Russian Revolution

CHAPTER 1

Introduction: 'Practical Critical Activity' and the Conception of Revolutionary Agency

'The question whether objective truth can be attributed to human thinking is not a question of theory but is a practical question. Man must prove the truth – i.e. the reality and power, the this-sidedness of his thinking in practice. The dispute over the reality or non-reality of thinking that is isolated from practice is a purely scholastic question.'[1]

We commence with the second of Marx's *Theses on Feuerbach* because an understanding of it here vitally informs the approach to the *historically precedent* question today for the survival of humankind: the question of revolutionary agency. The primary historical, and therefore theoretical, ground of this question is capital-in-crisis – what Mészáros refers to as the 'structural crisis of capital'[2] – and the relationship of the currently prevailing stage of political organization of the proletariat to this deepening crisis. Most students of Marx would readily concede the second thesis here on a *formal theoretical* level. They acknowledge its truth *formally*. However, and this is absolutely fundamental to the question of agency, it is quite a different matter to *integrate* Marx's incredibly profound thought here into a method of approach in the theoretical development of their work on revolutionary agency.

Does a conception of revolutionary agency truthfully *and actively* reflect the real, historically specific conditions in which a class, with its organizations and mediating forms of consciousness finds itself today? Does that conception actually address and serve to meet the real, practical needs of that class under those conditions? Does it (or does it have the potential to) 'grip the masses' as a 'material force' and serve as the 'realization of their needs'?

In order for any conception of agency to find roots and grow, it must be located within the life of the class movement of the proletariat; what Marx refers to as the 'real movement'[3] which, presently, is based on the trade unions. The addressing of the needs of this 'real movement' becomes the measure of the historic validity of any conception of revolutionary agency. To discount this presupposition is to 'speak over the heads' of the class movement of the proletariat. It is to posit a conception *contemplatively* as a 'rationalistic response' to the unfolding structural crisis of the capital order. To locate the question of revolutionary agency in 'the form of the object' and not 'subjectively' as existent 'sensuous practice'.

This unfolding and *necessarily deepening* structural crisis of capital does, of course, constitute the broad historical ground within which the need for new, *offensive* forms of agency asserts itself. These forms in and for themselves must be actually created by the proletariat in struggle. At the present stage, the proletariat is confronted by this crisis as it is currently organized 'within the framework of the existing institutions of the working class' (Mészáros, *Beyond Capital*, pp. 937–938). These conditions of deepening structural crisis will not 'spontaneously' generate the required forms of revolutionary agency which are historically adequate to move onto the offensive against capital. Once again, we turn to Marx's *Theses on Feuerbach*. In the struggle for the necessary (historically adequate) organizational forms of revolutionary agency, we are compelled to note that ...

> The materialist doctrine concerning the changing of circumstances and upbringing forgets that circumstances are changed by men and that it is essential to educate the educator himself. This doctrine must, therefore, divide society into two parts, one of which is superior to society. The coincidence of the changing of circumstances and of human activity or self-changing can be conceived and rationally understood only as revolutionary practice. (Marx, Theses on Feuerbach, III)

Marx here refers to a one-sidedly, deterministic and non-dialectical conception of materialism as we find amongst the French and English philosophers of the seventeenth and eighteenth centuries. He is drawing our attention to the truth that humanity is simultaneously both the creation and creator of its conditions of life and not simply a passive, 'dumb' and obedient creation and *tabula rasa* 'victim' of these impressing conditions. And that humanity can only create under the conditions with which it is confronted and which previous generations have created and passed down. The focus here is *activity under these confronting conditions*. The pivotal question is where the 'real movement' 'lives' at the historical moment, i.e. what are its moving, determining characteristics and relations at the current stage of the impact of the evolution of global capital-in-crisis on the life of the proletariat as a class.

Accordingly, any theory of revolutionary agency can only serve to orientate in activity if it is in direct communion with the current stage of what Marx refers to as 'the real movement'. This, in itself, means that it must be animated by and developed through and in relation to this 'real movement'. If a conception of agency has no real relation to this actual living movement then it becomes detached and stands in an *abstract* relation to this movement. In this 'confrontation', it can actually take on a 'sectarian', even 'alien', character because it is uninvolved with this 'real movement'. Moreover, this 'organic' relationship of a given conception of revolutionary agency to the 'real movement' implies a comprehensive grasp of the changed character of capital's crisis today and what this means for the future of humanity.

The *general* trajectory of development of capital-in-crisis can, of course, be understood but not in all the multiplicity and particularity of its unfolding detail and social expression. Luxemburg's maxim of 'Socialism or Barbarism' (*Junius Pamphlet*, 1916) is a clear manifestation of this when she boldly states that a system based on capital is inherently one of developing 'barbarism'. In this regard, in connection to the question of agency, if we can grasp the general tendencies of development of global capital-in-structural-crisis, then we can also orientate ourselves theoretically and politically in consonance with these tendencies. And, moreover, this understanding becomes absolutely pivotal in terms of the elaboration of any conception of agency, its nature, articulations, etc.

A conception of revolutionary agency must be founded on an understanding of these 'general tendencies of development' whilst being able to identify how these developments impact the traditional organizations of the proletariat, throwing them into their very own growing 'structural' crisis which reveals their historic inadequacy for both the immediate tasks and long term aims now confronting the proletariat. The conception needs to explain why there is a growing crisis within trade unionism and, moreover, indicate possible ways out of the impasse.

In other words, the whole conception must be a 'practical conscious' conception and not one passively divorced from the reality of people's lives. This is precisely why the most fundamental categories of this book are 'capital-in-structural-crisis' and 'trade unionism' and the relationship between them. Ultimately, the strengths and inadequacies of a conception of revolutionary agency are revealed, developed and superseded in the course of the activity of the class movement of the proletariat and the evaluation and 'lessons' of the results of this activity. They become subject to the practical, transforming self-criticism of such a movement.

When Marx writes of the 'real movement' he does not exempt this 'real movement' from the criteria developed in his *Theses on Feuerbach*. Quite the contrary, they apply no less to the 'real movement' itself. And that was the essential purpose of their formulation by Marx himself. To try to grasp and articulate the question of revolutionary agency in terms of the 'real movement' is to avoid approaching the question 'in the form of the object or of contemplation' and, on the contrary, to posit it in the form of 'sensuous human activity, practice'. That is, to pose it in terms of the 'subject of history', of the activity of this subject in its organization and consciousness. Marx's *Theses* directly impact the historically precedent question of revolutionary agency today. Hence the famous final thesis ...

> The philosophers have only interpreted the world, in various ways; the point is to change it. (Theses on Feuerbach, XI)

Epistemologically, analysis must start with global capital-in-crisis as the confronting whole and, specifically, with the *altered character* of capital's crisis from *cyclical conjunctural to enduring structural* as Mészáros correctly develops it in *Beyond Capital*.[4] This must move analysis on to a consideration of the changed occupational structure and social composition of the proletariat which implicates a critique of Marx's conception of the proletariat itself. The relationship between the intensifying structural crisis of the capital relation and this altered proletariat then leads, dialectically, onto the question of revolutionary agency and an examination of the present stage at which the proletariat finds itself in terms of its organization. We *cannot* start from the proletariat itself. That would be putting the proverbial 'cart before the horse'. The changes which have taken place over recent decades – especially those in the proletariat as a class – have been mediated by capitalist 'globalization' and the emergence of the structural crisis of the capital order.

We progress to the impact of 'globalization' and capital's crisis on the proletarian class in terms of its organization and consciousness. How have alterations in its occupational structure and social composition mediated and altered its traditional organization (trade unionism) and consciousness? What are its tendencies of development in terms of organization as a result of these mediations and impacts? How, therefore, does the proletariat now engage under the conditions of the structural crisis of capital in terms of its traditional mass organizations, viz trade unionism? How has the deepening of capital's crisis revealed, and is increasingly revealing, the historical limitations of trade unionism? Can we establish more adequate, higher forms of agency under these altered conditions of capital's global structural crisis? What are the conflicts being introduced into the body of trade unionism by capital-in-crisis? How are these conflicts driving the tendency towards higher forms of agency which are more adequate (fit for purpose under radically altered historical conditions) and suited for the struggles now emerging and to emerge under the changing conditions of capital's enduring structural crisis?

The development of a conception of higher forms of agency must endeavour to inform what the proletariat in its current mass organizations across the globe (trade unions) actually does in terms of a 'practical-conscious' orientation in conditions of structural crisis. Of course, it cannot 'proclaim and dictate' in the expectation that the class movement will 'dance to the tune'. But it must, at least in good faith, seek to inform and orientate as regards struggles present and future.

Any conception of revolutionary agency must be derived and located in the midst of where the proletarian class is today in terms of its mass organizations but, indispensably, within the changing conditions of capital's structural crisis and the developmental tendencies of these mass proletarian organizations. Conflicts *within* the trade unions – introduced or exacerbated by, and expressing, the deepening of capital's global crisis – can only sharpen as this crisis unfolds in the course of the twenty-first century. This will bring into relief the limitations of the trade union *form* under conditions of capital's structural crisis and, moreover, possibly provide the grounds for moving forward to a form of unionism which is not simply workplace-based. The intensification of capital's crisis as the century unfolds must, inevitably, become expressed within the body of trade unionism in the form of *'crisis of organization'*.

Hence, any conception of revolutionary agency must become 'relevant' and articulable to and within the *real life of the movement* of the class facing the deepening crisis and must be accessible by the proletariat in terms of the experiences which it makes as its trade unions (and other 'social movements') are impacted by the worsening structural crisis of the capitalist order.

A conception – to be fruitful – must not only help to orientate (not simply for the 'revolutionary') a whole movement. It must also serve to explain the experiences being made by the proletariat in the crisis of its own class organizations generated by the intensifying chaos of the capitalist order. Therefore, a theory of revolutionary agency *must* meet the proletariat where it is now at this historical moment (juncture) in terms of its mass organizations (trade unions) and related stage of consciousness. If the conception does not actually *seek to engage* with the real life and experiences of millions of people, then what use is it? Only on this basis can a theory of agency make itself available to address both the immediate and long term objectives of the 'real movement'.

Accordingly, in relation to trade unionism, a theory of revolutionary agency must incorporate a conception of the origins, historical evolution and the current tendencies of development of trade unionism in the age of the structural crisis of global capital. Specifically, that trade unionism originated and developed in the course of two centuries of capitalist expansion with intermittent conjunctural and displaceable cyclical crises of the capitalist order. The qualitative change in the nature of these crises into an enduring, universal structural crisis for the whole global capitalist order necessarily brings in its wake a profound 'crisis of organization' for trade unionism itself.

In Britain, trade unionism reached its 'high tide' with the historic miners' strike in 1984–1985. This was a watershed in its historical development in Britain. It is no accident that the defeat of the miners – the most 'militant' section of the organized workers' movement in Britain – took place against the background of the emergent structural crisis of capital as it started to unfold in the 1980s. The urgent question now facing the proletariat is how does it move forward – with all the historically imposed limits of its organization and consciousness – towards new forms of agency as the structural crisis of capital deepens? In other words, how to begin to transcend these limits?

For Marx, history was a living process and that is how he approached it in his work. He did not approach it as if it was 'something that had happened' and then had to be 'rationally debated and explained'. He did not approach the events of his time in the 'form of the object' but as 'sensuous human practice ... as activity ... subjectively' in relation to the human needs of the 'subject of history'. His critique was 'engaged' with the 'real movement' and not 'contemplative'. It is a critique to inform and orientate people in their activity to transform the world of capital into one beyond it. This is how we need to approach our critique of trade unionism within the conditions of capital's worsening structural crisis. A critique which references and orientates within existing, living conditions.

Marx's critical approach is not the approach of a form of philosophical rationalism. As if the object of the critique is merely a question or problem that needs to be answered or solved or a description of events that 'need to be explained'. His method of approach always involved and implicated the question of the real, living struggles of the day and their orientation in terms of perspectives in order to further the interests of the proletariat in the struggle to end the rule of capital. Surely this is the essence of Marx's final thesis: *'The philosophers have only interpreted the world, in various ways; The point is to change it'.*

Critique must be alive with the concerns and problems of the day in order to inform activity and struggle. Otherwise it presents itself with a 'detached, contemplative' character. Marx's criticism (*the 'critique of critical criticism*') in the 1840s was directed at criticism that was 'purely critical'. What emerged from this critique by both Marx and Engels was its *revolutionary content*.

In his writings on the great events of his time, Marx was elaborating his critique to inform and orientate people in their political activity. For example, if we look at *The Class Struggles in France: 1848 to 1850*, *The Eighteenth Brumaire of Louis Bonaparte* and *The Civil War in France*, we can see almost instantaneously this revolutionary critique of unfolding events. There is nothing 'dry', 'historicistic' or 'objectivist' in his approach.[5] Rather, in these texts, there is a real living engagement with the life and vitality of the struggles of the day and, critically, how the lessons of those struggles could inform present and future work.

His approach was rooted in his 'Critique of Critical Criticism' in the 1840s, i.e. in his critique of a criticism which is simply critically orientated and divorced from engagement with 'real life' and the organizations of the proletariat and their unfolding conditions of development. In essence, this is Marx contra 'objective conditions' (and 'objective historiography') or contra the doctrine of objectivism. It is Marx recognizing existent and mediating conditions whilst simultaneously putting forward a strategic line of march for engagement, for 'activity'. Such an approach must inform our approach to the question of revolutionary agency today. It is the relationship between the intensification of capital's global structural crisis and the trade unions (which remain the major political institutions of the proletariat globally) which forms the ground upon which the question is addressed in this book. This is a major theme pursued in the text.

For this is where the proletariat exists at this historical stage in terms of organization and consciousness as capital's crisis inevitably deepens. The following critique, accordingly, grapples with and references – and orientates people within – the existing, living conditions. The animating method of approach is not that of a form of philosophical rationalism, a mere detached contemplation. The object of the critique is not merely a series of questions that need to be solved. Neither is it simply describing and re-presenting events that 'need to be explained'. The main purpose is to inform and orientate in activity within the mass organizations of the proletariat, specifically within the trade unions.

All conceptions regarding agency can only be truly 'tested' and developed in the course of the unfolding of capital's global crisis and in the living struggle of the proletariat in relation to it. Such conceptions are not 'prescriptions' or 'predictions'. They are attempts (subject to alteration – even dismissal – as the crisis unfolds) to grapple with how we now proceed organizationally as a class under the altered conditions. However, they are not a 'doctor's prescription' as to *how we must now proceed* in terms of organization. Overshadowing this *contingent character* of conceptions of revolutionary agency is Marx's conception that ideas of revolution only grip and animate the lives of millions of people when these ideas are consonant with their real living experiences and when they actually address their needs which arise out of this collective experience ...

> The weapon of criticism cannot, of course, replace criticism by weapons, material force must be overthrown by material force; but theory also becomes a material force as soon as it has gripped the masses. Theory is capable of gripping the masses as soon as it demonstrates ad hominem, and it demonstrates ad hominem as soon as it becomes radical. To be radical is to grasp the root of the matter. But for man the root is man himself.[6]

And later ...

> For revolutions require a passive element, a material basis. Theory can be realized in a people only insofar as it is the realization of the needs of that people.[7]

In the theory of revolutionary agency, it is essentially a question of whether or not its conceptions 'grip the masses' (or contain the potential to do so) so that 'ad hominem' they become the 'realization of their needs'. A theory of revolutionary agency can only find a home in the class movement of the proletariat when it serves to realize its historic needs as a class. In so doing, it must serve to explain the living experience of millions. It must not simply and exclusively explain the nature of capital's structural crisis but must also guide and orientate the class movement itself in its organizational and political response to this crisis. If it merely 'explains' without adequately serving to orientate in practice then it becomes articulated rationalistically and takes on a disarming contemplative form which locates the whole question of revolutionary agency 'in the form of the object' and not 'subjectively', not as 'sensuous human activity'. Likewise, an adequate theory of agency cannot be developed without a comprehensive, detailed and profound conception and elaboration of the character of the structural crisis of capital as a global system. One aspect (realization of needs) cannot be divorced from the other (grasp of the structural nature of capital's crisis) if progress is to be made on the question of agency.

Any conception of revolutionary agency *'must prove the truth – i.e. the reality and power, the this-sidedness of its thinking in practice'*. In other words, within the context of agency, is the conception relevant to and realizable within what Marx terms the 'real movement'? Is it the 'realization its needs'? The struggle for new forms of revolutionary agency can only start from 'within the framework of the existing institutions of the working class' (Mészáros) where the historic outmodedness of this 'framework' is increasingly asserting itself with each twist and turn of capital's crisis. This old 'framework' becomes a hindrance to (a fetter on) the 'realization of these needs' and must be dissolved in the course of establishing the higher form of *revolutionary* agency with a new, historically more adequate 'framework' and *modus operandi*.

The 'revolution' lives where the 'real movement' lives. It does not live in the heads of assorted theoreticians, sectarians and dogmatists. Or in a world which may or might be. The real ground is a capital order which has entered the time of its structural crisis. Upon this ground lives the 'real movement' of the proletariat. Its current forms of organization were created in times of the expansion of the capitalist order and its recurrent cyclical crises. Accordingly, their character has been moulded and adapted by and to these former times and not by and to that of the currently unfolding structural crisis. This is where this 'ground' actually forms the basis for their developing 'crisis of organization' and generates the possibilities within them of movement towards higher forms of proletarian agency more suited to the structural character of capital's crisis in the twenty-first century. The conception of the historic outmodedness of trade unionism as a form of proletarian organization must emerge out of such relations.

Therefore, the historically precedent task on this global ground of capital-in-crisis can only revolve around the question of how the proletariat moves forward to higher forms of agency. How can these new forms of agency emerge and fuse the struggle to achieve immediate objectives with that of the realization of long term aims involving the transcendence of the capital order itself? These objectives and aims actually arise out of the social conditions generated by capital-in-crisis. They are imposed on the proletariat as a consequence of the structural nature of capital's inevitably deepening crisis. The proletariat is located here as the 'subject of history', the active antithesis and 'structural antagonist' of the capital order – confronted with social conditions which are themselves the outcome of the history of human activity – struggling to transcend these conditions in the course of transforming itself as subject.

As far as a theory of agency is concerned, we can only start with 'capital-in-crisis' which is a *more concrete category* than mere 'capital'. It is only within this unfolding 'structural crisis' (Mészáros) of the global capital system that the changes in the occupational and social composition of the proletariat (implying a critique of Marx's nineteenth-century conception of the proletariat) can be understood. And, moreover, how the alteration in the qualitative nature of capital's crisis underlies and has mediated the growing historic outmodedness of the traditional organizations of the proletariat, pointing the way towards new, higher forms of agency. We will now move on to a deeper and more comprehensive analysis of these changes and their historical significance for the organization of the proletariat as capital's structural crisis intensifies in the course of the coming century.

Notes and References

1 Marx, Karl, 'Theses on Feuerbach'. In *Marx-Engels Collected Works, Volume 5, 1845–1847*, pp. 3–5 (London: Lawrence & Wishart, 1976), Thesis II.
2 Mészáros, István, *The Structural Crisis of Capital* (New York: Monthly Review Press, 2009).
3 *Communism is for us not a state of affairs which is to be established, an ideal to which reality will have to adjust itself. We call communism the real movement which abolishes the present state of things. The conditions of this movement result from the premises now in existence.*

Engels, Frederick, and Karl Marx, 'The German Ideology'. In *Marx-Engels Collected Works, Volume 5, 1845–1847*, pp. 19–581 (London: Lawrence & Wishart, 1976), p. 49.

4   Mészáros, István, *Beyond Capital: Towards a Theory of Transition* (London: Merlin Press, 1995).

5   Even if he wanted to, Marx could not have pursued an 'academic career' because of the prevailing cultural and political conditions within the educational establishments of his time. Specifically, Marx would have been very quickly handed the status of *persona non grata* because he was a *revolutionary* in both outlook and activity and *not an academic*. Undoubtedly, he would have had to accommodate his whole mode of being and thinking to the ruling powers who employed him. It was no accident of his personal history that Marx was, for significant parts of his life, a 'kept man'.

6   Marx, Karl, 'Contribution to the Critique of Hegel's Philosophy of Law. Introduction'. In *Marx-Engels Collected Works, Volume 3, 1843–1844*, pp. 175–187 (London: Lawrence & Wishart, 1975), p. 182.

7   Ibid., p. 183.

PART I

Globalizing Capital-in-Crisis

CHAPTER 2

The Altered Character of Capital's Crisis

At the beginning of *The Uncontrollability and Destructiveness of Globalizing Capital*, István Mészáros writes ...

> We live in an age of unprecedented historical crisis. Its severity can be gauged by the fact that we are not facing a more or less extensive cyclic crisis of capitalism as experienced in the past, but the deepening structural crisis of the capital system itself. As such this crisis affects – the first time ever in history – the whole of humankind, calling for quite fundamental changes to the way in which the social metabolism is controlled if humanity is to survive.[1]

This unfolding of global capital's structural crisis[2] is determining every aspect, without exception, of the life and relationships of society. It is – moreover and critically for our conception of revolutionary agency – the deepening of this structural crisis-process of capital which is increasingly revealing and bringing into sharp relief the limitations of the traditional organizations of the proletariat and making socially necessary the creation of new strategies of struggle and forms of organization through which the proletariat can defend its class interests in the course of taking to the offensive against capital and its state powers. Taken as a whole, it has now become a question of defending both the natural and socio-cultural conditions of the future human society which capital's crisis – embodied in its increasingly *destructive reproduction* – is destroying on a global scale.

The very nature of this structural crisis of capital, the widening of its extensive, and especially the deepening of its intensive, character on a global scale, gives rise to the social need for higher forms of organization and strategies of struggle and opposition to its rule over society as the dominating social relationship of production and distribution. This defence of the natural and socio-cultural conditions of human life is a highly charged political process because it raises the question of who rules and on what basis. Accordingly, the direct challenge to the rule of capital actually raises the question of dispossession and appropriation. What is implied here is the appropriation of the powers of capital to defend these conditions of the future society in the face of the mobilization and resistance by the state powers that defend the rule of capital.

The capital relation is the foundation upon which the class relations of capitalist society both originate and unfold historically and the state power becomes established (United States, Canada, Australia, etc.) or modified and re-organized (Britain, France, Germany, Japan, etc.) as the political power of capital. The capital order over the previous centuries has expanded out of its European 'homelands' and has become established as a global order – so-called 'globalization'. This evolution towards an integrated world system based on the capital relation leads *necessarily* onwards towards the structural crisis of the global capital order. Capital's structural crisis is essentially a crisis of the reproduction of the capital relation itself. This is implicit in the very nature of the capital relation ...

> The real barrier of capitalist production is capital itself. It is that capital and its self-expansion appear as the starting and the closing point, the motive and the purpose of production; that production is only production for capital and not vice versa, the means of production are not mere means for a constant expansion of the living process of the society of producers. The limits within which the preservation and self-expansion of the value of capital resting on the expropriation and pauperization of the great mass of producers can alone move – these limits come continually into conflict with the methods of production employed by capital for its purposes, which drive towards unlimited extension of production, towards production as an end in itself, towards unconditional development of the social productivity of labour. The means – unconditional development of the productive forces of society – comes continually into conflict with the limited purpose, the self-expansion of the existing capital. The capitalist mode of production is, for this reason, a historical means of developing the material forces of production and creating an appropriate world-market and is, at the same time, a continual conflict between this its historical task and its own corresponding relations of social production.[3]

Capital has entered its terminal phase where globally its own character as capital becomes a progressively tightening fetter on its own expansion as self-augmenting value. It has entered the stage of the 'activation of its absolute limits' (Mészáros, p. 142 ff., *Beyond Capital*). This 'endless and limitless drive to go beyond its limiting barrier' in intrinsic to the very nature of capital itself ...

> Every boundary (Grenze) is and has to be a barrier (Schranke) for it. Else it would cease to be capital – money as self-reproductive. If ever it perceived a certain boundary not as a barrier, but became comfortable within it as a boundary, it would itself have declined from exchange-value to use-value, from the general form of wealth to a specific, substantial mode of the same. Capital as such creates a specific surplus-value because it cannot create an infinite one all at once; but it is the constant movement to create more of the same. The quantitative boundary of the surplus-value appears to it as a mere natural barrier, as a necessity which it constantly tries to violate and beyond which it constantly seeks to go. The barrier appears as an accident which has to be conquered.[4]

For capital, 'every boundary is a barrier' which is not the case for production in the ages beyond the capital relation. In the periods beyond capital, boundaries cease to be 'barriers' but simply become limits to be sustainably and ecologically managed by humanity and transcended (or even retracted and reduced) according to the needs of human beings in their relationship with nature. The tendency towards the deepening of this structural crisis-process – in capital's 'ceaseless drive to go beyond itself' – has profound implications for the proletariat and its class organizations through which it has traditionally conducted its struggle against capital. 'Going on' in the 'old ways' will not be possible.

The structural crisis of capital, on the whole, now means that capital's reproduction is a 'destructive reproduction' (Mészáros). In this sense, it is not simply 'developing' the means of production (as it has done previously, despite widespread destruction in wars, etc.) but is actually destroying the fundamental natural and socio-cultural conditions for human life itself on the planet and for its own self-reproduction as the dominant social relationship of production.

Consequentially, socialism now becomes necessary for human survival on the planet now that capital has entered this final phase of destructive reproduction as its structural crisis deepens and widens. Mészáros goes into this in *Beyond Capital*. The dictum of 'Socialism or Barbarism' has only now come into its own. What is implied in his conception of 'structural crisis' is the antithesis and end of the phase of 'conjunctural' and cyclical crises. These cyclical, conjunctural crises are part of a past historic temporal phase (during the nineteenth and twentieth centuries) beyond which the capital system has now moved globally into a terminal structural phase. This 'cyclical' phase necessarily leads to the 'structural' phase mediating which is the historic process of the tendency of the organic composition of capital to increase and the tendency of the rate of profit to fall. 'Capitalist breakdown' – within the context of structural crisis – can mean only one thing: the destruction of the necessary socio-cultural and natural pre-conditions for human life itself on the planet, for all sentient life.

The drive towards a continuously unhindered realization of surplus value implies a constantly expanding global market which is not possible. This 'drive' encounters the limiting parameters (engendered historically by the evolution and expansion of capital itself) which posits 'the activation of the absolute limits' of the capital system globally. Crises of overproduction, therefore, are not simply a question of the *realization* of value. They indicate that the forces of production developed within the framework of the social relation of capital have actually outgrown that framework. In other words, such crises demonstrate that capital itself has become a fetter on the actual development of these forces. Today, that conflict – between the further, ecologically sustainable development of these forces and the restrictive and destructive integument of the capital social form – is now being expressed in the widespread ecological, social and human destruction which comes with the destructive reproduction of capital on a global scale.

The *mass* of surplus value produced is actually increasing on a global scale. However, critically, the ratio of this surplus value to capital invested (machinery, etc., and labour power) is falling because of the increase in 'constant capital' investment (incorporating an increase in the ratio of the value of machinery and materials to labour power). The resulting augmentation in the productivity of labour is actually serving to intensify capital's crisis. It is the quantitative increase in this latter ratio (capital to surplus value, falling rate of profit) which is driving the mad rush for an *absolute* increase in surplus value. And this underlies the widespread ecological destruction and degradation of human beings.

Capital itself – as the outcome of its own historical development – posits its own limits with which it comes into direct contradiction. Its historic development has reached the stage where it is 'imploding in' on itself. Capital has fallen into its 'structural' stage where its very development is undermining its own nature. It is caught in an increasingly sharpening, self-contradictory and self-denying relation with itself as its structural crisis unfolds. This spells catastrophe for humanity and nature unless the capital epoch is globally superseded.

Before this stage emerged, crises were cyclical and capital could then displace its internal contradictions with a new phase of value expansion and accumulation into an expanding market which it had itself created historically. But in structural crisis, absolute expansion and accumulation merely serve to deepen its crisis. What previously served to attenuate and transcend crisis now serves to intensify and worsen capital's crisis. This drive to constantly increase the mass of absolute surplus value produced (for example, with more factories in China, India, Latin America, etc.) is a response to this self-abnegating and involutively self-destructive process and brings in its wake all the destruction we are seeing globally, the 'destructive reproduction' analysed by Mészáros.

And, of course, it does not matter (is *immaterial*) what is produced and destroyed as long as capital produces realizable value and it reaffirms itself as self-augmenting value. This is the irrepressible and insane logic of the capital relation. The drive for the realization of surplus value and capital accumulation regardless of the most terrible and apocalyptic costs on humanity and nature's magnificent creation.

The deepening of this structural crisis – disrupting and destroying nature's ecosystems – is the same crisis which is driving the destruction of public provision, its transference into the grasp of private capital for profit, mass structural unemployment and the driving down of workers' conditions of employment and wages. This is intrinsic to the tendency towards an increase in the rate of exploitation in the 'West' and the falling rate of utilization which comes with generalized waste production; disposability which services the needs of capital because it creates 'economic space' for value-production within whatever rapidly disposable use-value form it can embody itself.

All this, of course, introduces new, and intensifies, existing contradictions. For example, wage cuts must also mean less purchasing power and therefore less value realization (less profit) despite increasing the quantity of surplus value produced as a result of wage reductions and the increasing organic composition of capital. Wage reductions in the realm of productive capital means an increase in the surplus value produced whilst, simultaneously, reducing the overall social capacity for the realization of that surplus value.

Capital's offensive against labour arises – as with the destruction of nature – out of the developing intensification of its *enduring and intractable crisis of reproduction* on a global scale. This applies no less to the 'superstructural mediations' as its does directly within the realm of productive capital. The dismantling of adequate social provision and the state welfare system, privatization and the heightened pro-capital function and role of both the print and broadcasting media (Appendix II) have, amongst others, all become subject to the requirements of capital-in-crisis.

The traditional and enduring forms of 'defensively' evolved strategies and tactics of opposition to capital continue to determine the 'margins of action' of non-unionized as well as trade unionized workers. They continue to highly circumscribe their activity in the unfolding structural crisis of capital. It is within the context of the evolving conditions of this structural crisis that the trade union hierarchy becomes increasingly articulated as a body which opposes the historic interests of labour because the actual existence and interests of this bureaucracy are tied to the continuation of the capitalist system, standing as a proxy of capital within trade unionism itself. 'Defensively structured' must become transformed into 'offensively articulated'. This is the only way forward for labour if it is not to become increasingly subject to the unconditional dictat of capital-in-crisis.

But 'to embark on such an offensive' 'within the framework of the existing institutions of the working class' (Mészáros) inevitably means trade unionists increasingly coming into collision with that 'defensively constituted framework' as capital's crisis unfolds. It means the whole structure, organization and procedures of trade unionism being transformed (indeed superseded into a higher form of unionism) to fight for the class interests of the proletariat and the overturning of its 'current defensively constituted framework'. Such an overturn would have very deep, far-reaching historic implications for the class movement of the proletariat as a whole.

The increasing moribundity of the *trade union form* has become manifest in the growing ineffectiveness of the strike as a tactic for the realization of economistic goals. This tactic has become attenuated with the emergence of capital's structural crisis. When capital was in its post-war ascendant and expansionary phase – from the 1950s into the 1970s – the strike tactic was more effective because the conditions of capital's reproduction afforded capital more room to concede demands. These concessions to labour not only enabled the phase to unfold relatively unimpeded but they also served to feed consumer demand into this process of expansion. The NHS (National Health Service) in Britain was an example of this. Much vaunted by the sectarian left as a 'concession' which the post-war proletariat putatively 'forced out' of the state power, its establishment and financing simultaneously facilitated this expansionary phase of capitalist accumulation after the mass destruction during the second imperialist world war. The financing of public provision in general was a catalytic element in the post-war production of surplus value and the dynamic of credit-fuelled capitalist expansion and accumulation.

If conditions permit, capital is ready to concede the economistic demands of labour in so far as they do not actually interfere with the progress of accumulation and, in fact, can serve to energize production for profit and the accumulation of capital. This was one of the implicit principles of Keynesianism. It is quite different when capital as a global system enters its phase of structural crisis. Now the partition and distribution of every last quantum of value is vigorously disputed.

Inherent in this structural crisis is the drive to increase the rate of exploitation and adopt any measure to oppose the tendency of the rate of profit to fall. This whole crisis-dynamic implicates a sub-crisis in accumulation and the process of the reproduction of capital itself; in global capital's capacity to augment its value through the realization and capitalization of produced surplus value. So even though the *absolute mass of profit* has increased with 'globalization', the ratio of this mass to the total capital deployed (machinery, etc., and labour power) has continued to decline with catastrophic implications for the global capitalist system.[5] The structural crisis of the capital system is implicit within, and *necessarily* arises out of, the development of these latter relations fundamentally as a crisis of capital's self-reproduction as a *structured* social relationship of production and distribution such that ...

> the development of the productive forces brought about by the historical development of capital itself, when it reaches a certain point, suspends the self-realization of capital, instead of positing it. Beyond a certain point, the development of the powers of production becomes a barrier for capital; hence the capital relation a barrier for the development of the productive powers of labour. [...] the material and mental conditions of the negation of wage labour and of capital, themselves already the negation of earlier forms of unfree social production, are themselves results of its production process. The growing incompatibility between the productive development of society and its hitherto existing relations of production expresses itself in bitter contradictions, crises, spasms. The violent destruction of capital not by relations external to it, but rather as a condition of its self-preservation, is the most striking form in which advice is given it to be gone and to give room to a higher state of social production.[6]

Capital has now reached the stage where its *struggle for its own reproduction* has necessarily become destructive of the natural and social conditions of human culture itself and, by implication and paradoxically, of its own self-reproduction. The historically progressive moment in the development of capital is, in its self-evolution, that it has created and is increasingly creating the conditions necessary for its transcendence. This, of course, is posited dialectically with capital-in-crisis as a manically distending global system of 'destructive reproduction'. The fundamentally determining and 'negatively self-related' side of this dialectic is that capital's own struggle for self-reproduction is posited as the age of the destruction of the natural and socio-cultural conditions necessary for its own augmented reproduction; it destroys the very conditions which are necessary for it to simply 'be' or 'exist' as capital. The structural crisis of the self-reproduction of capital destroys the conditions for its own augmented replication and, in so doing, undermines its own existence as the dominant social relation of production and distribution.

The mass destruction of these conditions, a falling rate of utilization of products (more products bought, utilized and 'wasted' in a given period of time) and the systemic production of commodities into which is structured optimal 'disposability' in order to maximize the production of value, are now intrinsic aspects of this unfolding crisis-process. The terrifying and injurious creation of an economy of pollution and waste which services the needs of capitalist commodity production.

One of the most disturbing aspects of the reality of this insanity and nightmare of global capitalism is the widespread destruction, barbarism and cruelty to which the wonderful creation and beauty of living nature is being subjected. The destruction of whole ecosystems driving the extinction of species and daily threatening the additional termination of the life of more species of both plants and animals. This is being driven essentially by the capital system itself so that ...

> as the capitalist mode of production develops, an ever larger quantity of capital is required to employ the same, let alone an increased, amount of labour power. Thus, on a capitalist foundation, the increasing productiveness of labour necessarily and permanently creates a seeming over-population of labouring people. If the variable capital forms just one-sixth of the total capital instead of the former one-half, the total capital must be trebled to employ the same amount of labour-power. And if twice as much labour power is to be employed, the total capital must increase six-fold.[7]

This tendency – now operative in the epoch of globalizing capital – does not only mean the destruction of the lives of millions of human beings as 'surplus' to capital's requirements. The increasing productivity of labour under conditions of capital's intensifying structural crisis must have profound and the most terrible implications and ramifications for nature's creation in terms of 'waste production' and the precipitously 'falling rate of utilization' of the products of capital-dominated wage labour's relationship with this creation. The presently ongoing destruction of the magnificent Amazon Rainforest – largely to farm cattle for the transnational burger corporations – exemplifies in the most disturbing way possible this annihilistic destruction of the wondrous beauty of living nature in the interests of global capital.

A continuing and increasing production of surplus value must, necessarily, mean a burgeoning and systemic extension and intensification of capital's malignant crisis-phase of 'destructive reproduction'. In short, the relation alone – given by Marx above – signifies a tendency in capital towards an exponentially growing and irreversible annihilation of nature's creation if humanity cannot rise to the mighty historic task of putting a final and irreversible end to the rule of capital on the planet.

The inevitable presupposition of capital's intrinsic mode of existence (its inherent primary character being the continuously increasing augmentation of value, forever self-valorising value) is the unlimited expansion of the global market. Hence ...

> The market must, therefore, be continually extended, so that its interrelations and the conditions regulating them assume more and more the form of a natural law working independently of the producer, and become ever more uncontrollable. This internal contradiction seeks to resolve itself through expansion of the outlying field of production. But the more productiveness develops, the more it finds itself at variance with the narrow basis on which the conditions of consumption rest. It is no contradiction at all on this self-contradictory basis that there should be an excess of capital simultaneously with a growing surplus of population. For while a combination of these two would, indeed, increase the mass of produced surplus-value, it would at the same time intensify the contradiction between the conditions under which this surplus-value is produced and those under which it is realized.[8]

In other words, an excess of capital develops alongside a growing surplus, structurally unemployed population. Trying to bring the two together may increase the production of surplus value but the 'narrow basis on which the conditions of consumption rest' makes its realization – with the growing productivity of labour and the tendency towards the increase in the 'organic composition of capital' – increasingly problematic.

The immanently, value self-augmenting and expanding character of capital as a social relationship of production is premised on the basis of capital-created conditions of realization which directly contradict this character. This 'external' 'market' barrier is created by capital itself which then seeks to continually transcend it through enlargement and expansion of the global market in order to pass beyond its own internal barrier as limited yet necessarily self-expanding value. Clearly, the further evolution of such a relation beyond a certain stage of development is historically unsustainable and inevitably must confront humanity with the alternatives of annihilation or revolution. There is not, nor can there be, another, third road.

To continue down the current road of capital's 'destructive reproduction' must spell an intensification of the catastrophe and annihilation which is now actually unfolding. The only other alternative can and must be the creation of a globally sustainable socialist order of production and distribution in which both humanity's and nature's needs are complimentarily, symbiotically and socially located as pre-eminent and paramount. This can only mean the transcendence of the capital epoch and the dissolution of all those state and global agencies which rest on and defend capital's rule in the social metabolism.

The *absolute* increase in the demand for labour power necessitated by a 'continual extension of the market' – now taking place in the age of globalizing capital – is offset by the *relative* decrease in the magnitude of labour power employed in relation to the other major portion (constant capital) of capital. Increasing accumulation of capital extends production and population *absolutely* but then forms the basis for the growth in structural unemployment across the globe and pauperization, resulting in a greater restriction of the conditions of realization of surplus value by lowering consumption …

> the whole process of accumulation in the first place resolves itself into production on an expanding scale, which on the one hand corresponds to the natural growth of the population, and on the other hand, forms an inherent basis for the phenomena which appear during crises. The criterion of this expansion of production is capital itself, the existing level of the conditions of production and the unlimited desire of the capitalists to enrich themselves and to enlarge their capital, but by no means consumption, which from the outset is inhibited, since the majority of the population, the working people, can only expand their consumption within very narrow limits, whereas the demand for labour, although it grows absolutely, decreases relatively, to the same extent as capitalism develops.[9]

This, of course, takes place on the pre-determining basis of capital as a *value-relation* (the 'organic composition of capital' is a *value* relation) but also finds its direct reflection in the historic tendency towards a general increase in the productivity of labour; that is, the use of less labour power relative to machinery and materials deployed so that labour becomes more productive and the value embodied in commodities tends to fall with the result being a cheapening in price.

The net result for the life of the proletariat is expressed in the tendency for mass *structural* unemployment to rise. And this becomes a *structural prerequisite* for the continuation of capital's self-reproduction. This permanent unemployment and burgeoning social marginalization becomes, therefore, a historic necessity for the reproduction of capital itself in the epoch of its structural crisis. Capital's intensifying requirement for the reduction in 'the necessary labour time required for the reproduction of capital' and for a 'decrease of the quantity of labour power' employed relative to 'dead labour' generates and augmentatively mediates the creation of a permanently unemployed and marginalized social stratum. And, at the same time, tends to prolong and intensify the labour time of those in employment, resulting in a higher degree of exploitation. At one end of the social polarity, people lay idle, unfulfilled lives wasting and, at the other end, they are forced to work harder with greater intensity. The very existence of this contradiction serves the needs of capital.

The rise in the 'organic composition of capital' (ratio of machinery and materials used to labour power deployed), both on a technical level and in terms of value, means that mass structural unemployment takes place in a period of increasing productivity of labour, with all the dehumanizing consequences associated with it under capitalism (*Capital*, Vol. 3, Chapter 13, Part 3, q.v.).

In a socialist society, such an increasing productivity – suitably, ecologically and sustainably regulated by the associated producers – would be celebrated as an advance for humanity because it would release more free time for collective and individual human development. Under capitalism, it merely serves to augment immiseration in the service of profit and capital accumulation.

The *absolute* value of total capital invested – inclusive of labour power itself ('variable capital') – increases globally whilst the magnitude of the value of labour power and the number of people employed falls in relation to the total investment of constant capital. *Mass structural unemployment* – unfolding in the midst of increasing capital accumulation and labour productivity and inevitably leading to structural crisis – is a fundamental historic tendency of the development of production founded on the capital relation. Accompanying this tendency is a growth in the 'absolute mass of profit and a falling rate of profit' (*Capital*, Vol. 3, Chapter 13, p. 219).

Mass structural unemployment emerges in the presence of the increasing productivity of social labour, contrary to any Malthusian misconceptions. It develops – and intensifies in the course of capital's structural crisis – simply because advances in technique, in machinery and the science of the labour process generally means less labour is required to produce a greater quantity of products (and of higher quality) in a given period of time. Whereas in the past it may have taken fifty workers to produce x products in y time, today – as a result of technical advances in production – it takes 5 workers $y/50$ time to produce $10x$ products and with a higher, superior quality ...

> the possibility of a relative surplus of labouring people develops proportionately to the advances made by capitalist production not because the productiveness of social labour decreases, but because it increases. It does not therefore arise out of an absolute disproportion between labour and the means of subsistence, or the means of production of these means of subsistence, but out of the disproportion occasioned by the capitalist exploitation of labour, a disproportion between the progressive growth of capital and its relatively shrinking need for an increasing population.[10]

and ...

> in proportion as necessary labour is already diminished, the realization of capital becomes more difficult.[11]

The increase in the productivity of labour implicates a reduction in necessary labour time (i.e. the time in the production process during which the worker labours to reproduce the value equivalent of his or her subsistence). As the productivity of labour rises, the time required to reproduce this value equivalent *tends* towards zero but, of course, can never actually reach it in terms of the reproduction of the total social capital. With automation and computerization – and their integration in production – we see this tendency most clearly expressed.[12]

The resulting increase in the magnitude of *relative* surplus value produced does not rise proportionately with the growing productivity of labour. The rise in the magnitude of *relative* surplus value (relative to necessary labour time) never directly and proportionately corresponds to the increase in the productivity of labour. Rather an *inversely proportionate* relation unfolds. So, as Marx writes ...

> The multiplier of the productive force – the number by which it is multiplied – is therefore not the multiplier of surplus labour or surplus value [...]. The multiplier of the productive force is thus never the multiplier but always the divisor of the original relation.[13]

For example, if the productivity of labour doubles whilst the relation of necessary to surplus labour is 50:50, then this relationship becomes 25:75. Half as much labour is now required to produce the same quantity of use values and the value 'saved' is now transferred over as 'surplus labour time' The magnitude of relative surplus value has increased by 50 per cent (from 50 to 75) on the original magnitude with the fall of 50 per cent in necessary labour time (from 50 to 25). Productivity has increased by 100 per cent (doubled) with the magnitude of relative surplus value only increasing by 50 per cent (half of the original magnitude from 50 to 75 and has not doubled it to 100). If the productivity of labour doubles again within a fixed time period (say ten years), necessary labour time becomes reduced to 12.5 and surplus labour time rises to 87.5 (i.e. 75 plus 12.5). 12.5 divided by 75 multiplied by 100 is an increase of 16.7 per cent (compared to 50 per cent under the previous doubling of labour productivity) with another doubling in the productivity of labour. The relative rate of increase of the magnitude of absolutely increasing surplus value (resulting from the 'saving' of necessary labour time as a direct consequence of the repeated doubling of the productivity of labour) must constantly fall and tend asymptotically towards zero with each successive doubling of the productivity of labour. Given a temporally fixed working day, the value-equivalent of necessary labour time saved – with rising productivity – is transferred as an augmentation of *relative* surplus value.[14] The greater the fractional part of the working day becomes 'surplus labour time' with the growth in the productivity of labour, the more does the magnitude of the successively *newly added surplus labour time* fall and the less, progressively, does capital 'realize' itself as capital because this newly added surplus labour time as a fraction of the capital advanced tends, asymptotically, towards zero. This mechanism within the capital relation contains its inherent tendency towards its historic abnegation as a relationship of production. Capital – in the course of its historic accumulation process – posits ('activates') the 'absolute limits' of its own inherent nature and, increasingly, 'struggles' to reproduce itself as self-augmenting value.

The falling ratio of necessary to surplus labour time – resulting from technical innovation and development in production – expresses itself in a growth in the productivity of labour. Accordingly the ratio of *newly created* surplus value to the total capital value advanced (machinery, materials, labour power inclusive of newly capitalized surplus value) must fall. This, of course, is progressively expressed in the historic tendency of the rate of profit to fall.

This tendency (towards zero necessary labour time) in the historic development of capital is impossible to realize as is the inherent tendency towards zero circulation time (see *Capital*, Vol. 2) in order to maximize turnover time and, accordingly, value realization. However, the combination of both of these tendencies is mediating the deepening structural crisis of the capital relation on a global scale: an intensifying crisis of the reproduction of the very *structure* of capital which is now having, must continue to have and can only possibly have the most comprehensively devastating and destructive of consequences for nature and human culture worldwide.

The unplanned and anarchic tendencies in capital towards a stupendous increase in the productivity of labour is the operation of the intrinsic, internal and irrepressible logic of capital itself. It is the same logic – its historically inalienable tendency of development – which drives it *towards* its self-negation as a historical form of the development of the forces of production. However, this takes place in the epoch in which this drive becomes overwhelmingly one in which capital increasingly and more destructively struggles to reproduce itself with all the most terrible ramifications for nature's creation and human culture. And, as we have already shown by the numerical example given above ...

> the more developed capital already is, the more surplus labour it has created, the more terribly must it develop the productive force in order to realize itself in only smaller proportion, i.e. to add surplus value – because its barrier always remains the relation between the fractional part which expresses necessary labour, and the entire working day. It can move only within these boundaries. The smaller already the fractional part

falling to necessary labour, the greater the surplus labour, the less can any increase in productive force perceptibly diminish necessary labour; since the denominator has grown enormously *(i.e. as a result of the continuously rising productivity of labour – SM)*. The self-realization of capital becomes more difficult to the extent that it has already been realized. The increase of productive force would become irrelevant to capital; realization itself would become irrelevant, because its proportions have become minimal, and it would have ceased to be capital.[15]

Marx adds that this and previous concepts are 'correct only in this abstraction' and 'additional relations' will 'modify them significantly'. However – without ignoring these intimated 'counteracting influences' – the historic tendency couldn't be clearer. And the significance and ramifications are just as stark: the continuing existence of the epoch of capital is the positing of a path which *necessarily* leads to the deepening of structural crisis and an unfolding catastrophe for humanity and nature which harbours the possibility of annihilation. Humanity has now entered this terminal stage of capital's deepening structural crisis. Only by irreversibly transcending the epoch of capital – in a process of global revolution involving social restructuring and reconstruction – will this nightmare of history come to a final end and a truly sustainable and ecologically viable system of production be established beyond the era of capital.

Marx and Engels could not, of course, delineate the various and specific twists and turns of the future trajectory of the capitalist system and the class movement of the proletariat in Europe, the United States or elsewhere. They could not possibly have visualized these *specific and differentiated* social forms of the movement beyond the conditions of the time in which they lived and worked. However, what Marx could and did elaborate in his work were his conceptions of the historic tendencies of development of capital as a whole social relation of production and distribution. It is these very tendencies which we are now seeing manifest today as the structural crisis of capital opens up and broadens and deepens on a global scale.

The age of displaceable, cyclical, conjunctural crises is over. The twenty-first century is the unfolding of capital's structural crisis which can only manifest as an interconnected series of economic 'earthquakes, aftershocks, explosions and progressively more severe downturns' which 'play out' and express the deepening of this crisis of the whole global capital system. A fundamental qualitative break has taken place which defines two distinctive, determinate phases in the development of the capital system.

The most distinguishing feature that separates these phases is that of the 'organically structural' character of the crisis of the presently unfolding phase. Such a crisis of the global system of capital progressively and increasingly finds capital (as the root relation) 'hemmed in' in terms of its inherent character as capital. As its room for value-expansion becomes increasingly constricted, it must adopt measures in which anything and everything by means of which capital can expand its value will be appropriated. Social provision, human beings and nature all become subject to this appropriation, control and destruction in the service of capital-in-crisis.

It also explains why 'globalizing capital' now 'eyes' and inspects every sphere in all areas of human culture as potentially exploitable and that the intensity of established forms of exploitation of humanity and nature must necessarily accelerate as capital's structural crisis deepens. These are the direct manifestations of such a crisis which excludes the possibility of a return to the character of the former cyclical phases of 'boom and bust' of the nineteenth and twentieth centuries.

Prior to the 1970s, the antagonisms of capital's crises were displaceable. Capital had not yet become an ontologically intensive global relation entering its structural crisis phase. Various measures could be adopted and developed within conditions which continued to afford the capital system the room for expansion in a growing world market. Its structural crisis can no longer afford it this luxury of displacing its sharpening contradictions as in a conjunctural crisis. They are insoluble, deepening and intensifying on a global scale. George Liodakis writes that ...

> Although the potential for a (further) long-run development of capitalism should not be precluded, the tendency of the new stage of capitalism to exhaust both the external and internal limits of capital implies that this development will be prone to crisis and most likely approach the historical limits of the capitalist mode of production. This throttling effect on the conditions of capitalist accumulation will increasingly lead to more violent forms of class struggle and a progressive hardening of institutional structures and political practices, which bring forth the most essential aspects of an emerging totalitarian regime. This trend is already evident in the sphere of production and labor exploitation (more strict regulations, exhaustive exploitation, and elimination of established workers' rights). It is also manifested in

the relentless attempts to discipline and control all resistant social forces, and impose a capital-friendly world order, but also in the one-sided (profit-seeking) marshaling of all scientific and technological endeavors to serve the interests of capital, as well as in the cultural uniformity imposed by the totalizing impact of expanding market forces on a world scale.[16]

The economic 'crash' of 2008 is merely a minor prefiguration of the economic and ecological cataclysms and catastrophes which lie on the road ahead if capital's crisis continues to unfold without being resolved in the only way it can be, that is, by a complete and revolutionary restructuring of the social metabolism beyond the capital relation. The contradictions of its structural-crisis phase cannot be resolved within the historic parameters of capital; they are insoluble, deepening and intensifying and not displaceable as in previous cyclical stages of capital's development. These parameters are themselves intrinsic to the crisis of the capital system itself in this structural phase. *The temporal separation between the phases of conjunctural crises and the structural crisis of capital is a determinate separation between qualitatively and historically different phases of development of the capital relation. They are qualitatively distinct phases of development of the crisis of the capital system.*

A 'determinate phase' is simply one which is qualitatively different from the previous or succeeding one which displays features and characteristics which *essentially* distinguishes it from these other phases. For example, ice, water and steam are three physically different states ('determinate phases') of the substance with the chemical formula of H_2O. We have now entered the determinate phase of the structural crisis of capital in which the historically antecedent and determinately posited conjunctural character of capital's crises has disappeared. There will be *relative* 'ups and downs' and 'ebbs and flows' in the evolution of this structural crisis but it will remain, determinately and *absolutely*, an intensifying structural crisis, and not a series of forms of cyclical, 'boom and bust' conjunctural crises. This is why all the old 'certainties' about old forms of organization and methods of proletarian struggle are falling into historical 'outmode', crisis and chaos.

The global unfolding of this crisis of the capital relation must bring in its wake a deep crisis in terms of the way the proletariat has traditionally organized to fight for its interests against capital and its state powers. But it also mediates capital's *traditional authoritarian response* to its own previous crises amongst which was the imposition of fascist forms of rule. The possible use of such methods of rule becomes increasingly problematic for its state powers in an epoch where its crisis is structural and not conjunctural. The notion that capital has the historical room for manouevre to deploy fascism in order to serve to displace the ever-sharpening contradictions of its unfolding structural crisis – and in the same ways (deploying similar methods) in which it did with its conjunctural crises throughout the previous century – is misconceived and unsustainable.

Capital had not entered its phase of structural crisis in the 'Great Depression' of the 1930s and this gave capital more options and room to manouevre in terms of resisting its social effects. In those regions (Italy, Spain, Germany, Japan) without the outlets and 'cushion' of empires and 'spheres of influence' – such as Britain, France and the United States possessed – fascism was one of these options deployed in addition to 'war economies' which enabled the capital order to 'regain its equilibrium' and continue to expand after the mass destruction of the second imperialist world war. Thus, as Mészáros notes ...

> The world of capital weathered also the storm of its 'Great Economic Crisis' of 1929–1933 with relative ease, without having to face a major hegemonic confrontation from socialist forces despite the mass suffering caused by this crisis. For the fact is that 'Great' as this crisis was, it was very far from being a structural crisis, leaving an ample number of options open for capital's continued survival, recovery and stronger than ever reconstitution on an economically sounder and broader basis. Retrospective political reconstructions tend to blame personalities and organizational forces for such recovery, particularly with respect to the success of Fascism. Yet, whatever the relative weight of such political factors, one should not forget that they must be assessed against the background of an essentially defensive historical phase. It is pointless to rewrite history with the help of counter-factual conditions, whether they concern the rise of Fascism or anything else. For the fact that really matters is that at the time of the crisis of 1929–1933 capital actually did have the option of Fascism (and similar solutions) which it no longer possesses today. And objectively that makes a world of difference as far as the possibilities of defensive and offensive action are concerned.[17]

The structural crisis of capital cannot possibly form historically 'stable ground' for the establishment of fascism as we saw in the 1930s. Such a regime finds its historical presupposition outside such a structural crisis, in an age of conjunctural displaceable crises implying 'economic space' for capital to re-adjust and expand. To understand why Mészáros asserts in this passage that fascism is 'no longer an option' for capital today is, simultaneously, to conceptually grasp the deepest roots of capital's historic structural crisis.

Fascist rule in the service of capital presupposes a whole series of complexed historical conditions fundamental to which is a crisis of capital which is conjunctural and displaceable in its internal contradictory dynamic i.e. which is not structural, deepening, insoluble. The unfolding, global, widening and deepening structural crisis of the capital order cannot form a stable basis for the origination, enduring establishment and maintenance of fascist rule as we saw, for example, with Franco's thirty-five-year rule in Spain from 1939 to 1975. Hitler's regime in Germany had already entered economic crisis in the 1930s. It was the impetus given to the world capitalist economy by Roosevelt's 'New Deal' that came to the rescue of a failing economy in the Nazi Germany of the 1930s and enabled fascism to prepare for war.

Proletarian class movements *must* emerge in response to this structural crisis which is absolutely intractable and unresolvable within the parameters of the global capital order. Can fascism find solid, unshifting ground on which to settle in such a distinct and qualitatively new historic phase of development? No. fascism cannot resolve this unfolding structural crisis for capital. It can only be resolved beyond the parameters of the capital order itself. This widening and deepening crisis of the whole global capital order *necessarily* points towards a growing radicalization of the proletariat globally. It can only point, at most, to transitory fascistic trends – the echoes of past conditions – but not the imposition of enduring, determinate fascist forms of rule on behalf of capital-in-crisis.

The conflict – in the epoch of capital – between the conditions of the production of surplus value and the conditions of its realization is continuously reposited at a higher stage of existence until the contradictory dynamic of this relationship becomes established *on a global scale*. This is the historic moment at and within which capital arrives at the point of the 'activation of its absolute limits' and enters into its stage of structural crisis. The historic implications of this discovery are absolutely catastrophic for humanity if the capital system is not transcended on a global scale. Already, at the start of the twenty-first century, we are witnessing the manifestations of this conflict in the most disturbing forms of pillage and destruction of nature's creation and the dehumanizing malignancy of an unsustainable, utterly wasteful system of production.

We are now living through the unfolding of an 'unprecedented historic crisis' the likes of which humanity has never experienced before. It is not of the nature of previous crises of the capital order which were cyclical, conjunctural and, in the particularity of their contradictions, displaceable. It is a crisis which was always implicit in the very nature of capital itself but only comes to its fullest explicit development, realization and expression with 'globalization', when the capital relation itself generates the global conditions for the unfolding of this structural crisis and when it becomes 'ever-increasingly a system of destructive production'.

The reproduction of capital under these global conditions takes on the most wasteful and destructive forms which imperil the natural basis and cultural conditions of human life on the planet. Without 'fundamental changes', the downward spiral trajectory of 'destructive reproduction' of capital will undoubtedly continue. The question of 'Socialism or Barbarism' is one which resolves itself into the survival or destruction of human life on the planet.

Notes and References

1   Mészáros, István, *The Uncontrollability and Destructiveness of Globalizing Capital*. In *The Challenge and Burden of Historical Time. Socialism in the Twenty First Century* (New York: Monthly Review Press, 2008), p. 61.

2   Mészáros's conception of capital's structural crisis has been developed in his works, especially *Beyond Capital*. He released the more succinct *The Structural Crisis of Capital* which summarizes his conception of 'structural crisis'. According to Mészáros, we have now entered the period of 'the activation of capital's absolute limits' (*Beyond Capital*, p. 142 ff). He comprehensively elaborates his

conception of 'structural crisis' in part three of *Beyond Capital* (Chapters 14–20, pp. 521–871).

It is important that readers familiarize themselves with the conception of the *structural crisis of capital* found in the work of István Mészáros. There are no 'shortcuts' in this regard. A grasp of this conception forms the background to this text on revolutionary agency and mediates its content. To give a fully detailed account of this conception developed by Mészáros is beyond the scope and limits of this book. However, the conception is covered in the body of the text and regularly referenced.

3   Marx, *Capital*, Vol. 3, Chapter 15, II, 'Conflict Between Expansion of Production and Production of Surplus-Value', p. 250 (London: Lawrence & Wishart, 1974). On the question of 'structural crisis', see Chapters 13, 14 and 15, *Capital*, Vol. 3.
4   Marx, *Grundrisse*, Notebook III, 'The Chapter on Capital', pp. 334–335 (London: Penguin Books, 1973).
5   Carchedi, G., 'Behind and Beyond the Crisis', *International Socialism*, No. 132 (October 2011) <http://isj.org.uk/behind-and-beyond-the-crisis/> (Last accessed 2 November 2016).

Drawing on various statistical sources, Carchedi presents striking empirical and graphical evidence which clearly demonstrates the scientific character of the historic relationship discovered by Marx between the tendency of the rate of profit to fall and the rise in the organic composition of capital over the past seventy years.

6   Marx, *Grundrisse*, Notebook VII, 'The Chapter on Capital', pp. 749–750 (London: Penguin Books, 1973).
7   Marx, *Capital*, Vol. 3, Chapter 13, p. 223 (London: Lawrence & Wishart, 1969).
8   *Capital*, Vol. 3, Chapter 15, p. 245.
9   Marx, *Theories of Surplus Value, Part 2*, Chapter 17, 'Ricardo's Theory of Accumulation and a Critique of it. Crises (Introductory Remarks)', p. 492 (London: Lawrence & Wishart, 1969).
10 Marx, *Capital*, Vol. 3, Chapter 13, p. 222 (London: Lawrence & Wishart, 1969).
11 Marx, *Grundrisse*, p. 333.
12 Caixiong, Zheng, 'Robots go it alone at factory with no assembly workers', *China Daily* (5 May 2015) <http://www.chinadaily.com.cn/china/2015-05/05/content_20620184.htm> (Last accessed 3 November 2016).

'More than 80 percent of manufacturing operations in Guangzhou, the province's (Dongguan) capital, will be using industrial robots and related "intelligent" technologies by 2020, according to official projections'. Automation itself forms the technical basis for so-called 'Lights Out Manufacturing'.

13 Marx, *Grundrisse*, p. 336.

14 See *Grundrisse*, pp. 333–341, for a more detailed explanation of this relationship.
15 Marx, *Grundrisse*, pp. 340–341.
16 Liodakis, G., 'The New Stage of Capitalist Development and the Prospects of Globalisation', *Science & Society*, Vol. 69, No. 3 (July 2005): pp. 341–366.
17 Mészáros, István, *Beyond Capital*, Section 18.1.2, p. 678.

CHAPTER 3

A Century of Lenin's *Imperialism*

In the Preface to the French and German editions of *Imperialism, the Highest Stage of Capitalism*, Lenin writes ...

> the main purpose of the book was, and remains, to present, on the basis of the summarised returns of irrefutable bourgeois statistics, and the admissions of bourgeois scholars of all countries, a composite picture of the world capitalist system in its international relationships at the beginning of the twentieth century – on the eve of the first world imperialist war.[1]

Almost a century of development of the capitalist system has taken place between the writing of Lenin's famous work on imperialism and the stage at which the capitalist system has arrived today. One can observe, of course, certain features of Lenin's description of the pre-First World War imperialism of his time, historically modified and presented today. However, what we have to consider is the nature of the new stage of development of the capitalist system. It is a stage – not described in Lenin's conception – which is fundamentally characterized by its structural crisis and the 'activation of its absolute limits'. The capital order's capacity to displace its sharpening contradictions are becoming exhausted as the actual reproduction of capital as a structure becomes increasingly problematic; capital becomes 'hemmed in' and 'self-negating' as a result of its own historical trajectory and tendencies of development. Hence ...

> despite the major defeats of the past the deciding issue is that the end of capital's historical ascendancy in our own age – through the extension of its domination even to the most distant and formerly isolated pockets of the planet – has brought with it the activation of the absolute limits of this system of social metabolic control. [...], the margin of displacing the system's contradictions becomes ever narrower and its pretences to the unchallengeable status of causa sui palpably absurd, notwithstanding the once unimaginable destructive power at the disposal of its personifications. For

through the exercise of such power capital can destroy humankind in general – as indeed it seems to be bent on doing just that (and with it, to be sure, also its own system of control) – but not selectively its historical antagonist.²

When Lenin was writing *Imperialism*, capital had not at that time entered its period of structural crisis. It is within this newly posited historical context that we must now re-evaluate Lenin's contribution. The basic features of Lenin's conception of imperialism are outlined in his book. These are ...

> (1) the concentration of production and capital has developed to such a high stage that it has created monopolies which play a decisive role in economic life; (2) the merging of bank capital with industrial capital, and the creation, on the basis of this 'finance capital', of a financial oligarchy; (3) the export of capital as distinguished from the export of commodities acquires exceptional importance; (4) the formation of international monopolist capitalist associations which share the world among themselves, and (5) the territorial division of the whole world among the biggest capitalist powers is completed. Imperialism is capitalism at that stage of development at which the dominance of monopolies and finance capital is established; in which the export of capital has acquired pronounced importance; in which the division of the world among the international trusts has begun, in which the division of all territories of the globe among the biggest capitalist powers has been completed.³

The 'truth' (the outcome) of the dynamic and capital-expansion of the century-long phase of 'capitalist imperialism' is the currently unfolding phase of capitalist globalization which is the epoch of capital's structural crisis with all those relations and features which Mészáros describes comprehensively and in detail in *Beyond Capital*.

The impression we are presented with above in Lenin's five part characterization of imperialism is a system which is primed for growth, dynamic and moving forwards into its latest phase. It is not industrial capitalism in the course of its historic ascendancy during the eighteenth and nineteenth centuries. Rather it is the development of its twentieth-century phase of 'monopolist' expansion at the end of which it has truly become a global system of production and distribution. Towards the end of this century-long phase, its structural crisis becomes posited (long ago implied by Marx, specifically in Vol. 3 of *Capital*) which is historically potentiated within the capital relation itself.

In the 'imperialist' stage of capital's evolution, the capitalist 'free competition' of the eighteenth and nineteenth centuries is replaced with 'monopoly capitalism'. Large scale industrial and financial conglomerates supplant small and medium sized 'business concerns' with centralization and concentration of production in both industry and finance whose interests increasingly 'merge' into integrated and colossal capitalist 'ventures' …

> Economically, the major feature in this process of imperialist expansion is the displacement of capitalist free competition by capitalist monopoly. Free competition is the basic feature of capitalism, and of commodity production generally; monopoly is the exact opposite of free competition, but we have seen the latter being transformed into monopoly before our eyes, creating large-scale industry and forcing out small industry, replacing large-scale by still larger-scale industry, and carrying concentration of production and capital to the point where out of it has grown and is growing monopoly: cartels, syndicates and trusts, and merging with them, the capital of a dozen or so banks, which manipulate thousands of millions.[4]

This was a phase of capitalist development in which there was still room for international capital to move, maneouvre and expand. The epoch of 'wars and revolutions' turned out to be more imperialist wars for the redivision of resources and markets than socialist revolutions. Imperialism was indeed the '*highest* stage of capitalism' but not the '*final* stage' as it was understood to be by many communists. Clearly this was not the case.

Hegel taught us that the 'highest point' (zenith) of development of any society is that point at which it also starts to decline. Ancient Rome reached its highest point of development in the second century (CE) under the Antonine emperors but the end of this same century witnessed the start of the stormy crisis of the third century and long term decline and dissolution. The return to a degree of stability in the fourth century – after major structural reforms in production (making it more autarkic) and administration beginning with Diocletian at the end of the third century – did not halt the decline. Another example: the Athens of the first Delian League entered its 'Golden Age' in the fifth century (BCE) but by the end of the century it was on its knees after defeat in the Peloponnesian War. The second Delian League subsequently established was a pale imitation of its antecedent.

The point of flowering of a culture is also that point at which it begins to go to seed. All cultures start to degenerate at their height so that even when a culture is starting to enter its terminal period of decline and decay, it can give the *appearance* that it is on the threshold of a 'Golden Age'.

The 'globalized' phase of development is pre-figured in the developmental tendencies of the previous 'imperialist' phase. Taking capitalist development as a whole over the past 500 years, 'capitalist globalization' is the epoch of capital's structural crisis and, accordingly, its post-zenith, terminal crisis-phase which is the epoch of its 'destructive reproduction' on a global scale.

Implicitly, the 'highest point' or 'phase' of capitalist development cannot be the 'final phase' but merely a prelude to this later stage in which its decline and degeneration become fully developed and expressed. Within the imperialist phase, there was not a single successful revolution in any major capitalist country. The revolutionary struggles of the German proletariat (the most politically advanced section of the international proletariat) were crushed or hobbled by the capital-agencies of Social Democracy, Stalinism and fascism.

'Imperialism is capitalism at that stage of development … in which the division of the world among the international trusts has begun'. This phase had only 'begun' when Lenin put pen to paper and wrote *Imperialism*. His conception that the coming century would be a century of wars and socialist revolutions was demonstrated to be misplaced by the actual unfolding of the historical process itself. Rather, imperialism was a period in which Lenin himself, paradoxically, viewed capitalism as …

> growing with the greatest rapidity in the colonies and in overseas countries. Among the latter, new imperialist powers are emerging (e.g. Japan). The struggle among the world imperialisms is becoming more acute. The tribute levied by finance capital on the most profitable colonial and overseas enterprises is increasing. In the division of this 'booty', an exceptionally large part goes to countries which do not always stand at the top of the list in the rapidity of the development of their productive forces.[5]

The expanding productive and money capital of Lenin's 'monopolies and banks' has been replaced by that of transnational corporations which astride the globe like *colossi* and giant Leviathans of finance capital. Capital 'for export' – as distinct from, and as well as, commodities 'for export' – from within the realms of 'nation states' no longer holds the same degree of significance in terms of the quantitative expansion of the capital order as it did at the start of the twentieth century. Lenin emphasized this export of capital when he wrote that the world is 'divided up' amongst 'capital-exporting countries' but it is finance capital itself in its roaming role in seeking to augment its value which has 'led to the actual division of the world' …

> The capital-exporting countries have divided the world among themselves in the figurative sense of the term. But finance capital has led to the actual division of the world.[6]

The whole globe today is simply the captured *ontological arena of capital per se*. Rather than being a global arena into which it is actively creating an expanding market ('implicitly global') for the growing production and realization of value, the world is now wholly enmeshed within and dominated by the capital relation. The market is now 'explicitly global'.

The barriers which capital now encounters in their opposition to its 'self-valorisation' are not so readily transcendable as they were when it was a dynamically expanding system of production and distribution in previous centuries. The chief problematic confronting the capital order and its state and global agencies becomes one of self-valorisation ('growth') under conditions where capital has become a global relation, has created and reached the 'limits and finitude' of the world market and posited, through its very development, its own structural crisis. Capital's internal contradictions sharpen and intensify under conditions where its capacity to displace them becomes increasingly limited and 'hemmed in' as a result of the globalization of capital itself within its own self-created arena. In essence, the scenario for capital, at the end of its long historical road, is one where displaceability of the intensifying contradictions of its structure is becoming increasingly more problematic and tending towards an absolute non-displaceability.

Capital is free to move around the global organism (using the totality and complexity of its circulatory system) wherever it can find the highest rate of surplus value. The are no *colonialist* 'spheres of influence' inhibiting this surplus-value-seeking movement. What were formerly some of the biggest capitalist powers have become reduced and supplanted in importance for capital by powers that were formerly colonies or in the grip of foreign domination or influence. India and China are the obvious examples here, but increasingly Brazil and other economies in Asia.

Global capital now has its own 'representative' global organizations acting independently of the separate interests of 'nation states'. Organizations such as the World Bank, the IMF and the WTO have been formed to articulate the interests of capital on a global scale by attempting to bring together, 'mediate' and consolidate the interests of different and competing sections of transnational and finance capital. The 'division of the world amongst the biggest capitalist powers' (Lenin) has given way to a world in which capital itself is the 'biggest power' and the 'capitalist powers', taken collectively or competing with each other individually, pledge fealty and merely serve as proxies at the table of this global power.

With Lenin, we have the division of the world between the most powerful capitalist nation states and their appropriation of the natural resources of the colonies, exploitation of their seemingly endless cheap labour-power and the use of these parts of the globe as captive markets for their 'home-produced' commodities. In the 'imperialist' period, the activities of the monopolies and cartels are mediated by the political domination of the competing major European powers, Japan and the United States in their different and varied 'spheres of influence'. The political centrality of the nation state exists in the regulation of monopoly capital as does the constant possibility and threat of war between the rival imperialist powers for the conquest and re-conquest and for the division and re-division of the globe and the planet's resources in the service of rival capitals. The twentieth century is shaken by two world wars and many other rivalries and conflicts between the imperialist nation states.

In Lenin's conception of imperialism, the world is still divided up between the capitalist powers and monopolies to such a degree – 'spheres of influence' – that the free flow of capital is still hindered by these political 'spheres of influence' and the economic 'interests' of different capitalist nation states. In other words, capital has still not become a truly 'global system' in its actuality. A 'territorial division of the world, of the struggle for colonies, of the struggle for spheres of influence' still underpins and articulates the interests of 'nation-states' and those in 'alliance' with each other ...

> The epoch of the latest stage of capitalism shows us that certain relations between capitalist associations grow up, based on the economic division of the world; while parallel to and in connection with it, certain relations grow up between political alliances, between states, on the basis of the territorial division of the world, of the struggle for colonies, of the 'struggle for spheres of influence'.[7]

These same nation states today now actively encourage the free flow of transnational capital into their geographical demesnes and work to facilitate the flow of capital to areas of the globe where the rate of exploitation of labouring humanity is nothing short of obscene. Nation states are now so totally enthralled to and in the grip of transnational capital, which is so powerful, that it can play one state power off against another in order to get the best deal and national conditions and parameters for its 'investment'. And this is not simply a matter of global capital utilizing the cheapest sources of 'unskilled' labour-power wherever it can find them. For example, India and China are turning out significantly more and equally well-qualified Chemistry and Engineering graduates as Britain and the other major European countries every year.[8] This is a bonanza for transnational capital. For the chemical and pharmaceutical corporations, for example, there is absolutely no compelling reason whatsoever for them to invest in Europe, Japan or the USA when all the technicalized labour-power can be employed at a fraction of the cost in India, China or elsewhere and specialists can be imported on 'flexible' contracts when and if required.

Capital now finds itself in a qualitatively different epoch beyond the stage described in Lenin's *Imperialism*. Some writers[9] are describing the current stage as the 'empire of capital'. If this is apt, then it is indeed a global 'empire' where boundaries – unlike with previous empires in human history – have ceased to be geographical. Its 'boundaries' now become a function of the degree of exploitative intensity to which it subjects labour-power and a function of the degree to which nature in all its magnificent creation and beauty becomes subjected to the most nauseating and disturbing forms of destruction, barbarism and 'trashing'. And, as Mészáros shows in *Beyond Capital*, the production of 'generalized waste' becomes endemic or intrinsic to this destructive reproduction of capital-in-crisis.[10]

Within this horrific, psychotogenic world of the 'Daily Nightmare', the free-flow of capital is not hindered but actually encouraged and facilitated. Capital dictates the rules of the game globally and the 'division of the world between rival imperialist powers' – which characterized most of the last century – no longer serves as a brake on its global adventures.

Capital itself is highly mobile. Factory units are now designed for dismantling, shipping and re-erection in different parts of the globe. Workers on strike in the United States, for example, can find themselves 'locked out' one week and a month later 'their' factory simply 'asset-stripped' or actually re-located to China, India or Indonesia where workers are paid one-tenth the wage or paid a low enough wage to make the move worthwhile for capital.[11] Casualization and precarization in employment are the necessary corollaries which accompany this high global mobility of capital. In this movement within its own self-created global arena, it becomes articulated as the dominant, all-powerful social relation of production and distribution which controls every aspect of the reproduction of the social metabolic process. It controls the press and broadcasting media (Appendix II) and dictates its terms to governments and nation-states, revealing their impotence in the face of this omnipotent relation.

The new 'globalized' situation is the age of the extension and consolidation of the global dominance of transnational capital which is a development onwards from the mere 'monopoly or cartel' of Lenin's *Imperialism*. The capital assets of a single transnational corporation can equal the 'Gross Domestic Product' of many small countries put together. Compared to these transnationals, the assets of Lenin's 'monopolies' pale into insignificance. The IMF, World Bank, US Federal Reserve, WTO and, increasingly, Chinese financial institutions serve the interests of global capital more than any fundamentalist fanatics could ever serve their god.

Today China is the world's banker. The vaults of its banks are stuffed with 'hard currency' and bullion.[12] The capital loaned out by China is not only used by debtors to purchase commodities produced in China itself but this loan capital is serviced as short or long term debt. Posited in this relationship between China (creditor) and the rest of the world's economies (debtors) is the explosive potential for a massive deepening of capital's crisis and the profound and utterly disruptive dislocation of the transference of value around the globe. The credit system drives investment in production in an already glutted world market, facilitates consumption and financial speculation whilst also encouraging 'the elements of disintegration of the old mode of production'.

Credit today is not only driving production but also consumption and, of course, ever-burgeoning financial speculation, in its various guises. Every major financial speculation tends to be the 'mother' of the next so any of these many dual 'mother-children' credit ventures can become the 'mother' of the next stage of the unfolding credit crisis of the capital order if debts cannot be 'honoured' to creditors. This is what we witnessed with the 'sub-prime crash' in 2008 which originated in the inability to meet loan repayments in the American mortgage market and to sell the collateral in the form of housing.

Credit 'worthiness' – in an anarchic system with inherent contradictions and instabilities – can very rapidly become 'unworthiness' and lead on to 'crashes' and 'credit crises'. Credit is deployed to expand the capital system, to develop production and the world market whilst simultaneously creating conditions for the deepening of capital's structural crisis and the actual breakdown and disintegration of the capital order globally ...

> The credit system appears as the main lever of overproduction and overspeculation in commerce solely because the reproduction process, which is elastic by nature, is here forced to its extreme limits, and is so forced because a large part of the social capital is employed by people who do not own it and who consequently tackle things quite differently than the owner, who anxiously weighs the limitations of his private capital insofar as he handles it himself. This simply demonstrates the fact that the valorisation of capital based on the contradictory nature of capitalist production permits real, free development only up to a certain point, so that in fact it constitutes an immanent fetter and barrier to production, which is continually broken through by the credit system. Hence, the credit system accelerates the material development of the productive forces and the establishment of the world market. It is the historical mission of the capitalist system of production to raise these material foundations of the new mode of production to a certain degree of perfection. At the same time credit accelerates the violent eruptions of this contradiction – crises – and thereby the elements of disintegration of the old mode of production.[13]

The astronomical (unearthly) figures for the magnitude of what Marx refers to as 'fictitious capital'[14] is not one but many 'ticking timebombs' waiting to detonate in the course of this coming century within the body of the global capitalist system. A default in the United States debt alone will start to throw the world's capital markets and system of production and distribution into utter and complete chaos. The question is not 'if' but 'when' this US default will happen. And, of course …

> the aggravating condition today is that the rest of the world – even with the massive Chinese contribution to the balance sheet of the American Treasury – is less and less capable of filling the 'black hole' produced on an ever-growing scale by America's insatiable appetite for debt financing, as demonstrated by the global reverberations of the recent U.S. mortgage and bank crisis. This circumstance brings the necessary default of America, in one of its more or less brutal varieties, that much nearer. The truth of this disturbing matter is that there can be no way out of these ultimately suicidal contradictions – which are inseparable from the imperative of endless capital-expansion, irrespective of the consequences – without radically changing our mode of social metabolic reproduction. This demands adopting the responsible and rational practices of the only viable economy – an economy oriented by human need, instead of alienating, dehumanizing, and degrading profit.[15]

Politically, we have witnessed the emergence of the United States as capital's policeman of the globe with its client states behind it. Those states which refuse to sign up to the *Pax Americana* become liable to military action in order to bring them into its orbit. The *Pax Romana* employed remarkably similar tactics in order to establish, expand and consolidate its rule. But here, in the form of the American state power of capital, we have the chief political and military representation of the interests of global capital. Formally, there is no 'global government' which articulates the interests of capital uniformly across the world. However, taken informally and substantially, it is quite clear that the United States – as the principal and pre-eminent state power of capital in the world – along with the major financial institutions and transnational corporations on the global stage, constitute the main collective powers of 'governance' to defend the interests of the 'empire of capital'.

Retrospectively, we can now recognize that Lenin's imperialist epoch was not one of a series of socialist revolutions taking place across the world to eliminate the capitalist system. In his book, *Not Without A Storm*, Cliff Slaughter writes that ...

> Contrary to what we believed and based our political lives on, then, the twentieth century was not the 'epoch of working-class socialist revolution'. Rather, it was the epoch of the maturing of the conditions for socialist revolution, by way of great increases in the productivity of labour and 'globalisation', bringing the capital system to the onset of its structural crisis; and within this process, the transition of historically backward countries to capitalism.[16]

The simple truth which we have to face today, painful as it may be for some, is that in the course of the unfolding of the twentieth century ...

> the objective conditions for the social revolution had in fact not matured; and this is contrary to what many of us – not without cause – believed. They were coming to maturity only over (say) the last quarter of the century – in today's conditions of the onset of capitalism's structural crisis and globalisation.[17]

The twentieth century did not generate the conditions necessary for the socialist revolution. Indeed, capital still had 'room' to displace its contradictions and enter a final period of expansion after the Second World War. It was only with the emerging and maturing structural crisis of capital from the 1970s onwards that the global conditions have started to mature for the socialist offensive. This conception also helps to explain the different defeats and losses of the proletariat in the course of the unfolding of the last century; an epoch which was more 'imperialist wars' than 'socialist revolutions'.

Although the conditions are now maturing for the establishment of socialism, this is profoundly tempered by the phase which the capital order has now entered. Capital's 'destructive self-reproduction' actually degrades the natural and cultural conditions necessary for socialism. Side by side with the development of the latest innovations in technique, capital destroys those conditions necessary for socialism. As its structural crisis unfolds, capital will find it increasingly more difficult to reproduce itself as its internal contradictions intensify, implying an even greater devastation of nature and culture. And this must inform and 'change our ideas of how the workers' movement orientates itself, its strategy, and tactics, its alliances' (Cliff Slaughter., ibid., p. 283).

It is within this presently evolving context (the key to understanding the past is furnished by and found in the developing relations and conditions of the present) that we can locate and understand the whole nature of capitalist development within the twentieth century. And, more critically, our response to it and our activities as communists in the course of this past century's development. Moreover, we can proceed – with a *more* concrete degree of political adequacy – to seek to grasp the underlying conditions which led to defeats and betrayals of one kind or another in which millions of proletarians and revolutionaries perished under the rule of capital. We can also *fully grasp* why Social Democracy (and especially its *opportunism* which Lenin refers to in *Imperialism*, as does Trotsky in later writings) and Stalinism were capable of delivering millions into the hands of fascism and the Gulags.

Today, as capital's structural crisis worsens, the roadblock of Stalinism to the emergence of higher forms of revolutionary agency has vanished with the fall of its socio-historical basis since 1989. Stalinism has done significant ideological damage to the struggle for socialism but its fall has removed an obstacle – to that same struggle – the significance of which cannot be overestimated.

The existence of the Soviet system served to discredit socialism and when the whole edifice collapsed, this served to ideologically and morally reinforce the capital order and its guardian state powers and global agencies. However, it is also vitally important to recognize that its disintegration across the globe has removed one of the major obstacles to the unfettered development of the agency of revolution globally. A survey of the history of the twentieth century reveals the counter-revolutionary role which Stalinism played in all the major struggles of the proletariat for its emancipation. Stalinism – like Social Democracy – was *essentially* a proxy of capital in the international proletarian movement. The historical basis of that agency within the proletarian movement has now collapsed and disappeared.

Stalinism has clearly done enormous damage both ideologically and politically to the class movement of the proletariat. But a new generation of people coming forward in struggle against the capital system will no longer be hobbled by the counter-revolutionary character of Stalinism. In this regard, the demise of Stalinism has removed an obstacle on the road to revolution.

The deepening and sharpening of the contradictions of the global capital system in crisis starts to comprehensively destroy the social and natural conditions for the new society. But in this unfolding crisis it also drives the necessity for the movement towards socialism. It heightens the possibilities of the growth of movements against the capital system. But, as we can see, it is a contradictory development. Socialism is not the inevitable outcome of the present stage. It only becomes an inevitability beyond a certain point globally when the process of eliminating capital from the 'social metabolic process' has commenced and its state powers have been irreversibly defeated and dissolved. The further descent into barbarism is equally possible without the positing of the necessary, irreversible conditions for socialism which can only exist and evolve as a *global* formation and never 'in a single country' alone and in isolation. The agency for this overturn can only be the organized global proletariat.

Marx himself wrote[18] that the global movement towards communism would be a long, drawn-out, 'painful', historical process which would 'pass through different phases of class struggle'. In the course of this enduring process, the class of capitalists will offer resistance and, of course, at times they will have their victories and this will, to a certain degree, serve to impede the movement towards communism. But the unfolding of this historical process towards communism has actually started and this tendency will intensify in the course of the coming century. There are not and will not be 'any speedy solutions through the success of political revolutions'.[19] Marx's 'guiding principles' in regard to 'time scale' remain 'valid'. Mészáros further writes – in regard to the transition to socialism – that ...

> the undeniable deviation of the objective historical trends from the 'classical model' raised with a certain urgency the complications of any transition to socialism, carrying with it the necessity of elaborating specific theories of transition, in accordance with the new modalities of crisis and the changing configuration of socio-economic conditions and historical circumstances. It was in response to such trends of development that [...] Lenin defined Imperialism as the 'Highest Stage of Capitalism'. [...][20]

Lenin's 'highest stage of capitalism' was also, in his conception, the 'final stage' and, therefore, accordingly, in the light of developments over the past half-century or so, must be ...

equally subject to major historical qualifications. Nevertheless, he pushed into the centre of analysis the problematic of capital's ruthless global expansion and its manifold contradictions as graphically exemplified by the inherent structural weaknesses – to the extent of a potential rupture – at determinate linkages of its global chain.[20]

Lenin therefore 'saw the new, higher stage as the last phase of capitalism'. Today, as the twenty-first century opens up, many 'Marxists' still doctrinally hold to Lenin's conception of 'imperialism' which the developing global conditions of the rule of capital-in-structural-crisis have 'subjected to major historical qualifications' or even superseded (sublated). According to Cliff Slaughter ...

> Some would-be Marxists hold that Lenin's 'Imperialism, the Highest Stage of Capitalism' is still the key to our epoch, even though it has been left behind by history. More important for our purposes is the way in which his writings on leadership and class-consciousness, developed in conditions of Tsarist oppression and illegality, were taken by Communist Parties all over the world to be the recipe for 'vanguard parties' in all conditions. Trotsky wrote brilliantly and led the principled fight against the Stalinist distortion of Lenin's heritage, but his notions of leadership, party and the nature of the epoch now need a thoroughly critical review. Mészáros makes the clearest case for a renewal of Marxism: his reaffirmation of the revolutionary role of the working class, however, poses the most difficult question of all – how in practice will this social agency necessary to put an end to the rule of capital be prepared, forged, organized?[21]

We will try to address this latter question in the coming chapters.

Notes and References

1   Lenin, Vladimir I., 'Imperialism, the Highest Stage of Capitalism'. In *Lenin's Selected Works, Volume 1*, pp. 667–776 (Moscow: Progress Publishers, 1963) <https://www.marxists.org/archive/lenin/works/1916/imp-hsc/index.htm#ch10> (Last accessed 2 November 2016). Preface to the French and German editions <http://www.marxists.org/archive/lenin/works/1916/imp-hsc/index.htm#ch10>.

2　Mészáros, István, *Beyond Capital. Towards a Theory of Transition* (London: Merlin Press, 1995), p. 145.
3　Lenin, ibid., Chapter 7, 'Imperialism as a special stage of capitalism'.
4　Lenin, ibid., Chapter 7.
5　Ibid., Chapter 7.
6　Ibid., Chapter 4, 'Export of Capital'.
7　Ibid., Chapter 5, 'Division of the world amongst capitalist organizations'.
8　ICEF Monitor, 'China and India to produce 40% of global graduates by 2020', *ICEF Monitor* (16 July 2012) <http://monitor.icef.com/2012/07/china-and-india-to-produce-40-of-global-graduates-by-2020/> (Last accessed 3 November 2016).
9　For example, see Hardt, Michael. and Antonio Negri, *Empire* (Cambridge, MA: Harvard University Press, 2000); and Meiksins Wood, Ellen, *Empire of Capital* (London: Verso Books, 2005).
10　Mészáros, *Beyond Capital*, Chapter 15, p. 547 ff.
11　McCormack, Richard A., 'America's Biggest Companies Continue to Move Factories Offshore and Eliminate Thousands of American Jobs', *Manufacturing and Technology News*, Vol. 20, No. 10 (31 July 2013) <http://www.manufacturingnews.com/news/TAA0731131.html> (Last accessed 3 November 2016).
    This website lists a large number of American companies and corporations which 'moved factories offshore' during or before the summer of 2013.
12　Financial Times, 'Record profits for global banking as China dominates list of top banks', *Financial Times* (30 June 2014) <http://aboutus.ft.com/2014/06/30/record-profits-for-global-banking-as-china-dominates-list-of-top-banks/#axzz3Rw8ZKPVu> (Last accessed 2 November 2016).
    Palma, Stefania, 'Top 1000 World Banks: Chinese banks go from strength to strength', *The Banker* (29 June 2016) <http://www.thebanker.com/Top-1000-World-Banks/Top-1000-World-Banks-Chinese-banks-go-from-strength-to-strength> (Last accessed 3 November 2016).
13　Marx, *Capital*, Vol. 3, Chapter 27, 'The Role of Credit in Capitalist Production', p. 566 ff.
14　Marx, *Capital*, Vol. 3, Chapters 29–33.
15　Mészáros, *The Structural Crisis of Capital*, 'The Unfolding Crisis and the Relevance of Marx', p. 35 ff (New York: Monthly Review Press, 2009).
16　Slaughter, Cliff, *Not Without A Storm: Towards A Communist Manifesto for the Age of Globalisation*, Chapter 8, 'The Twentieth Century: A Hypothesis', p. 285 (London: Index Books, 2006).
17　Ibid., p. 286.
18　Marx, *The Civil War in France* (Peking: Foreign Languages Press, 1966), p. 172.

19 Mészáros, *Beyond Capital*, 'Marx's Unfinished Project', p. 438.
20 Ibid., p. 438.
21 Slaughter, Cliff, *Bonfire of the Certainties – The Second Human Revolution* (Lulu.com, 2013), Introduction, p.xviii.

CHAPTER 4

On Changes in the Proletariat with Capitalist Globalization and the Need for a Critique of Marx's Conception of the Proletariat

It is now necessary to make a general survey of how the 'globalization' of capital has altered the occupational and social composition of the proletariat over the last half-century. How does this inform the question of revolutionary agency?

Marx's conception of the proletariat is the *point d'appui*. His conception was essentially one of nineteenth-century industrialized workers exploited by *productive* capital i.e. an overwhelmingly surplus value producing proletariat as opposed to a more heterogeneous ontology within which a proletariat, paid out of revenue, is, as we observe today, a socially and politically significant component of the labouring class.

In the nineteenth century, at the time of Marx's analysis, the labour of the proletariat was essentially *productive* in nature[1] and concentrated in the newly industrialized or industrializing regions of the planet, primarily Europe and increasingly the United States. Capital was established yet still 'in its little corner' in Europe and only starting to spread itself across the globe. Now, at the beginning of the twenty-first century, we have a qualitatively different situation where *global* capital and an occupationally and socially more complex proletariat increasingly confront each other as the structural crisis of the capital order unfolds. The proletariat is itself now a 'globalized' class. Capital has become a world relation which has captured and enmeshed the whole globe, in each area and in toto. The 'globalization' of capital has also given birth to the 'globalization' of the proletariat as a class.

Today, the proletariat remains a class – like its predecessor in the previous two centuries – which can only survive, without descending into destitution, by selling its labour-power to the owners of capital and its various state powers or other agencies. It shares this *absolute* characteristic with its ancestors regardless of the *historically relative* alterations which have taken place over the past fifty years or so. Socially and technically it has moved on and now has characteristics not possessed by its predecessors. It is the historical development of technique and capital itself which has been the source of these changes in the character of the proletariat.

The global proletariat today – in comparison to its nineteenth-century antecedent – is highly mobile, adaptable, multilingual, technically and socially more diverse and proficient in the latest forms of communication. These alterations in its character have been necessitated to service the needs of capital. Globally, the *productive surplus-value producing* proletariat is now augmented by a growing *'service sector' revenue-consuming* proletariat. Marx (after Adam Smith) distinguishes between 'productive labour' (labour producing surplus value) and 'unproductive labour' (labour which does not produce surplus value but is paid out of the surplus value (revenue) 'productively' produced by the former.) The so-called 'service sector' is an area of this 'unproductive labour' because it does not directly produce surplus value as in production. In connection with these different forms of labour, Marx writes, in the middle of the nineteenth century, that ...

> the extraordinary increase in the productivity of large-scale industry, accompanied as it is by both a more intensive and a more extensive exploitation of labour power in all other spheres of production, permits a larger and larger part of the working class to be employed unproductively.[2]

Marx refers to this class of 'unproductive labour' as the 'servant class'. Today we could locate millions of these 'unproductive labourers' in the so-called 'service sector'. He adds ... 'What an elevating consequence of the capitalist exploitation of machinery!' (p. 575, *Capital*, Vol. 1, Penguin Edn, 1976) with this reproduction of 'the ancient domestic slaves, on a constantly extending scale' (p. 574, ibid.).

With capitalist 'globalization' what has emerged, and is becoming more established and pronounced, is a geographical polarization between regions of 'productive' and 'unproductive' labour (i.e. between labour that reproduces the value of labour power and simultaneously creates surplus value compared to labour that distributes and serves to realize that value and is paid out of revenue).[3]

A significant component of the contemporary proletariat in the 'older' capitalist countries is now made up of *unproductive* (not producing value but living off the revenue produced by *productive* labour) 'service sector' workers and the *structurally unemployed* subsisting on payouts of state welfare benefits. Added to the millions who work in the 'service sector' is the so-called 'middle class' or 'professional' workers like medics, clerical staff, engineers, teachers, etc. They are as much a part of the proletariat as the factory worker or the care assistant, i.e. they can only survive by selling their capacity to labour to capital or its agencies (if they are fortunate enough to find employment) regardless of this labour-power's character as more complex, skilled and highly technicalized labour.

Teachers, nurses, doctors, journalists, lecturers, engineers, architects, etc., would not consider themselves to be part of the 'working class' or to be 'proletarians'. Rather they would, generally, refer to themselves as 'middle class'. 'Working class' has, for many of them, manual wage labour and 'blue collar' connotations or today even carries the 'stigmata' of 'benefits culture'. But all, generally, can live only by selling their labour power to capital, its state power or its various agencies. Regardless of the form which this labour power takes. Today a teacher, architect or engineer on £40,000 or more per annum could very easily tomorrow be standing in the dole queue with the structurally unemployed next to the migrant cleaner or a redundant steel worker: a new 'professional' addition to the 'benefits culture'. The 'professions' are as much a part of the 'precariat' as the 'blue collar' or 'unskilled' worker.[4]

It is true that some workers (a steadily decreasing number) hold pensions, have shares and savings, own their own homes and some even have second homes but all these are the outcome of their labours in the service of capital and rest upon continued employment or a retirement income. Besides, with the precariousness of their property and savings, etc., and with the anarchy of the capitalist market and unfolding crisis-process of capital, the termination of employment brings the prospect of liquidation of any assets to the fore simply in order to maintain their current living standards. A worker – retired or not – with a pension, his own home, a car and a slim portfolio of savings and shares does not a finance capitalist make. The criteria of precariousness apply no less to his/her mode of life as they do to any other worker.

Likewise, the so-called 'intelligentsia' are also proletarianized, 'casualized' and 'precarized', often with zero hours and 'flexible' contracts. The university teacher, for example, is subject to the same precarious forces of capital's structural crisis today as the manual or office worker.[5] The 'intelligentsia' is now, on the whole, an intrinsic part of the proletariat of the twenty-first century even though it may be – if in political outlook acting ideologically in the service of capital – hostile to its own class interests as a part of this proletariat.

It is the structural crisis of capital which is driving changes in the proletariat itself. This crisis demands a more readily exploitable and dismissable workforce under optimal conditions for the benefit of capital. Anti-labour legislation, 'zero hours' contracts, cutting 'red tape' (i.e. health and safety regulations), 'casualization' of employment and mass structural unemployment are all the necessary creations and corollaries of this unfolding crisis.

At the opening of the twenty-first century, capital has at its disposal – on a globally integrated scale – computerization, robotics, automation and satellite and internet communication systems. The actual source of the increasing polarization between, on the one hand, the 'productive' labour of Latin America, Asia and parts of Africa and, on the other hand, the increasingly 'unproductive' labour of Europe, Japan, US, Australia, etc., is the obscenely high rate of surplus value (rate of exploitation) to be found for capital in the regions of Asia and Latin America compared to those in Europe, the US and elsewhere. The creation of most of the surplus value in the former and its conveyance in stupendous quantities into the latter is indicative of the inhuman and destructive superexploitation taking place.

The global transfer of value from its regions of production to its regions of consumption – becoming increasingly wasteful and destructive with what Mészáros refers to as the 'decreasing rate of utilization' – to a certain degree 'featherbeds' the existence of the proletariat in these 'older' capitalist regions.[6] The mass transfer of value from these 'productive' regions arises out of the most brutal forms of superexploitation of wage labour and serves to propagate those 'consumerist service industries' in the 'older metropolitan' capitalist countries which corresponds approximately to a growing division between the production of value, in one part, and its realization, in another part of the globe.

For example, the transnational technology corporations in China can produce laptop computers and mobile phones at a fraction of the sale price we find in European and American retailers, indicating a phenomenally obscene rate of exploitation of Chinese workers on its eastern seaboard. Not only is the rate of exploitation (rate of surplus value) extremely high but such a global mechanism of production and distribution represents a stupendous transfer of value from regions such as China, India and Latin America to the 'older' regions of the capitalist world. This mechanism of conveying vast magnitudes of value from one part of the world to another takes place at the human cost to the lives of the extremely exploited and degraded proletariat in regions of production such as China, Asia and Latin America. This, of course, does not ignore capitalist development which has also taken place in parts of east Asia where the 'standard of living' of some sections of the proletariat is higher than its counterpart in regions of Europe and America.

The proletariat of the traditional capitalist countries as a whole is in a 'privileged' position compared to the workers of the rest of the globe. The obscene rate of exploitation in China and India, for example, serves to attenuate the rate in Europe and the US. The transfer of value to the older capitalist countries 'cushions', to a certain degree, employed and unemployed workers in these countries. In this sense only can we deploy the notion that one section of the global proletariat is 'featherbedding' another more privileged section.

The relatively 'privileged' mode of life of the employed workers in these older capitalist countries also exhibits certain 'parasitic' characteristics in their consumption in that their whole mode of life is subsidized by this mass transfer of surplus value from the superexploited labour of workers in other parts of the globe. Without this most terrible exploitation, the mode of life of the employed proletariat in these major capitalist countries would be completely altered. It would decline, if not 'take a dive'.

The implications of any disruption or significant alterations in this aforementioned dynamic of value transfer are absolutely explosive for the capital order and especially for the historically established proletariat in Europe and the US. The unfolding of the structural crisis of global capital will tend to remove the 'cushion' (subsidy) of value-transference afforded workers in the 'West' with the growing tendency towards the equalization of the rate of exploitation of labour across the globe. In other words, the rate of exploitation of workers in the capitalist countries of Europe, North America and Japan will tend to increase towards ('harmonise with') that of workers in the 'superexploited regions' of Asia and Latin America. This must mean an intensification in class antagonisms and struggle. And if, under the changing global conditions of the increasingly problematic reproduction of capital, workers are not employable (i.e. not *exploitable*), then, increasingly, the pauperization of the many millions we see in these other 'productive regions' in Asia and Latin America (the so-called 'BRICS' regions: Brazil – Russia – India – China – South Africa) awaits the proletariat in the older, major capitalist regions of Europe, Japan and North America: *de te fabula narratur*. Mass structural unemployment in the latter regions is a pre-figuration of this historic tendency towards a proliferating pauperization of the proletariat. The stories of workers' lives we see unfolding in the 'BRICS' regions of the globe gives an idea of the future existence of those workers' lives in the older metropolitan capitalist areas.

Today we are witnessing the widespread liquidation of social provision and services as a consequence of the global crisis of banking capital. But the disruption of this dynamic of value transference would profoundly alter the life of the proletariat in Europe and the US. Mediating this transference is the incredible increase in the productivity of labour since the end of the last world war after 1945. We mention here the tendency which Marx noted, namely that …

> every advance in the use of machinery entails an increase in the constant component of capital […] and a decrease in the variable component […]. We also know that in no other system of production is improvement so continuous and the composition of capital employed so subject to variation as in the factory system. This constant variation is however equally constantly interrupted by periods of rest, during which there is a merely quantitative extension of factories on the existing technical basis. During such periods the number of workers employed increases.[7]

Capitalist globalization has actually served to accelerate and accentuate the trend towards the increase in the 'organic composition of capital'. A relative decrease in variable capital compared to constant capital (that is, wage labour to machinery and materials employed in the process of production of capital) is accompanied by an absolute increase in the number of workers employed globally with the extension of capitalist production. More workers are now employed globally but a progressively declining number *relative* to the value of machinery as productive technique advances. This expresses the unceasing drive of capital to increase the *absolute* mass of surplus value produced whilst, at the same time, compensating (Marx's 'counteracting tendencies' in Vol. 3 of *Capital*) for the historic tendency of the rate of profit to fall.

The growth in the mass of surplus value produced takes place side by side with the growth in mass structural unemployment. This trend, noted by Marx in the middle of the nineteenth century, now replicates itself on a global scale with the most profound implications for the capitalist order and the life of the global proletariat as a whole, but especially for that section in the historical 'homelands' of capital as capital's crisis deepens within the coming century.[8] This drive for profit drives capital-in-crisis increasingly and ever onwards towards an increasingly more 'destructive reproduction' with all the inhuman and barbarous consequences for humanity and nature.

As the organic composition of capital (ratio of the value of machinery and materials to that of labour-power employed) has a historic tendency to increase then, ultimately, it is only the unplanned extension of production which can serve as a medium for the realization of value and the source of revenue for consumption. Capital now enters its degenerative global phase of development which is increasingly a crisis of the reproduction of the capital relation itself. A phenomenal and grotesque expression of this crisis is the utter wastefulness and destructiveness wreaked on humanity and nature as a consequence of the intensifying contradictions of capital-in-crisis. This 'destructive self-reproduction' of capital being the inevitable outcome of capital's structural crisis of value-realization and self-reproduction.

This progressive increase in the organic composition of capital is at the root of the 'activation of capital's absolute limits' and has driven and irreversibly locked capital into its developing structural crisis on a global scale. This, necessarily, brings in its wake the entrenchment of structural, irredeemably persistent, growing mass global unemployment. This phenomenon (mass structural unemployment) is intrinsic to the logic of development of capital itself. It must include in its deathly embrace all sections of the proletariat, highly skilled or 'unskilled'. Mass structural unemployment is intrinsic to capital's unfolding crisis and, indeed, absolutely necessary for capital in its attempts to attenuate this crisis inherent within itself as a social relation of production.

The proletariat as a whole has become more universal and flexible in its labouring capacities as the capitalist system has evolved because this is precisely what capital itself demands. This, of course, has implications for the labourer in terms of the degradation and further dehumanization of his/her role in production in which s/he becomes a 'mere appendage of the machine' and is employed to work monotonously in a 'supervisory capacity'. His/Her labour-power is dehumanistically calculated as the 'labour' component of capital itself in the reproduction of capital. It is activated, for capital, as a mere material element in the reproduction of capital with all its dehumanizing, alienating consequences for the labourer in his/her relationship with his/her labour, his/her fellow men and women and with him/herself.

The increasing degradation of labour and the labourer alongside the growth in structural unemployment becomes functionally related to the progressive increase in the organic composition of capital which tends to transform the 'skilled worker' into a mere 'supervisor' of production. The machine is constantly – in one form or another – replacing human labour. At the same time, the worker in this supervisory function, is expected to be able to move effortlessly from one area of production to another with the breaking down of divisions and barriers in production. Today, a person can move through different occupations (if they are lucky enough to find work in an age of structural unemployment) in the course of life whereas in Marx's time this was not so easy.

Capitalist globalization inevitably signifies mass unresolvable unemployment in the presence of a phenomenal increase in the productivity of labour; starvation and malnutrition in the presence of the overproduction of food; mass homelessness in cities full of empty habitable buildings; the deprivation and destruction of public healthcare and education facilities where humanity now has the knowledge and potential to eliminate both common health problems and mass ignorance; mass overwork with increasing rates of exploitation at one end of a polarity and mass destitution and idleness at the other with all the social consequences and ramifications necessarily implied by all these glaring and painful contradictions.

Global capital-in-crisis is driving the human species and the natural conditions necessary for a higher form of human life towards a 'black hole' of history. This is the 'truth' (outcome) for the proletariat of the unfolding of this inherent trend of the capital order. Towards an abyss into which it is drawing and destroying the whole of human culture and the amazing, wonderful beauty of nature's living creation unless humanity embarks on and prosecutes an ultimately successful global struggle against the capitalist system itself and for the elimination of the capital relation (*the 'cube root' of capital-ism*) from the social metabolism as a whole.

Capital only employs labour-power insofar as it can make a profit off it. This is the motive of capitalist production and the subsequent accumulation of capital. This means that capital only innovates, applies and develops technique with the aim of augmenting its own value. Any innovation will always be subject to the pre-eminent economic criteria laid down by capital regardless of the benefits to or detriment of humanity as a whole in the epoch of capital.

For example, if medical technology is discovered to treat a specific disease or disorder, it will not be developed unless it can be produced in the service of profit. Capital is not advanced without the prospect, at least, of a return and augmentation of its originally advanced value. Otherwise, this would be capital 'wasted' and, as such, the negation of its own intrinsic character as capital.

This also applies directly to human labour power. The bearer of a specific skill will only be employed by capital if a profit can be made off the activation of that skill. If the employment of any skill at any level cannot yield surplus value for capital then it is *not* a skill as such *for capital*. This is the source of the under-utilization and social waste of the highly skilled insofar as they cannot be exploited by capital in the actual execution of these skills.

People with doctorates in Engineering, for example, may find themselves in a desk-based managerial position in the service of capital rather than developing their technical knowledge and skills acquired over many years in training and production. Today many highly qualified and skilled people are unemployed or may even be found 'tossing burgers' in 'Macs' or 'Kings'. In this sense, many workers are, indeed, not only overskilled for capital's requirements. But – in the course of being used in the service of capital – they have their more advanced skills denuded and wasted in the course of 'de-skilling'. Acquired skills are not developed and put to full use in the service of humanity and, more often than not, they become 'atrophied'.

It is 'the theft of alien labour time' (Marx) by capital which constitutes the active basis of its valorisation and self-reproduction. This is the ontological root of capital's exploitation of labour. The worker reproduces the value of his own wage in the product plus an incremental surplus value. The value equivalent to the wage is used by the worker to purchase the means for reproducing and sustaining his labour-power as a commodity for re-sale to the owners of capital or its various agencies. It is labour (i.e. wage labour) that *must* produce surplus value or, if not, it ceases to be variable capital for capital as a whole and becomes useless and *unemployable because unexploitable* labour for capital.

The purchase of labour power takes place on condition that the value produced by the labourer is always greater than the actual value of the labour power itself. Otherwise, no surplus value could be produced and therefore no profit made on its realization. The negation of capitalist commodity production means, necessarily, that this alienated character of labour will be supplanted by the 'free activity of the social individual'.[9]

Today, across the major capitalist countries, many millions are condemned to the reality or the prospect of indefinite, endemic, structural unemployment. Millions will never work again and these numbers increase globally by the day. This structural unemployment is multiplied many times over in the so-called 'underdeveloped' regions of the globe. In India alone, for example, more people are actually registered unemployed than are employed and this is only those who are *registered* jobless.[10] The statistics are staggering. Add to this the many millions in India who are *unregistered* as jobless, destitute, homeless, begging and pauperized, diseased without nourishment, healthcare or education and social services. The promised wonderland of capitalist globalization is a distant mirage for these millions of human beings living in grinding, abject poverty and despair.

This social stratum of the structurally unemployed (the capitalist media in Britain refers to it derogatorily as the 'benefits culture' or as 'the underclass' which has the sinister ring of *'untermensch'* to it) is distinct from the unemployed of previous centuries. The prestructurally jobless were a quantitatively variable reservoir of potential labour power ('industrial reserve army') for when capitalist production and circulation picked up. But this new stratum of the structurally unemployed has now become *absolutely* superfluous to the needs of capital. It is the direct, immediate relationship between this stratum and the capitalist state which is so potentially explosive. It is a relationship which is unmediated by any traditional organization of the proletariat such as trade unions and their conservative bureaucracy. This downtrodden layer of the proletariat has literally 'nothing to lose'. It is not even burdened down with the 'golden chains' of wage labour. It was, more or less, this social stratum which rose in revolt and opposed the police with mass street resistance after the killing of Londoner, Mark Duggan, by the Metropolitan Police in the summer of 2011.[11] Duggan was labelled as a 'gangster' by the capitalist media.

The capitalist system itself – based as it is on exploitation and injustice – is, of course, an *inherently crimogenic* social system. 'Crime' is the creation of such iniquitous conditions and not separate or separable from them as social conditions of human life based on the rule of capital and its state powers and global agencies. These powers defend the very system which breeds 'criminality' and subjects the 'criminal' to the punitive measures of its so-called 'criminal justice system'. *They jail those who are the social creations of the very system which they defend.*

In terms of its occupational and social composition, the proletariat of today is virtually unrecognizable compared to that at the time of the Russian Revolution. The vast majority of the world's population is now proletarian, either urban or rural. And this number increases by the day. The process of the proletarianization of the peasantry and rural poor in China and India, for example, is proceeding apace to service the needs of capital in both city and country. It is being mediated, at root, by the historic process of global capital-in-crisis and the drive to increase the mass of profit and accumulate capital through the superexploitation of countless millions of human beings who are dehumanistically identified as disposable material components in the destructive and increasingly problematic process of capital's reproduction.

We have already observed that globally, and in each area of the world, the proletariat is far richer and complex in its occupational structure, social composition, technical and mental capacities and in its geographical mobility. And, of course, that there are many divisions and even conflicts within the proletariat itself. But this, despite all the difficulties in regard to the question of revolutionary agency which that implies, can also constitute a source of its strength and political development. This heterogeneity and plurality need not necessarily mean internecinity. This diversity within and richer composition of the proletariat can actually serve to facilitate the emergence and development of the requisite forms of revolutionary agency in the course of the coming century as we shall see later.

Can we proceed today on the question of agency – specifically in regard to the original metropolitan centres of capitalist production, the capitalist 'homelands' – on the basis of Marx's or Lenin's conception of the proletariat? Can we develop an adequate theory of revolutionary agency without a comprehensive re-characterization of the current nature of the proletariat in its altered composition and structure under the prevailing conditions of the global rule of capital-in-crisis?

A century of development compels us to recognize the radically different social ontology of the proletariat in Russia at the start of the 1900s and the global proletariat today in 2017. In Tsarist Russia, the proletariat was a minority fraction of the total population. Its social composition was largely industrial in the major urban centres. A significant portion of the proletariat was no more than second or, at most, third generation removed from its peasant or semi-peasant origins. During the civil war period after 1917, many peasants were drafted in from rural socio-cultural backwardness into the cities/factories in order to replace the most class conscious and militant sections of the industrial proletariat who formed the shock troops and bulwark of the Red Army. Here, in essence, we have a picture of a relatively small, very young and historically immature proletariat impoverished in social composition and supplemented by conservative rural elements. Today, of course, with the unfolding of twenty-first-century capitalist globalization, we have a completely altered picture.

A comprehensive critique of Marx's conception of the proletariat (which was of the nineteenth century) is necessary because of the changes which have taken place in the proletariat arising out of the conditions created by globalizing capital-in-structural-crisis. The social character and occupational composition – and the geographical distribution in terms of a global polarization of productive and unproductive labour – of the proletariat has altered to such a degree over the last half century that a critique of Marx's conception is unavoidable.

Such a critique must, accordingly, have implications for the development of the conception of revolutionary agency in the epoch of capital's structural crisis. These changes in the capitalist system with 'globalization' in the past half-century now require new strategies of struggle and higher forms of organization of the proletariat. New forms of agency are now required through which the proletariat can conduct its struggle to put an end to the epoch of capital.

More immediately, what are the implications of such a critique for the development of conceptions of revolutionary agency? A critique of all the old organizational forms (especially trade unions but also workers' councils and the political 'Party-form') is required and these forms must be located within the historical conditions of their creation, evolution and decline in the past two centuries.

For if we accept that there have been historically significant changes in the structure and nature of the proletariat itself since Marx developed his conception – as manifest in its current global situation, social composition and changed occupational structure – then does this not indicate a thorough re-appraisal of those organizations through which the proletarian class has traditionally conducted its struggles, be they defensive or offensive, trade union, workers' council, Party-form, etc.?

Such a critique can only take place on the ground of a comprehensive understanding of the evolving structural crisis of capital. The principal 'target' of this critique must be the prevailing mass, bureaucratized organizations of the proletariat across the globe, namely trade unionism. In other words, a critique of Marx's conception of the proletariat *implicates* a comprehensive analysis and critique – relative to the changes which have taken place in historical conditions since Marx elaborated his conception of the proletariat – of all those organizational forms through which the proletarian class has traditionally conducted its struggle against capital. The results of such a wide and detailed critique would serve to inform perspectives and orientation in the current global situation in relation to the 'practical critical' elaboration of the conception of revolutionary agency.

Marx's conception of the proletariat therefore needs to be brought forward and superseded (sublated) for this vital purpose; for the purposes of transforming the 'real class movement' of the proletariat in struggle. It must incorporate an understanding of the 'globalization' of the proletariat itself as inseparable from capital's 'globalization' into its stage of structural crisis.

The historical validity and degree of 'outmodedness' – the 'historical time' – of all previous forms of proletarian agency are now subject to critique under the impact of the altered global conditions (created by globalizing capital itself) within and through which the capital order is now developing in its structural crisis. The trade unions – as the prevailing mass organizations of the proletariat worldwide – cannot be exempted from this critique.

The question of revolutionary agency is the historically precedent question which needs to be addressed by the class movement of the proletariat globally if humanity is to transcend the epoch of capital. This, of course, necessitates a characterization and grasp of the nature of the global situation in which the proletariat now finds itself. And this, in turn, requires a comprehensive critique of Marx's conception of the proletariat which is over 150 years old. The changes in the character of the proletariat since Marx (regardless of the continuing relative correspondences between Marx's conception and its current nature) is demanding such a critique. This work would feed into and serve to inform work on the question of agency. In fact, this critique of Marx's conception of the proletariat is absolutely indispensable in order to develop a comprehensive theory of revolutionary agency for the twenty-first century.

Today – as we move into the century of capital's structural crisis – the initial forms of agency of revolution must and can only be the *modes within which the revolutionary self-activity of the proletarian class temporally manifests itself in its organization and struggle to terminate the very existence of capital itself and, in the course of this mighty historical process, the political rule of capital in the form of its state powers and global political agencies.* This can only start to come about now because of the historic *ontological* maturation of the proletarian class as a global class which has taken place over the last century. This global quantitative growth, qualitatively altered structure and social composition of the global proletariat has very important implications for the question of agency as capital's crisis inevitably deepens in the coming century.

Notes and References

1. Marx, *Theories of Surplus Value, Part 1*, Chapter IV, 'Theories of Productive and Unproductive Labour', pp. 152–305, (London: Lawrence & Wishart/Progress Publishers, 1969).
    Marx, *Capital*, Vol. 1. Appendix: 'Results of the Immediate Process of Production, Productive and Unproductive Labour', pp. 1038–1052 (London: Penguin Books, 1976, Introduction by Ernest Mandel).
2. Marx, *Capital*, Vol. 1, Chapter 15, 'Machinery and Large-Scale Industry' (London: Penguin Edn, 1976), p. 574.
3. Marx, *Theories of Surplus Value, Part 3* (London: Lawrence & Wishart Edn, 1972, translated by Jack Cohen and S. W. Ryazanskaya).
    '*The main difference between productive and unproductive labour noted by Adam Smith is that the former is exchanged directly for capital and the latter for revenue...*' (p. 426).
    Marx later writes in relation to the work of Richard Jones that ... *'Jones quite correctly reduces Smith's productive and non-productive labour to its essence – capitalist and non-capitalist labour – by correctly applying the distinction made by Smith between labourers paid by capital and those paid out of revenue'* (p. 432).
4. See, for example, Guy Standing's work *The Precariat – The New Dangerous Class* (Bloomsbury, 2011).
5. Datablog, 'University funding cuts: which institutions are worst hit?', *The Guardian* (17 March 2011) <http://www.theguardian.com/news/datablog/2011/mar/17/university-funding-cuts-institution-hefce-universities> (Last accessed 4 November 2016).

6   Mészáros, *Beyond Capital*, pp. 547–596.
7   Marx, *Capital*, Vol. 1, p. 578.
8   Marx, *Capital*, Vol. 3, Chapters 14 and 15.
9   Marx, *Capital*, Vol. 3, 'The Trinity Formula', pp. 958–959 ff (London: Penguin Classics Edn, 1991, translated by David Fernbach).
10 Jobless levels in India (February 2015) are approximately 45 million *registered* unemployed and 30 million *registered* employed in a total population of 1.3 billion. This means that only 2.3 per cent of the *total* population is *registered* as employed. The same website (given below) expects the registered employed in India to rise to approximately 32 million and the registered jobless to 56 million by 2020. Accordingly, the trend is towards an even lower percentage of the total population 'registered employed' as the population continues to increase towards 2020.

Trading Economics, 'India Unemployment Rate 1983–2016', *Trading Economics* <http://www.tradingeconomics.com/india/unemployment-rate> (Last accessed 4 November 2016).
11 Prasad, Raekha, 'English riots were "a sort of revenge" against the police', *The Guardian* (5 December 2011) <http://www.theguardian.com/uk/2011/dec/05/riots-revenge-against-police> (Last accessed 4 November 2016).

CHAPTER 5

The Impact of Capital-in-Crisis on Nature

Capital's structural crisis is a crisis of the *reproduction* of its structure. This crisis expresses the truth that capital as a social relationship of production has come to the end of its long historical road, implying the untenability and negation of the capital relation itself. That the productive activity of humanity has arrived at a stage of technical development which is increasingly incompatible with the existence of the capital relation. This posits, directly, the historic necessity for the 'destructive reproduction' of capital, arising out of the 'activation of capital's absolute limits'. At the same time, it posits the driving necessity for humanity to go beyond the capital relation.

Capitalism, in previous times, was seen as a historically progressive social system. It served to dissolve the remnants of feudalism, to break down parochial modes of life and to create the necessary conditions for a more advanced way of life for humanity, despite its destructive effects on humanity and nature in the course of its historic ascendancy, development and hegemony. The rapidity and scale of capital's advance – and its destructive effects – were seen as the 'price which had to be paid for social progress'. The onset and unfolding of capital's structural crisis now brings in an epoch of 'destructive reproduction' in which the 'destructive' element 'becomes more and more disproportionate and ultimately quite prohibitive'. Any vestiges of 'social progress' have been eclipsed by the entry of capital into its structural crisis of 'destructive reproduction'. Mészáros writes ...

> Once upon a time the defenders of the capital system could praise with some justification its power of 'productive destruction' as inseparable from the positive dynamics of advancement. This way of seeing things was well in line with the constant extension of capital's scale of operations, truly in the form of 'productive destruction'. The successful encroachment of capital over everything that could be encroached upon – that is, before the system had to overreach itself in the way we have already seen – made the notion of 'productive destruction' tenable, even if progressively more problematic as

the scale itself increased. For the destruction involved could be generously written off as a necessary part of the 'costs of production' and expanded reproduction, while the constant extension of capital's scale of operations had brought with it the displacement of the system's contradictions as an additional benefit. However, things have changed for much the worse with the consummation of capital's historical ascendancy and the activation of the system's absolute limits. For in the absence of further possibilities of encroachment on the required scale, the 'destructive' constituent of the overall 'cost of production' – to be met within progressively constraining limits – becomes more and more disproportionate and ultimately quite prohibitive. We have historically moved from capital's reproductive practices of 'productive destruction' to a stage where the predominant feature is increasingly and incurably that of destructive production. It is not too difficult to see – even if the personifications of capital find it impossible to admit – that no system of social metabolic reproduction can indefinitely survive on this basis.[1]

The increasingly rapacious destruction of nature's creation is a direct manifestation of this crisis of reproduction. It is inseparable from the 'triumph of generalized waste-production' and the 'decreasing rate of utilization' (see Mészáros, *Beyond Capital*, Chapters 15 and 16, pp. 547–600) which have become indispensable for the constant renewal of the value-realization process and therefore for the continuation of the process of the reproduction of capital as a whole in the unfolding of its structural crisis. New versions of established (and perfectly adequate) products are continually being re-designed and re-presented in order to confer on the older versions a fake obsolescence.

Marketeers encourage people to discard and spend and repeat the actions. A whole mass psychology has grown up and has been 'cultivated' around habitual 'shopping', encouraged by advertisement which serves to feed this alienating and ecologically destructive 'consumerist' activity and mentality. Credit has financed this 'consumerism' in the service of the continuously and destructively wasteful realization of value and the accumulation of capital. Nature and humanity are being sacrificed on the high altar of profit and capital accumulation. All this has a *brutalizing and degrading* effect on human beings, on their psychology and physical organism, in their relations with each other and with nature's creation.

The irrepressible and untransgressible logic of capital is to locate human beings and nature as disposable objects for exploitation. Every aspect of culture and human relationships becomes subject to this brutalization and degradation. It becomes expressed in the predatory wars of the state powers of capital and yet can be found residing in the most intimate interpersonal relationships between people. The wonder and beauty of nature's creation is under the scourge of a profit-driven daily destruction as capital's structural crisis widens and deepens.

Everywhere we look, we see nature's creation is being subjected to the most disturbing forms of destruction, barbarism, cruelty, torture, pillage and annihilation for profit and sadistic 'pleasure'. Personal gratification, often in the most narcissistic and voyeuristic forms, has become the preoccupation of the age at the expense of anything and everything. Legalized brutality, gratuitous cruelty and sadism have become widespread, intrinsic to which is this regarding of people and animals as mere objects for use, mere objects for exploitation to serve certain ends. And this has invaded every aspect of human life and relationships as a reflex of this age of 'destructive reproduction'.

The motivating force behind capital's widespread devastation and exploitation of nature's creation is the uncontrollably destructive dynamic, expansion and accumulation of capital-in-crisis, its relentless drive for profit. The actual dynamics of the capital order in crisis demand (necessitate) this 'destructive reproduction' of capital. This is the immanent dynamic of the enduring and unfolding historic crisis of the very structure of the capital relation itself and not simply a displaceable cyclical or conjunctural crisis.

For humanity to transcend the epoch of globalizing capital must also mean, therefore, the overcoming of the dehumanizing effects on people of the continuation of this age. And the irreversible establishment of a totally transformed and truly nurturing and symbiotic relationship with nature itself. The destructive relations of the capital epoch must be replaced with a paradigm shift involving the establishment of creative and life-enhancing relations with nature. The destruction of nature is humanity's self-destruction. Humanity's symbiosis with nature is the beneficial development of both.

We would be forgiven for thinking that the word 'progress' has no historical meaning whatsoever unless within the present age we could discern the possibilities for a human life free of the domination, destruction, exploitation, brutalization and the despair which now characterize human relationships and humanity's relation with nature.

For example, if we consider the barbarism, destruction and a multitude of forms of cruelty daily inflicted on living nature. These activities are linked directly or indirectly to the drive for profit and/or for sadistic 'pleasure' in an age when capital needs to place *destructiveness* as its *modus operandi* in order to reproduce itself. This, of course, *en passant*, raises the question of the origins of sadism, cruelty and other 'transhistoricals' in human beings. *However, undoubtedly, as long as cruelty and sadism continue to mediate humanity's conscious relationship with nature, this must indicate that humanity, and therefore nature, has not truly become disentangled from the relations and psychosocial legacies of bourgeois society in particular and from the psychopathology of the history of class society and the rule of private property in general.*

This sort of behaviour is not inherent in human beings any more than slavery is inherent. It can be eliminated with revolutionary social change and subsequent development. This means that it is only in the transformation of human social relations that an increasingly more humane and compassionate approach to all living creatures can be truly cultivated by humanity as a whole. Only through the revolutionary transformation of human beings (the elimination of capital from society's landscape) by human beings themselves will the social-human conditions and pre-requisites be posited for the rest of living nature be able to live free from human predation and cruelty. Inevitably, this will and must involve changes in agricultural and nutritional practices and the move towards a diet where the destruction of other living creatures is eliminated. As long as capitalism continues globally, the establishment of this new relationship to and with living nature remains impossible. The rule of capital must be transcended and humanity must advance to socially transform itself if living sentient nature is to live without the human predation, persecution, barbarism and cruelty which we are increasingly witnessing today.

Once again, the urgent and historically precedent question of revolutionary agency raises its head: the creation and development of organizations – with the initiation and elaboration of necessary global perspectives, strategies and tactics – to prosecute the struggle beyond the point of return for capital, its state powers and its global agencies.

The *opening of this path* to this 'true realm of freedom' (Appendix I) (Marx, *Capital*, Vol. 3)[2] is through those consciously organized forms of revolutionary agency which are capable of uprooting capital from the social landscape and toppling the state powers which defend capital. Only in the transformation of humanity can the relationship to living nature be truly transformed. And such a transformation can only take place in the course of a long, enduring and unfolding period of social revolutionary changes central and essential to which is the progressive transcendence of the capital relation. The barbaric mass destruction of nature's creation will only end when humanity is emancipated globally beyond the capital system and the state powers and global agencies which defend it have been irreversibly dismantled.

There are those who assert the possibility of the 'greening' of capitalism. For example, the Green Party in Britain advocates a 'responsible capitalism' as if the global existence of the capital relation in an apparently and bizarrely postulated 'responsible' form is compatible with an ecologically sustainable future for the planet.[3] The politics of the Green Party despise the destruction which the transnational corporations are bringing down on the planet. However, they consistently fail to address the root of the problem which is the existence of the capital system itself. The resulting conception is the fabulous 'greening of capitalism' which is as chimeric as mermaids, unicorns and the fabled medieval dogheads (Cynocephali). Underlying the untenability of a 'green capitalism' is the simple historic truth that ...

> The capital system's blind expansionary drive is incorrigible because it cannot renounce its own nature and adopt productive practices compatible with the necessity of rational restraint on a global scale. Practising comprehensive rational restraint by capital would in fact amount to repressing the most dynamic aspect of its mode of functioning, and thereby to committing suicide as a historically unique system of social metabolic control [...] It cannot revert to a previous – less globally integrated and expanded – condition; nor can it move forward in its restless global expansionary drive on the required scale.[4]

A 'green capitalism' is an impossibility. It is neither establishable nor, if it were remotely possible, would it be sustainable. Which is most definitely *not* to assert that the struggle for an ecologically sustainable future does not start within the present epoch of capital. But it is only truly realizable 'for itself' beyond the capital relation.

This means that the long term aims of the struggles of the 'animal welfare and rights' and 'grassroots green' movements only become actualizable as an intrinsic, organizational part of a broad movement to terminate the epoch of capital. Only as an integrated and 'organic' part of the proletarian movement in the fight for this sustainable, communist future. Their struggles for animal welfare against the manifestations of an inherently barbaric system are integral to the struggle to put an end to the epoch of capital once and for all.

Accordingly, any form of revolutionary agency must contain intrinsically within itself the struggles and activities of these 'eco-movements'. The emancipation of humanity as a whole from the rule of capital is also the emancipation of living nature from the barbarism of that rule. This human liberation (the second 'human revolution') becomes a historical pre-condition for the complete liberation of nature from the barbarism and destruction of previous epochs.

Marx wrote in his time that it is the development of capitalism itself which generates the material conditions necessary for socialism. This remains a positive aspect in its historical development. However, this aspect has become, with the onset of capital's structural crisis, subsumed and subordinated to the 'destructive reproduction' of the capital order. The frenetic, uncontrolled 'drive' for profit and capital accumulation in the time of its structural crisis is destroying those conditions which are necessary for the creation of a socialist society. However, at the same time, this relentless 'drive' simultaneously generates opposition to this destruction. Already, this opposition is taking the form of various campaigns and movements across the globe. Some are conscious and others are not conscious that such opposition to this destruction is, implicitly, opposition to the very existence of capital. Yet some still think it is possible to have a 'greening' of capitalism. It is a mistaken conception which belies the nature of capital itself.

Inevitably, as this destruction and wastage unfolds, it must serve to intensify the opposition that already exists and open out into new movements against the destructive manifestations of the capital order in crisis. Such movements oppose this ecological/environmental carnage of capital's rule but this is qualitatively different from actually addressing the rule of capital itself. Analogically speaking, to tackle the symptoms of an unfolding, chronic planetary illness is not the same as tackling the root causes of the illness itself, out of which the symptoms of the 'illness' tend to constantly arise, replicate and manifest. The causality must be grasped, pulled up 'root-and-branch' and transcended.

Capitalist commodity production in the age of its structural crisis becomes the time of the phenomenal waste and destruction of the natural and cultural conditions of human life. The most terrible wastefulness and most barbaric forms of destruction of the age now constitute a *fundamental presupposition* for the continuation of the capital order. At the same time, capital's capacity to displace its growing and sharpening contradictions in this reproduction is becoming more limited, more constricted and making social explosions and cataclysms more likely with each passing day. This destruction and waste production is inherent ...

> in the nature of capital that it cannot recognize any measure by which it could be restrained, no matter how weighty the encountered obstacles might be in their material implications, and no matter how urgent – even to the point of extreme emergency – with regard to their time scale. For the very notion of 'restraint' is synonymous with crisis in the conceptual framework of the capital system. Neither the degradation of nature nor the pain of social devastation carries any meaning at all for its system of social metabolic control when set against the absolute imperative of self-reproduction on an ever-extended scale.[5]

The historical paradox presents itself that only now are the conditions being created for socialism in the midst of the destruction of those same natural and cultural conditions by the unfolding of capital's crisis. This developing contradictory state of affairs stands in contrast to the 'imperialist' expansion of capital in the twentieth century.

We can observe directly the detrimental alteration of these natural conditions of life on the planet by studying climate change. The science of studying climate change (Climatology) is now an established discipline. The uncontrollable character of capital's crisis is having the most profound effects on the planet's climate systems. These effects can only worsen as this crisis deepens.

The reciprocality of the relationship between capital-in-crisis and nature's ecosystems contains within it the possibilities of the deepening of this structural crisis. This is very clearly exemplified in the relationship between 'global warming', the melting of the ice-sheets in the polar regions and the effect of this on maritime climates.

The relationship between global warming, the disappearance of the icesheets and the operation of the Gulf Stream (the 'Conveyor') which regulates the maritime climate[6] of north-western Europe is a very specific example of this reciprocality of capital's pollution-generating crisis and the alteration of nature's cycles. The chief characteristic of a 'maritime climate' is the small differences between summer and winter temperatures reflecting a certain equability in the changing seasons of these types of climate.[7]

Geoscientists have investigated and analysed the historical deposition, over many millenia, of the different layers in the ice-sheets of Greenland and the Arctic. From inspecting this layered record in ice-cores, they have discovered direct correlations between the degree of salinity in the water of the Atlantic Ocean throughout its history and the actual flow-speed or the suspension of this flow in the Gulf Stream itself.[8] They have found that as the salinity of the ocean drops (as more freshwater enters it from melting ice sheets), the Gulf Stream has a tendency to slow down or 'switch off' and fall into a state of suspension. It effectively decelerates or ceases to flow, to circulate as a 'conveyor' of warm air and water from the equatorial regions to the North Atlantic, north-western Europe and, of course, Britain's shores.

The influence of the Gulf Stream is very important in the regulation of the maritime climate of north-western Europe, and especially Britain which is in its direct path. This influence tends to warm up the climate in the winter months and cools it down in the summer months. By doing this, it maintains the maritime character of the climate. The continued melting of the ice-sheets will lower the salinity of the North Atlantic waters and tend to increase the possibility of the Gulf Stream 'slowing down' or even 'switching off'. Geoscientists have discovered that it may not necessarily be a gradual process of switch off. It could be sudden, abrupt, catastrophic. Once the salinity drops beyond a certain point, it could trigger the immediate 'turning off' of the Gulf Stream over a period of years, not decades or centuries. A United States National Research Council report on climate change posed the question as to what defined a climate change as 'abrupt'. It answered ...

> Technically, an abrupt climate change occurs when the climate system is forced to cross some threshold, triggering a transition to a new state at a rate determined by the climate system itself and faster than the cause. Chaotic processes in the climate system may allow the cause of such an abrupt climate change to be undetectably small.[9]

This would have catastrophic consequences for the maritime climates which are subject to the Gulf Stream's influence in western Europe. If it 'switches off', it will, from all the geoscientific records and studies, radically alter these maritime climates by ushering in long, freezing sub-zero winters and baking hot summers. It will polarize the temperatures between the seasons. In other words, 'maritime' will cease to be 'maritime' and the climate will be more like a 'continental climate' which we find in the interior of Asia or North America.[10]

Changes in climate, as we have exemplified above, can be abrupt and leaps forward from one state to another qualitatively different one can take place relatively quickly, with catastrophic consequences for all life. It is not 'man in the abstract' which is the main source for generating these alterations in climate but rather human society at a certain stage of historical development where capital is the dominant relationship of production. Unplanned production for profit based on this relation-in-crisis is the fundamental causality behind socially mediated climate changes. Not the Malthusian 'man as a species' per se, not 'man in the ahistorical abstract', which we sometimes find with the liberalisms of 'green' or 'ecopolitics'.

The denial of climate change has become a professional pre-occupation of all manner of right-wing 'think (sic!) tanks', system ideologues and chattering media charlatans. Such nefarious activities are a conscious or unconscious ideological defence of the global capitalist order and its unfolding, malignant destructiveness of the Earth's planetary and localized climatic and ecological systems. It ineffectually seeks to dissociate such changes in these systems from capital's global crisis by endeavouring to reduce them to the 'cyclical' rhythms of nature itself independently of the workings of the structural crisis of the global capitalism of the twenty-first century. Unfortunately, for individuals like Nigel Lawson[11] who was Thatcher's long-serving Chancellor, a *non-ideological* mountain of scientific data and research too bountiful to cite is daily demonstrating the effects of global capitalism on the planet's ecology and climate. No amount of 'cooking the books' or ideological 'saucing' will be able to smother the increasingly evident truths presented by these peer-reviewed scientific investigations.

With millions in deep poverty and struggling to meet their energy bills, what sort of a social crisis would the onset of such a climate change precipitate in Britain and in other areas? Many elderly (and not so elderly) people become ill or die every winter in Britain from hypothermia or extreme cold because they cannot afford to heat their homes. They die not because of the absence of available energy but because they do not have the income to pay for enough of it which will enable them to survive the winter. The immoral position of the capitalist energy companies is 'pay up or get disconnected' from the energy grid. People only keep warm in winter on condition that the energy companies can profit from it. People freeze to death as well as keep warm as victims of the profit system. The elderly and the homeless living on the street are particularly vulnerable to illness and hypothermia with falling temperatures.

Capital's crisis today is intractable, inescapable and irresolvable within the conditions and parameters of the global capitalist order. It is not a crisis which is displaceable within these parameters. It is structural and enduring with all the ramifications implied for nature and human culture. On the one hand, the development of its dynamic necessarily drives it towards the destruction of the full panoply of nature's creation, human beings and therefore of all those natural, social and cultural conditions which are required for the establishment and development of socialist society. But this self-same destruction also destroys the very material basis for the continuation of the capital order itself whilst, simultaneously, starting to posit a dynamic of social revolution. Capital-in-structural-crisis actually contains and gives birth to all the necessary conditions for its own transcendence as a result of the unfolding of its own internal-crisis mechanisms.

The only social class which can resolve this structural crisis in favour of the continuation of society is the proletariat organized in its necessary forms of revolutionary agency.

The proletariat is the only class, the only force, that can put an end to the epoch of global capital and create the social basis for a new future for humanity established on the foundations of the common ownership of the entire planet arising out of the abolition of private property. This, of course, does not mean that the capital order will *inevitably* give way to socialism. Quite the contrary, the proletariat organized as revolutionary agency will have to fight to put an end to its existence once and for all. However, one thing is *absolutely beyond doubt*: there is no future for a global order based on capital. Either it will self-destruct and take humanity and the world's current and increasingly threatened ecosystems with it or the organized proletariat will go forward, put an end to it and create the basis for a new human future and new relations between humanity and nature. This is precisely why the question of revolutionary agency has historical precedence today over all other questions.

A planned socialist system of production and distribution – worked and democratically controlled by a free association of producers with all the advances in science and technology at its disposal – will be one which places humanity's relationship with nature at the forefront of all actions and considerations in the course of human activity and planning.

The climate changes taking place since the Industrial Revolution commenced in the eighteenth century in England can only now be the result of the continual and ruthless drive of capital to augment its value which is, at its very core, an unplanned and anarchic system as Marx noted many years ago.

The rising levels of greenhouse gases in the atmosphere and oceans are serving to alter climate. It is only since the beginning of the capitalist Industrial Revolution that the concentration of carbon dioxide has been consistently rising as a trend in the planet's atmosphere. Before that records indicate a relatively stable and circumscribed, equilibrated concentration.[12] The crisis of the global capital order is serving to accelerate the rate of damage already done by capitalist development to the planet's ecosystems and is altering its climate to a significantly different degree to that which previous centuries of social development has done.

In truth, the whole question of climate change is intimately connected with the global existence of planned or unplanned production in the broadest sense of the term and not simply in the narrow economic sense. Ostensibly, the Soviet system was a 'planned' economy but one which was a 'forcing house' for the development of production after the Russian Revolution from a society based on peasant labour to an urban industrial society. In a certain sense, it was a totally 'unplanned' form of 'planning' which inevitably brought destruction and the pillage of nature in its wake. There are many examples of this from the Soviet era but perhaps the most poignant is the destruction of the ecosystem of the Aral Sea.[13] The term 'planned' here in this text does not, therefore, refer to the bogus 'top-down' Stalinist system of 'planning' in the now defunct Soviet system.

To point to the Soviet system as a 'model' for 'socialist development and planning' is clearly inadequate when the operational criteria of capital were continuing to influence the 'mode of social metabolic control' and development of production within this system. The murderous destruction of humanity in its millions in the Gulags, Stalin's genocidal purges of whole peoples and any political opposition took place alongside the widespread ecological destruction and disruption of nature's ecosystems in the Soviet Union of 'really existing socialism'. To identify the Soviet system as an exemplification of 'socialist economy' or 'socialist centralized planning' is nothing short of a complete misconception of the nature of the Soviet system itself. We cannot take the Soviet Union, China, Cuba, etc., as models for 'socialist planning'.

The Soviet system was never a 'socialist economy' and 'central planning' was not and never can or could be 'socialist' because it involves the imposition of alien bureaucratic state structures and directives on the self-organization and self-direction of the proletariat as a revolutionary class in its historic global movement for self-emancipation. The restructuring and re-planning of the whole of society's social and economic landscape beyond the capital epoch will be an intrinsic part of this struggle for emancipation. It cannot be realized by means of structures which are alien to that process of revolutionary transformation.

The assertion that it would make no difference if production were planned or unplanned (with fossil fuels as the major energy source) and that both forms of production would equally damage the planet's ecosystems is a false ahistorical identity. This identity contains the pessimistic implication that climate change and ecosystem disruption/destruction are simply a function of *technological* development and not of the prevailing character of the dominant social relations or of the socio-economic mode in which this technology is engineered and utilized. It is not only pessimistic but also a *fetishistic* conception which abstracts from the real social conditions of technology's creation, development and operation.

Changes and shifts in climate and increasing ecological destruction are not simply the consequences of developments in technology but are directly bound up with the historically specific character of capital as the dominant social relation. A consideration of why these changes are taking place fundamentally revolves around the question of whether or not production is planned or unplanned and, accordingly, is intrinsically connected with the existence or non-existence of capital as the dominant global social relation.

To try to understand these developments merely and exclusively in terms of 'technological evolution' is bound to lead into a *fetishistic* conception. In other words, to divorce technological innovation and its social mode of utilization from capital – as the ruling relationship of production and distribution and as the dominant operative 'mode of control of the social metabolism' – leads directly to the conception that the ecological crisis can be resolved within the continuation of the framework of the capital system. Either by modifying technology (which would undoubtedly contravene the interests of capital-in-crisis) or by the 'greening' of capitalism: a self-contradictory assertion which, as we have already seen, will not 'stand' in any real or theoretical form ...

> to say that 'science and technology can solve all our problems in the long run' is much worse than believing in witchcraft; for it tendentiously ignores the devastating social embeddedness of present-day science and technology. In this respect, too, the issue is not whether or not we use science and technology for solving our problems – for obviously we must – but whether or not we succeed in radically changing their direction which is at present narrowly determined and circumscribed by the self-perpetuating needs of profit maximization.[14]

In truth, the worsening ecological crisis is an organic and intrinsic product of capital's intensifying structural crisis and cannot be metaphysically divorced from this crisis or from the history of the capitalistically determined design, engineering and production of the employed technology. They are two inseparable aspects of the same crisis.

This ecological crisis will only start to be resolved with the global termination of the epoch of capital and, subsequently, in the course of the evolution of the post-capital aeons within which the forms of technology will be re-designed and re-engineered to actually develop (nurture) humanity's relationship with nature further beyond previous eras.

If we conceive that there can be no difference between the planned socialist and unplanned capitalist systems of production in terms of their destructive effects on nature's creation, then we do, indeed, replicate the ahistorical and abstract 'man is the destroyer of nature' notion which is sometimes put forward by certain sections of the 'Green' movement and 'ecopoliticians'. Humanity 'in the ahistorical abstract' is not destroying nature but rather this destruction is only taking place under a system of social relations of production and distribution in which capital-in-crisis is the dominant relation.

A socialist society would not fetishistically approach humanity's relationship with nature purely as a function of the stage at which scientific knowledge and technique had arrived. The nub of the question in regard to climate change and ecological destruction/sustainability is the existence or non-existence of capital as the dominant relationship of production. And, accordingly, of the social mode within which technology is actually utilized which must itself have consequences for the design and technical character of technology in general. To assert that it does not really matter (for these questions of climate change, ecology, etc.) whether global society is socialist or dominated by capital – because it all depends on knowledge, technology and scientific discovery – is a bogus conception which separates the actual design, production and use of technology from its actual *socio-historically conditioned mode of utilization*. Whether or not capital is the ruling relation of production and distribution is the *fundamental consideration* at the core of ecological/climate questions.

This, of course, is not to dismiss the environmental consequences of the actual physical operation of technology itself. In a planned, socialist system of production – as knowledge and technology advance – we will be able to adjust and modulate (i.e. plan) our activities accordingly (re-design, re-engineer, alter modes of usage, etc.) in order to minimize or eliminate any environmental damage to nature and its ecosystems which may stem directly from the actual physical-operative character of technology used. This is not the primary consideration for capital in its crisis of destructive reproduction.

The degree of damage which human society does to nature's creation is a function of the character of its dominant social relations and the social mode within which technology is actually operated and applied in order to wrest our needs from nature. It is not simply and exclusively a function of knowledge, technology or innovation. The material process of technology itself has been developed to serve capital in the present epoch. Its ecologically and environmentally destructive character is not the primary consideration for capital. In this sense, socialist humanity will have to radically alter and innovate technology itself so that its materially destructive capacities on nature (including on human physiology and psychology) are eliminated or are subject to modifications which progressively and increasingly minimize such deleterious effects on nature and humanity.

In the epoch of capital, the actual *material character* of technology itself – and its operation arising directly from this character – is engineered and developed to service the requirements of capital. To maximize profit and accumulation. Implicitly, in an evolving age beyond capital, technology will have to be constantly materially re-engineered and re-modulated in order to establish – and maintain into the future – an ecologically sustainable relationship with nature. Hence, both the mode of utilization and the material engineering (and disposition as material process) of technology arise out of the pressing requirements of the prevailing social relations. Accordingly, in the present epoch, the material character of technology and its mode of operation are inseparably linked to and mediated by capital as the pre-eminent social relation controlling the whole social metabolism. In the epoch of its structural crisis, this necessarily implies an increasingly more destructive deployment and operation of this technology and a design process which panders to this profit and capital-accumulation driven crisis-process.

In the ages beyond capital, a totally different mode of utilization is deployed in accord with both human needs (in contrast to those of capital's needs) and in consonance with the wider needs of the *natural conditions* of human life. The alteration in both the character of the production of the means of production (and means of subsistence) and their mode of utilization implies a qualitatively different relationship with nature's creation. The forms of mediation between man and nature are fundamentally altered because the social relations have become revolutionized. Capital has become transcended as the dominant relation and replaced by the identification, refinement and realization of human needs. A totally transformed relationship with nature's creation – which will be nurturing, creative and respectful of the 'needs' of nature – becomes intrinsic to the realization of these historically created and developed human needs.

We can clearly observe the conflict between the requirements of capital and those of human beings in a very specific example: coal-fired power stations. Their design and subsequent operation takes place with the emission of many thousands of tons of greenhouse gases (mostly carbon dioxide) into the Earth's atmosphere every year. And, as we have seen, with increasing ramifications for catastrophic changes in the planet's climate systems. But already we have the technology to design and operate coal-burning power stations which are 'emission free'. All gases can be separated out, concentrated and even liquified or solidified for use in other productive chemical processes without a single molecule escaping into the planet's atmosphere or biosphere. Likewise the heat and liquid effluents from the burning of coal and gas could be processed and used without polluting the planet. Different ways of producing 'clean coal technology' are already established and being researched and developed.[15] For a society where the fundamental cultural paradigm has shifted from *profit* (the historically specific form taken by the product of surplus labour in the age of capital) *to need*, this movement from 'polluting' to 'pollution free' would be a relatively simple transition to make.

The deleterious and destructive effects of capitalist production on nature were known at the time of Marx and Engels.[16] But, as we note above, in a planned economy, even the controlled use of fossil fuels need not be polluting as we have (and have had) for many years the science and technology to prevent this and, indeed, to utilize the by-products of burning fossil fuels. The fact that the atmosphere and oceans are concentrating carbon dioxide and other greenhouse gases is the result of the fact that, under capitalism, the universal implementation of technical processes to stop it are not profitable and would take a massive 'unsustainable' bite out of the produced surplus value and thus interfere with capitalist accumulation. Even the 'recycling' and 'landfill mining' practised today are only done on condition of capital turning a profit.

Mészáros summarizes these relations of the capital-determined expediency of scientific knowledge and technological innovation when he writes that ...

> even the already existing forms of scientific knowledge which could to some extent counter the degradation of the natural environment must be left unrealized, because they would interfere with the imperative of mindless capital expansion; not to mention the refusal to pursue the necessary scientific and technological projects which could, if funded on the required monumental scale, redress the worsening state of affairs in this respect. Science and technology can only be pursued in the service of productive development if they directly contribute to capital-expansion and help to displace the system's internal antagonisms. Nobody should be surprised, therefore, that under such determinations the role of science and technology must be degraded to 'positively' enhancing global pollution and the accumulation of destructiveness on the scale prescribed by capital's perverse logic, instead of acting in the opposite direction, as in principle (but today in principle only) they could.[17]

There is much in Marx which history has left behind. However, his method of working and grappling with problems is just as relevant today in the area of the impact of capital's crisis on planetary climate and ecosystems. In this sense – and with the unfolding of capital's global structural crisis – Marx is more relevant today in regard to understanding the effects of this crisis on the planet's ecosystems than he was in the nineteenth century.

The questions which we are raising here concern specific eco-historical problems which are now in development or are in the process of formation as mediated and deepening by capital's crisis. We recognize them as the products of the historical development of the capital relation which stands as the basis (cube root) of the whole capitalist social formation which is destructive of nature's creation.

However, these questions can only be fully and comprehensively addressed *in practice* in the course of the period of transition to and evolution of a global socialist society. They cannot, therefore, be addressed simply within the realm of an advocacy which remains locked within the parameters of the capital system. Most critically, they cannot be *fully addressed, without hindrance*, within the framework of a destructive order which is the really existent historical source of the actual problems we seek to resolve. That capitalist framework must be utterly smashed and broken up if these problems are to be resolved in the long run.

We cannot truly approach these questions outside of practice, that is, outside the actual living struggle to restructure the social metabolism beyond capital which must involve a historic struggle with the state power of capital itself and the life-and-death struggle to break and dissolve it. Once again, the urgency of the question is raised: how do we move forward to the formation of agencies of revolution which will form the basis for going beyond the capital relation itself and really tackling the problems which we are considering here?

These enormous, historically posited problems can only be progressively diminished and resolved, therefore, in the actual process of actively countering and resolving them. And this means the commencement of a joined-up international struggle to eradicate the capital relation from the global social metabolism in the violent presence of the state power of capital itself and the global agencies of capital. We simply do not know what we are to inherit if the state powers of capital are irreversibly dismantled globally and we fully enter – unhindered with a clear view of an open horizon – this period of revolutionary transition. We can, however, be certain that what we inherit from the capitalist epoch will be a whole mass and complexity of global and localized problems and contradictions which are both social and ecological in character.

We will have no option but to address the living reality as we inherit it in the transition period and this means, of course, proceeding with the resolution in practice, over lengthy periods of time, of all these various contradictions and problems inherited from the epoch of capital. History does not present a smooth line of unproblematic, uncomplicated, unparadoxed development. This is the only way in which we can really proceed since only when the necessary 'social conditions are actually in existence or are in the process of formation' – to paraphrase Marx – can we truly address the specific complexity of the questions raised here in this chapter. The conception and associated perspectives on how to address and solve these capital-created and mediated ecological and environmental problems can only be developed in the course of the unfolding of actual human activity based on the prevailing conditions and possibilities of the time.

Notes and References

1   Mészáros, István, *Beyond Capital* (London: Merlin Press, 1995), pp. 186–187.
2   See Appendix I: *Marx's Realms: Capital, Natural Necessity, True Realm of Freedom.*
3   Green Party, 'Capitalism should exist for the good of the people, not the other way round', *Green Party* (20 January 2012) <https://www.greenparty.org.uk/news/capitalism-should-exist-for-the-good-of-the-people-not-the-other-way-around.html> (Last accessed 3 November 2016).
    The Green Party in Britain is another party of the state power of capital. Whether it is conscious of this elementary truth or not. This is incontrovertible from a mere cursory inspection of its programmes and manifestos. Essentially, it envisages 'environmental' reforms and an 'Old Labour' style social programme *within* the continuation of the global capitalist order. It does not fundamentally question or address the origins of the 'ecological crisis' within the operation of the global *capital* system itself and, specifically, within the conditions of its unfolding structural crisis.
4   Mészáros, *Beyond Capital*, Chapter 5, 'The Activation of Capital's Absolute Limits', p. 179.
5   Ibid., p. 173.
6   A maritime climate (sometimes referred to as an 'oceanic', 'marine' or 'west coast' climate) is a temperate climate with cool summers and mild winters with relatively narrow temperature range, fluctuations and differences between the different seasons. This type of climate is often contrasted with 'continental climates' where

winters tend to be cold, summers warm or hot and temperature variation wider and more polarized at their extremes. Such climates are characteristic of the inland regions of North America and Asia. The character of maritime climates is markedly influenced by oceanic currents – such as that of the Gulf Stream on the climate of north-western Europe – and localized marine weather systems.

7   Science@NASA, 'A Chilling Possibility. By disturbing a massive ocean current, melting Arctic sea ice might trigger colder weather in Europe and North America', *Science@NASA* (5 March 2004) <https://science.nasa.gov/science-news/science-at-nasa/2004/05mar_arctic/> (Last accessed 3 November 2016).

8   Alley, Richard B., 'Ice-core evidence of abrupt climate changes', *Proceedings of the National Academy of Sciences of the United States of America* (PNAS), Vol. 97, No. 4 (15 February 2000) <http://www.pnas.org/content/97/4/1331.full> (Last accessed 3 November 2016).

9   National Research Council, *Abrupt Climate Change: Inevitable Surprises* (Washington, DC: The National Academies Press, 2002) <https://www.nap.edu/catalog/10136/abrupt-climate-change-inevitable-surprises> (Last accessed 2 November 2016).

10 University Of Illinois At Urbana-Champaign, 'Shutdown Of Circulation Pattern Could Be Disastrous, Researchers Say', *ScienceDaily* (20 December 2004) <http://www.sciencedaily.com/releases/2004/12/041219153611.htm> (Last accessed 2 November 2016).

11 Nuccitelli, Dana, 'Nigel Lawson suggests he's not a sceptic, proceeds to deny global warming', *The Guardian* (28 July 2014) <https://www.theguardian.com/environment/climate-consensus-97-per-cent/2014/jul/28/nigel-lawson-suggests-not-a-sceptic-denies-global-warming> (Last accessed 4 November 2016).

12 Climate Emergency Institute, 'Atmospheric Greenhouse Gases & Greenhouse Emissions', *Climate Emergency Institute*, n. d. <http://www.climateemergencyinstitute.com/greenhousegases.html> (Last accessed 3 November 2016). [See graph of greenhouse gases (methane, carbon dioxide and nitrous oxide) concentrations over the last 2,000 years.]

13 Howard, Brian Clark, 'Aral Sea's Eastern Basin is Dry for First Time in 600 Years', *National Geographic* (2 October 2014) <http://news.nationalgeographic.com/news/2014/10/141001-aral-sea-shrinking-drought-water-environment/> (Last accessed 3 November 2016).

14 Mészáros, *Beyond Capital*, 'The Necessity of Social Control', p. 877.

15 'Clean Coal Technology' enables power stations to be designed which cut out the emission of polluting and greenhouse gases (such as carbon dioxide, sulphur and nitrogen oxides) into the Earth's atmosphere. The burning of 'fossil fuels'

becomes a potentially 'clean' source of energy and recyclable materials with the need-based, stringent application and development of this technology.

16 See, for example, John Bellamy Foster, *Marx's Ecology. Materialism and Nature* (New York: Monthly Review Press, 2000).

Also Bellamy Foster's *Monthly Review* article *Marx and the Rift in the Universal Metabolism of Nature*: <http://monthlyreview.org/2013/12/01/marx-rift-universal-metabolism-nature/> (Last accessed 2 November 2016).

Paul Burkett, *Marxism and Ecological Economics: Toward a Red and Green Political Economy* (Chicago: Haymarket Books, 2009).

Engels, *The Part Played by Labor in the Transition from Ape to Man* in *The Origin of the Family, Private Property and the State* (New York: International Publishers, 2007), pp. 260–261.

Marx, *Capital*, Vol. 1 (New York: International Publishers, 1967), pp. 505–507.

17 Mészáros, *Beyond Capital*, Chapter 5, 'The Activation of Capital's Absolute Limits', p. 175.

CHAPTER 6

The Trajectory of Trade Unionism under Capital's Unfolding Structural Crisis

The deepening of capital's structural crisis brings in its wake growing mass structural unemployment, increasing competition between workers for employment and falling wage levels. The 'wages and conditions' trade union militancy of the post-war (1939–1945) Keynesian expansion has vanished. Increasingly, the unfolding of capital's crisis signifies a legislation-backed slavery (the minimalization of trade union rights) in the employed section of the proletariat and an enforced state-sponsored pauperization of that constantly growing section which is 'surplus' to capital's requirements.

The structural crisis of the whole system of the 'theft of alien labour time' tends to push capital into measures which create a proletariat of wage *slaves* (with minimal, if any, trade union rights), paupers and beggars. But the continuing privileged existence of the trade union hierarchy actually rests on the maintenance of this capital system; on the continued flow of member subscriptions and on the 'returns' on union funds (money capital investments) circulating in the world's capital markets. The 'truth' (outcome) of these relations is 'Business Unionism' as the crisis-mediated product of hierarchical trade unionism's relationship with capital as the epoch unfolds. The trade union bureaucracy articulates, consciously or unconsciously, capital's interests inside the labour movement. Recent events in the past decade in both Britain and the United States have very clearly illustrated this conception.

In 2008, the owners of the Petroineos Refinery at Grangemouth near Edinburgh introduced plans to radically alter the pension scheme of workers at the refinery. Approximately 97 per cent of UNITE's members at the plant voted to strike. Again in 2013, capital insisted on radical changes in employment conditions and pensions with the threat that the plant would be closed if these changes were not accepted by the unions. The workers rejected the plans but the UNITE bureaucracy agreed to capital's 'restructuring' which involved a no-strike deal, wage freeze and changes in the pension scheme after Petroineos prepared the plant for complete closure. Len McCluskey, General Secretary of the UNITE trade union, explaining the position of the top stratum in the union, said ...

> What's different? The company's closure of the plant has led our stewards to believe the priority is to keep the plant open. We have to say to the company that the survival plan is something we are prepared to embrace and go along with if, if you like. But that includes discussions and consultation and we will see what comes out of those discussions. I wouldn't want to mislead you. Their survival plan requires us to accept certain things and our stewards' position is that we are accepting those issues. It's not that it's all up for negotiation. They are demanding we accept their ultimatums and we have decided to accept their ultimatums. The consultation will be around the logistics of those issues and the practicalities of those issues. There will be no doubt some alterations within the context of those discussions. What has changed is the company have closed the plant and have put it into liquidation and we are not going to allow that to happen and the stewards are now responding to the wishes of our members who may feel outraged by what has happened but the priority is to keep the plant open and we will see what the future brings.[1]

This was not a 'tactical retreat'. It is the irreversible tendency and future of 'business trade unionism' in the epoch of capital's structural crisis. In the 1960s and even 1970s, such closure threats would have been dismissed as bluff and bluster; a means to try to end a troublesome strike. And under the conditions of capital expansion and accumulation at the time, such intimidation would have been rejected and not worked. Today, we have entered a different epoch where the bluff of strikes and mass walk-outs no longer trump capital's threats of closedown and asset-stripping.

Capital-in-crisis knows that it is 'holding all the aces' when it looks *this trade union bureaucracy* squarely in the face. It knows that because the *caste* interests of this stratum ultimately rest on the rule of capital, it likewise knows that this rule – under the presently unfolding crisis conditions – highly circumscribes the limits of activity of the trade union hierarchy and therefore, in the finality of matters, restricts and controls its space for manoeuvre. Whither the strike as a tactic of struggle? Whither the 'economistic' (wages and conditions) struggle against capital?

The strike as an 'economistic weapon' – under conditions of structural crisis – is now 'in serious trouble'. Today, generally, threatened strikes within the realm of private productive capital are often met with counter-threats of closure, redundancies, layoffs or even plans to re-locate production. Counter-threats which usually carry weight in an age of structural crisis. Another alternative at the disposal of capital is legal action which shackles the capacity to strike.

In the 1960s, the mere threat of a strike would often bring capital to the negotiating table. Mediating these new tendencies today is the overbearing and dominating needs of capital in the epoch of its *structural* crisis as opposed to its more flexible approach in previous cyclical, conjunctural and displaceable crises. And this is reflected in the concordat between the trade union elite ('business unionism') and capital. An *entente cordiale* between capital and the labour bureaucracy. At Grangemouth, the UNITE bureaucracy totally caved in and conceded everything to capital. Such abject subservience can only mean, at best, a temporary reprieve for workers at the plant.

Workers in both Europe and North America can see how precarious their employment is with the options which are now available for globalizing capital. The playing out of capital's structural crisis is already driving it towards the destruction of whole sections of the proletariat, its communities and immediate industrial and civic environment which are identified as being superfluous to the needs of capital. And such options not only in Asia or Latin America.

If we look at what has happened to the city of Detroit[2] in the United States, we can see what the future possibly holds for countless millions across the globe in Europe and North America if we do not commence the necessary restructuring of the social metabolic landscape. If we do not establish the necessary forms of agency to commence this mighty historic process of transition.

Detroit was, of course, 'Motown City', the mass production of cars, with a massive and, at times, militant proletariat. In Detroit, we are observing a possible pre-figuration of the future but we are also seeing the seeds of how people can organize in opposition to capital's destruction of the cultural conditions of the future society. People have been left to rot by capital and its state power but they are, in response, starting to take matters into their own hands. For example, in the establishment and development of a program for the urban farming of food by returning wasteland in the city of Detroit back to agricultural/horticultural land.[3]

Under conditions of structural crisis, capital stands *in relation to the trade union bureaucracy* (both its national and international forms such as the United Nations ILO) as the organ grinder does to the monkey. The whole structure and organization of official trade unionism is now completely integrated into the capitalist order, including on a financial level. The financial portfolios and pension funds of trade unions are managed as capital on the world market so that any increments accruing to these funds are as likely to have their origins in the uncompensated labour of sweatshops in Asia or Latin America as they do in the parasitism of money capital circulating in the world's capital markets.

It is not in the *caste* interests of the top stratum of the trade unions to carry forward a struggle against capital to its historic conclusion. And that conclusion is the transcendence of the capital relation globally and the establishment of a world socialist society. Its interests are inextricably tied to the continuation of the capital order and its state power. The continued historic existence of the whole labour and trade union bureaucracy is indissolubly tied up with the continuation of this destructive, increasingly barbaric, outmoded capitalist order. The termination of the epoch of capital would mean, beyond doubt, the end of the existence of this labour stratum. That is why betrayal is not an option but a necessity. Today, the example of the ex-miners and their now decaying, jobless communities in Britain illustrates the 'solidarity' and 'support' of the TUC in the year long strike of 1984–1985.

Indeed, the interests of the trade union bureaucracy are so closely interwoven with the continuation of the capital system to such a high degree, that it will be impossible for organized labour to take to the offensive against capital and its state power without simultaneously coming into direct conflict with this reactionary labour hierarchy. Accordingly, in the struggles to come, a 'revolution' within trade unionism itself (against its hierarchical structure which is a product of and serves the requirements of the social relations of the capital order) must be an ongoing and intrinsic part of the unfolding of the offensive against capital. But even this will not be enough. The question of higher forms of agency is now most definitely and undoubtedly on the agenda. Without a definite move forward against its current conservative organizational structures and bureaucratic administration, trade unionism can only continue on its path towards an increasing historic vestigiality and extinction as the structural crisis of capital widens and deepens. The dilemma increasingly facing trade unionized workers – as the global process of capital-in-crisis intensifies – is 'revolutionization or cipherization'.

Accordingly, the struggle against this labour hierarchy is absolutely implicated as a pre-requisite for the refoundation of the class movement of the proletariat; that is, for trade unionists – as organized workers – to form part of an unfolding offensive against capital and its state power. The fight for the dissolution of this bureaucratic caste becomes an intrinsic part of the unfolding struggle against the capital order as a whole.

The present, hierarchically dominated, trade union form of labour organization (the universal historic form of labour organization globally) cannot stand. It must be dissolved into a new higher social form of unionism or it will perish in all but name, leaving behind only a vestige of its former self.

Trade unionism alone, in and by itself – and especially within its current structures and form of organization – is totally inadequate to deal with the maturing, intensifying crisis. Trade unionism has now entered an impasse. However, the movement into this impasse actually begins to generate the potential for the development of the class movement of the proletariat; a 'qualitative leap' as it were in organization and consciousness.

The actual arrival at this impasse has generated a very profound conflict (of which many trade unionists are, as yet, unaware) between, on the one hand, the demands being placed on the proletariat by the unfolding structural crisis of capital and, on the other, by the simple truth that the traditional organizations of the proletariat – specifically the trade union form – are historically outmoded and no longer suited not only for their original 'economistic' purposes but also to address the tasks emerging under the necessarily worsening conditions of the structural crisis of the capital order.

This conflict now mediates the *political disorientation* in the proletarian class movement; the old no longer 'works' but what to do? How to move on and create something new which does address and articulate in practice the needs of the proletariat as a class in the epoch of capital's structural crisis? This conflict cannot be left unresolved because it will continue to serve as a source of the degeneration of the whole movement. 'Re-foundation' means moving forward offensively (in the course of which any process of resolution will be initiated and evolved) in terms of tactics, strategy and class organization.

The proletariat, as a class, cannot 'go on in the old way' with its trade unions. Not simply in their current structural and organizational form. But *in any form at all*. They are useless as they stand in the midst of the structural character of capital's crisis and will become increasingly more so. Unfit for purpose. Historically outmoded. We have passed beyond the question of 'winning' or 'losing' strikes. The trade unions are no longer capable of consistently delivering such victories. It has now become a question of what forms of agency will be necessary to take humanity beyond the capital order itself. We need to move forward to a fundamentally new type of unionism which is based in the whole class and not simply in the workplace. And such a new type of unionism would indeed be more capable of articulating the class interests of the proletariat both *inside and outside* the workplace.

The strike itself as a tactic of struggle must now be re-evaluated and re-articulated within and according to the altered conditions generated by capital's structural crisis. For example, we have to consider the question of how strikes for better wages in the 'public sector' can detrimentally affect people who use these services, especially when the effects of strikes on people using the services are distorted, whipped up and bent for their own political purposes by capital and its media.

The trade union strike itself needs to be understood historically as a response to the impositions of capital on labour under specific conditions. Conditions can alter to such a degree that strikes may sometimes become counter-productive to the interests of the class and this necessitates the adoption and elaboration of new forms of struggle. In other words, the strike must not be *abstractly and ahistorically apotheosized as an absolute and unconditionally apposite ideal* so as to be posited as the only necessary form of struggle for all situations. This may appear to be offering comfort to capital. In truth, when the strike tactic is automatically rolled out every time as a 'reflex' response to capital's offensive, this may serve to deepen established divisions within the proletariat. It betrays the limited character of the strike tactic under very specific circumstances where new strategies and tactics are clearly required which meet the interests of the proletariat *as a whole*. The strike must be grasped in terms of the specificity of its validity for the class as a weapon of struggle within the altering situations and circumstances in the history of the capital order. Here valid, there not appropriate, etc.

In retrospect – returning to our example of UNITE at Petroineos – the limits of trade unionism have impressed themselves in practice on the workers at the Grangemouth refinery. The acceptance of the conditions dictated by capital at the Petroineos plant bears this contradictory character. On the one hand, it reflects the subservience of the trade union bureaucracy to capital. And yet, on the other hand, it is a sober acceptance by workers that their present class-based organizations are no longer fit for their original purpose. And to seek to fight for their class interests through such impotently structured and compromisingly led organizations would be tantamount to signing up with millions of others to permanent unemployment and everything which that implies for their mode of life.

Accordingly, any approach of the workers at Petroineos – subsequent to the threat to close the plant – which may appear to be a 'surrender to capital' could be viewed as (1) workers 'buying time' on the basis of a sober acknowledgement that their traditional organization are no longer fit for purpose under the conditions of structural crisis and (2) that a postponement ('keeping your powder dry in the pouring rain') of confronting capital is rendered necessary for the time being but, sooner or later, must come and is in process of coming to be.

This scenario was, once again, recently reflected in events in the United States. In February 2014, the car workers at the Volkswagen (VW) plant in Chattanooga, Tennessee, in the United States voted by a simple majority *not* to be unionized.[4] The United Automobile Workers of America (UAW) had the actual support (sic!) of the Chief Executive Officer at VW Chattanooga for unionization and for the formation of a 'German-style works council'. The leadership of the UAW had reached a 'neutrality agreement' with VW in which it included a clause which effectively vowed to keep wages and benefits low relative to other car manufacturers. When asked why he had included this in his agreement with VW, the President of the UAW, Bob King, stated that ...

> Our philosophy is, we want to work in partnership with companies to succeed. Nobody has more at stake in the long-term success of the company than the workers on the shop floor, both blue collar and white collar. With every company that we work with, we're concerned about competitiveness. We work together with companies to have the highest quality, the highest productivity, the best health and safety, the best ergonomics, and we are showing that companies that succeed by this cooperation can have higher wages and benefits because of the joint success.[5]

This 'oath of fealty' to capital is tantamount to a declaration of intent to commit a crime before it is actually carried out. With this sort of union leadership, who needs capitalist management at VW Chattanooga? Simply 'outsource' the management of VW to the UAW executive.

Many workers now see 'their' trade unions – managed by a governing labour elite – as part of the whole problem which they are now facing. As they stand, they are *certainly not* part of the solution. The trade unions take their subscription fees and offer workers almost nothing in exchange for them (possibly legal representation) except bluster, obfuscation, excuses, betrayal and dirty deals with capital in which everyone is happy except the sub-paying worker.

Many trade unionists would agree that 'their' trade union does not really 'belong to them' but rather that 'they belong' to 'their' trade union. In the way of an insurance policy belonging to the holder which the company refuses to pay out when legitimate circumstances demand. In other words, the policy does not really belong to the holder but to the company. The serf 'belonged' on (was tied to) the demesne of his lord. The demesne did not 'belong' to the serf. The distinction may seem to be oversubtle but it is real and critically important nevertheless. 'Trade Union Baron' is indeed a very apt description when we consider the nature of the relationship between the top governing stratum and the broad membership of the trade union branches.

The trade unions are not 'their' (the workers') unions but stand confronting them as alien bodies (which, like capital, they themselves have created) and which operate to service the requirements of a six-figure, pensioned and perked salariat which puts its own caste interests before the class interests of the proletariat as a whole or even in part. In other words, they are alienated from the very organizations which they themselves as a class originally created to represent and articulate their class interests in the struggle against capital. The dual financial basis of the existence of this salaried bureaucracy (member fees from wages and money capital investment to augment union funds) further cements the top stratum of trade unionism into the dominant socio-economic order as adjuncts and proxies of capital. Once again, on all levels, 'business unionism' is the inevitable corollary of these relations.

At Chattanooga, the car workers clearly recognized that the whole structure of their lives – under conditions where losing your job means a possible lifetime of unemployment or low-wage, casual employment at best – depended on whether or not they were to keep their jobs at the Volkswagen plant. They clearly did not consider trade union membership to be vital for that. Implicitly, they considered that their conditions of employment and wages would be the same or even worse whether or not they were members of the UAW.

They made a 'Faustian deal' with capital. Under the worsening conditions of capital-in-crisis, people in workplaces will form an alliance with whosoever they think is the *best bet* for guaranteeing prolongation of employment. Any worker would vote for such a deal with capital if s/he thought that it would save his/her job and therefore life's 'normal' structure of family, home, children, holidays, car, etc. But you would only make such a deal if you thought that the class organizations (capital-enthralled trade unions) which had traditionally represented your interests had utterly failed and had even abandoned you and gone over to the side and ways of the enemy.

This is what has happened at the Volkswagen plant in Chattanooga, Tennessee. Official trade unionism is so 'close' to capital than many workers today – across Europe and North America – simply cannot see any reason for subscribing. The 'fees due' can be deployed in more productive and pleasurable directions. Rather than ending up in a pension fund and later in the pension pot of a retired General Secretary. If even the Chief Executive Officer at the plant recommended a vote for unionization, then what does this say about the leadership of the UAW?

The vote of the car workers in Tennessee may appear to be a vote against trade unionism and for capital. *It is not*. It is a vote *against* 'Business Unionism'. It is a vote against this form of unionism, its corruption, its inertia under the conditions of capital's structural crisis, its own structural and organizational integration into the whole capitalist order, its constant refusal to even attempt to mobilize the class in struggle. It is *not* a vote *for* the organ grinder but rather a vote *against his* monkey.

The vote of car workers at the VW plant in Tennessee does not express any confidence in capital to deliver full and lasting employment. Rather it is a *class* expression that workers have lost confidence in the capacity of the trade union structures and bureaucratically evolved organization to articulate their class interests. And because, in time of crisis – when 'business unionism' is sinking fast into the quicksand of history and, relatedly, totally enthralled to capital itself – it sees the false promises which capital offers as the only straws which are worth grasping. A majority vote against unionization is not necessarily a vote against trade unionism per se or for capital. But rather an expression of profound dissatisfaction of workers with trade unions in their current form. A deep, crisis-mediated distrust of official trade unionism.

Workers – all over the world – are not so easily swayed by capitalist media propaganda. They do not need to be lectured on the subject of class interests and the differences between them. They almost 'instinctively' know where their own interests are located. The UAW executive has placed responsibility for the outcome of the vote at the door of the Republican Party in the US and the capitalist media. Not at their own front door or at more remote sources.

Moreover, the UAW leadership actually spurned the support of the local community in Chattanooga. One American journal, *In These Times*, covering the dispute and vote wrote that …

> pro-union community activists, who spoke with 'In These Times' on condition of anonymity out of fear of hurting their relationships with the UAW, spoke about difficulties in getting the UAW to help them engage the broader Chattanooga community. Many activists I spoke with during my two trips to Chattanooga said that when they saw the UAW being continually blasted on local talk radio, newspapers and billboards, they wanted to get involved to help build community support.
>
> However, they say that the UAW was lukewarm in partnering with them. Indeed, when I attended a forum in December organized by Chattanooga for Workers, a community group designed to build local support for the organizing drive, more than 150 community activists attended – many from different area unions – but I encountered only three UAW members. Community activists said they had a hard time finding ways to coordinate solidarity efforts with the UAW, whose campaign they saw as insular rather than community-based.
>
> 'There's no way to win in the South without everyone that supports you fighting with you,' said one Chattanooga community organizer, who preferred to remain anonymous. 'Because the South is one giant anti-union campaign.'[6]

In other words, rather than reaching out to the broad layers of the proletariat in Tennessee, the UAW bureaucracy opted to maintain the car workers in isolation from this tappable, potential support of their local brothers and sisters within the wider community in Chattanooga.

The vote against unionization amongst the car workers in Tennessee is an expression of the globally acting contradictory forces to which workers are now being subjected in the epoch of capital's structural crisis. The result of the vote itself bears a contradictory character. It appears to be a vote for capital and against worker organization. However, on closer inspection, it remains a vote against capital's proxies in the UAW and, in this way, contradictorily, a vote which, in the long term, will tend to gravitate against the interests of capital.

As the crisis deepens, for millions of wage labourers across the globe, the *immediate questions* are very simple and direct: Do I have a job or don't I, bearing in mind that employment is becoming increasingly difficult to secure? Will I be able to pay the rent, the mortgage, feed and clothe myself and my family? Will I have the money to survive and live? The car and holiday abroad once or twice a year? Do I have a better chance of keeping my job if I accept the terms offered by capital or if I reject them? If capital states that being in a trade union will lessen the chances of keeping my job and keeping my workplace open, do I accept it and leave the union to its fate? Or do I risk unionization, the possibility of strikes and that the threats issued by capital will be carried out? Do I do a 'Grangemouth' or a 'Chattanooga' or do I do the opposite and mobilize for a fight with the presently inadequate form of union organization available?

The strike weapon has now, taken by itself, become highly circumscribed by the conditions imposed by capital's structural crisis either as a means to defend public provision against the assault by the state power of capital, or to further the interests of productive wage labour in the surplus value-producing factories and plants. Indeed, with the onrush of 'globalization', over the past thirty years or so, capital has increased significantly the number and different types of weapons in its armoury to tackle the strike weapon. From shipping in desparado strikebreakers from overseas territories to simply dismantling or closing and selling off plant and moving where labour power is significantly cheaper.

Within months or even weeks, capital can 'close down' a business, the factory infrastructure dismantled, shipped abroad in containers and re-assembled ready for production with labour power at a fraction of its price beforehand. It is not only furniture which is now 'flatpack'. This prefabricated character of the production of the means of production ('modular construction') enables capital to assemble, disassemble and re-assemble its production units and simply ship them around the globe where conditions are more favourable for exploitation. This global mobility of constant capital (aka 'plant' or 'industrial relocation services') affords the greatest potential and opportunity to maximize profit. Sometimes it's cheaper just to build a completely new production system abroad (combined with relocation of some machinery/materials) and sell off the original for local use, even scrap, etc. The transnational corporation Nestlé has adopted this strategy in its exploitation of labour in 'Asia, Oceania and Africa'. According to its website, its 'modular factory' can be 'expanded, moved or its function transformed without having to start from scratch'.[7]

Globalization has afforded capital a greater degree of strategic and tactical flexibility in regard to the exploitation of human labour. An example of this 'flexibility' for global capital is the wages of call centre workers. According to a BBC report in 2003 *'average call centre salaries in the UK are about £12,500 ($22,000) a year, compared with £1,200 ($2,100) in India.'*[8] Many companies and corporations are 'going offshore' because of such graphically obscene rates of exploitation.

English-speaking and equivalently educated people in India are trained to do the same job as a worker on ten times the salary in the US or Europe which is equivalent to a transfer of 90 per cent of the salary of the worker replaced in Europe into the profit coffers of the corporations as a result of employing an Indian worker. In China, workers are slaving for 40 cents per hour[9] making computer parts for major corporations, with labour costs at a tiny fraction of the retail price in stores in Europe and the United States.

Such examples demonstrate that capital's options in its global strategy to maximize the extraction of surplus value have actually increased and diversified. Why make laptops in the UK when the mass of profit per unit is so much higher as a result of producing them in India or China and shipping them across the globe? Why even bother with all the hassle of dealing with possible strikes, etc., when you can just move abroad where the rate of exploitation is so much higher? And where you can establish and dictate slave labour conditions and simply hire and sack at will with the support and corruption of local state powers and officials?

Any strike against capital is, of course, legitimate in itself in so far as it is a struggle against capital in pursuance of the class interests of the proletariat, regardless of whether it is 'sectional' or not. Only the likes of IBM, Microsoft, etc., and corrupt local officials would question the need for the Indian and Chinese workers above to form militant unions and launch all-out strikes and occupations in order to pursue their interests and strive to smash slave-labour conditions. However, by exclusively focusing on the strike weapon – determining it as the highest form of struggle – and thinking that this type of action alone can solve workers' problems and serve to meet their demands, means that they effectively remain circumscribed within the socio-economic parameters of the capital system in an age when those parameters have been remoulded by capital in its attempt to transcend its own, intractable structural crisis.

The continuing deployment of the strike weapon as it was traditionally used in the past period of *conjunctural, cyclical* crises of the capitalist system is now confronted by the altered (*structural*) character of capital's crisis. Implicitly, these new conditions demand new forms of struggle, higher forms of agency and the transformation in class consciousness which is necessary to orientate the proletariat in the struggle to end the epoch of global capital. What is now really required is a leap in organizational and structural-political form and a corresponding development in consciousness which will begin to place the struggle against capital, its state powers and global agencies on a qualitatively new footing.

That is not to assert that strikes are no longer important. In certain respects, they are now *more* important. For example, strikes by the 'information proletariat' working in ICT and techno-scientific workers could be extremely effective and dangerous to the capital system. We also have to recognize that there are aspects of any strike which are going to have indirect or 'knock-on' effects on the lives of the proletariat because of the integrated and implicate character of social production in its totality as a unity of diverse interconnected processes. For example, a strike in the computerized processing of salaries and benefits, etc., in the interface between the state and banking sector, would directly affect people's lives and their families, etc. And of course, it would be precisely this aspect amongst others which the state power of capital and its media would exploit to try to break such a strike. All these considerations raise the fundamental and historically precedent question of the forms of agency now required for the proletariat to conduct the struggle against the capital system.

Under the deepening crisis of the capital order, a strike could, in certain circumstances, actually play into the hands of the state and even offer it the opportunity and excuse to close services or tender them out to private capital. Therefore, there is now a real need to deploy the strike weapon intelligently, strategically, selectively and politically to advance the interests of the proletariat in its struggle against capital and its state power. This, once again, is not to deny the importance of the strike weapon but to re-appraise its role and employment under changing conditions.

Under certain conditions, therefore, strikes – to oppose privatization, for example – would not always be the appropriate response by workers and their communities. Under other conditions, the strike would be the best weapon. The strike weapon has now – taken by itself and independently of more historically appropriate tactics of struggle – become insufficient to defend public provision against the assault by the state power of capital.

The emergence of the new form of capital's crisis brings in the need to discern the best times and conditions in which to use or not use the strike weapon. Consider the following scenario. A Health Trust wishes to close a hospital, return privately owned infrastructure to capital for sale and transfer facilities to another hospital as part of privatization which will mean a direct attack on health provision for local people. Would a strike at the threatened hospital be the best response? It is threatened with actual closure because the trust is on a privatization trajectory and wants to 'economize' services. Surely here a better response by workers and the local community would be the widespread organization of an occupation followed by actual community appropriation: *'This hospital has been saved from closure and is now communal property'.*

Appropriation would mean taking hold of all infrastructural and medical assets, including land and financial assets. The repudiation of the financial liabilities and debts of the hospital would be open to debate and action. Small businesses and the self-employed would be exempt from the repudiation of debt but the banks, insurance houses, and health corporations certainly would not. Debts to these latter would be repudiated immediately and all their assets seized for communal use. This would raise the question of re-organizing and restructuring how the hospital is run, turfing out the bureaucrats and establishing democratic bodies and committees to administer the affairs of the hospital and, most importantly, to *defend and palisade* the communal appropriation of all assets.

An example where a strike, or even a 'work to rule', would be productive is, for example, where civil servants are refusing to impose draconian measures on unemployed workers like slashing benefits or subjecting the jobless to a even harsher regime of punitive measures than already exists at the moment for millions. The imposition of such a regime is not simply an attack on the unemployed but also on the conditions of work of civil servants. It raises the stress and problems of front line staff working with unemployed people. Here we can discern an actual merging of interests of civil servants with the jobless people they are working with. A strike or refusal to implement such measures would stop the state power in its tracks. Here a strike or 'work to rule' would be more appropriate than an occupation. The refusal by civil servants to implement such measures against the jobless would serve a strategic and political purpose in facilitating the disruption of the operation of the state power of capital against unemployed workers and also mean that civil servants were acting to attenuate the additional stresses and problems of such a repressive system. People could still be receiving their allowances without being subject to harsher measures.

Likewise the transfer of public assets to speculators or the threatened closures of schools, care homes and libraries might be opposed by the 'occupation and appropriation' tactic. We would need, therefore, to develop the tactic of the selective or strategic strike to oppose the plans of the state power of capital to destroy our public provision. Anti-labour legislation – and the constant possibility of more in the pipeline with the practical compliance of the labour bureaucracy[10] – has served to curtail the initiation of strikes and their actual tactical development in the course of struggle. The precipitous fall in trade union membership since 1979 (from 13.2 to 6 million individual members) and the demolition of employment rights ('zero hours' contracts, etc.) have also significantly attenuated the strike as a weapon of mass struggle.[11]

Strategic strikes would further the interests of the proletariat as a whole by undermining the capacity of the state power to function and impose its will and rule. But to *occupy and appropriate* as communal property is to begin to make inroads into the actual basis of the rule of this state power by starting to re-organize and restructure the whole social metabolism in favour of human need against capitalist private profit. It is to begin to undermine the rule of the capital relation itself. It is a question of control: who owns, runs and organizes for the future, the social and economic infrastructure and metabolism? How can it be re-organized and restructured to meet human need? How can the exploitative and dehumanizing capital relation be eliminated from the social metabolism?

It is not simply a question of fighting for better conditions and wages (the immediate demands confronting the proletariat) which has been the traditional role of the trade unions and which, of course, never leaves the agenda and can be incorporated into a higher form of proletarian organization. The change in conditions with capital's deepening structural crisis means that the question of who owns and runs the whole social metabolism and for what purpose – and not just for a bigger wage or better working conditions under the rule of capital – must increasingly raise the fundamental question of rule and power.

In other words, the actual living struggle to realize these immediate demands must be combined with the long term objectives of social transformation. This dynamic can only be fully posited and realized through profound changes in the way the proletariat organizes as a class. It forces the question of organization and agency directly onto the agenda. A question which can no longer be ignored as capital's crisis deepens.

The limitations of the trade unions in their traditional role of fighting for better conditions and wages are evident. But even if workers recognize the limitations of trade unionism today, what alternative is there at the present stage? Workers only have these organizations, at this point, through which to try to articulate their 'economistic' interests. And this approach still carries a certain legitimacy according to where and under what conditions a strike is taking place. At the moment, what else have workers got for defence but their trade unions? At this stage, they remain with their traditional organizations and its associated forms of consciousness.

Despite all the 'left discussion' about 'social movements' and 'radical extra-parliamentary activity', etc., the proletariat – as a class – still, at the present stage, essentially remains with its traditional trade union organizations which – despite precipitously falling membership since 1979 – remain the mass organizations (with membership in many millions across the world) of the proletariat globally.

However, even if we can conceive a radicalized trade unionism which overturns all the old bureaucratism and conservatism, this would still be, in and by itself *as trade unionism per se*, absolutely inadequate to form a spearhead against capital and its state power under the altered conditions of the structural character of capital's crisis. The traditional forms of struggle such as the strike tactic for increased wages and better working conditions, or even just to keep your job, must now be re-contextualized and their limitations grasped within the altered conditions.

The limitations of trade unionism today do not simply arise out of 'failures of leadership' or out of not being 'militant enough'. These limitations have emerged as barriers to struggle and organization which result from the altered character of capital's crisis. 'Militancy' and threats of strikes were more productive of short term objectives in capital's cyclical phases of 'boom and bust' when the economic conditions afforded capital 'room' to retreat and manoeuvre. But under conditions of structural crisis, this 'room' becomes progressively constricted so that the manoeuvrability of capital tends to diminish towards a vanishing point. This is why strikes today may be countered with *genuine threats* of closedown or mass sackings. Threats under crisis conditions which force the hand of employers to actually carry out. Structural crisis means that capital's approach towards trade unionism is one where it either expects total subservience or it adopts an increasingly authoritarian stance in its state power, anti-labour legislation, brutality and thug-policing, etc.

As a class, the proletariat can only start with the immediacy of the conditions which confronts it. But these 'immediate conditions' are mediated by the worsening situation for global capital which impacts on the *totality* of the life of the proletariat as a class. A class which can only survive by selling its labour-power to capital and its various agencies or live a state-dependent pauper-subsistence. Without the historically legitimate and offensive organizations of class struggle, the proletariat must truly continue to reside and sink deeper into a de-unionized, universalized wage 'slavery'. Necessarily associated with this state of affairs lies the realm of state-sponsored beggardom, criminalization and pauperization within which millions across the globe already exist, awaiting supplementation from those still 'fortunate' enough to be exploitatively employed by capital.

The historic tendency of the living struggle of the 'real movement' today can only be towards the refoundation of the class movement of the proletariat as a whole within the immediacy of the grounding historical conditions and arising out of the conflicts with capital and its state powers within these evolving conditions of structural crisis. This implies working to create an organization of struggle which can both address the immediate tasks confronting the proletariat under the prevailing conditions whilst also integrating in its activity those long-term and 'far-reaching' perspectives based on a grasp of the general trajectory of the mediating structural crisis of capital. To neglect or focus on one at the expense of the other is to either become lost in or buried under the immediacy of the 'economism' of the moment or to become divorced from the present day tasks by exclusively focusing on the long-term objectives ...

> Men make their own history, but not of their own free will; not under circumstances they have chosen but under the given and inherited circumstances with which they are directly confronted. The tradition of the dead generations weighs like a nightmare on the minds of the living.[12]

To actually make this 'connection' – between the dialectics of the immediate and the mediate, the particular and the universal – means to participate in the present struggles (e.g. a strike, campaigns, etc.) not simply in order to fight *exclusively* for their success but to participate in order to politically mediate the realization of the historically necessary higher form of revolutionary agency. Raymond Williams touches on this relationship when he writes that ...

> The unique and extraordinary character of working-class self-organization has been that it has tried to connect particular struggles to a general struggle in one quite special way. It has set out, as a movement, to make real what is at first sight the extraordinary claim that the defence and advancement of certain particular interests, properly brought together, are in fact in the general interest. That, after all, is the moment of transition to an idea of socialism. And this moment comes not once and for all but many times; is lost and is found again; has to be affirmed and developed, continually, if it is to stay real.[13]

Today – at the present stage in the unfolding of capital's structural crisis – this means *identifying (locating) in activity* what is actually done now, in the immediacy of the continuously arising and vanishing moments of everyday campaigns, strikes, marches and demos, etc., *with* the struggle for the agency/organs of revolution to go beyond the capital relation and its state powers.

The historically fundamental questions and problems which immediately confront the proletariat can only be truly addressed – under the conditions of the deepening crisis of the capital order – through the innovation of a fundamentally new type of proletarian organization. This must involve elaborating new, higher strategies and tactics of struggle which are offensively articulated and develop in practice ('practical consciousness') the overall perspective for the eradication of the capital relation from the life of the social metabolism itself in combination with the overthrow of the state powers of capital and its global political agencies.

The pre-eminent consideration within this perspective is the historically precedent question of agency. It is question which cannot be left unanswered any longer as capital opens up its offensive against workers generally and against the full panoply of public provision which the proletariat has historically taken for granted but which is now beginning to disappear into the whirlpool of capital's inexorable crisis-movement.[14]

The theoretical and political characterization of the current stage at which the capitalist order has now arrived in the course of its long historical development inevitably compels us to critically evaluate the relationship between trade unionism and capital (and its state power). How has the unfolding of capital's structural crisis impacted on the traditional 'economistic' role of the trade unions? How, in struggle, has this crisis served to bring into sharp focus the historical limitations of trade unionism and its accompanying forms of 'militant' and 'economistic' consciousness?

Trade unionism, as the universally prevalent form of organization of labour's 'economistic' struggle against capital across the globe, has been in decline over the last three decades. How does this decline relate to the emergence and development of capital's structural crisis? And, moreover, to the bureaucratic structures (mediated by the class relations of bourgeois society) of trade unionism tied to the past, dead conditions of previous centuries?

How does the class movement of the proletariat actually address and develop these questions in the unfolding of the life of what Marx refers to as 'the real movement'? What are the capital-in-crisis mediated limits of the current form (trade unionism) of the proletarian class movement? How can it commence the process of transcending these historically imposed limits of its organization and consciousness? How do we struggle and organize to move that process forward as the structural crisis of capital opens up and deepens?

As early as 1940, Trotsky, shortly before his death, wrote that ...

> There is one common feature in the development, or more correctly the degeneration, of modern trade union organizations in the entire world: it is their drawing closely to and growing together with the state power. This process is equally characteristic of the neutral, the Social democratic, the Communist and 'anarchist' trade unions. This fact alone shows that the tendency towards 'growing together' is intrinsic not in this or that doctrine as such but derives from social conditions common for all unions.[15]

This conception is more concrete and germane today than it was when Trotsky actually wrote it. These 'social conditions common for all unions' are now rendered more uniform and homogeneous by the unfolding of capital's structural crisis; a crisis which is daily becoming more 'globalized' and concentrating and intensifying the actual historic process of 'modern trade union organization ... drawing closely to and growing together with the state power'.

It is one of the author's basic contentions in this work that trade unionism per se (not simply its *form of organization*) has been delivered into a state of historic outmodedness by the emergence and unfolding of capital's structural crisis. And, accordingly, *trade unionism is now more useful for capital than it is for the proletariat and becoming increasingly more so as capital's crisis proceeds to deepen and intensify*.

We, the proletariat as a class, need to move forward to a fundamentally new type of unionism which is based in the life of the whole class and not simply in the workplace. And such a new type of unionism will, indeed, be more capable of representing the class interests of workers *both inside and outside* the workplace. The new historic form of the 'Social Union' would articulate and fight for the immediate and long term interests of the proletarian class as a whole. And not, supposedly and exclusively, for one section of it employed by capital and its agencies. Trade unionism itself may be pivotal in the actual creation of this higher form of unionism.

Notes and References

1. Farrell, Sean, 'Grangemouth crisis: Unite union now accepts plant rescue plan', *The Guardian* (24 October 2013) <https://www.theguardian.com/business/2013/oct/24/grangemouth-crisis-unite-accepts-survival-plan-ineos> (Last accessed 4 November 2016).
2. Wolff, Richard, 'Detroit's decline is a distinctively capitalist failure', *The Guardian* (23 July 2013) <https://www.theguardian.com/commentisfree/2013/jul/23/detroit-decline-distinctively capitalist-failure> (Last accessed 4 November 2016).

   Hackman, Rose, 'Detroit demolishes its ruins: "The capitalists will take care of the rest"', *The Guardian* (28 September 2014) <https://www.theguardian.com/money/2014/sep/28/detroit-demolish-ruins-capitalists-abandoned-buildings-plan> (Last accessed 4 November 2016).

   Onesto, Li, '"Dying Detroit": The Impacts of Globalisation. Social Decay and Destruction of an Entire Urban Area', *Global Research. Centre for Research on Globalisation* (23 June 2010) <http://www.globalresearch.ca/dying-detroit-the-impacts-of-globalisation-social-decay-and-destruction-of-an-entire-urban-area/19856> (Last accessed 3 November 2016).
3. Michigan Urban Farming Initiative, 'All About MUFI' <http://www.miufi.org/about> (Last accessed 3 November 2016).
4. DePillis, Lydia, 'Auto union loses historic election at Volkswagen plant in Tennessee', *The Washington Post* (14 February 2014) <https://www.washingtonpost.com/news/wonk/wp/2014/02/14/united-auto-workers-lose-historic-election-at-chattanooga-volkswagen-plant/> (Last accessed 3 November 2016).

   Rushe, Dominic, 'United Auto Workers union drops lost vote appeal at VW Tennessee plant', *The Guardian* (21 April 2014) <https://www.theguardian.com/world/2014/apr/21/volkswagen-tennessee-auto-workers-union-drops-appeal-lost-vote> (Last accessed 4 November 2016).
5. Ibid., *Washington Post* (14 February 2014).
6. Elk, Mike, 'After Historic UAW Defeat at Tennessee Volkswagen Plant, Theories Abound', *In These Times* (15 February 2014) <http://inthesetimes.com/working/entry/16300/after_uaw_defeat_at_volkswagen_in_tennessee_theories_abound> (Last accessed 2 November 2016).
7. Nestlé, 'Flexible, fast and functional: Nestlé to adopt modular factories', *Nestlé.com* (4 July 2014) <http://www.nestle.com/media/newsandfeatures/modular-factories> (Last accessed 3 November 2016).

8   BBC News, 'Call Centres "bad for India"' (11 December 2003) <http://news.bbc.co.uk/1/hi/world/south_asia/3292619.stm> (Last accessed 3 November 2016).
9   Thomson, Rebecca, '"Prison-like" conditions for workers making IBM, Dell, HP, Microsoft and Lenovo products', *Computer Weekly* (17 February 2009) <http://www.computerweekly.com/news/2240088431/Prison-like-conditions-for-workers-making-IBM-Dell-HP-Microsoft-and-Lenovo-products> (Last accessed 3 November 2016).
10 Wintour, Patrick, 'Biggest crackdown on trade unions for 30 years launched by Conservatives', *The Guardian* (15 July 2015) <https://www.theguardian.com/politics/2015/jul/15/trade-unions-conservative-offensive-decades-strikes-labour> (Last accessed 4 November 2016).

    This legislation is merely the next (and not the final) stage in the process of capital's plan to legally shackle the trade unions to the point of absolute impotence. The state power of capital has been elaborating this trajectory since the election of Thatcher in 1979.

11 '*In all capitalistically advanced countries we are confronted by numerous instances of authoritarian legislation, despite the past traditions and constantly reiterated present claims to "democracy". The authoritarian measures are made necessary by the growing difficulties of managing the deteriorating conditions of socioeconomic life without the direct legislation of the state. They are designed to underpin with the threat of law and, whenever needed, the use of force, the more aggressive posture of capital towards its labour force*' (Mészáros, *Beyond Capital*, p. 251).

    And such measures are orchestrated and articulated with universal approval amongst the triad of reaction constituted by the capitalist print, internet and broadcasting media (see Appendix II).

12 Marx, Karl, 'The Eighteenth Brumaire of Louis Bonaparte'. In *Surveys From Exile*, edited by David Fernbach, pp. 143–249, 146 (New York: Vintage Books, 1974).
13 Williams, Raymond, *Resources of Hope. Culture, Democracy, Socialism* (Verso, 1989), p. 249.
14 '*Under the circumstances of the system's structural crisis, however, even the once partially favourable elements in the historical equation between capital and labour must be overturned in favour of capital. Thus, not only there can be no room now for granting substantive gains to labour [...] but also many of the past concessions must be clawed back, both in economic terms and in the domain of legislation. This is why the "Welfare State" is today not only in serious trouble but for all intents and purposes dead.*'

Mészáros, *Beyond Capital*, Section 5.4.4, 'The Activation of Capital's Absolute Limits', p. 240.

15   Trotsky [1940], *Trade Unions in the Epoch of Imperialist Decay* (New York: Pathfinder Press, 1990).

CHAPTER 7

Capital's Offensive against Social Provision

The social gains made in public provision (health, education, housing, social services, etc.) after 1945 were, contradictorily, 'a necessary and positive constituent of the inner dynamic of capital's self-expansion itself' after the carnage and destruction of the second imperialist world war.[1] Not only did they provide a direct social medium for the realization of value, resulting capital accumulation and expansion. The actual salaries paid out also augmented the increase in the post-war circulation of capital. This post-war inflationary expansion of the capitalist order was only made possible on the bloodied ground of the mass destruction of imperialist war.

Today, in the age of increasing labour productivity, the falling rate of profit and the growing destructive overproduction mediating capital's crisis, such Keynesian economics of displacement could not find an enduring, long-term ontological foothold. Such measures would, if attempts to apply them today were universally activated, only serve to exacerbate the historic and daily worsening problems of the capitalist mode of 'destructive' reproduction.

The structural crisis of the capitalist order has now driven it on to a trajectory (since 1979) of the progressive withdrawal of the funding and continuation of social provision. However, by running down this provision it must, at the same time, necessarily constrict an arena in which capital finds an important outlet for the sale of its commodities. Increasingly, capital seeks to resolve this contradiction through the transfer of all public provision and assets into the domain of capital exploitation so that all these services operate exclusively on a profit-only basis. The privatization of public provision is, therefore, not only an attack on the proletariat. It also begins to erode, at the same time, an arena within which the state power directly subsidizes capital. This 'double-edged' sword also applies to the attack on the so-called 'benefits culture' which is again, indirectly, a subsidy for those areas of capital producing the means of subsistence and for the landlords and utilities.

Private capital is only invested in the provision of 'public services' on strict condition that it can make a profit out of this investment. Otherwise, this 'investment' ceases to function as capital. A recent manifestation of the operation of this maxim has been observed with the withdrawal by private capital from the contract to run the Hinchingbrooke Hospital in Cambridgeshire.[2] According to Julian Huppert, Liberal Democrat and erstwhile MP for Cambridge ...

> the private provider has found it couldn't make a profit and it's pulling out leaving the whole future of the hospital hanging in the balance.[3]

Attempts by the state power to resolve the contradictions – arising from withdrawal of state provision and its attempted relocation into the realm of private capital – are potentially explosive. It must serve to fuel the drive of the proletariat as a whole towards re-constituting itself offensively with new strategies of struggle and opposition to capital and its state power in the form of new, more broad-based, organizations.

The process of capital seeking to resolve the current contradictions which it faces in the provision and management of public services is effectively under way. As the structural crisis deepens, it must move increasingly towards the completion of the trajectory of 'public provision' for profit. Just to take one well-known prefigurative example in healthcare: the establishment of the National Institute for Health and Care Excellence in Britain.[4] The fundamental purpose of this quango of accountants is to look at healthcare and medication provision through 'cost/benefit' financial calculations and decide whether or not sick or dying people's lives are 'worth' prolonging on the basis of such hideous formulae.

This capitalist 'cost/benefit' ethos of the ledger book has permeated the whole of the health care system in Britain. In the United States of America, millions of people are still not treated for curable illnesses (despite the 'reforms' of the Obama administration) because of the long-term operation of this ethos, reflecting the malignant requirements of capital. If you cannot afford the astronomical and rising cost of health insurance in the

United States, you do not receive the latest and optimal treatments for life-threatening illness.

The unavoidable implications of these continuing developments are, for example in healthcare, that if the provision of a vital treatment or use of a specific medication cannot yield a profit then it will not be made available and people will be left to deteriorate or die. And, indeed, this is already starting to happen in Britain in which cheaper, less effective medications are being used instead of more expensive and more therapeutic methods of treatment. If the treatment which people need in order to have an optimal chance of survival comes out on the 'wrong side' of the 'cost/benefit' calculations, then they are left with inferior treatments which are cheaper but less life-prolonging and/or life-enhancing. For many, this means deterioration and early death.

This is the immovable logic of capital itself: hospitals and schools (and social provision in general) run on the basis of the most sacred principle of 'production (read 'provision') for profit'. The pre-eminently determining maxim of 'No Profit. No Service' must prevail under conditions where private capital is 'providing' public services. Service will only be provided on condition that profit is made as we have already seen at Hinchingbrooke.

This transfer en masse of the public services into the clutches of private capital was initiated by the Tory government of John Major from 1992 onwards but accelerated significantly under Tony Blair's 'New Labour' with the further rolling out of the Private Finance Initiative (PFI).[5] Private capital, for example, now owns much of the basic infrastructure of many hospitals, schools, health centres and other 'public facilities' and annually reaps a very fat interest from the 'public purse' for investing the capital to construct them. It is perfectly feasible to envisage a situation where fiscal conditions alter to such a degree that the 'interests' of capital are not met by the state power and so, under such conditions, hospitals, infrastructure, etc., could be closed, sold off and assets ('collateral') liquidated to land or property speculators, etc. The public infrastructure now stands as 'security' pledged for the repayment of the financial investment ('principal' plus interest, of course) used to build it by private, value-augmenting, money capital. Again, what is operative here is the untransgressable logic of capital and the crisis-mediated momentum to drive forward with a general programme for the complete privatization of all public provision ...

> Over the next few decades, the current welfare state will become unsustainable. We need to come to terms with the fact that the universal welfare state is over: a radical refounding of the relationship between the individual and the state is necessary.[6]

The Tories' 2010 election mantra of 'The Big Society' was a menacing prefiguration of this strategy. Such notions simply mean that the state power of capital is going to transfer all public provision into the profit-ruled clutches of private capital and, accordingly, if capital cannot make a profit out of human illness and despair then people will have to turn to their 'own endeavours and resources' or to charities, if any are available. Capital will run any services (the 'choice cuts') out of which it can make a profit and simply leave the non-profitable remainder (the 'scrag ends and offal') to 'extra-capital' agencies.

Privatization of social provision is effectively equivalent to the withdrawal of this provision if no profit is made. But anybody with even a cursory knowledge of the latent 'structural problematic' (described in Marx's *Capital* and developed by Mészáros in *Beyond Capital*) found in the inevitable historic projection and trajectory of the social relation of capital could see that this was bound to unfold and manifest sooner or later. Privatization had to become an intrinsic part of capital's structural-crisis process: social provision on condition of profit. All 'public provision' subject to the inflexible, operative criteria – as of an 'iron law of nature' – of profit-driven and self-augmenting value as it enters its period of structural crisis.

Capital itself ceases to be capital – it becomes divested of its character as 'capital' – if it cannot augment its own value through its circulation in the social metabolism. Profit is therefore its most sacred objective and anything that hinders that must be pushed aside and jettisoned. The return of the value advanced together with the holy increment is the inalienable and inexorable doxology of capital. Without it there could be no accumulation of capital or a charmed lifestyle for the capitalist class which lives a life of sybaritic luxury through its ownership of the whole exploitative capitalist process.

The politicians of the capital order are peddling an outright lie when they state, with a breathtaking degree of unequivocation, that private capital running the public services will not affect the nature of that provision. On the contrary, it will profoundly alter it – more or less beyond recognition – to the detriment of many millions and is already doing so as many are already experiencing.

Such developments, in themselves, arise out of and are animated by the deepening of the structural crisis of capital which eyes, *and must eye*, every area and sphere of society for capture and expansion. The extension of capital's domain is complemented by the progressive and most crippling increase in the intensity of its exploitation of acquired resources. Nothing is excluded. Nothing is sacred. Except the drive to perpetually augment the value of capital itself. The self-valorisation of capital is the highest, the most sacred principle to which everything else is subservient and subordinate, including (especially!) human life and well-being. And in the course of the unfolding of its structural crisis, this principle must be multiplied many times over with the most disturbing and devastating impact on nature and the life of humanity.

The depth of capital's crisis could not be made any clearer by the crisis of banking capital in 2008 and its impact on social provision. The inherent requirements of capital-in-crisis are hoovering up every last ounce of value as manifest in the wake of this banking crisis. Any available value in the whole system of welfare and public provision is being sucked unceremoniously into the gilded chambers of global finance capital as the 'return' for money borrowed by the state power, in Britain and the United States, to prop up the tottering banking system after the crisis of 2008.

What is approaching, very rapidly – unless capital can directly make profit out of it – is 'provision' and 'welfare' run by charitable endeavours, unpaid do-gooders and Christian salvationists. The real outcome will be more misery, suffering and people's lives sacrificed on the high altar of the Moloch of capital. On both a physical and psychological level, this means the continuity and deepening of human suffering as a consequence of capital's predations which are arising directly out of the current crisis-nature of the epoch of the rule of capital.

To pay back the global creditor parasites of finance capital, the whole system of public provision in Britain (hospitals, schools, housing, municipal services, social support, welfare provision, etc.) is progressively being liquidated into the coffers of capital in the form of the repayment and augmentation ('principal plus interest') of loan capital. With more crises of banking capital inevitable (the latest one 'brewing', in October 2016, relates to the equity and liquidity problems of the transnational Deutsche Bank after it was slapped with a $14 billion fine by the US Department of Justice for its implicated role in the selling of 'sub-prime' mortgage-backed securities whose non-realization (default) served to precipitate the banking crisis of 2008) sooner or later, the implications for social provision of this ongoing process of value-appropriation are socially explosive. The inevitable outcome flowing from this deepening structural crisis is the transfer of the whole of social provision into the hands of capital for profit or, if a profit cannot be 'turned' on their appropriation, their liquidation or demotion to charity. The 'payback' must come from somewhere. Value does not materialize out of thin air or droppeth from the sky like kind mercy.

Capital is hard-nosed, hard-faced and driven by its own uncompromising logic of exploitation, accumulation and value augmentation. Absolutely nothing must stand in the way of its untransgressable logic. For the state power of capital, the major tappable source of repayments for loans is state-owned assets, revenue from taxation on income and capital and the whole system of financing social provision. Sale of state assets, increased levying of taxes on income and withdrawal of social provision become the mechanisms for keeping the banks afloat as more 'debt crises' inevitably erupt onto the surface of the socio-economic landscape of the global capitalist order.

The state power of capital must defend and take measures to defend the social relations upon which its own existence rests. The liquidation of state assets and increased rate of extraction of revenue from income is the 'pot' from which this power takes the financial means to try to prop up banking capital. Where the state borrows money from the capital markets to prop up failing banks, those loans remain recallable (formally or informally) on collateral which is state assets and revenue, social provision and, of course, any state 'share' in the propped up banks themselves.

Such crises of the global capitalist financial system must mean successive, massive transfers of 'state value' to finance and prop up the capital order. The necessary consequence of this transfer is the further and intensifying destruction of living standards, public services, jobs, housing, healthcare, education, amenities, benefits and taxation increases on people who cannot afford to pay and, in many cases, are already impoverished; the so-called 'working poor'.

Debt crises are serving – as specific manifestations of capital's overall structural crisis – as drivers for the capture of the totality of exploitable social provision by capital. The increasingly heavier social burden of these crises of the bankrupt, outmoded and unsustainable capital system fall on the shoulders of the proletariat. The agency of this imposition is the state power of capital. Nobody is exempt – those in employment, the sick, homeless, pensioners, jobless, elderly, needy, vulnerable, students, self-employed, etc. Those in work today are only too aware that tomorrow they could be joining the dole queue with the long term, structurally unemployed.

The only way to fully and effectively oppose these imposed measures is to organize, work and fight *collectively as a class*. Trade unionism is irreversibly inadequate. To begin to mobilize and organize the resistance to the destruction and devastation already taking place and rapidly worsening. This implies the need to work towards the establishment of new forms of agency which are adequate enough to build and spearhead resistance to the capital order itself. Such an independent mass mobilization would inevitably find itself in confrontation with the governing castes of the established, historically outmoded organizations of the proletariat. With the top stratum of 'business unionism' and its political arm which identifies the continuation of the capitalist order as the historic basis for its own privileges, including its six-figure salaries.

For the proletariat, the emphasis and awareness must be on the perspective that ...

> under the new historical conditions of capital's structural crisis even the bare maintenance of the acquired standard of living, not to mention the acquisition of meaningful additional gains, requires a major change in strategy, in accordance with the historical actuality of the socialist offensive. Capital's growing legislative attack on

the labour movement underlines the necessity of such a change in the strategic orientation of its adversary.[7]

The introduction of anti-labour legislation by Tory and its maintenance by Labour governments demonstrates the necessity for such changes in strategy and organization. And the continued prostration of the trade union bureaucracy to these laws necessarily brings the struggle for a higher social form of agency into collision with this hierarchical form of organization.[8]

We can expect – in addition to the legislation now passed into law in May 2016 (Trade Union Act 2016) which limits the right to strike by placing more draconian conditions on the validity of strike ballots – more anti-labour legislation in due course from 'our representatives' residing in their more or less clapped-out, graft-ridden, capital-subservient, corrupt parliamentary system of governance. The whole purpose is to legally shackle trade unionism to the point where strikes effectively become increasingly difficult to organize and ineffective when they do actually take place. Mussolini, Hitler and Franco used the 'gun and the jackboot'. Today, in Britain, capital is using 'Parliamentary Democracy' to realize, essentially, the same objectives.

Equally as threatening and sinister is the continuing Tory government's posturing against 'human rights' and 'extremism' which is not a movement-specific term (for example, against the Islamists and Jihadists exclusively) but is being articulated as a 'blanket' to 'tackle extremism in general', that is, for all those 'on the wrong side of the blanket'.

The toothless bark of the Trades Union Congress (TUC) in Britain that the privatization of public provision is merely 'ideological' is a smokescreen to cover for their own abject subservience to capital and Keynesian delusions. Despite all the 'left-wing' rhetoric, any Labour government headed by Corbyn would very soon encounter the constricting and overwhelming pressures of capital's structural crisis. Any attempts at returning to Keynesian economic programmes would 'hit the buffers' of this crisis. The inspirational mass movement behind Corbyn (presently, October 2016, around 600,000 people) would very soon realize the political limitations of the figurehead of their movement. His social democratic outlook remains bounded within and circumscribed by the economic parameters of the capital order.

The most recent (Summer 2015) significant political manifestation of these 'buffers' (capital's crisis in the social metabolism) has emerged in Greece where the so-called and much media-vaunted 'radical left' party of Syriza failed to organize the Greek proletariat in opposition to global finance capital. Rather than repudiating the astronomical debt imposed on the Greek people, it decided to act as the proxy of capital and impose the burden in a 'deal' where it totally surrendered to the demands of the European and global political agencies of capital. Meanwhile, the extra burden imposed – by the 'revolutionaries' in Syriza – on the already overburdened Greek proletariat can only become heavier with all the social and psychological consequences for millions of Greeks.

The historical truth of the matter is that capital has entered – as Mészáros has very clearly shown in his work – the period of its structural crisis on a global scale. And it is this crisis which drives it into areas formerly considered to be 'out of bounds'. The transgression into these areas is intrinsic to its own crisis-ridden nature and the 'violation of its own barrier' as a social relation in the twenty-first century. It necessitates the complete appropriation of all public provision for exploitation and profit. This is the simple truth of the matter and hence the agenda of capitalist governments – of whatever hue – to transfer all public provision into the hands of the financiers and transnationals.

The darkening and looming shadow of the TTIP initiative is a clear invite to 'further privatization' in this regard. No amount of mealy mouthed evasion or mendacity can hide that simple historical truth. The ideological posturing of parliamentary politicians is merely the justificatory gloss employed to consummate this predatory process. Already much of the infrastructure is actually owned by private capital. TTIP (The Transatlantic Trade and Investment Partnership)[9] will provide the global 'connections' for the further complete privatization of social provision and state assets across North America and Europe. What we are now witnessing is only the beginning of an agenda to completely 'privatize' all the public services, excepting none. Those which cannot be 'privatized' (made available for profit) will be discarded or farmed out to charities and do-gooders.

Capital-in-crisis must constantly invade and drive to appropriate the different spheres of public provision for the purpose of its self-valorisation i.e. to take over public provision provided by its state in order to invest for profit. The PFI (Private Finance Initiative) in Britain is an example of this predation by capital. The labour performed by workers in these areas of social provision must become targeted by capital as an actual or potential source of profit. To exchange these concrete forms of labour directly for capital which returns the value of the wages advanced together with an increment. Under such conditions, public provision – once appropriated by capital – becomes provision on condition of profit. No profit means no provision.

This capital offensive against social provision spells catastrophe for millions. Capital engages in this predatory, profit-seeking drive to counter the effects of its own structural crisis on itself as a social relation of production and distribution. For example, where a capitalist corporation runs a health service or school, the labour of the health service worker or teacher, etc., must be exchanged for capital rather than for state revenue in order to open new vistas to continue with the process of the accumulation of capital. The state then uses revenue from tax or the liquidation of assets to pay the corporation. People also start to pay directly for the health and education services which were previously 'free at the point of use'. The corporation must 'turn a profit' otherwise its capital ceases to be capital and its ownership and/or management of a service becomes 'financially unviable'.

Nothing must stand in its way in this, its untransgressable logic. This unfolding structural crisis is the historic driving force behind capital's need to appropriate and run public services on the basis of profit only. This arises directly out of the onset of capital's structural crisis which is the primary causality mediating the privatization of public provision in Britain since Thatcher came to power in 1979 and continued by 'New Labour' thereafter.

The privatization of social provision and state assets (starting in the 1980s with the transfer of state utilities and 'streamlined' industries into the hands of private capital) is symptomatic of the depth of capital's crisis. It must now expand into any areas left for exploitation where it can make profit and accumulate. This privatization of the 'utilities' and the remnants of state-run 'heavy' industry in the 1980s (such as steel and deep-mine coal) prefigured the transfer of all public provision into the profit-seeking grasp of capital. The first depositions of mass structural unemployment arose out of this closedown and destruction of state capitalist industries and the transfer of any viable remnants into the hands of private capital.

If the trade union form of organization displays its impotence in the face of capital's unfolding structural crisis, then consider the plight of the many millions who are now condemned to the prospect of indefinite unemployment across the regions of Europe and North America. This structural unemployment is multiplied many times over in the so-called 'underdeveloped' regions of the globe in Asia, Africa and Latin America.

In the 'aboriginal' capitalist countries – those regions of the world which led the advance charge of capital onto the scene of human history – this structural unemployment has given rise to the so-called 'benefits culture'. As with social provision in general, the relationship which capital has with this 'welfare culture' is charged with, and is becoming augmented with more, conflict as capital's crisis opens up like a Pandora's Box of human history.

The established relationship between capital's state power and the jobless has always been founded on the former's capacity to fund the system of so-called 'welfare benefits'. The fiscal crisis of the state power of capital will increasingly become an ongoing spur to axing benefits, to transfer revenue from the jobless, sick and retired and place it directly into the coffers of finance capital as debt repayment.

This is where the present 'cuts' in social provision are ending up.[10] To finance a parasitic lifestyle of an obscenely wealthy, useless, featherbedded class of idlers and their managerial elite who receive the highest form of 'benefits' known as 'bonuses' and 'dividends' on capital. The ultimate human source of this wealth is the labour and pockets of millions of working people across the globe and those in the 'developed' regions whose public services are under assault.

In these latter regions, capital and its state power have declared economic war on the proletariat and its public services. When a hospital closes or a social service is eliminated, the funds used to maintain that provision are being transferred by capitalist governments into the treasure chests of global finance capital. It is these organizations on whose behalf the Syriza government in Greece has arrived at a 'historic compromise', and is now acting to keep the flagging capital order on its feet. So much for 'socialist movement'. So much for 'revolutionaries'. So much for 'the future of socialism'.

In 2008, when Gordon Brown's Labour government went to the capital markets to borrow the 'principal' to prop up the collapsing banking system in Britain, the only possible form of destruction which the repayment of this 'principal' plus interest could have possibly taken is the destruction of social provision by this state power or its transfer into the grasp of capital for purposes of profit and accumulation. This is why all social provision – health, education, housing, social services, employment in local and national government, recreational amenities, etc. – are all being 'downsized', sold off or given their marching orders to operate on the basis of making profit. In essence, the state power of capital can no longer – with the onrush of capital's crisis – afford to provide and develop these wider, overarching social functions as it did in bygone days. This is the socio-economic ontology of crisis underlying the ideology of the so-called 'reduction of the state' in some areas (social provision, education, state-owned landed property, welfare, etc.) whilst the state power has become more 'attuned' and 'steeled' to altering conditions in other areas (intelligence agencies, police and armed forces training and provision, etc.).

The falling revenues resulting from capital's crisis drives the capitalist state to pauperize the jobless and sick regardless of non-payment of bills, rents, increase in petty criminality, etc. In the long term, as these measures against the welfare-dependent section of the population work their way through the socio-economic landscape, it will make matters worse for the capital system. This is why, in the fight against cuts in social provision, the proletariat needs forms of organization which can bring together the jobless, the employed and all those who are dependent on the 'benefits system'.

The trade unions, in their present structure and organization, have completely abandoned the jobless and are, in themselves and in their self-subsistence, not only utterly useless for this unificatory purpose. They are inadequate as a vehicle to fight for and articulate the interests of the proletariat as a whole in the oncoming collisions with capital and its state power.

This outmodedness of the trade unions will become increasingly more evident as capital's global crisis progressively unfolds. They have become 'funnelled' and 'bottlenecked' into an 'impasse' as a result of the fact that their *modus operandi* reflects the existence of superseded conditions with the emergence and development of capital's *structural* crisis. This must tend to posit a growing internal crisis of their organization taking the form of the opposition between membership and hierarchy. The 'stopper' in the 'bottleneck' (hindering further development towards a new form of organization) is constituted by the caste interests of the trade union bureaucracy whose privileged 'gravy-train' mode of existence – six-figure salaries, hefty pensions, golden hellos and goodbyes, trade union residences, trips abroad, etc. – is predicated on the basis of the continuation of the capitalist system itself. This is precisely why the ideological ideal of this labour hierarchy is a *reformable capitalism* which leaves the existence and rule of *capital* in place and, indeed, is supported by this hierarchy. The privileges of the trade union hierarchy ultimately rest on the existence of the capital system. Accordingly, they live and fall with this selfsame system.

The unemployed population today is distinguished from its 'reserve army' role in the previous cyclical phases of capital's crises. The emergence of *structural* unemployment means this 'benefits' social layer has now become historically posited as a permanently jobless, determinate social stratum. Countless millions across the globe are now forced into this burgeoning cul-de-sac of unemployment. A dead end of destitution, dehumanization and misery with all the social and psychological problems and ramifications associated with it.

The superfluity of this stratum for productive capital – as a direct source of surplus-value producing labour – can only express itself in an increasingly state-sponsored pauperization and beggardom. Contradictorily, such an increase in mass pauperization, however, will undoubtedly have unpalatable consequences for the process of the reproduction of capital itself in certain sectors because it will serve to interfere with the circular process of value realization. In pauperizing millions who live on state benefits, the state power would effectively be withdrawing a socially mediated subsidy for that sector of capital which provides housing and produces the means of consumption for this layer. The pauperization of millions will, in the long term, only serve to sharpen the contradictions within this process of value realization because the unemployed and disabled remain necessary for very limited but specific sectors of capital as a mediating source for the sale of its commodities and hence for its reproduction in these sectors.

This social layer – dependent on state welfare – has, ontologically speaking, become posited as a determinate, dependent, 'parasitic' social stratum. Not, of course, a sybaritic parasitism as we see with the capitalist class. But a type of dependency of a meagre, soulless, life-draining character where a bare subsistence is hardly guaranteed. The term 'dependent' or 'parasitic' is not, of course, employed pejoratively here in relation to welfare but rather is descriptive of the fact that this stratum – ironically like the capitalist class itself – lives off revenue produced by the labour of others which is mediated by handouts from the state power.

All benefits and allowances ultimately arise out of the surplus which workers are producing globally through their productive labour and which is partially appropriated as revenue by the respective state bureaucracies. Out of this revenue the state pays benefits and allowances as well as the salaries of its employees like civil servants, teachers, medics, etc. This unemployed stratum lives off the surplus which workers are producing globally. It is *producing no value* whatsoever (consuming without producing) and is totally dependent on the state power.

Accordingly, if the state continues to remove state benefits (welfare), it will also block off a source for the market realization of the value produced by employed workers (i.e. for the reaping of profit by capital) which will only serve to deepen the crisis of the capital order by narrowing the 'market space' for the realization of value.

All this must become expressed politically. In so far as the 'benefits culture' is a mediating component in the realization of value and thus in the circulation of capital, it must, by virtue of this, be drawn into it as a necessary part of this whole process. However, in essence, the 'benefits system' effectively constitutes an indirect subsidy to capital from its state power so that this benefits parasitism is partly serving to perpetuate the higher form of parasitism of the capital relation. A dual parasitism prevails – capital and the structurally unemployed – with the source of the surplus being the labour of the employed global proletariat.

Both social strata (the capitalist class and the structurally unemployed) are, therefore, living off this surplus and, although the fiscal position of the capitalist state may temporarily stabilize, capital's crisis will worsen with cuts in benefits in the long run. The system of regular welfare payments constitutes a state subsidy for capital mediated by those directly receiving them and exchanging them for the means of survival. The value created by productive labour serves not only to maintain its own wage enslavement. It also serves as the source of the revenues which keep the state power of capital in its rule over society. The value created by this productive labour of the proletariat serves to maintain the welfare system (in the form of a state- appropriated and re-distributed value arising out of tax on profit and wages), the capitalist class and the state power which defends the latter's interests in direct and alien opposition to the proletariat as a class.

Axing benefits, therefore, becomes a 'cut' for commercial capital like shops, food companies, the utilities and, of course, for landlords. To defer cutting benefits would contribute to intensifying the fiscal crisis of the capitalist state, the conflict between its revenue and its obligations to loan capital (hence the obsession of government with 'turning a surplus in public finances'). And yet to continue to cut them and fill the coffers of finance capital can only serve, in the long run, to sharpen class antagonisms and actually encroach on the interests of those spheres of capital providing the means of consumption for those living on welfare benefits.

The growing use of charity and so-called 'food banks' by millions is a response to these 'cuts' and a drain on the potential realization of value. This is why some big businesses and food outlets refuse to donate to food-banks and prefer to destroy food regardless of the fact that millions on state welfare benefits are finding it increasingly difficult to 'heat and eat' at the same time.

Many now face the dehumanizing dilemma of having to feed their families *or* to keep them warm in winter at the same time. Sometimes both hungry and cold at the same time as we are commonly witnessing with the growing homeless and rootless living in the doorways of city streets whilst thousands of habitable 'buy-to-let' properties remain empty and unoccupied.

In Marx's conception of the proletariat in the nineteenth century, the unemployed were a quantitatively varying reservoir of potential labour power for when production and circulation picked up after the 'down' phase of cyclical crises. Today, this jobless stratum is permanently lodged in a state of structural unemployment and is superfluous for capital as a direct source of value production. However, they remain a mediating component in the overall circulation of capital. They are not value-producing proletarians but they are value-realizing through their sundry purchases despite their parasitism.

The only other way for the state power to subsidize commercial capital would be by *direct payments to capital without mediation via this social stratum*. The human significance, implications and ramifications of such a conception are too horrific to contemplate but the fact that it is *not 'illogical' within the actual operation of the 'logic of capital' to do this needs to be faced*. A deep cesspit of possibilities of the inhuman brutality of the capital system awaits to be actualized and every day, as the crisis unfolds, they are coming more fully into view.

Implicitly, as the fiscal crisis of the state deepens, there will be the most profound consequences for this so-called 'benefits culture'. It is interesting to note here *en passant* that both the English (1640s) and French Revolutions (1790s) were animated by – and emerged against the background of – a worsening fiscal crisis of the respective absolutist states.

Sweeping cuts in benefits and allowances represents a qualitative realignment in the direct relation between this permanently unemployed stratum and the state itself, raising the possibility of the growth of mass opposition movements where a subservient dependency on state handouts can be pushed to breaking point, exploding into open hostility and conflict.

We witnessed a pre-figuration of this when the youth took to the streets in the Summer of 2011 after the Metropolitan Police execution of Londoner, Mark Duggan. Because there exists no arbitrating and mediating regulatory mechanism whatsoever between this stratum and the state (as there is, for example, between organized labour and the state in the form of the trade union hierarchy, ACAS, etc.), then any conflict would likely to be more untempered and directly charged with an open hostility.

Through what forms of organization can this 'benefits' stratum participate, represent itself, conduct, initially, a struggle against the onslaught of the capitalist state which is surely to worsen and intensify? We will address this and other such vital questions in later chapters.

The relatively more 'privileged' mode of life of the employed proletariat in the capitalist 'homelands' also exhibits certain parasitic characteristics in that it is subsidized by the global mass transfer of value created by the labour of the proletarians of other parts of the globe where the rate of exploitation is nothing short of horrific. Without this most terrible 'superexploitation', the mode of life of the employed proletariat in these major capitalist countries would be completely altered. Accordingly, it may be asserted that the proletariat of the 'older' capitalist countries is in a relatively privileged position compared to the workers of the rest of the globe and certainly, in this regard, economically, they do indeed have 'more to lose than their chains'.

As the structural crisis of capital deepens, this 'benefits' layer will increasingly face the prospect of a deeper pauperization and beggardom. Sections may even gravitate towards fascism as they scapegoat migrants and ethnic minority groups. We are seeing this, for example, with the attraction of some sections of the proletariat in Britain towards UKIP (United Kingdom Independence Party) and towards the 'National Front' in France. If it remains as it is, without a fundamental political re-orientation under radically altering conditions, then utter degradation and slavery awaits this layer. The pitiful position of many migrant workers in Britain today – under 'gangmasters' – and the most dehumanizing and degraded condition of workers in other parts of the globe is the fate which awaits large sections of the proletariat in the capitalist 'homelands' without the necessary strategic and organizational re-orientation and transformations. The position of these so-called 'Third World' proletarians is a prefiguration of what awaits the 'First World' proletariat if it cannot rise to the challenge and move onto the revolutionary road.

The so-called 'safety net' of the 'benefits culture' is being minimally maintained for the present because the state power of capital cannot risk the socio-economic and political consequences of removing it, not only for itself as the organizing centre for the rule of capital but for some minor sections of capital itself, for the realization of a part of its value in the circulation process.

How much longer can this last? The unemployed are already being subjected to a punitive, degrading and humiliating 'sanctions' regime by the state power in Britain. Many are 'cut adrift' for weeks, if not months, without payments so they are forced to the soup kitchens and 'food banks'. The state attack on the unemployed ('cheats' and 'scroungers') and the sick ('work-shy' and 'shirkers') is supported by its ideological cheerleaders in the print and broadcasting media who whip up the hostility and hatred towards this pejoratively attributed 'underclass'.

Hitler's ideologists termed whole peoples as *untermensch*. Capital's media never stops reminding us of the existence of an 'underclass' which sounds just as sinister. This so-called and pejoratively termed 'underclass' is actually an intrinsic part of the proletarian class which has been abandoned by capital (necessarily so from capital's vantage point) into structural unemployment. Politically and organizationally, they can and must form an organically integrated part of the mass proletarian movement now being made necessary by capital's deepening structural crisis.

Systematically, this criminalization of the jobless by the state power is part of the overall, insidious strategy to drive them further into pauperdom or into a twenty-first-century version of the workhouse: punitively managed forced labour for a state pittance.

The sick and incapacitated are already being forced off sick benefits and onto the dole queue in order to make them 'available for work' where none is actually available. The real, motivating reason is simply to reduce the level of payments which the state gives to the disabled and ill. Today (October 2016) the government in Britain is not only forcing people off sickness benefits onto the dole queue. It is also reducing payments (for those who are sick and disabled) from the sickness rate to the jobless 'available for work' rate. A person who is most fortunate to find work saves the state a welfare payout but also pays a premium into the state treasury in terms of any taxation and national insurance. Human needs are totally swept aside and disregarded on the basis of these 'cost cutting' measures. These assaults by the state power on the jobless and sick are, of course, impacting people psychologically with a growth in the number of suicides recorded which are undoubtedly linked to this state persecution of people.[11]

With the state power deploying unscrupulous and inhuman methods (it regularly finds those, for example, with heart disease, cancer or terminal illness, 'fit for work') of forcing people off sickness benefits, the financial savings are not insignificant and can be transferred into the coffers of finance capital to pay off debt. How long will it be before the state power of capital points the baton and barks: all must work for their handout or lose it? The return of a twenty-first-century version of the Victorian workhouse.

Notes and References

1 Mészáros, *Beyond Capital*, p. 941.
2 BBC News, 'Hinchingbrooke Hospital: Circle to withdraw from contract' (9 January 2015) <http://www.bbc.co.uk/news/uk-england-cambridgeshire-30740956> (Last accessed 3 November 2016).
3 Cambridgelibdems.org.uk, 'Huppert fights to bring Hinchingbrooke Hospital back to the NHS' (9 January 2015) <http://www.cambridgelibdems.org.uk/huppert_fights_to_bring_hinchingbrooke_hospital_back_to_nhs> (Last accessed 3 November 2016).
4 The National Institute for Health and Care Excellence is an agency of the Department of Health in the British state. It advises on the present and possible future use of technologies, procedures and medicines in the National Health Service. Fundamental to its assessments is the application of 'cost-benefit' calculations. This government 'quango' – originally established as the 'National Institute for Clinical Excellence' – is, with a certain comedic irony, known by the acronym of 'NICE'. The pre-determining criterion in its assessments of treatments and medicines is the evaluation of their 'efficacy' on the basis of their 'cost'. Accordingly, healthcare in Britain becomes subject to the constraints of financial parameters which can overrule specific and beneficial treatments on financial grounds.
5 The following website gives a succinct and accurate description of what the PFI involves: Benjamin, Joel, 'Seven things everyone should know about the Private Finance Initiative', *Open Democracy* (17 November 2014) <https://www.opendemocracy.net/ournhs/joel-benjamin/seven-things-everyone-should-know-about-private-finance-initiative> (Last accessed 3 November 2016).

6   Skidmore, Chris, MP, *A New Beveridge: 70 Years on – refounding the 21st century welfare state* <https://chrisskidmoremp.files.wordpress.com/2012/11/beveridge2.pdf> (Last accessed 6 November 2016).
    Skidmore is a Tory MP for Kingswood, Gloucestershire. The document is published by the Free Enterprise Group of right-wing Tory MPs.
7   Mészáros, *Beyond Capital*, 'Radical Politics and Transition to Socialism: Reflections on Marx's Centenary', p. 941.
8   It was a *Labour* government which first considered a post-war hobbling of the trade unions in Britain in the form of the 'In Place of Strife' white paper which was not passed into law. Drafted, in 1969, by the then Labour Prime Minister Harold Wilson and that oft-celebrated late (died 2002) 'leftie', Barbara Castle, Baroness and formerly seated as a member of her majesty's most honourable extra-parliamentary Privy Council. 'In Place of Strife' legislation would have rendered illegal the trade union struggles in 1979 which toppled the Callaghan government. Ironically, it was Callaghan himself in cabinet who opposed the white paper becoming legal statute.
9   Jeffries, Stuart, 'What is TTIP and why should we be angry about it?', *The Guardian* (3 August 2015) <https://www.theguardian.com/business/2015/aug/03/ttip-what-why-angry-transatlantic-trade-investment-partnership-guide> (Last accessed 5 November 2016).
10 Ownership of UK government debt. The major owners are institutional finance capital such as insurance and pension funds and the banks, including the Bank of England. A significant portion is in the form of overseas money capital. The government does not provide access to specific details of overseas gilt holdings. However, a significant investment must come from countries which are money-capital rich such as institutional investors in China, oil-exporting countries, etc. Global finance capital is the Moloch to which every national government pays homage and at the shrine of which they most devotedly worship. The value historically deployed to fund public services in Britain is now being sucked into the distended accounts of the institutions of global money capital. This is where public provision in liquidation – health, education, social services, etc. – is ending up. To augment the value of the money capital of these obscenely wealthy organizations and the various investors and individuals owning them.
    Reuben, Anthony, 'Who owns the UK's debt?', *British Broadcasting Corporation News (BBC News)* (26 February 2010) <http://news.bbc.co.uk/1/hi/business/8530150.stm> (Last accessed 3 November 2016).
11 McVeigh, Karen, 'DWP urged to publish inquiries on benefit claimant suicides', *The Guardian* (14 December 2014) <https://www.theguardian.com/society/2014/dec/14/dwp-inquiries-benefit-claimant-suicides> (Last accessed 4 November 2016).

PART II

Impasse and Outmodedness:
The Twilight of the Trade Unions

CHAPTER 8

The Organization of the Proletariat under Cyclical and Structural Forms of Capital's Crisis

The emergence of capital's structural crisis is altering the outlook of the trade unionized proletariat. The 'militancy' of the 1960s into the 1980s has become impacted by defeats, anti-labour legislation and the decline in trade union membership. At the root of the effects on the consciousness of trade unionized workers is the supersedence of the cyclical and conjunctural by the structural and enduring form of capital-in-crisis. The ghost of 'militancy' continues to haunt the trade unions despite the fact that conditions have moved on beyond the phase of capitalist development characterized by the expansion and accumulation of the post-war (1945) period.

The current phase of consciousness (characterized by caution, reluctance, circumspection and even cynicism arising out of the limits imposed by capital's growing structural crisis) has emerged as a result of the termination of the previous, historically lengthy phase of cyclical crises. The old methods of 'militancy' of the post-war period are now approached with a political 'ambivalence' and are identified as an 'ideal' which delivered results in the past but today are 'unrealistic', etc: 'We are in different times' is an oft-heard refrain.

Disorientation and disaffection with the whole hegemonic system of capitalist governance – and with the traditional forms of proletarian struggle and organization – are symptomatic of the termination of this period and the emergence of the structural period of capital-in-crisis. The old methods are no longer adequate but trade unionists have not, as yet, made a step beyond them.

As the crisis is deepening, the consciousness which corresponds to, or is umbilically connected to, past conditions is stubbornly holding on but it cannot endure. The limitations of the traditional forms of struggle are already revealing themselves to trade unionized labour in attempts to launch various campaigns against the 'cuts' and 'austerity'. This, of course, implies that these older forms of consciousness (corresponding to the prestructural phases of capitalist development and crises) are outmoded and that the proletariat is now their *prisoner* under qualitatively higher conditions which have superseded the previously posited 'cyclical and conjunctural' determinations. The 'line of least resistance' is being held but it must start to give way sooner or later.[1]

The structural crisis of the capital system must 'bite deeper' into the life of the proletarian class and this posits the possibility of 'refoundation' and 're-organization'. The strike and the demonstration however, taken by themselves, cannot address the needs of millions in their real, broad historical scope. Indeed, such methods could only serve to further the 'economistic' requirements of the proletariat when the capital system still had 'room to maneouvre' and afford the proletariat such 'economistic' concessions. That age is now over and raises directly the question of offensive forms of struggle to put an end to the whole system of capitalist commodity production.

New strategies and tactics are necessary for the unfolding conditions of structural crisis. However, in regard to previous forms and tactics of proletarian struggle, strikes and marches will continue to have their strategic and political uses but these forms of struggle taken in and by themselves (which are more appropriate to those past conditions of the 'prestructural' capitalist age) are becoming increasingly inadequate to deal with the intensity of the crisis coming towards the proletariat as the twenty-first century unfolds.

Certainly, the political operation of labour strictly within the parameters set down by the capital order (as we see with the British TUC, for example, or the American AFL-CIO) can only mean a continued and deeper descent into extreme precariousness in employment and destitution, pauperism and beggardom outside of it. In Britain, at the present time (Autumn 2017), the total trade union membership is approximately 6 million in a national population of about 60 million people. Down from 13.2 million at its height in 1979 at the time of the election of the first Thatcher government.

The Organization of the Proletariat

A 'silent conflict' has become posited *between* the unfolding of the conditions of the higher structural stage of the crisis of capital *and* the continuing existence of the forms of proletarian class organization and consciousness corresponding to past 'cyclical' conditions of crisis. The strike, the demonstration, petitions, marches, etc., can no longer, in and by themselves, address the needs of millions as this crisis deepens. *Official* trade unionism (bureaucratically and hierarchically controlled by a well-paid and compromised labour elite) continues to operate strictly within the constantly narrowing political parameters set down by the capital order because to start to go beyond those parameters means the beginning of its own demise and that of its hierarchically mediated privileges.

The only way that the trade unionized proletariat can go forward and open up a breach against capital as a system is in the struggle to go beyond the traditional forms of organization and older methods of struggle. And, in the course of this struggle, to transform its consciousness and bring it into direct relation (ontological consonance and resonance) with the altered conditions which now confront it as a class. A recognition in practical organization and consciousness that the proletariat is now confronted with radically different conditions of capital's rule compared to those of the previous centuries.

In a discussion with fellow socialists, István Mészáros encapsulated the essence of this problematic in relation to the whole question of agency in the epoch of global capital-in-crisis ...

> The structural crisis and its deterioration mean that the mass organizations of the working class tend to follow the line of least resistance. Instead of embarking on a different and more radical strategy they follow on whatever seem to be the dominant trends – the social democratisation of the Communist parties, the liberal-bourgeois-ification of the social democratic parties. It all plays into the hands of established power relations. It is crucial to grasp this. But it must reach a point at which this will change. I am convinced that we must see a revival of labour activity ... not in this category or that category, but in the labour movement as a whole. I think this is the answer to the question of agency. It is the only agency that I can see. Of course this doesn't mean that women, and other movements, cannot be part of it. Indeed they must be part of it. That is vitally important. But such movements on their own have no totalizing strategy. It is labour as such – as the structural antagonist of capital – which has this, or rather it potentially has it. It has such a strategy given favourable

> historical circumstances. And I am convinced that the circumstances must develop in the direction of providing them, that we are heading toward an ever-deepening crisis with some quite horrendous developments on the horizon, the revival of imperialism in its most aggressive form. And what can then oppose that? Certainly not some marginal force. It has to be the system's most elementary antagonist ... elementary in the sense that it can have an alternative mode of social-metabolic reproduction to capital. The alternative to capital has to be at the level of control – the overall control of society.²

We also need to add the so-called 'radical left' of the likes of Syriza in Greece to those which have 'followed the line of least resistance'. Syriza – which was proclaimed by 'radical lefts' all over the globe as the 'avant-garde' and 'future' of revolutionary politics – totally submitted (Summer 2015) to the demands of the 'Troika' of globalizing money capital. Rather than even attempting to mobilize the Greek proletariat into new, independent and qualitatively higher forms of mass organization to oppose capital, the leadership of Syriza remained within the political parameters set down by capital and its state/global powers and has, accordingly, handed the Greek proletariat over to the predations of global capital. So much for 'radical left' and 'the future'. Aeschylus, Euripides and Aristophanes would have fallen over themselves to acquire such material for their dramas.

This sad and sorry episode in Greece very clearly illustrates the simple truth that ...

> As far as the political representatives of labour are concerned, the issue is not simply that of personal failure or yielding to the temptations and rewards of their privileged position when they are in office. It is much more serious than that. The trouble is that when as heads or Ministers of governments they are supposed to be able to politically control the system they do nothing of the kind. For they operate within the political domain apriori prejudged in capital's favour by the existing power structures of its mode of social metabolic production. Without radically challenging and materially dislodging capital's deeply entrenched structures and mode of social metabolic control, capitulation to the power of capital is only a matter of time; as a rule almost managing to outpace the speed of light. Whether we think of Ramsay MacDonald and Bettino Craxi or Felipe Gonzales and François Mitterrand – and even long imprisoned Nelson Mandela, the newly found champion of the South African arms industry – the story is always depressingly the same. Often even the wishful anticipation of the 'realistic and responsible role' which is supposed to be

appropriate to an expected future high ministerial position is enough to produce the most astonishing somersaults.[3]

Mandela yesterday ... Tsipras today ... Corbyn tomorrow ... if elected. Corbyn abandoned the principled socialist position to withdraw from the European Union capitalist club (the proletariat of Britain disagreed with him) and his deputy, John McDonnell, has already fondly embraced so-called 'fiscal responsibility'.[4]

Only in the living experience of struggle do many thousands, if not millions, come to a practical-conscious realization of what is required in the form of organization, the changes in structure and organization which are required to move forward. Such changes cannot be 'delivered from outside' or 'from above'. This is the mantra which we repetitively find – ideologically and ahistorically – enshrined with the various left-wing sectarian groups who are ready to deliver the solution, fully formed, as the 'democratic centralist party', if only they could, apparently, recruit sufficient numbers into their midst.

The results and lessons of such experience can only be generalized and organically articulated in practice in the re-organization and restructuring of the class movement as a whole. Changes in 'mass consciousness' require such learning experiences by millions in struggle. Marx wrote of the alteration of the consciousness of people (*The German Ideology*, 1845)[5] on a mass scale as an epoch-making step forward. 'Communist consciousness' must grip and move people on a mass scale if it is to be epoch-changing. But this 'communist consciousness' can only arise out of millions of people in struggle changing themselves in the course of changing their conditions of existence. People in struggle against the manifestations of capital-in-crisis are simultaneously the producers and the products of the alterations in their conditions of life, including their organizations of class struggle.

The refoundation of the proletarian class movement can only be based on this collective living experience of the class in struggle. And such a refoundation can only take place 'given favourable historical circumstances'. Accordingly, as capital's crisis deepens and impacts the life of the proletariat, the most immediate question which confronts us is not really that of 'agency' as determinate organizational structure. The *more fundamental* consideration is the need for new forms of struggle required to oppose capital and its state power.

It is the lessons actually learnt by millions which have been derived from the living experience of struggle which must inform the 'practical-consciousness' of the proletariat in terms of the next steps in its re-organization and refoundation. It is this engagement and experience of the proletarian class as a whole (and not the 'Trotskyist' or 'Leninist' political papalism of the 'high priests' of the left-wing sectarian grouplets) which is critical and fundamental.

It is only in the course of the prosecution of new, temporally more adequate, 'offensive' strategies and tactics of struggle that the need for a corresponding new form of 'overarching' agency will assert itself under the prevailing and developing conditions. These new forms of revolutionary agency will only come into being within and out of the strife of conflict and out of the experience and lessons of these struggles. Essentially, these struggles – if they are to be 'not some marginal force' – must start from and arise 'within the framework of the existing institutions' of the proletariat with all the current limitations in methods of struggle, organization and level of consciousness.

The proletariat can only start where it is located and 'grounded' at this point (trade unionism) in the historical development of its organization. A higher form of agency – as a historically more adequate form to 'deal with' the conditions of structural crisis – can only arise out of struggles against capital and its state powers. These struggles must engender associated conflicts emerging within the established forms of proletarian organization which will create opposition in terms of the way forward and act as a source of the development of a 'practical consciousness'. This must arise on the ground of the stage of consciousness which the proletariat stands with at the moment, and will be a development on from, or a qualitative break with, the established forms of organization and consciousness. Conflict and experience and the practical assimilation of its lessons in terms of organization constitute the source of the movement of a mass consciousness itself. The necessity to move forward to more offensive, higher forms of agency suited to the age of capital's offensive against the proletariat in its time of structural crisis must assert itself as this crisis unfolds and intensifies.

The Organization of the Proletariat

Since dialectical thinking involves the study of the world in its development (and not as a static, fixed formation), this 'world in its development' is grasped as the identity and conflict of arising and vanishing moments, giving it its immanently contradictory character, the tendency to return to the old but at a different stage or higher phase of development, the 'leap' forward to a qualitatively new set of relations, etc. As one determinate formation or stage of it is passing away this becomes identified with and makes room for a new formation or stage which is emerging out of its passing and which is connected with it yet distinct from the older, dying phase, etc. Contradiction is precisely this identity of vanishing and arising moments which are nevertheless essentially distinct and opposed in their identity.

We need to grasp the importance of dialectics in relation to the present stage of the development of the crisis of the capital order and especially in regard to trade unionism because the crisis of the former inevitably forms the historical ground of and gives rise to a most intense crisis within the latter. A crisis of organization which is already starting to mature.

To *rational contemplation*, trade union organization appears to be caught in a trajectory of irreversible decline and that it cannot possibly contain 'in embryo' a higher form of unionism. That the decline of trade unionism contains no indwelling possibilities of a move beyond the trade union form. But the truth of this decline contains the possibility (which dialectical thinking recognizes) of a re-birth (a negation of the decline itself which re-posits a return to a higher form of unionism) which will bring proletarian organization into a historically more adequate form and directly confrontational relation with capital's structural crisis, with capital and its state power and its global agencies of control. The great historical role of trade unionized labour is potentially to prepare – in the very process of negation of its organizational form – the ground and conditions for the birth a higher form of unionism which unifies and steels the whole proletarian class for the struggle to terminate the epoch of capital.

The development of the crisis of the capital order creates the conditions for the intensification of the internal contradictions within trade unionism as the primary universal historical form within which the proletariat worldwide has traditionally organized and evolved the forms of consciousness corresponding to it. Labour remains in its movement and consciousness with its traditional 'economistic' organization. How can this be otherwise given the legacy of two centuries of capitalist expansion across the globe? But today trade unionism faces the all-pervasiveness, malignancy and gravity of capital-in-crisis; a crisis of the structure of capital itself where the former mechanisms of displacing the antagonisms arising as a result of its expansion and accumulation are increasingly narrowing, becoming constricted ('hemmed in') and 'seizing up'. This confers on trade unionism *per se* (and not simply in terms of its bureaucratized and hierarchical structure) its historically outmoded character as a form of proletarian organization for the epoch of capital's deepening structural crisis. *This is not simply the recognition of the hierarchical form of trade unionism as being historically outmoded but trade unionism itself as a form of proletarian organization for the age of capital's structural crisis. Trade Unionism as being more suited to the previously dominant form of capital's crisis (cyclical/conjunctural) and not its terminal, structural form.*

The bureaucratized character of official trade unionism itself implies a differentiation of interest based on and arising out of the prevailing class relations of the capitalist system. Of course, many trade unionists dispute this 'stratification of interest'. They see that officials are elected to their positions with 'responsibilities' and this confers, in their eyes, a certain legitimacy to their methods of administrating the affairs of the union and even to six-figure salaries, large pensions, perks, etc.

However, what many trade unionized workers do not (and many do!) see behind the veil of formalities is that hierarchically structured trade unionism itself necessarily involves *governance by a caste-stratum* whose interests – in contrast to the broad membership of the branches – ultimately lie in *the continuation of the capital order*. This must have explosive implications for the current structures and form of organization of trade unionism tied, as it is, to the history of the 'cyclical, conjunctural, displaceable crisis-phases' of the capital order. And, of course, this applies especially in Britain where the roots of trade unionism have become intertwined with the roots of capital over two centuries of empire and imperialism. But not exclusively in Britain, of course.

This is the generalized, stratified structure of trade unionism which we see around the world. And this structure has always rested on an expanding capital system, augmenting its value in the course of the accumulation of capital throughout two centuries. As a universal and traditional form of the organizing proletariat, the structural crisis of the capital system brings in its wake the emergence of conflicts within the structure of trade unionism itself which must animate an irreversible trend towards its dissolution or its transformation into higher forms of proletarian organization. And this must apply globally, to trade unionism in every part of the planet. For hierarchically organized trade unionism per se is historically outmoded and even a 'trade unionism' without such a hierarchical structure could not possibly articulate and represent the interests of the proletariat as a whole class in its struggle to terminate the epoch of capital.

As the crisis of capital unfolds and deepens, what will inevitably become sharpened is this difference of interest within trade unionism itself – between top stratum and members – placing on the agenda the absolute necessity to overturn trade unionism in its current defensive form and moribund structure. The necessity to replace it with a higher, more democratic, offensive form of 'unionism' – which is not exclusively based in the workplace – must increasingly assert itself.

The old defensive form must be cast off and replaced with a form which corresponds to the historical needs (the newly emerging content) of the proletariat as a whole in the age of capital's structural crisis. The resulting organizational form of the proletarian class must correspond to the altered conditions which now animate and infuse the life of the proletariat as a class.[6] It must be a re-birth of forms of proletarian organization which are inherently capable of comprehensively addressing the effects of the death throes of the capital system on the life of the proletariat.

Accordingly, this structural crisis increasingly brings in its wake a very deep and profound crisis for labour as regards the old defensive forms of organization. The old ways of organizing in trade unionism are fundamentally unfit – even for their original purpose – in their present structure and organization and this will become increasingly evident as capital's crisis matures. The need to throw off the old defensive forms and replace them with new offensive forms of struggle against capital and its state powers will increasingly assert itself.

The historic precedence of the question of revolutionary agency now becomes clearly posed and articulated around the question of new offensive forms, strategies and tactics of struggle against the capital order and its state power. Therefore, on this immediate question of agency, how can the proletariat, in its present global situation and changed occupational structure, move onto the revolutionary road, that is, initiate the historical process of the transcendence of the capital order?

Trade unionism in its current hierarchical form and structure is effectively acting as a policeman of the trade unionized proletariat; as a proxy of capital and its state power in the trade union movement. The real historic dependence of the existence and privileges of the trade union bureaucracy on the continuation of the capital order is a fundamentally mediating relation which has underpinned its servility to capital and its state power for the past century and more. This relationship can only be sustained, as capital's global crisis widens and deepens in its extent and intensity, at the expense of the proletariat as a whole.

Historically, this trade union elite and capital have squabbled over the distribution of value, its partition and relative division but the 'trade union barons' have never questioned the right and legitimacy of capital and its state power to rule. If it were to do this, and act on it, it would throw its own parasitic existence as a labour caste into question.

Moreover, the state power has effectively shackled trade unionism through legislation. It could not have done this without the compliance and submission of the bureaucratic elite which controls significant sections of the employed proletariat through the mechanisms of official trade unionism. The mandarins and ideologues of the state power of capital recognize the conservative role of this labour elite because these state bureaucrats are 'class conscious' enough to acknowledge that the caste interests of this elite are intrinsically connected to the continuation of social relations based on capital whose 'ruling interest' this state articulates and defends. And those 'ruling interests' are the class interests of the owners of capital.

The state power in the current epoch is the organized political power of the capitalist class. It is in its interest to maintain an increasingly 'integrated' 'business unionism' but it would prefer no unionism at all to one which is 'revolutionizing' under conditions brought on by the historic trajectory of global capital-in-crisis. That would be the worst scenario of all for capital because then labour is beyond its control and has declared political independence from both the state power and its functioning proxies in the trade unions which have been left behind.

In a certain sense, the conception of the 'independence of the workers' movement' has always been unrealized and unrealizable within its currently hierarchically structured relations. The possibility of such an 'independence' can only flow from the demolition of this labour hierarchy and can never exist in its controlling presence. Those who continue to issue clarion calls for the so-called 'independence of the workers' movement' imprisoned within the present hierarchical structures are ignoring the historical truth of the tethering of this movement – through these same structures – to the state power of capital and the defended social system.

Real 'independence' can only come about once labour has rid itself of this hierarchy. To issue such 'clarion calls' therefore can only be historically legitimate if they are an invitation to topple the rule of the trade union bureaucracy and to free the workers' movement for real advances in organization.

The present relations between the state power and the trade union bureaucracy are therefore a product of the antecedent conditions of existence of the capital order where its contradictions were displaceable according to the ebb and flow of economic 'boom and bust' cycles. This relationship altered and shifted according to whether capital was in a period of expansion and accumulation or had passed into a 'bust' or 'downturn' period.

Today, these repeating cycles have become superseded and replaced by capital's deepening structural crisis-phase. We can expect changes and qualitative shifts, if not disruptions, in this relationship between capital and the trade union hierarchy as the crisis of this order deepens in the course of the coming century. The structural character of this crisis is working its way through and must become expressed in this relation between state and labour hierarchy. And, more specifically, changes and shifts as a result of the opening up of an offensive against capital itself.

The present arrangements can only hold at the expense of the proletariat as a class. However, we cannot discount the possibility that sections of this bureaucracy will break away and come over to the proletariat. However, on the whole, it will try to maintain the equilibrium of its subservient relationship with the state power of capital because its historic position as a privileged caste depends on the continuation of this relation. Anything that threatens it – including and especially offensive struggles to pass beyond the current form of organization and structure of trade unionism – will be opposed and attempts made, with the help of the state power if necessary, to defeat such struggles. To challenge the capital order implicatively and simultaneously becomes a challenge to the whole bureaucratized structure of trade unionism itself.

The development of capitalism in the nineteenth century required workers to form trade unions to fight for their 'economistic' interests, for better wages and conditions, a reduced working day, removal of child labour, etc. Retrospectively, it appears as if trade unionism was 'spontaneously' generated by capitalist development almost as a 'law of nature'. The *conditions* for the emergence of trade unions were generated by industrial capital itself. However, their actual formation had to be fought for by real, living, acting, thinking workers. Likewise, there is nothing inevitable – as if by some sort of historical default – that trade unionism must always exist under the aegis of the capital system, never mind outlive it. There is no 'law of nature' or iron law of historical development which explicitly states or implies that a capital order without any trade unionism whatsoever is impossible. Quite the contrary, with each passing year of capital-in-crisis, it is perhaps becoming increasingly necessary for this order to dispense with trade unions or, at least, completely neutralize them. If not this worst scenario for workers then completely integrated and corporatist trade unions which would be no more than members insurance or provident societies legally bound without strikes.

The aspirations of the 'branch members', of course, are a different matter. If they don't fight for broader, class-based organizations, they will lose everything and effectively become de-unionized and leave behind only the name of trade unionism without anything substantial remaining. So there is no cast-iron guarantee that the trade unions will actually survive within the capital order itself never mind outlive it as the conditions of this order's continuing existence alter with the unfolding of its structural crisis.

The gratuitously assumed notion that capitalism will always spontaneously generate trade unions and that trade unionism will outlive the capital order remains an oft-repeated dogma of 'the left'. Wage labour is not necessarily unionized wage labour. For capital, within the economic sphere more than the political, 'unionization' is a dispensable characteristic of wage labour. The actual qualitative nature of wage labour remains unaltered regardless of whether it is 'unionized' or not. In either case, capital, as Marx wrote, continues to live 'vampire-like' off it.

Capitalism could survive without 'business unionism' but it would lose a conservative mechanism for the control of labour. This is why 'business unionism' is the optimal form for capital. However, the intensifying contradictions of capital's structural crisis are increasingly suggesting that not even the proxy of 'business unionism' will be exempt from possible elimination as the needs of capital-in-crisis increasingly assert themselves.

The trade unions are financially dependent on and integrated into the functioning of the global capital order.[7] Millions of pounds worth of their assets are invested in its operation in the form of bonds, pension funds, shares, etc. In certain respects, the trade unions function like investment companies which guard, augment and pursue their financial interests as money capital on the world's markets. Inevitably, with the flow and reflux of capital in its multifarious and nefarious guises, funds which grow as part of their portfolios must arise, partially at least, out of the sweated, uncompensated and superexploited labour of others. Today, the existence and value-augmentation of the assets of the trade unions are so closely bound up financially with the operation of the capitalist order that the deepening of its crisis could very easily bring in a financial/fiscal crisis for the trade unions themselves. It is in the financial interests of these labour bureaucracies not to challenge the rule of capital never mind to seek to overthrow it.

If we substituted the term 'provident society' for trade union – abolishing the right of its members to strike – a minimal internal adjustment would be required in order to bring the bureaucratized organizations into a resonating consonance with their new name. General Secretaries would slip effortlessly into the same office chairs the next morning but now as Chief Executive Officers in the same fluent way that many have readily placed themselves on seats in the House of Lords. It is not in the caste interests of the top stratum of the trade unions to carry forward a struggle against capital to its historic conclusion. And that conclusion is socialism.

The high tide of trade unionism in Britain was the miners' strike of 1984–1985. This year-long strike was of fundamental historic significance for the proletariat. It truly revealed the limits of trade unionism per se – as a form of organized proletarian activity – circumscribed by the parameters of the capital order within which it was formed. But without the proletariat as a class struggling to go beyond such limits, the re-birth of the class movement is impossible. Over three decades have passed and it is as if trade unionism has been tamed by the state power. Today, the beast growls, sometimes, but never bites.

Arthur Scargill (who led the National Union of Mineworkers) was, at the time, the personification of the left wing of the trade union bureaucracy. The attempt of Scargill and the cohort around him to establish a new post-strike party (the Socialist Labour Party, SLP) on the rebound from Blair's 'New Labour' represented an aborted articulation of the interests of the left wing of this bureaucracy.

Scargill's whole political approach was animated by bureaucratic Stalinistic methods which served the needs of capital. And this became directly manifest in his style and methods of governance of his now essentially defunct Socialist Labour Party. Any opposition within it was countered with threats of expulsion followed by actual expulsion on non-compliance. There was no room for broad democratic discussion and expulsion became the 'norm'. Democratic discussion was, in all but name, closed down.

Trade unionism can no longer operate within the capital order in the same way it operated in the 1960s and 1970s because the conditions of capital's reproduction have completely altered. The crisis of this order dictates otherwise. In truth, trade unionism per se is as historically outmoded as the valve-engineered computer. It is, however, for the 'lefts' within its ranks, merely a question of putting the appropriately 'militant' leadership in place and, as if conjured up by magic, the formula of trade unionism plus the left-wing militant leadership equals socialism. This is the liturgical formula which every left-wing sect chants and to which it pays homage. Ironically, and perhaps unconsciously, the cynicism of the *realpolitik* of the

TUC in Britain, and trade union hierarchies around the world such as the AFL-CIO in America, is a more truthful acknowledgement in practice of its own caste interests than the posturing of its 'left wing' is in ostensibly representing the interests of trade unionized labour.

Any future attempts by the 'left wing' of the top stratum in the labour movement to create 'parties' or 'alliances', etc., will articulate a same or similar caste interest as mainstream hierarchy but merely a 'left' version of it. It was the miners' strike in 1984–1985 which circumscribed the political limits of trade unionism in its 'official' form, including its 'left' varieties. This is not to state unequivocally that such a 'high tide' will not arise again but such a 'tide' will not be any higher. It will certainly not transcend its limits without a 'revolution' within trade unionism itself.

The Trades Union Congress (the highest body of trade unionism in Britain) has evolved into the direct agent of capital at the head of the workers' movement. Its trajectory has complemented that of the Labour Party leadership which, despite the election of Jeremy Corbyn, will and must continue to do capital's bidding no matter how 'left' that bidding is presented to be. Any attempt to re-inaugurate Keynesian economics (if a Corbyn government is elected) must remain within the parameters of the realm of capital.

The TUC now views trade unionism as a movement to be governed, ruled, controlled, chanelled and contained within manageable parameters which define not only the interests of this top bureaucratic layer but also, simultaneously, provide a supporting prop for the capital order itself. The capital order is the historic ground on which the privilege and interests of this layer rests. Accordingly, this stratum is not going to 'pull the rug' from underneath itself. Quite the contrary, it must maintain it. This bureaucracy will strive to contain all future struggles of trade unionists within these parameters. This means, necessarily, with the deepening of capital's crisis, that the broad membership of the trade unions is on a collision course with this bureaucracy and, by implication, with the whole outmoded and moribund structure and form of organization of trade unionism as it has existed over the past century and more. If the struggle to transform trade unionism into a higher form of 'unionism' falls by the wayside, then the historic impasse or 'bottleneck of outmodedness' – into which trade unionism has now entered – must result in the further degeneration of trade unionism and its total, most abject surrender to capital, possibly followed by its complete extinction.

Following the mass slaughter and destruction of the second imperialist world war (1939–1945), capital was able to displace its accumulated contradictions and undergo a period of expansion and development into a global stage. Only in the 1970s, with the emergent structural crisis of the capital order, have the conditions started to develop which point towards the possibilities of a global offensive against the capital system.

The major historical landmark in Britain – which indicated an entry into a qualitatively new period – was the defeat of the miners in 1984–1985. The miners' strike in 1984–1985 was the high point of post-war trade union militancy in Britain and a watershed in trade unionized labour's unconscious response to capital's deepening structural crisis. The defeat of the miners by the Thatcher regime was the beginning of trade unionism's entry into its historic 'bottleneck of outmodedness' as a form of 'economistic' struggle against the predations of the capital order.

A sampling and significance for people's lives of these new conditions of structural crisis. Whether people work for private capital or for the so-called 'public sector' (the difference is sometimes difficult to identify these days), when workers are given notice of redundancy or sacking, their trade union is highly unlikely to fight for their jobs. A week does not pass without factories closing and more public provision eliminated with the usual bleating, toothless and inactive response of the trade union leaderships. And yet many within the union hierarchies peddle the myth that the trade unions are 'member-led'.

Today – unlike in the 1960s and 1970s – when people lose their jobs, it means the distinct possibility of terminal unemployment and the prospect of never working again. This is why people feel that they have 'too much to lose' if they go on strike. They are afraid of losing their jobs – and they will make any compromise necessary (this compromising has its limits, of course) to keep them – if they enter struggle.

You lose your job and the whole structure of your life starts to fall apart. Your mortgage or rent on your home, car, holidays, family relationships, etc: a lifetime of unemployment faces you with all the devastating consequences for your personal life and those of others. Not a single job is 'safeguarded' today under the conditions of crisis, whether you are working for private capital or for the so-called public sector. The days of capital expansion in the 1960s – when you could walk out of your old job in the morning and walk into a new one in the afternoon – have gone forever. This crisis of capital is structural and is enduring. It will worsen. It must worsen. Undoubtedly. The age of full employment is over for good. Unemployment is, like capital's crisis, structural and increasing globally. Millions today and succeeding generations tomorrow will never work again. Capitalism has entered its final period of breakdown and dissolution.

If you strike today and man the factory gates the employers can simply close down and/or move abroad. At Grangemouth they 'saved' their jobs but at what cost? The ultimate, logical implication of all this is that it is a choice between being (1) a low-paid slave for private capital or for the state power with worsening conditions and wages, where trade unions have no muscle to fight back (2) being a pauper on the dole or on sickness benefits with no prospect of future employment or (3) being a homeless, wandering beggar on the street. Such are the stark choices increasingly facing people in the epoch of capital's worsening structural crisis.

The trade unions are run by a self-serving, privileged stratum on executive salaries, fat retirement pensions, greeted with 'golden hellos' or 'golden handshakes' of hundreds of thousands of pounds or quitting/retiring with similar 'golden goodbyes'. Former UNITE General Secretary, Derek Simpson, received a nauseating 'golden goodbye' of £500,000.[8] Meanwhile, everyday, people are losing their jobs and sinking into penury. The unemployed, sick and disabled are persecuted, humiliated and bullied by the state. You fall into joblessness or long term sickness and you really do feel the oppressive power of the capitalist state bearing down on your shoulders in all its tyrannical immediacy.

The jobless directly experience its real nature as the state *power of capital*. It truly feels like a malevolent power over you and 'inside your head' (psychologically). You don't have to grasp it theoretically in Marx or Lenin to feel it on a human level. It defends the owners of capital and not the rest of us. In London particularly, and elsewhere generally, people are being made homeless because of the savage attacks on welfare; the 'social cleansing' of whole neighbourhoods in order to provide the resources for the property speculators and capitalist 'developers'. And 1001 other injustices and oppressions are all unfolding on a daily basis.

We cannot continue with the present state of affairs and go on with what we have in the form of the hierarchically structured and paternalistic form of organization we find in the trade unions. They are, in the current form, outmoded. Unfit for purpose to deal with the deepening and intensifying crisis. If we do not move on to something more radical, more offensive against capital and its state power, then we will continue to 'sink'.

This has been the unfolding trend since 1979; approximately 13.2 million individual trade unionists in that year. Today (November, 2017) about 6 million and falling. That is an average haemorrhage per annum of over 200,000 people from the trade unions. With supporters, part-timers, etc., an average of about a quarter of a million people every year since 1979. At what point apoplexy? Or have we already reached it?

Up to the present, trade unions – formed and developed under 'defensive historical circumstances' of capitalist expansion – have adopted a wholly inadequate, defensive posture in relation to capital's structural crisis. The traditional methods of struggle are anchored in the old conditions and cannot serve workers in the struggles to come as the crisis-process deepens. Trade unionism – if it continues in its presently defensive, hierarchical organizational and structural form – will continue to decline. This decline will be associated with a bureaucracy which increasingly acts as the policeman of its falling membership on behalf of capital. Either that or a 'revolution' within trade unionism itself where it forms a point of departure for a higher, more radical form of agency against capital of and for the proletariat as a whole class.

We cannot, of course, discount the possibility of it gradually sinking and disappearing completely within the unfolding conditions of capital's structural crisis. The emergence of a 'trade unionism' which is essentially a 'provident society' integrated into the state power as its proxy and shackled by anti-labour legislation cannot be discounted. Trade unionism as a vestige of its former self; a cipher governed by an utterly subservient elite which has totally surrendered to capital.

Under the deepening, worsening conditions of this crisis, the state power of capital will be in a position to pose to itself (and is already doing so with more anti-labour legislation passed into law in May 2016, the Trade Union Act) the question of whether to accelerate the pace of trade unionism's complete destruction or maintain a grip on trade unionized labour through the subservience of the trade union bureaucracy. It could very easily employ a dual strategy and 'hedge its bets'. But the primary focus and consideration for capital is on the irreversible establishment of a wage-labour force which is totally and absolutely subservient to the needs of capital. Accordingly, for the proletariat as a class, 'socialist strategy badly needs restructuring in accordance with the new conditions'.⁹

The formation of the trade unions took place under different conditions in a different epoch to those which are now posited and developing with capital's structural crisis. Trade unions later were the main force in the formation of the Labour Party in Britain at the beginning of the twentieth century. They supported and financed the Labour Party. The trade unions would fight for better conditions and wages by means of the strike when and where necessary and the Labour Party would work through the capitalist parliamentary system to bring in legislation to further the aims of trade unionism and improve the social and economic position of the proletariat as a whole.

The high point of development of these endeavours was the thirty-five-year period between 1945 and 1980. It corresponded to the post-war period of global expansion where capital was temporarily able to displace its contradictions by adopting Keynesian economic measures after the catastrophic destruction of the second imperialist world war. It was in this period that the strike weapon most effectively won improved working conditions and better wages.

Trade unionism and Social Democracy served to defend gains made in social provision within this period of capitalist expansion. However, trade unions could operate in this role – under such conditions of capitalist expansion and accumulation – only where 'concessions' made by capital were not so much 'sacrificial' but rather served the purpose of augmenting capital's process of self-expansion and development in this post-war period. For example, much of the state spending on the NHS has gone directly into the coffers of capital either as a supplier of infrastructure, equipment, drugs, etc., or as return payments to capital as the owners of assets (for example, under the Private Finance Initiative, PFI). And, of course, the salaries of workers in the 'public sector' have been ploughed back into consumption in its various forms.

The Keynesian economic measures after the second world war served the needs of capital. And this was reflected in the expansion of public provision. It was not a 'retreat' by capital as some on 'the left' assert but a strategic means of displacing its post-war contradictions and stabilizing and expanding the post-war global capital order. It may be argued that the whole of state expenditure on social provision since 1945 has been a direct or indirect payout to capital.

However, since the 1970s, we have witnessed the emergence and the steady intensification of a qualitatively different type of crisis for capital. The trade union militancy in Britain in the 1970s and 1980s can be traced as an active, though unconscious, response to this growing crisis as articulated in the defensive struggles against the attempts of the capitalist state to impose the consequences of this crisis on the shoulders of labour. Thatcherism and the 'mission' of Blair's 'New Labour' (Blairite Thatcherism) have developed this political course of and for capital in the process of privatizations, casualization, 'precarization', anti-labour legislation, etc., because such measures and actions have corresponded to the needs of capital as it attempts to manage the impact of its own structural crisis on itself as a social relation of production and distribution.

In this regard, the election of the Thatcher government (1979) was a watershed for trade unionism. The capitalist class and its state power 'woke up' to the reality and gravity of the historic structural crisis of its own system. Heavy industries and the 'utilities' run and subsidized by the state were now placed under the constraining criteria of the untransgressable logic of private capital: make profit and accumulate without state subsidy or perish. The trade unions responded to closures and the destruction of working conditions in the 1980s by deploying the same forms of 'militancy' of the previous two decades. But this was no longer a cyclical, conjunctural crisis. It was the personifications and representatives of capital starting to respond to the onset of capital's structural crisis. The state power brought in anti-labour legislation limiting the activity of trade unionism. This has continued over the last three decades. The trade union bureaucracy, on the whole, and the Labour Party top stratum submitted to the needs of capital-in-crisis.

The openly 'pro-capital' trajectory of the Labour Party in Britain (Kinnock, Smith, Blair, Brown, Miliband) and the prostration of official trade unionism to capital over the decades since Thatcher's 'decade' have very definite roots in the transition to an epoch in which the capital order has no more room for compromise with trade unionized labour because its own space for manoeuvre is rapidly diminishing as its structural crisis deepens. Capital – backed by its state power – demands absolute subservience and, if it does not get it, will adopt the necessary legislative and material measures to enforce it.

These new relations correspond to the new epoch of capital's structural crisis. It is an age which demands, at the same time, new forms of proletarian organization which can take to the offensive against capital and its state powers. Hence the urgency of the need to address the question of the historic inadequacy of the older, established forms of proletarian organization (primarily the trade unions) under evolving conditions which are qualitatively different from those of the past under which workers formed their organizations to fight for their class interests. This question is, as we shall see later, intrinsically connected with that of revolutionary agency.

The continuation of capital's offensive can only create the conditions for the re-emergence of open class struggles but in more explosive and protracted forms directed against capital's state power. And in forms which go beyond the traditional 'strike tactic'. Such struggles will serve to bring into focus both the reactionary, 'class collaborationist' character of the trade union hierarchy and the class character of the prevailing state power with its 'armed bodies of men', courts, prisons and government bureaucracy.

The most urgent question of the age is, therefore, how do we put an end to the rule of capital, bearing in mind that, at the current stage, our class organizations in themselves are totally inadequate for carrying through this task? The trade unions in their present form are no longer fit for 'economistic' purposes (which was the purpose of their original formation), never mind the mighty historic tasks of putting an end to the age of capital. We need to create new, *offensive forms* of organization to conduct this struggle to put an end to capitalism as a global system. To go forward and create a totally different type of society for future human generations. But pivotal in this question is what sort of organizations will we need to carry through this great historic task?

Notes and References

1. Mészáros, *Beyond Capital*, Chapter 20, p. 771 ff.
2. Mészáros, István, in Terry Brotherstone, Theodore Koditschek, István Mészáros and Cliff Slaughter, 'Discussing Marxism at the Millennium. Appendix I: Marxism, history and the future', edited by Terry Brotherstone. In Cliff Slaughter, *Not Without A Storm – Towards A Communist Manifesto for the Age of Globalisation* (London: Index Books, 2006), pp. 294–295.
3. Mészáros, *Beyond Capital*, p. 731. Also see Gilmore, Inigo, 'Mandela applauds South Africa's rising arms trade', *The Times* (23 November 1994).
4. Rentoul, John, 'John McDonnell: Shadow Chancellor is the new voice of fiscal responsibility', *The Independent* (13 March 2016) <http://www.independent.co.uk/voices/john-mcdonnell-shadow-chancellor-is-the-new-voice-of-fiscal-responsibility-a6927926.html> (Last accessed 3 November 2016).
5. Engels, Frederick, and Karl Marx, 'The German Ideology'. In *Marx-Engels Collected Works, Volume 5, 1845–1847*, pp. 19–581, 52–53 (London: Lawrence & Wishart, 1976).
6. Lenin, Vladimir I., *Lenin Collected Works, Volume 38. Philosophical Notebooks* (Moscow: Progress Publishers, 1972), pp. 220–222, 'Elements of Dialectics'.
   Lenin writes (in his analysis of Hegel's dialectics) of the old form being thrown off by the newly emerging and unfolding content (the conflict between this arising content and the older, established constraining form which is inconsonant with this content) and replaced by a form more appropriate to the character of the new content and through which it can be fully expressed and freely articulated and developed. If this does not happen with trade unionism towards a new, higher 'social' form of unionism, (and there is no inevitability in it) then the trajectory of trade unionism is undoubtedly further downwards towards socio-cultural vestigiality and extinction.

7   The TUC documents at the following two links make interesting reading. Especially for those trade unionists working for the named companies in the documents.
    TU Fund Managers Limited, 'Trade Union Unit Trust. Manager's Final Report. For the year ended 15 August 2015. 108', *TU Fund Managers Limited* <http://www.tufm.co.uk/tufmwordpress/wpcontent/uploads/2015/10/Trade-Union-Unit-Trust-ANNUAL-15-08-15.pdf> (Last accessed 3 November 2016).
    TU Fund Managers Limited, 'Trade Union Unit Trust. Monthly Factsheet as at 31 December 2014', *TU Fund Managers Limited* (January 2015) <http://www.tufm.co.uk/tufmwordpress/wp-content/uploads/2015/01/TUUT-Factsheet-31Dec-2014.pdf> (Last accessed 3 November 2016).
8   Milmo, Dan, 'Former Unite leader paid £500,000, sparking "golden goodbye" row', *The Guardian* (18 July 2011) <https://www.theguardian.com/politics/2011/jul/18/unite-leader-golden-goodbye-row> (Last accessed 4 November 2016).
9   Mészáros, *Beyond Capital*, p. 673.

CHAPTER 9

Labour's Growing Crisis of Organization

The formation of the traditional political parties of workers (Social Democratic and Communist Parties) took place in the nineteenth and twentieth centuries. These periods were times of the growth and expansion of the capitalist system across the world. From Europe into the Americas and then into Asia and Africa. It was an age of colonialism, of capitalist accumulation through the normal cyclical course of 'boom and bust' expansion and by means of war, conquest and the partition of the globe's resources between the major, competing capitalist powers. During these centuries – despite and also because of the wars, death and destruction – the capitalist system continually regained its equilibrium after various dislocations and re-stabilized itself out of its periodic 'conjunctural crises'.

The 'Great Depression' of the 1930s was the major example of such a crisis in the twentieth century whose contradictions could only be displaced by world war and the later phase of inflationary expansion which reached its end point during the 1970s. The displaceability of the accumulated contradictions of the 'Great Depression' of the 1930s was an indication that the capital system had not, at the time, entered its terminal phase of structural crisis. Post-war developments from 1944 onwards (the Bretton Woods Agreement) into the 1970s vindicates this conception.

What has emerged and is evolving today is a capitalist epoch of a qualitatively different order. The epoch of capital's *structural* crisis.[1] In Britain, we are witnessing the effects of this crisis on trade unionism and the Labour Party. The formation of the Labour Party as a putative representation of the interests of the trade unions took place at the beginning of the last century; 'Old Labour' and its social basis in the hierarchically structured trade unions. The trajectory of the Labour Party since Neil Kinnock's witchhunt of Labour Party socialists in the 1980s – and the prostration of official trade unionism to capital over the past quarter of a century – has very definite roots in the transition to an epoch in which the capital order has no more room for compromise with labour because its own capacity for expansion and accumulation is rapidly diminishing as its structural crisis deepens. The election of 'left-wing' Social Democrat Jeremy Corbyn in the summer of 2015 will make no *fundamental* alterations in this trajectory of the Labour Party which is driven by forces beyond the control of the Labour hierarchy. A 'borrow and spend' strategy (Keynesianism) will not resolve capital's crisis but will merely serve to aggravate and intensify it within the very parameters of the capital order. Capital will continue to demand absolute subservience from labour and, if it does not get it, it will adopt the necessary measures of state to enforce it. This, of course, is what we have seen developing in legislation since Thatcher's anti-labour laws in the 1980s. The movement which has developed behind Corbyn – currently (Autumn, 2017) half a million strong – is, however, a real tangible social expression of the dissatisfaction of millions with the 'austerity' of the capital order imposed by its politicians. Such a movement has arisen as a form of opposition of the proletariat to the manifestations of capital's crisis and cannot be simplistically identified as 'Corbyn's foot soldiers' or 'messengers'. The potential for further developments here needs to be considered.

This movement's opposition to 'austerity' posited the conflict between the broad party membership and MPs in the Labour Party (Autumn 2016). Corbyn has been painted as the 'left-wing' 'unelectable' bogeyman by the pro-capital, Labour Party Blairite establishment, the bulk of its MPs and their friends and supporters in the capitalist print and broadcasting media. However, despite its obvious limitations, the ground swell of support for Corbyn (specifically around the 'Momentum' movement) reflects a profound dissatisfaction with the trajectory taken since Kinnock. It is a desire and attempt to return to a radicalized 'Old Labour' as capital's crisis impacts the lives of millions but which must inevitably come up against the brick wall of this structural crisis.

Any attempt to return to and implement the politics of 'Old Labour' reformism will only serve to bring into focus and relief its (and hierarchically structured trade unionism's) utter inadequacy, indeed bankruptcy, in the shadow of the deepening structural crisis of the capital system. And this not simply in labour's currently bureaucratized organizational form and structure but even in any 'radicalized' forms which may emerge.

Those explicitly pro-capital and anti-socialist political relations which were established within the Labour Party by the Blair leadership corresponded to the requirements of capital in the epoch of its structural crisis. It is an age which demands, at the same time, new forms of proletarian organization which can take to the offensive against capital and its state powers. Hence the urgency of the question of agency which needs to be addressed under developing conditions which are qualitatively different from those of the past under which workers formed their organizations to fight 'economistically' for their class interests.

These methods of struggle and the 'radical' reformist politics corresponding to them (as we found expressed politically during Corbyn's election campaign in the Summer of 2015) are anchored to past conditions and cannot serve workers in the emerging struggles. And any Labour Party government, led by the Corbyn type of social democrat, will undoubtedly find that any attempt to return to Keynesian economics will only serve to intensify the manifestations of capital's crisis. The 'Corbynist' project is locating its aims entirely within the parameters dictated by the capital order. But this order has now entered its terminal structural crisis. Accordingly, this order, in its structural crisis, delineates and dictates the terms and conditions of programme and action in any attempt to return to Social Democracy and Keynesian expansionary economics. Corbyn's deputy, John McDonnell, is already referring to a programme which remains within the limits of 'fiscal responsibility'. Repudiation of debts to global capital is not on the cards.[2]

These 'defensively structured' strategies continue to determine the 'margins of action' of non-unionized as well as trade unionized workers which can only highly circumscribe their activity in the unfolding situation. Workers all over the world created their trade unions as 'instruments and institutions' to fight for and articulate their interests in the struggle for improved wages and conditions of employment. And likewise, globally in all the major capitalist countries – including in all the 'BRICS'[3] regions – the proletariat still remains with this universal historic form of its organization.

Capital and its state power now confronts the proletariat organized in its trade unions (with a trend towards diminishing membership) inside the workplace and that broad section outside which is essentially disenfranchised without political organization and representation. With this in mind, what clearly imposes itself on the proletariat is the need to embark on ...

> the socialist offensive under the conditions of its new historical actuality. This implies also the necessity to face up to the major challenge of being compelled to embark on such an offensive within the framework of the existing institutions of the working class, which happened to be defensively constituted, under very different historical conditions, in the past. Both going beyond capital and envisaging a socialist offensive are paradigm issues of a transition to socialism.[4]

But 'to embark on such an offensive within the framework of the existing institutions of the working class' means, inevitably, trade unionists coming into collision with that 'defensively constituted framework'. In concrete terms, it means, in trade unionism, a struggle to go beyond the present conservative form of labour organization. To transform these latter forms into organized structures with procedures which are adequate to fight for the class interests of the proletariat as a whole against the capitalist order in crisis which is intensifying its offensive against the proletariat. It means the dissolution of hierarchically structured trade unionism as the proxy of capital in the movement of the proletariat. It means opposing capital and its state power as the principal enemy and not trying to accommodate interests to it which are utterly opposed to it.

This accommodation is the path which the British Trade Union Congress (TUC) is following and will continue to do so regardless of closures, job losses, pay cuts, attacks on public provision, pensions, etc. The opposite path must be taken. It means fulfilling and realizing the project Marx himself set out for trade unionism when he wrote that the trade unions must act as the 'organizing centres of the working class in the broad interest of its complete emancipation'.

The 'socialist offensive' is understood here to be a 'process of transformation', an unfolding, complex 'historical phase' arising out of the contradictions and conflicts of the capitalist epoch (ibid., *Beyond Capital*, p. 940).

It is neither a 'sudden event' nor a 'linear' progression but contains the potential for setbacks, reverses, 'lapses', etc. It is the 'unfolding actualization of a trend'; the major, characteristic tendency of historical development of the epoch regardless of 'all fluctuations, unevenness and even relapses'.

Revolutions do not unfold according to dictionary definitions or with the linearity of straight line graphs. They are real living struggles containing all the contradictions and cultural baggage of the place and age and through which the aspirations of revolution are expressed. In the unfolding of these revolutions, the revolutionary class embodies in its struggle and life the living contradictions bequeathed by the past and the aspirations towards the new socialist world which it is striving to create.

All revolutions unfold as 'dialectical movements' beyond the old and so, accordingly, sometimes turn back on themselves and are forced to return to situations which appear to be what they have just transcended. But contained within this 'spiralling', returning movement, there is always an irreversible advance beyond the old.

What is critical here in relation to the supersedence of the capital order is that an unfolding and driven process of transcending its fundamentally controlling social relation is opened up and its state power is dismantled by peaceful means if possible or by war if necessary. But there are no formal 'definitions' of revolution to which the real events of living struggle must or can correspond. No definition against which real living struggle and the unfolding of events are compared and measured in order to see if the reality in revolution fits it.

We locate, essentially, the 'existing institutions of the working class' as its trade unions which were indeed 'defensively constituted, under very different historical conditions'. In 1979, at the time of the election of the Thatcher government in Britain, there were approximately 13.2 million individual trade union members.[5] The latest TUC figure for January 2016 is approximately 6.5 million.[6] If we take the total loss of members over the period between 1979 and 2014, and average it out, then about 200,000 people per annum have become 'de-unionized' in the land of the Tolpuddle Martyrs since 1979. A long-term, stark, graphical illustration of this trend of falling trade union membership is given in recent, government statistics.[7]

It is critical to recognize here that the trade union – as a determinate, historically enduring form – is the globally established ('first line of defence') and universal form of proletarian organization. The form of organization which is common to different national sections of the proletariat across the globe and through the medium of which it has traditionally conducted its struggle for the realization and defence of its class interests in different parts of the world. Essentially, we can still identify the trade union form as the fundamental 'substance' which continues to 'fill' the 'framework of the existing institutions of the working class'.

The dizzying and precipitous fall in trade union membership over the last four decades has clearly revealed that organized labour in this trade unionized form is heading further into the 'swamp' and continuing to sink into the quicksand of history under the impact of capital's deepening structural crisis. The unfolding of this crisis is indicating that the proletariat cannot go on in the old way with its hierarchically structured trade unions and its traditional parties which are the creations of past, dead historical conditions of capital's rule.

The 'Social Democratic' and so-called 'Communist' (read Stalinist turned Social Democrat or even 'Blairite') Parties across the globe are all now secondary political articulations of capital and its state power. They do not pose a serious threat to the rule of capital and, indeed, are often to be found 'in' or even 'as' governments which are managing the affairs of capital and its state power. The so-called 'radical left' of Syriza in Greece has recently (Summer 2015) joined this ignominious club of 'radicals' who have managerially submitted to the value-augmenting requirements of global capital. All the bluster and rhetoric from the 'lefts' of various hues about Syriza being the 'revolutionary form of the age', 'the future of socialism', etc., has disappeared – with the 'promise' of Syriza – into the ancient dust of the Athenian street.

This decline in trade union membership stands out as a historical trend causally mediated by capital's structural crisis. This has been accompanied by the growing inability of trade unionism to defend the interests of the employed proletariat (never mind the other sections). With every week that passes, capital closes 'unviable' operations to which we hear the usual toothless bark of the trade union leaders. A recent example of this (January

2015) was the closure of the parcel delivery firm CityLink in Britain with thousands of redundancies. The most 'militant' trade union in Britain (the Rail, Maritime and Transport Union, the RMT) supposedly 'representing' workers in this company effectively stood by like a defenceless infant whilst his bag of sweets were unceremoniously snatched by a bullying, beefy playground adolescent. Its response – which has now become more or less customary or 'standard' for trade unions – was to yell, cry, stamp its feet and whine to the capitalist media.

The emergence of the beginning of the structural crisis of the capitalist system in the 1970s signified the need for capital and its state power to constitute a more repressive relationship with organized labour as this crisis unfolded, exerting its effects on capital and impacting the effectiveness of the traditional 'economistic' role of trade unionism.

The 'militancy' of the 1970s and the struggles of the trade unions in the Tory decade of the 1980s was an unconscious response to the actual deepening of this structural crisis. On a phenomenological level – but essentially mediated by the emergence and maturation of capital's underlying structural crisis throughout this two-decade period – these struggles were fought out over the need to maintain and preserve wage levels, jobs, working conditions and, of course, whole industries and communities. The high point of these battles was the miners' strike of 1984–1985.

The fall in the membership of the trade unions is therefore a direct manifestation of the widening and deepening of this crisis. *It is a capital-in-crisis mediated trend.* And therefore, as such, will continue in its downward trajectory. It is important to note that the category here is not simply 'capital' but the historically more concrete 'capital-in-crisis'. Trade unionism is itself now slipping deeper into crisis as a result of the impact of the development of this crisis of capital. The unfolding of this trend in membership-decline is therefore inseparable from the emergence and development of this structural crisis of the capital system.

To understand why there is an inability of trade unionism to defend the interests of the employed proletariat in today's altered conditions, we need, firstly, to understand how trade unionism itself came into being in the course of the capitalist expansion in the past two centuries. Furthermore, how the defensive posture which it has taken historically is the product of these past conditions of its emergence and development *within* the capitalist system. And specifically, how this posture relates to the 'accommodating' relationship of trade unionism's governing elite to the state power of capital itself. But secondly, and more critically, how the unfolding of capital's structural crisis is actually impacting on the traditional 'economistic' role of trade unionism. It truly becomes a question of transformation or death.

Trade unionism in Britain came into being in the cauldron of capitalist expansion in the course of the nineteenth and early twentieth centuries. European colonialism was expanding and consolidating itself in various parts of the globe. The colonial territories provided a readily available supply of cheap raw materials and labour power for British capital and captive markets for its produced commodities. British rule in India was a primary example of this. Within this historical context of colonialism and world empire, trade unionism in Britain and in Europe was born.

The trade unions were established under totally different conditions to what are developing today. They were primarily and remain, in all essentials, 'economistic' 'wages and conditions' organizations with a *remedial* character, born in a period when capitalism was still a growing, expanding system of commodity production and circulation and which still had the capabilities to concede the demands made on it by employed workers or at least maintain a degree of stability or equilibrium in its relations with labour.

In this formative period, trade unionism took on and became ingrained with a reactive and defensive character because it was formed under conditions where such a way of proceeding delivered the necessary advances and improvements in wages and working conditions. That period has gone forever and is not coming back. Contrary to the demands and delusions of the Keynesian advocates in the Labour Party and elsewhere (reinforced with the election of Corbyn), global capital has now entered its period of terminal decline, its structural crisis, and *only storms and not sunrises* lie ahead for the capital order. New types of organized and offensive forms of struggle against the capital order and its state powers will be required as the crisis unfolds; the opening up of a broad offensive front against the capital order itself and against the state powers defending that order.

Initially, an example of a 'grassroots' movement of labour organized directly within the workplace, as trade unionism started to develop within conditions of capitalist expansion, it soon became bureaucratically structured and governed by a privileged ruling stratum. Its principal objective – under these conditions of expansion – became consolidated as a movement through which workers struggled to improve and consolidate their wages and working conditions. Trade unionism became rapidly adapted to the fortunes and trajectory of the capitalist order with a settled parasitic and privileged governing caste ...

> The years of comparative industrial peace, between the 1850s and 1880s, had seen 'a shifting of leadership in the trade union world', as the Webbs put it, 'from the casual enthusiast and irresponsible agitator to a class of permanent salaried officials expressly chosen from out of the rank and file of trade unionists for their superior business capacity'. To the epoch of 'defence, not defiance', corresponded the emergence of a generation of trade union leaders of a different type from those who had laid the foundations in the bitter days of the Combination Acts and Tolpuddle. It was between these 'sober, business-like' men and sections of the capitalist class 'that the political alliance was forged which, in different forms and phases, has been with us ever since – "the bourgeoisie cannot rule alone"'.[8]

The creation and transfer of value in the era of British colonialism served to modulate and attenuate the degree of exploitation of the proletariat living in the 'homeland' of British colonialism. In this way, indirectly, the value created on the back of colonial slavery served to underpin and cushion the position of this top bureaucratic stratum in the trade union movement. Today the transfer of astronomical magnitudes of value, from areas of the globe where the rate of exploitation is obscenely and shamelessly high compared to the 'metropolitan' capitalist countries of Europe, the US and Japan, resonates with a similar subsidizing function.

The defensive posture which trade unionism had taken historically received a further boost with the post-war expansion (1945–1975) of capital. This period of expansion and accumulation enabled the capitalist order to displace its historically accumulated contradictions for the next three decades. It provided the conditions within which the leaden, conservative structures of trade unionism could become further consolidated as the bureaucratic expression of capital's interests inside the workers' movement. This consolidation integrated a 'reformist' perspective in relation to the capitalist system.

> *The conception of a reformable capitalism without actually going beyond the capital relation itself was the ideal articulation of the interests of the trade union bureaucracy in the age of its birth and subsequent development.* It arose in a definite historical phase of development where the structural crisis of capital was in the future and the integration of the interests of the trade union and labour bureaucracy into the whole hegemonic superstructure of the imperialist capitalist order was taking place.

In Britain, this process of 'integration' has deep nationalistic roots which reach downwards into the substratum of the history of British capitalism at a time when it still 'ruled the waves', lived on the bloody fruits of colonialism, the exploitation of slave labour and the first forms of trade union organized labour to be established were the craft unions of the skilled 'aristocracy' of labour.

This 'aristocracy' of labour carved out a position for itself within capitalist society which placed itself 'above' 'unskilled', non-unionized labour. This has profoundly influenced the historic structure and organization of British trade unionism. It was only later that the unionization of unskilled labour arrived, in the later part of the nineteenth and early twentieth centuries. The ideological legacies of this division between 'skilled' and 'unskilled' labour remain and are refracted within trade unionism itself today despite the tendency towards 'de-skilling' (the worker as a superintendant of the production process based on a continuously increasing component of constant capital (machinery and materials) relative to labour-power in this process) and the widespread levelling of wages and conditions.

Historically, therefore, the trade unions and Social Democratic parties established themselves and gravitated ...

> in opposition to capitalism (not to capital as such) and in a fundamentally defensive way.[9]

In their origins and development, trade unionism and Social Democracy always took for granted – either explicitly or implicitly and despite any pretensions to the contrary – the continuing existence of that which they sought to reform. They always accepted the notion that capitalism could be reformed, made more humane, but that the capital relation itself – *the cube root of capitalism* – had to remain the fundamental, controlling social relationship of production and distribution. Marx, for very good reason, gave his major work the title *Capital*. The capital relation is the most essential problem. How to remove it from the social metabolism.

The capitalist state can be overthrown. But if the capital relation remains after that overthrow and is not uprooted and eradicated, then the restoration of capital-ism lies dormant and the possibility of its actual return, its state et al, remains. The capital relation does not disappear overnight with the state power that has always maintained the historic task of defending it. Once that state power is defeated and dissolved politically in the globally significant regions of the planet, then begins the less hindered social revolution of transcending the capital relation itself, of going beyond it, and beyond the commodity-form, both of which are historically much older than capitalism itself. The task of truly freeing human social life from their degrading and dehumanizing mediation then unfolds without the obstructing presence of the state power of capital. Only with the irreversible dissolution of this state power can the historic horizon to be fully opened up, unhindered, for the prospects, purposes and perspectives of the revolutionary process of eradicating capital as existent relation which historically precedes capitalism itself by many centuries. In this historic sense, it may be asserted that capital and the commodity form both precede capitalism and, for a period, will continue to survive it as humanity gets to work to eradicate both the capital and commodity forms from the social metabolism.

The historically outmoded character of trade unionism is clearly manifesting itself in its falling membership which reflects its growing ineffectiveness as both an 'economistic' organization in the struggle for improved wages and employment conditions and as a general centre of opposition to capital. The decline of trade unionism does not simply arise directly out of the 'objective conditions' being created by capital's structural crisis including defeats in past struggles. It also arises out of the very way in which trade unionism is hierarchically structured and organized in terms of its established bureaucratic procedures and alienating mechanisms. In the age of social media, the bureaucratic and self-serving management of the trade unions is observable by millions. And, of course, trade unionized and other workers boggle at the stupendous salary differences between top officials and branch members. Some General Secretaries are paid six-figure salaries whilst the workers which they are supposedly representing barely cross the threshold from a four-figure to a five-figure salary.

Historically, in relation to the trade union bureaucracy in general, we have observed, with unseemly regularity, how frictionless it has become for a trade union leader to readily make the profitable transition to the post of government minister, peerage or even a governor on the board of the Bank of England.[10] As the once jailed, late UCATT activist, Des Warren, observed in his book *The Key to my Cell*: trade union leaders always stand at 'the front of the queue when honours are dished out'.[11]

The hierarchically governed trade unions – with their conservative, leaden structures and well-paid and pensioned, elected-for-life general secretaries and top officials – are now integrated into the capital system and completely inadequate to deal with the demands now being placed on millions by the depth and severity of the intensifying crisis of the capital system. And this 'inadequacy' means both in terms of 'immediate demands' in their traditional 'economistic' role as 'wages and conditions' organizations and in any wider 'long term' social objectives. In the epoch of capital's structural crisis, trade unionism per se becomes historically outmoded and is now subject to a trajectory of either dissolution or supersedence into a higher form of unionism. Either it will become a vestige of its former self or it will become constituted as a 'platform' for a higher, more open, transparent and mass participatory form of unionism based in the whole of the proletariat as a class.

The internal organization and structure of this higher form will be decided through the direct participation of all concerned. Needless to say, the foundation of such a movement – if it is to truly articulate the interests of the proletariat in the age of capital's structural crisis – must be constituted as a qualitative break with previous types of organization such as we find in the current structure of the trade unions. The principle of continuously active revocable delegation (more about this later) will be central rather than having officials and 'representatives' either elected 'once in a blue moon' or even appointed for life on featherbedded salaries, 'golden handshakes' and equally lucrative 'golden goodbyes'.

The governing caste of trade unionism will try to maintain the impotent, dead strategy of protest and the reform of a system which is beyond reform. A 'revolution' within labour's political organization is now rendered necessary. Trade Unionism has become totally outmoded historically even in terms of its original foundational purposes, that is, as an agency for improved 'wages and conditions' in the workplace. In this regard also, the ruling stratum has effectively become an accomplice seeking to accommodate the interests of labour to the requirements of capital.

Effectively, the age of trade unionism per se has now come to an end because the epoch of capital's all-pervading structural crisis now demands that new adequate forms of proletarian organization are absolutely necessary for the purpose of conducting the struggle against capital; to put an end to the epoch of the existence of capital itself. The separate existence of the 'wages and conditions' form of organization – independently of the life of the class movement of the proletariat as a whole – has entered a 'bottleneck' of history (become 'funnelled' into it by the character of capital's structural crisis) within which it is slowly but surely suffocating.

What is now required is a real move forward in terms of organization and consciousness; changes which will bring into being a type of organization capable of conducting the struggle to put an end to the existence of the capitalist order itself and therefore, necessarily, the state powers which defend that order.

Trade unionism cannot be organized as a platform to move towards a higher form of agency as it is currently governed in its prevailing, hierarchically and bureaucratically organized and structured form. Or rather can only be organized as such a platform in direct opposition to this bureaucratic-caste system of governance. Any politically radical coalescence ('mergers') with any 'social and political movements' – for example, those which are tending to emerge in those regions most directly affected by the so-called 'sovereign debt crisis'[12] such as in Greece and Spain – will inevitably come up against these conservative trade union bureaucracies whose interests are more closely integrated with the continuation of the rule of capital rather than its termination. Long ago Marx wrote that the trade unions are ...

> too exclusively bent upon the local and immediate struggles with capital, the trade unions have not yet fully understood their power of acting against the system of wage slavery itself. They therefore kept too much aloof from general social and political movements.[13]

And today, we can see that this characteristic determination of trade unionism identified by Marx in his time has been preserved and maintained over 150 years. It has become congealed in the very structure, procedures and organization of the trade unions. In the course of these 150 years, they have failed to …

> consider themselves and act as the champions and representatives of the whole working class … *and to* … convince the world at large that their efforts, far from being narrow and selfish, aim at the emancipation of the downtrodden millions.[14]

With his customary dialectical foresight and summary concreteness, Marx then reveals the limits and the possibilities of trade unionism …

> unconsciously to themselves, the trade unions were forming **centres of organization** of the working class, as the medieval municipalities and communes did for the middle class. If the trade unions are required for the guerilla fights between capital and labour, they are still more important as **organized agencies for superseding the very system of wage labour and capital rule.** *(emphasis Marx).*[15]

Marx – in his subsection titled 'Their Future' - then proposes that the trade unions must …

> Apart from their original purposes … now learn to act deliberately as organizing centres of the working class in the broad interest of its **complete emancipation.** They must aid every social and political movement tending in that direction. *(emphasis Marx).*[16]

This latter proposal is, incredibly, more valid and concrete today than when Marx actually wrote it. Regardless of the notion that some (the 'militant anti-prescribers' in some left-wing grouplets) may consider Marx to have committed the grave heresy of 'prescription' or even tentatively stepped over the proverbial line into the infernal regions of near 'prediction'. It is only when the 'sinful' fall …

into the same error as Proudhon, of not seeking the real basis for (his) agitation in the actual elements of the class movement, but of trying to prescribe the course of the movement *according to a certain doctrinaire recipe ... (emphasis SM)*.[17]

... that we can give credit accordingly to the 'Marxist' 'anti-prescription' lobby who presumably are not involved with 'the actual elements of the class movement ... according to a certain doctrinaire recipe' and are not caught in the politically apoplexizing and paralysing pre-occupation of 'contemplating' these 'actual elements' *'in the form of the object'*.

This raises the question of how trade unionized workers (not six-figure salaried officials) are to relate to the so-called 'social and political movements'. This question actually implicates the trajectory which the trade unions are taking under the impact of capital's crisis. The approach (or rather its absence) of the trade unions to these 'external' 'social movements' is mediated by the bureaucratized power relations within the trade unions in which the top stratum has carved out a privileged mode of life for itself.

This present organizational form of the trade unions is actually serving as a fetter on establishing any productive relationship of trade unionists with these 'social movements'. The interests of the top stratum and the continuous reproduction of these interests – as a caste – is inextricably connected (interwoven even financially in terms of union funds and investments) to the continuation of the very system which these 'social movements' are actually challenging. The implication here is that any movement from within the body of the trade unions which threatens these relations will be opposed by this ruling stratum. Only by trade unionized workers actually coming into direct collision with this bureaucracy (in fact displacing it) will any radically significant and coherent organizational step forward be made in relation to a deeper political relation between trade unionized workers and the emerging 'social movements'.

In other words, as the crisis deepens and trade unionized workers increasingly realize that their 'vertically structured' trade unions are inadequate for the demands confronting them, this must become manifest in an open conflict between workers and the 'vertical structure' of their trade unions which are integrated functionally as part of the capital order.

The prognosis is an open confrontation with the 'old forms' which must be 'thrown off' if a real move forward is to be made by the trade unionized proletariat. The posited outcome of this 'throwing off of the old forms' – if it is to serve as an organizational means of furthering and articulating the interests of the proletariat as a whole class – can only be one which moves beyond the historically narrowed confines of trade unionism regardless of how radical and democratic any established structures may be. Without such a movement against the present hierarchical arrangement, the unfolding trajectory towards historic vestigiality must continue.

Trade unionized workers are increasingly becoming the prisoners of their 'own' organizations. The 'old forms' are acting as barriers ('fetters') to the development of their class interests in the midst of a deepening structural crisis for capital. The bureaucracy (the 'prison guard') has caste interests distinct from the 'prisoners'. This relation can only endure on the foundation of the rule of capital. It cannot do so on the grounds of its transcendence and common ownership. This bureaucratic caste naturally gravitates towards defending the capital order and, by implication, its state power.

From the perspective of the worker in struggle, hierarchically structured trade unionism increasingly takes on the form of a barrier which must be transcended. The trade union bureaucracy – under the rule of and in thrall to capital and its state power – becomes the warder of trade unionized workers. The forces unleashed by capital's structural crisis direct trade unionized workers towards the creation of a higher form of unionism – in collaboration with 'social movements', etc., and in opposition to labour-caste interests – or these forces will continue to push trade unionism as a whole further down the road towards extinction as we have witnessed since 1979. But 'branch level', 'broad membership' trade unionists will only be able to do this if they move to go beyond the current, hierarchically structured set up within 'their' organization.

The top stratum needs to maintain the established structures. It does everything possible to maintain them. This set-up is intrinsically associated with its privileges as a ruling caste. *But even if we, as a class, radicalize the trade unions – in terms of structure, activity and 'leadership'- this, in itself, would still be inadequate organizationally to address the impact of capital's evolving structural crisis on the life of the proletariat if trade unionism continues to retain its self-subsistent, self-sufficing, discrete character separate from the life and interests of the class as a whole.* A 'revolution' within trade unionism can, therefore, only mean the historical movement towards a higher form of unionism, that is, the use of this 'revolution' to move forward (as a means or 'platform') towards a higher *social* form of unionism.

In passing, it is important to note here that the conception of 'Social Unions' being developed here in this text is *not* that found in the work of Kim Moody.[18] It is not simply the re-articulation of trade unionism in a broader, more 'socialized' and 'networking' form: radicalized 'shop-floor' trade unionism *prosthetically connected* to various 'social movements', campaigns and community groups, etc: so-called 'Social Movement Unionism'. Rather, the conception in development here signifies the transcendence of trade unionism itself simultaneously resulting in a higher form of unionism incorporating all the previous functions and activities of trade unionism but in the form of what we may call 'Social Unions' which will articulate the historic interests of the proletariat both 'inside' and 'outside' the workplace as a coherent, unified, organizational whole. A 'Proteus' which is capable of retaining, modulating or altering its form, internal structures, procedures, etc., according to the demands placed on the proletariat by the changing conditions of the struggle against capital and its state and global powers.

One determinate form of unionism is superseded by a higher, historically more adequate form. Implicit in Moody's 'Social Movement Unionism' is the continued historical legitimacy of trade unionism per se (only more militant plus a 'networking' with the 'social movements') as a form of organized proletarian struggle in the epoch of capital's deepening structural crisis.

Moody's conception, however, must not be rejected outright because it possibly holds the promise of a 'transitional form' through which the proletariat must pass in the unfolding struggle against the capital order. But it cannot possibly be the historically adequate and universal, determinate, relatively enduring form necessary for the commencement of the negation of the capital order.

The question of trade unionists 'relating to social movements' actually implicates the impasse within the traditional forms of organization of labour. It cannot be separated from this growing crisis. Either the 'traditional form' 'revolutionizes' and moves forward or it continues to thrash around, 'grasping at straws' and sinks. To continue to assert the dogma of the impossibility of the capitalist system without trade unionism is merely the wishful thinking of the labour bureaucrat or the leader of the left-wing sect.

What is becoming increasingly evident is the need for an overarching, coherent, organizational framework which arises organically from within the participatory elements of the class. And, indeed, a framework which is not imposed from 'above and outside' (again in the style of the sectarian left or the labour bureaucrat) is the only form which will serve to necessarily preclude the dead weight of 'ossifying doctrine'. The real living unity of the agency of revolution will only come about through participation in practice. And not through any 'insistence' on 'doctrinal unity'. This 'doctrinal unity' is a 'driver' of the practices of the left sectarian groups.

Any theory of agency must relate to the present life and historical experience of 'the real movement' of the proletariat as it stands and is currently evolving and not distance itself from it. The urgent question of revolutionary agency is an intensely political question of 'practical consciousness' arising directly out of and within the current impasse which the traditional organizations of the proletariat have entered. It is a question which must impress itself on the organized proletariat as capital's structural crisis intensifies.

Accordingly, it is not a question which is posed as 'narration' or 'recount' but necessarily as 'practical consciousness' arising out of the conditions presently bearing down on the proletariat with capital's deepening structural crisis. The 'real movement' is conceived and articulated 'as sensuous human activity, as practice'. It is grasped 'subjectively' (the subject of history) and not discursively (anti-Marx) 'in the form of the object or of contemplation' found in 'narrative'.

Without a doubt, the conditions necessary for the emergence of the 'required forms of social consciousness' and the 'strategic/instrumental mediations' are not fully developed today in 2016 but these conditions are *now in the process* of emerging. History is a dialectical process (a coming to be (positing) out of negation in which such conditions are present implicitly – in Hegel *'an sich'* meaning ontologically undeveloped, yet potentiated – as opposed to actually posited, *gesetzt*) and not simply a joined-up series of concatenated events, one emerging from the other without each being 'embryonic' or 'implicit' in the antecedent conditions of the others.

It is necessary to start, simultaneously, both in theoretical orientation and in 'sensuous human activity' with this presupposition in regard to activities within and through the currently 'available instruments and institutions'. Necessity is, indeed, the 'mother of development' but social development does not take place simply and exclusively as a result of the operation of 'driving necessity'. If this were the case, then the whole of human history would become fatalistically reducible to a 'waiting game' and, as Paulo Freire implies, we would be justified in residing in 'accommodation' rather than being immersed in 'transformation'. [19]

The trade unions were established essentially as 'wages and conditions' organizations in order to secure a greater share of the value which living labour itself produces. This tussle was always rooted in the presupposition that the rule of capital remained unchallenged so that such 'economistic' differences were fought out and negotiated strictly on the ground, and within the parameters, of the capitalist system. The expansion of the capitalist system throughout the last two centuries enabled gains to be made in terms of wages, conditions and social provision in general.

However, the trade unions were never intended – nor could they have been intended – to form the organizational basis for overthrowing the rule of capital and its state powers. The conception that the trade unions plus 'the revolutionary party' ('the vanguard') was, and still is, regularly articulated by the left-wing sectarian grouplets as the magic formula which will take humanity beyond capitalism to a socialist society. However, this ignores the fundamental historic process whereby trade unionism very rapidly became integrated into the whole hegemonic superstructure of the capitalist order. This is especially notable in Britain where the trade union bureaucracy threw in its lot with the ruling class during the period of empire.

However, the epoch of a 'reformable capitalism' where this labour bureaucracy (TUC/Labour Party bureaucracy) could feed off the fruits of labour and imperialist exploitation over the course of two centuries has now passed through the hour glass of history. We have now entered an epoch where the traditional forms of struggle and 'defensive' organization are becoming increasingly inadequate as a means to not only win new gains but also defend the old ones. This raises the direct question – mediated by the impact of capital's inevitably deepening structural crisis – of 'restructuring' and 'refoundation' of the established 'institutions of struggle' of the proletariat. Accordingly, we are confronted with a situation where …

> the increasing difficulty and ultimate impossibility of obtaining defensive gains – on the model of the past – through the existing defensive institutions […] and the objective pressure for radically restructuring the existing institutions of socialist struggle so as to be able to meet the new historical challenge on an organizational basis which proves itself adequate to the growing need for a strategic offensive …

increasingly and imperatively asserts itself.[20] Fundamentally …

> what is at stake, then, is the constitution of an organizational framework capable not only of negating the ruling order but simultaneously also of exercising the vital positive functions of control, in the new form of self-activity and self-management, if the socialist forces are to break the vicious circle of capital's social control and their own negative/defensive dependency on it.[21]

What is required is the creation by the proletariat – in a truly radical rupture with the past – of a *new universal historic form of organization of a fundamentally and qualitatively higher typicality*. A new type of organization which will be comprehensively adequate and equipped in the widest possible social sense (synthesizing 'immediate demand' with 'long-term objectives') to 'take on' and defeat capital and its state powers on their own ground.

The path taken from 'Old' to 'New' Labour in Britain (inclusive of any attempt at a 'Corbynista' 'return' to 'Old Labour') corresponds to the supersedence of the age of reformable capitalism. And Corbyn's attempt to put matters into 'reverse gear' will merely serve to bring this into sharper relief. There can be no return – within the crisis-ridden parameters of the capital order – to the period of full employment and the creation and expansion of social provision which was based on the final post-war 'boom' of the global capitalist system after 1945. On the contrary, this provision is deep in process of being withdrawn. Herein lies the political significance of the path which the Labour Party in Britain has taken since Kinnock removed the socialist 'enemy within' in the 1980s and Blair went forward to repeal 'Clause Four' and create 'New Labour' in the 1990s.

Labour's growing crisis of organization therefore, necessarily, arises out of the unfolding and intensifying structural crisis of the global capitalist system itself. This crisis of capital, accordingly, brings in its wake a very deep and profound crisis for labour as regards the old defensive forms of organization. They – the old ways of organizing trade unionism – are fundamentally unfit for purpose in their present structure and organization and this will become increasingly evident as capital's crisis matures and its assault on public welfare provision and the proletariat as a whole develops to more intense and comprehensive levels. The need to throw off the old defensive forms and replace it with the new offensive forms directed uncompromisingly against capital and its state powers will increasingly assert itself. This, of course, is no guarantee that the required historic metamorphosis will actually take place. Fatalistically leaving the task to a driving, inevitabalistic – almost 'Spinozistic' – historic necessity alone is not sufficient in itself to posit this higher offensive form.

Hence, it is vital to stress that as the structural crisis of capital deepens in the course of the coming century, major changes will be necessitated in the 'instruments and institutions of socialist struggle' in order to 'bring to fruition the historical tendency in question' (i.e. the fullest development of the actuality of the socialist offensive). This is because these previously established 'instruments and institutions' have been formed in different times and under different conditions and circumstances ('at a qualitatively different historical conjuncture').

For trade unionists and for the proletariat as a whole, therefore, the emphasis must be on the perspective that the deepening of the structural crisis of capital – where 'even the bare maintenance of the acquired standard of living' as well as defence of any past gains remaining and any attempts to acquire new ones – will necessitate the active initiation and elaboration of major changes in strategy and organization in 'accordance with the historical actuality of the socialist offensive'. Indeed ...

> there will be no advance whatsoever until the working class movement, the socialist movement, is re-articulated in the form of becoming capable of offensive action, through its appropriate organizations and through this extra-parliamentary force.[22]

The introduction of anti-labour legislation since 1979 and its statutory maintenance by successive Labour governments demonstrates the necessity for such changes in strategy and organization. In May 2016, more anti-labour legislation (Trade Union Act 2016) has been passed into law by the 'liberal democracy' in Britain with lots of indignation and words but no action from the TUC. The trade union bureaucracy has, since the first anti-labour legislation was enacted under Thatcher, continued to prostrate itself to these governments' (Tory and Labour) refusal to remove the anti-union laws from the statute book. This amounts to over thirty years of abject subservience and refusal to mobilize against these anti-labour laws.

The opening up of an offensive against capital and its state power would bring into sharp relief the organizational fetters and historic limitations of trade unionism itself (if it is still around!) which shackle trade unionized workers, tethering this section of the proletariat to the capital order itself. The trade union 'defensive' form in conflict with capital and its state power can only mean, increasingly, the realization in the consciousness of the proletariat of its historical outmodedness and inadequacy as a form of organization of struggle of and for the proletariat in the age of capital's structural crisis. This must impact workers' consciousness and become a source of conflicts within it which animate its political development. Capital's crisis and the response of the proletariat within its traditional forms of organization will (must) serve to facilitate such developments in consciousness.

The fetters and dead weight of tradition must be thrown off if the proletariat is to move forward in struggle against capital. Older, pre-trade union 'traditions' may need to be 'disinterred' and 're-discovered'. There is an unconscious or even conscious *leitmotif* operating within the governing stratum of the trade unions; a dilemma wherein it is dimly perceived that to comprehensively oppose the capital order would sound the death-knell of this ruling stratum and yet not to oppose it also spells a slow and lingering death. The only way this stratum can attempt (totally ineffectively, of course) to resolve this dilemma is to 'oppose' by using the impotent and outmoded methods presented by the bourgeois order itself which is, at the same time, no real opposition at all. Such 'opposition' undoubtedly corrals trade unionism within the limits of the capital order and slowly sends it towards its death. To be 'in dilemma' is, of course, to be subject to an alien social power which, in this case, can only be capital itself. Incidentally, *en passant*, this is precisely why dilemma – as a psychosocial form – must and will tend to disappear in the commune once the latter has globally established itself and is evolving on the basis of its own self-created and socially self-mediating foundations and relations.

Trade unionism, under the weight of the present hierarchical organization and structure, is shackled and tethered to the capital order itself. Those fetters must be thrown off. Otherwise trade unionism itself as a whole will begin to perish without moving on to a higher form of organization. The major problem which confronts labour today is how to move forward in struggle when the old forms of organization are clearly outmoded. What emergent forms of struggle will place the feet of the proletariat on the road towards the creation of the 'new universal historic form' of proletarian organization? It is not so much a question of the 'radical restructuring of politics itself' but rather of the initiation and development of consistently effective tactics and forms of struggle as part of an overall strategy to establish the higher form of proletarian agency in the struggle against capital-in-crisis.

The crisis for labour is a crisis of organization imposed on it by the unfolding and deepening structural crisis of the capitalist order which demands solutions for the class as a whole and not simply for one ever-diminishing employed and exploited section of it, supposedly represented in 'its' trade unions.

Trade Unionism has become totally unfit for the realization of 'economistic' aims never mind for challenging the capitalist system itself. Even in terms of its original foundation 'wages and conditions' purposes, it has become outmoded. Rather than being the agency for challenging capital's rule, its top ruling stratum is continuing to serve as one of its most important props and loyal supports.

Effectively, the age of trade unionism as an organizational form of proletarian struggle is at an end. The epoch of capital's all-pervading structural crisis now demands that new, more adequate forms of organization are absolutely necessary for the purpose of conducting the struggle to put an end to the epoch of capital. In a certain sense, the traditional form of proletarian organization – namely trade unionism – is also sinking deeper into its very own 'structural crisis'.

What is now required is a real move forward in terms of organization and consciousness; changes which will bring into being a type of organization capable of conducting this global struggle to put an end to the existence of the capitalist order itself and therefore, necessarily, the national state and global powers which defend that order. This has clearly become indicated and manifest in the limitations of the traditional strategies and tactics of struggle of the proletariat and the historically outmoded character of its traditional organizations.

The socio-economic conditions generated by the unfolding of capital's structural crisis is pushing the trade unions further into a historical 'bottleneck'. Within this confinement, they are 'stuck', struggling to manouevre 'economistically' and politically, and settling into a terminal slumber and irreversible state of growing historical outmodedness. Trade unionism has been driven irreversibly into a cul-de-sac of history as a result of the impact of this developing structural crisis.

The developing conditions of this unfolding structural crisis are circumscribing the limits of this traditional form of organization and revealing its comprehensive historical inadequacy as an organization through which the proletariat can conduct its struggle against capital in the age of its structural crisis. This implies a historic trajectory of outmode and dissolution as evidenced by the decline of trade unionism in the 'homelands of capital' over the past four decades from the early 1980s to the present.

Increasingly, its governance by the top strata of its hierarchies and financial connections with the capital markets, ensures that trade unionism actually becomes more integrated into the capital order. The existence and caste interests of its governing structure have become inseparable from the continuing existence of the capital order itself. This means that in its present hierarchical structure and form of organization, trade unionism cannot continue without functioning, in one way or another, as a proxy of the capital order and its state power. The dominating criterion for capital today in its relationship to trade unionism is whether or not it is useful in serving its interests and in helping to perpetuate the socio-economic order based on capital.

What the capital system has entered is no longer an escapable or displaceable cyclic crisis. Capital has itself entered its very own cul-de-sac; the cul-de-sac of its long historic journey which predates capitalism itself. This has very profound consequences for the modes in which the proletariat has traditionally organized to oppose capital and its state power. Capital 'threw down the gauntlet' in the 1980s and the proletariat has yet to pick it up.

Structural crisis means trade unionized workers must move forward and work to form a qualitatively different, broader form of 'Social Unionism' or the evolution of the trade unions will effectively tend towards extinction. It is capital's structural crisis which is the source of a growing crisis within labour's traditional organization and strategies of struggle which have become ineffective in the face of this intensifying crisis. The conflicts generated within trade unionism between the historic needs of the proletariat as a class and the hierarchically structured and governed form of trade unionism serve as a potential source of movement towards a higher form of unionism.

Notes and References

1 Mészáros, István, *Beyond Capital. Towards A Theory of Transition* (London: Merlin Press, 1995) (approx 1000pp.).

Mészáros's work represents a fundamental, ground-breaking and important development for socialism in the twenty-first century. Its central concept is that capital has now entered its period of structural crisis. It is an essential study for all those who want to fight for an end to the age of capital.

More accessible works by Mészáros are *The Challenge and Burden of Historical Time: Socialism in the 21st Century* (2008) and *The Structural Crisis of*

Capital (2010). Also of note is his work *Marx's Theory of Alienation* which has become a 'standard text' on the question of alienation.
2   Rentoul, John, 'John McDonnell: Shadow Chancellor is the new voice of fiscal responsibility', *The Independent* (13 March 2016) <http://www.independent.co.uk/voices/john-mcdonnell-shadow-chancellor-is-the-new-voice-of-fiscal-responsibility-a6927926.html> (Last accessed 3 November 2016).
3   'BRICS' countries: Brazil – Russia – India – China – South Africa.
4   Mészáros, *Beyond Capital*, pp. 937–938.
5   TUC (Trades Union Congress in Britain) statistics on trade union membership. Trades Union Congress, 'TUC Directory 2016', *Trades Union Congress* <https://www.tuc.org.uk/sites/default/files/TUC_Directory_2016_Digital_Version_AW.pdf> (Last accessed 3 November 2016).

This TUC document presents statistical evidence to support the conception of 'bottleneck' and 'outmodedness' in relation to the trajectory which trade unionism has taken with the unfolding of capital's crisis since the late 1970s.
6   *TUC Directory 2016*, ibid., p. 32.
7   See the graphically presented data on page 6 of the government document given at the link below which gives membership figures over 120 years from 1892 to 2014.

Department for Business, Innovation & Skills, 'Trade Union Membership 2014. Statistical Bulletin', *Department for Business, Innovation & Skills* (June 2015) <https://www.gov.uk/government/uploads/system/uploads/attachment_data/file/431564/Trade_Union_Membership_Statistics_2014.pdf> (Last accessed 3 November 2016).
8   Pearce, Brian, 'Some Past Rank-and-File Movements', *Labour Review*, Vol. 4, No. 1 (April–May 1959): pp. 13–24 <https://www.marxists.org/history/etol/writers/pearce/1959/04/rankandfile.html> (Last accessed 2 November 2016).

Pearce, Brian, 'Some Past Rank-and-File Movements'. In Brian Pearce and Michael Woodhouse, *Essays on the History of Communism in Britain*, pp. 105–137 (London: New Park Publications, 1975).
9   Mészáros, *Beyond Capital*, pp. 940–941.
10 The Curriculum Vitae of Bill Morris, for example, reveals the steady rise of a trade union careerist from shop floor to seat in the House of Lords. A common trajectory of a typical 'lord of unionized labour' or 'union baron'. 'Union baron' is probably the most apt description of the relation between trade union leader and branch member – despite its origins in the capitalist press. The baron was a privileged and parasitic tenant within the relations of the feudal order who 'lorded it over' his subinfeudated serfs and villeins on his demesne. But the baron was himself subinfeudated to his greater lord. Morris's path perfectly describes

the elevation of an individual who has never posed (and has, accordingly, been 'elevated' because of this) a serious challenge or threat to the capital order or its state power. On the contrary, he has faithfully served that order and its state. Morris epitomizes the 'Lathe to Lords' path of the trade unionized servant of capital who scaled the trade union ladder in order to step into the 'establishment lounge' and emerge dressed in ermine on the seats of the upper chamber of the bourgeois parliament in Britain.

See also Arnot, Chris, 'Society Interview. Great Expectations', *The Guardian* (3 October 2007) <https://www.theguardian.com/society/2007/oct/03/guardi-ansocietysupplement. communities2> (Last accessed 4 November 2016).

11 Warren, Des, *The Key to My Cell* (London: New Park Publications, 1982).

12 The latest phase of capital's crisis is becoming manifest in the debt-ridden problems of so-called 'sovereign states' which are being revealed to be not so 'sovereign' as they formerly assumed. It is only a matter of time before a new, higher stage of this crisis opens up. These 'sovereign' problems are the surface expression of the historically intractable debt problems (astronomical magnitudes of what Marx refers to as 'fictitious capital') of global finance capital itself as expressed directly in its precarious banking system. This crisis of the capital order cannot be solved within the parameters of that order. Humanity will have to go beyond capital itself in order to end the worsening global crisis. And that must mean the break up and dissolution of the national state and global powers of capital which serve to defend the present iniquitous order. What is at stake here is the very future of humanity. Either the rule of capital and its state powers must end or humanity will sink deeper into barbarism.

13 Marx, Karl, 'Instructions for Delegates to the Geneva Congress'. In *The First International and After. Political Writings. Volume 3*, edited by David Fernbach, pp. 85–94 (London: Penguin Books in association with New Left Review, 1974), p. 91, Section 6, 'Trade Unions. Their Past, Present and Future'.

14 Ibid., p. 92.

15 Ibid., p. 91.

16 Ibid., p. 92.

17 Karl Marx to Johann Baptist von Schweitzer (13 October 1868). In *Marx-Engels Collected Works, Volume 43* (London: Lawrence & Wishart, 1988), p. 132.

18 For example, see the following:

Moody, Kim, 'Kim Moody interview: the superpower's shopfloor', interview with Martin Smith and Chris Harman, *International Socialism*, No. 115 (July 2007) <http://isj.org.uk/kim-moody-interview-the-superpowers-shopfloor/> (Last accessed 3 November 2016).

Moody, Kim, *Workers in a Lean World: Unions in the International Economy* (London: Verso, 1997).

Schavione, Michael, 'Moody's Account of Social Movement Unionism: An Analysis', *Critical Sociology*, Vol. 33 (2007): pp. 279–309.

19 'It is necessary that the weakness of the powerless is transformed into a force capable of announcing justice. For this to happen, a total denouncement of fatalism is necessary. We are transformative beings and not beings for accommodation' Freire, Paulo, *Pedagogy of the Oppressed* (London: Penguin Books, 1996).

20 Mészáros, *Beyond Capital*, p. 941.
21 Ibid., p. 941.
22 Ibid., p. 985.

PART III

Breaking Out of the 'Bottleneck' of Historically Limited, Self-Subsistent Trade Union Organization

CHAPTER 10

'Socialist Pluralism' and the Conception of the 'Social Union'

Without confronting the destructive consequences of the rule of global capital-in-crisis prior to the dissolution of the national state and global powers of capital, there can be no emergence of an 'organizational framework' for revolution. Such a 'framework' will only arise in the struggle against the destructive manifestations of capital-in-crisis. This 'pluralistic' process of confrontation has, in the form of various campaigns and movements, already begun and will inevitably intensify. The overriding consideration here is how this 'pluralism' of the movements of millions against the effects of capital's crisis on humanity and nature can be articulated – i.e. posited in its negativity – into a coherent form of organization which can constitute itself determinately as the social and political agency of and for revolution.

Without the origination and development of endogenous, organically integrated and 'overarching', unifying and positive structural determinations (an exponential force expressing the movement of the totality) arising within the relations between these 'pluralities' – which co-ordinates and constitutes the 'pluralities' into a fighting socialist unity of revolution through participation – what will result is not successful revolution but 'disarray and defeat'.

This continually arising 'negativity' of 'radical pluralistic' confrontation incorporating the power and momentum generated by it – without bringing together this pluralism into a coherently posited 'organizational framework' for revolution – is one which will recurrently dissipate and disperse in the maelstrom of global capital's crisis no matter how often it rises to confront the effects of this crisis. For example, factory occupations, the occupations of public spaces, struggles to oppose ecosystem destruction, formation of anti-capitalist and anti-militarist 'networking' through the internet, trade union strikes against cuts in public provision, etc., are all movements opposing the effects of capital's structural crisis on the immediacy of people's lives and on all those natural and socio-cultural conditions necessary for the future society. These are ways of trying to preserve these conditions and they constitute the nascent material for the formation of revolutionary agency. However, in their separation and fragmentation from each other – regardless of how militant and radical they may be – they cannot challenge the national powers of capital and, of course, its global agencies.

Without taking on board this fundamental consideration of a coherent organizational framework, the concept of 'pluralism' gets us no further up the road towards the required forms of agency. The fragmentary, isolated and 'marginal' character of many of the emerging movements against the devastating consequences of the destructive reproduction of capital-in-crisis must be overcome if the aims of these movements are to be fully realized. Capital functions as a transglobal socio-economic and political power over the proletariat through its nation states, 'blocks' and various global agencies. To truly challenge its rule is to challenge this power across the globe. A transglobal power which is compounded out of different, often conflicting, socio-economic, political and ideological organizations, institutions and services.

The different capitals compete against each other globally but they all constitute themselves as an opposing power – not necessarily and directly expressed in and through the form of unitary and 'overarching' 'established' institutions – when it comes to their common interest in the face of the 'structural antagonist' in the form of the proletariat. They are acutely conscious of the substantiality of common interest and rush to each other's defence in times of crisis when the capital order is truly threatened. It is only when the movements opposing the manifestations of capital's crisis come into relation with each other within an 'organizational framework' that they then have the potential to challenge this transglobal power of the capital order. And it is only within this context that …

> the elementary condition of success of the socialist project is its inherent pluralism. It sets out from the acknowledgement of the existing differences and inequalities;

not to preserve them (which is a necessary concomitant of all fictitious and arbitrarily enforced 'unity') but to supersede them in the only viable form: by securing the active involvement of all those concerned.[1]

This is ...

> impossible without the elaboration of specific strategies and 'mediations', arising from the particular determinations of changing needs and circumstances, which represent the greatest challenge to contemporary Marxist theory.[2]

The establishment and development of this 'participatory unity' which 'actively involves all those concerned' must involve the variety of different interests coalescing and working together on the basis of their *common class interest* whilst being able to pursue the realization of their specific aims and objectives as an intrinsic part of this 'participatory whole'.

The 'most urgent demands of our times' and the forces behind them can no longer be 'incorporated into capital's objective dynamics of self-expansion'. They are directly and ontologically incompatible with these 'objective dynamics'. They must and will motivate the struggles 'for the foreseeable future'.

The notion of the creation of 'a genuinely pluralist framework of common action' (ibid., p. 702) indicates the direction in which we have to move, to actively engage for the purpose of establishing the necessary form of revolutionary agency in the unfolding of the 'socialist offensive'. For the re-foundation of the class movement of the proletariat.

Moreover, it is paramount to note that the historically defensive conditions of the past meant that socialists had a tendency to focus 'on the general principles of the socialist alternative'. Under the changing conditions of structural crisis which are necessitating, increasingly, offensive strategies, this 'declaration of faith ... in the abstract ... is completely out of place' (ibid., pp. 702–703). The need to integrate the ...

> totality of social demands, from the most immediate 'non-socialist' everyday concerns to those openly questioning capital's social order as such, into a theoretically coherent as well as instrumentally/ organizationally viable strategic alternative.[3]

now comes into view on the historical horizon as a most urgent task ...

> Thus, the real issue is how to set firmly an overall direction to follow while fully acknowledging the constraining circumstances and the power of immediacy opposed to ideal shortcuts.[4]

Any form of 'agency' would be unsustainable under the intensifying conditions of capital's structural crisis if it were simply a loose, merely 'interfacial', confederation of different organizations and campaigns, etc., without a coherently established and functioning 'organizational framework' which constitutes a unification through participation of its various components. Under the weight of worsening conditions of crisis, a loose, informal confederation would be more likely to disintegrate whereas the overarching, determinate organization of some kind of established 'union', as long as it is adaptable and able to be restructured 'en route' in the process of 'transition', would be more likely to maintain its cohesion as it moves into the 'breach'.

In other words, there must be a real, determinate, substantial organizational and participatory coherence of the 'pluralities' and not simply a formal conferentiality in which the 'pluralities' merely 'interface'. What is required is an organically integrating and participatorily developing movement which still retains a degree of distinction of the 'pluralities' (does not wholly extinguish and subsume them) within the established organizational and 'overarching' coherence of the 'greater than the sum of its parts' whole. It is only within this organizational and political coherence that objectives which point beyond the age of capital can be developed, refined and fought for against the social and political power of capital itself.

On a phenomenological level, confronting the destructive consequences of capital's rule is therefore not necessarily identical with confronting that rule itself. And we observe this today all over the planet in the form of various disparate and disconnected struggles against those consequences.

There is a real distinction here, an ontologically and consciousness-mediated 'gap' which needs to be bridged between addressing the *phenomenological manifestations* of capital-in-crisis (structural unemployment, ecological devastation, mass poverty, disease and starvation, etc.) and the *real historic taproot* of these manifestations which is the actual existence of the capital relation in crisis as the pre-eminent, globalizing social relationship of production and distribution mediating these phenomena. And this

'Socialist Pluralism' and the Conception of the 'Social Union'

is where the question of agency comes into its own, mediated – as it must be – by the necessary requirement of a 'socialist pluralism'. Essentially, the ...

> meaning of socialist pluralism – the active engagement in common action, without compromising but constantly renewing the socialist principles which inspire the overall concerns – arises precisely from the ability of the participating forces to combine into a coherent whole, with ultimately inescapable socialist implications, a great variety of demands and partial strategies which in and by themselves need not have anything specifically socialist about them at all.[5]

This pluralism is fundamental. It mediates both the popular democracy of social revolution and the 'autonomous' and 'self-managing' yet co-operative character of all the 'participants' in the actual restructuring of the social metabolism beyond the capital relation such that ...

> the socialist enterprise is structurally unrealizable without its full articulation in the manifold autonomous ('self-managing'), and thus irrepressibly pluralist projects of the ongoing social revolution.[6]

'The most urgent demands of our times' – in their *ersatz* and 'single issue' separation from each other – are demands which every 'liberal could embrace'. However ...

> it is rather different, though, when we consider them not as single issues, in isolation, but jointly, as parts of the overall complex that constantly reproduces them as unrealized and systematically unrealizable demands [...] it is the **condition** of their realization that ultimately decides the issue, (defining them in their plurality as **conjointly** socialist demands) and not their character considered separately. Consequently, what is at stake is not the elusive 'politicization' of these separate concerns through which they might in the end fulfil a direct political function in a socialist strategy, but the **effectiveness** of asserting and sustaining such largely self-motivating 'non-socialist' demands on the broadest possible front.[7] (emphasis – IM)

The political expression and articulations of this 'overarching form' must arise organically and democratically out of the relations between the pluralities which constitute the whole movement. The explicit political forms and structures must not be superimposed on this movement either 'from outside' or 'from above' which would serve to undermine the 'self-managing' character of the differing 'pluralities and the democracy of the movement as a whole. And this ties in with 'what is at stake' which is ...

> the constitution of an organizational framework capable not only of negating the ruling order but simultaneously also of exercising the vital positive functions of control, in the new form of self-activity and self-management, if the socialist forces are to break the vicious forces of capital's social control and their own negative/defensive dependency on it.[8]

The only real structural antagonist to capital is the proletariat itself. There is, and can be, no other. It is the only conceivable agency of revolution organized in historically adequate form for the tasks now emerging as capital's crisis inevitably deepens in the course of the unfolding of the coming century.

In the 1960s and even later, the so-called 'revolutionary left' sampled (and regularly became politically infatuated with) a variety of 'alternative' forms of revolutionary agency. Through their fickle hands passed the putative 'agencies' of students, armed peasants, the intelligentsia, black power groups, radical feminists, racial egalitarians, urban guerillas, etc., anyone of which could supposedly and bizarrely constitute the agency of revolution. In fact, almost anybody other than the class of wage labourers (employed or unemployed, manual or mental) in their historically determinate, antagonistic relation to capital and its state power. The proletariat as a class is the only class that can put an end to the epoch of capital as Marx and others since have clearly shown, simply by virtue of its *historically and organically antagonistic relationship* to capital itself.

Take, for example, the so-called 'feminist movement' which is and has always been 'embraced' by 'every genuine liberal'. This movement in and by itself (or any other movement which is not a participating and integrated part of an overarching class movement of the proletariat) is totally inadequate to put an end to the rule of capital. In Britain, a significant section of feminism *isolated from the proletarian class movement* has become a movement – largely located in the capitalist media – whose principal objectives are to simply give women the opportunity for advancing their careers in the management of the capitalist system. The leading figures in this movement think they have achieved something if the head of a big capitalist corporation, bank or political organization is a woman and not a man. Certain sections of feminism have degenerated into becoming a mantraic war cry or an indignant *cri de coeur* of the aspiring female careerist.

This movement today (in contrast to the great struggles for women's suffrage in the past) has not substantially touched the lives of millions of working class women. Because their social lives are *essentially governed* by their existence as members of a *specific social class* rather than by being governed by their status as 'women'. 'Woman' is a less historically concrete (more abstract) and a more transhistorical category than 'woman worker'.

Feminism has merely sought to address *formal and not substantial* relations of equality and, as such, in its isolation from the class movement as a whole merely articulates a *liberal agenda* which can be ostensibly accommodated within the modulating parameters of the capital order. In fact, the capitalist media has virtually appropriated feminism as its own just as it has hypocritically co-opted anti-racism as a moral crusade whilst defending the very system which breeds and perpetuates it.

Feminism in and by itself will not and cannot be the agency of revolution which emancipates humanity from the epoch of capital. All of these characterizations – gender inequality, the dispossession and impoverishment of the rural poor, racism, patriarchy, etc. – are not 'self-standing', exclusively self-mediating determinations but are all rooted in the primary mediation of the rule of capital.

The system of the reproduction and circulation of capital is the root, fundamental, socio-historical relation mediating all these secondary, organically interconnected social phenomena. Fascism, racism, gender relations, etc., cannot be adequately grasped separately – as if they are self-subsistent determinations without connection to the whole – in isolation from the mediation of the primary relation. Capital is the cube-root of capitalism and its historic structural antagonist is the proletariat.

The real emancipation of womanhood can only be realized with the emancipation of the proletariat as a class which means the emancipation of humanity per se from the rule of capital.[9] To postulate that the real, substantive social and sexual emancipation of women is possible and fully realizable in the epoch of capital-in-structural-crisis is a mirage which the ideologues of capital perpetuate daily in their broadcasting and print media.

Historically, the struggle for women's suffrage was a vital part of the struggle of the proletariat to broaden and deepen its democratic rights under capitalism. It was not simply a 'women's question' but rather a class question; a part of the broader class struggle. In Britain, many of the leading figures for women's enfranchisement were socialists, not liberals. It is a profound error to separate women's emancipation from the emancipation of humanity from the rule of capital. 'Women' are not women in the abstract (without historical characterization) but real women as determined through their position in the prevailing class relations. The only historic force which is capable of carrying through this emancipation is the proletariat (men and women) organized as revolutionary agency. This is an absolute relation within the development of the capital system.

Marx is the consummate 'feminist' in the history of human thought. Marx's life work is the highest form of 'feminism'. Accordingly, to be a feminist today necessarily means being a student of Marx and a theoretical and practical developer of his legacy. All other forms of feminism in relation to Marx are simply by-words, openly or disguised, for the continuing submission and oppression of women because they do not address the fundamental root causality of these forms of inequality which is the existence of capital itself as the ruling relationship of the whole social metabolism.

Politically, of course, it would be an abrogation of responsibility to neglect any struggle against oppression – whatever its form – but it would also be a serious political error to not fully recognize and comprehend the root relation which is mediating the different forms and manifestations of oppression. The *discreteness* of each struggle is not neglected but is always understood in relation to the major relationship which *primarily mediates* the whole. The primary relation at work in the multiplicity of these details is capital. The struggle for women's emancipation therefore becomes intrinsically linked to the struggle to end the epoch of capital.

The key, in this respect, to grasping the root problem of human emancipation is not to understand revolutionary agency as a formal 'intertwining and overlapping' of different struggles to constitute a singularity but rather grasping these struggles in their 'unity-in-diversity' as mediated by the continued dominance of the capital relation. It is not a question of reducing them to a 'single struggle against capital' but rather as grasping each struggle in its specific organic relation to the rule of capital; how each struggle – 'anti-racist', 'women', 'anti-fascism', etc. – has many mediating links to this rule. And if we detach them from these links, they tend to become abstract, single-issues of a liberal character, divorced from their real mediatively determining historical locus which is the existence of the capital relation in the epoch of its deepening and intractable structural crisis.

These considerations on isolated struggles lead directly onto the question of revolutionary agency and the historic need for an overarching, participatory form of organization which can articulate the interests of the class as a whole and not simply 'women', 'migrants, 'oppressed minorities', 'the unemployed', etc. To simply see the category of 'proletariat' as just another one on parity with 'women', 'migrants', etc., is a liberal and not a socialist position. The fundamental problem confronting us today is: how do we go beyond the epoch of capital and what kind of agency/ies will be required for that transformation?

'Women' or this or that force or group 'independently' of the proletariat organized as agency are not the historic structural antagonists of the capital order. Only the proletariat *as a class* fulfills this historic role and function. It is true, of course, that the proletariat has diversified (its occupational structure and social composition has altered with globalization) but in this diversification it remains 'the proletariat as a class'. Within the historically relative, this absolute character continues to assert itself. And today, as at the time of Marx, it can only survive by selling its labour power to capital or its various agencies. Its *productive* labour remains the source of the growing and augmenting value of capital and the proletariat therefore is, and can only be, *the* truly adequate, comprehensive and revolutionary historic antagonist of capital.

Any form of these isolated movements is, as such, in its separation from the class movement, a *faux form* for the substantial historic realization of its long term objectives such as women's emancipation, elimination of racism, ending of war, etc. However, in their intrinsic and integrative relationship to the proletarian class movement, a different side emerges.

For the class movement to integrate these *faux* forms is to make them an intrinsic part of that movement and strip them of their *ersatz* character. It is an enrichment of the movement itself and the consummate realization of the principle that genuine unity and comradeship is found only in participation and struggle. Whilst abolishing this separate, self-subsistent *faux, ersatz* character, it preserves its 'moment of distinction' within the continuum of an overarching class movement within which it can truly develop and become expressed as part of the movement for human emancipation from the rule of capital.

Indeed, this 'unity' cannot be a truly self-sustaining, revolutionary 'singularity' without being an overarching form of organization which brings together all the different aspects of the *faux forms* and, in the course of integrating them, *actually transforms* (divests these forms of their *ersatz* nature) them as essential participants ('ingredients') in the higher form of revolutionary agency. By bringing the different aspects into a singularity of organization, it is their mutual participation in struggle which becomes the key to its continuous reproduction as a singularity.[10] But in their separation from each other these various movements take on a 'liberal', and therefore 'bourgeois', character in that the realization of their goals is posited as achievable within the capitalist order.

This class character of these movements-in-separation is transformed when they coalesce and are integrated into an overarching form of proletarian revolutionary agency. Their class character as articulating the historic interests of the proletariat as a whole then becomes directly expressed through and in the actual struggle of this revolutionary agency against capital and its state power. Each aspect becomes an integrated and integrating aspect of the whole which both enriches the whole and expresses itself through it as a moment of this whole. The actual 'bourgeois' class character of the separated movements becomes altered as they become integrated into an overarching singularity of organization of the proletariat in struggle against the capital order and its powers and agencies.

Organizing today against capital and its state power means bringing the legacy of Marx and others forward and developing it for the new conditions of rule of capital-in-structural-crisis now confronting us. It means starting out from where the proletariat is today in terms of its principal forms of organization and the attendant forms of consciousness. And moving into the struggle on the basis of the limitations of this organization and consciousness. And, moreover, showing how these currently 'principal forms' are inadequate for the conditions of struggle being generated by capital's structural crisis which is now unfolding. Hence the need for profound and far-reaching organizational change in the proletarian class movement.

In the major capitalist countries – and across the globe generally – the proletariat remains with its trade unions (the 'old universal historic form' of proletarian organization) in terms of organization and consciousness. But these trade unions are now completely inadequate even for their traditional 'economistic' purposes and functions. They are outmoded in their current form. But their potential as a medium within which to create new forms of agency for the structural-crisis-conditions of capital's rule cannot and must not be discounted.

Here, in this conception of 'socialist pluralism', we have a theoretical framework on which to base and develop our conceptions in regard to the question of agency and the emergence of the abovesaid opposition movements to the destruction and havoc being wreaked by capital in its unfolding crisis. The work of Marx and Mészáros constitutes a theoretical basis – which does, however, need to be developed in relation to the question of revolutionary agency – for informing our practical-conscious activity in relation to the development of forms of agency which can begin to challenge the rule of capital itself.

It is precisely within this activity in common of 'constantly renewing socialist principles' and through the 'ability of the participating forces to combine into a coherent whole ... a great variety of demands and partial strategies' that the real steps forward will be made on the formation of revolutionary agency. To 'define them in their plurality as conjointly socialist demands' by 'asserting and sustaining' them 'on the broadest possible front' is the start of 'the constitution of an organizational framework capable not only of negating the ruling order ... etc.'. Herein lies the potential linkage (joining up and coalescence) between those movements now emerging to oppose the devastating socio-cultural and ecological effects of capital's crisis. The potential of a movement towards an 'overarching' form which constitutes the beginning of the necessary form of agency to oppose and begin to transcend the capital order.

The conception of 'socialist pluralism' in *Beyond Capital* (Section 18.3, pp. 694–703) contains and implies, in undeveloped form, the general conception of the organizational form of the 'pluralistic' 'Social Union'. Social Unions would be 'inherently pluralist' organizations in which the constituent cells would preserve their 'autonomous, self-managing' character whilst this higher form of unionism (compared to trade unionism) itself would 'secure the active involvement of all those concerned'. This participatory involvement would seek to supersede (sublate, not abolish) in practice these 'acknowledged existing differences and inequalities' through this active participation rather than seeking to preserve them through a 'fictitious and arbitrarily enforced unity'.

The Social Union would bring together the proletariat, with its 'non-socialist everyday concerns', and the 'most enlightened elements of the proletariat' (Marx). Such an organization would 'arise precisely from the ability of the participating forces to combine into a coherent whole, with ultimately inescapable socialist implications, a great variety of demands and partial strategies which in and by themselves need not have anything specifically socialist about them at all'. And such an organization would be 'impossible without the elaboration of specific strategies and "mediations", arising from the particular determinations of changing needs and circumstances'. And, very importantly, they would integrate the 'totality of social demands, from the most immediate "non-socialist" everyday concerns to those openly questioning capital's social order as such, into a theoretically coherent as well as instrumentally/ organizationally viable strategic alternative' (Mészáros).

The 'Social Union' against capital would more concretely accommodate – and be more adequate historically in terms of proletarian organization under developing conditions of structural crisis – the altered social and occupational composition of the proletariat created by globalizing capital. It would, therefore, – in terms of its organization and social composition – not only be *more concrete historically* (greater diversity/plurality, more widely embracing, and rich in social composition, constituting an evolving, organizational unity of the proletarian class) but also *more consonant* as a means of addressing the problems of the proletariat in the age of capital's structural crisis.

This is precisely where a comprehensive critique of Marx's 150-year-old conception of the proletariat is not only made possible but also absolutely necessary as a consequence of these globally altered conditions of the capital system. Such a critique must, undoubtedly, throw into sharp relief the question of the historical adequacy of previous forms of agency such as trade unions, political parties, soviets, workers' councils, etc., in the present epoch. However, from where we stand at the moment, at this historical juncture, trade unionism may well become important in the formation and development of a higher form of revolutionary agency. 'Trade union consciousness' possibly exhibits the increasing potential – if we may be allowed to spontaneously 'tread on a few dead toes' – to pass into a higher form of revolutionary 'social union consciousness' as capital's structural crisis deepens and intensifies globally.

In relation to the past structures, class composition and 'conjunctural' social context of the workers' councils, for example, the Social Unions would – in their creation and development – more specifically be inclusive of the social interests of those wage workers who otherwise, in previous times, would have been considered to be part of the 'middle-class' and not to be an intrinsic part of the class movement of the proletariat. Compared to the workers' councils of the twentieth century, the creation and altering character of the Social Union as a mass 'organizationally viable strategic alternative' would more closely reflect and assimilate both the changed global conditions of capital's unfolding crisis and the altered occupational structure and social composition of the proletariat.

In other words, a Social Union as opposed to a trade union or workers' council is more embracing under the presently unfolding conditions, and unifies a greater diversity of people into a single body. In the course of doing this, it serves to transcend – through the active participation of all in the struggle of the whole against capital – traditional lines of social division between differentiated sections of the proletariat such as 'white' and 'blue collar', manual and professional, men and women, industrial and service worker, local and migrant worker, 'productive' and 'unproductive' labour, employed and unemployed, etc. The trade union form is more strictly limited (historically 'more abstract') in these manifold respects.

The 'advantages' and 'benefits' gained for all its members/components by the emergence and 'evolution' of this type of overarching organization would be socially 'selected' – under intensifying conditions of crisis – as to facilitate its consolidation and further development. Only within such an 'overarching organization' could the political character of separated 'liberal' demands actually become altered and emerge as 'conjointly socialist demands' capable of challenging the capital system itself. The emergence, sustainability and momentum of such a movement presupposes a deepening and intensification of the unfolding structural crisis of capital i.e. the historical ground and conditions would have to be such that the conflicts and antagonisms of the developing crisis would be the 'motor' or 'engine' for the birth and continuous propagation and development of such a movement of social unions.

Retrospectively, we can recognize that the workers' council as a historical form was more directly associated with the trade union-organized industrial proletariat i.e. with those workers engaged in productive industrial labour (reproducing the value of their labour power as well as producing surplus value). The structure and operation of the social unions (based on the principles of socialist pluralism) must be broader, more comprehensive, more embracing and complex enough – in comparison to the traditional trade unions and workers' councils – to accommodate the multiplicity of the varying interests of different sections of the proletariat in its more complex and more demanding present global situation and changed occupational structure.

In a certain sense, it would be a dialectical return (negated negation) to the workers' council but simultaneously the positing of a body which is beyond both this proletarian organization and the limits of trade unionism of previous times. It would be socially more complex in its creation and evolution which could possibly contain within itself (integrate as an active component) a radically re-constituted trade unionism. However, a 'trade unionism' which would be totally transformed compared to its present state as a result of its new organic relations with the Social Union as a whole. However, we have to conceptualize the Social Union as an initial – if not *the* initial – form of agency directed against the capital order. It is vital to recognize that we are not, at the moment, pre-occupied with the conception that ...

> the social form which defines itself through the [...] 'expropriation of the expropriators' [...] could not be considered a truly self-sustaining form, because of the contradictions arising from its continued dependency on the negated object.[11]

We take it as given, on grounds of historical dialectics alone, that the further resolution of these 'contradictions arising from its continued dependency on the negated object' will lead on towards more 'truly self-sustaining forms' of agency.

However, what is not taken as given is the nature of the 'social form' in the present global situation i.e. the form of agency through which the proletariat will embark on and start to conduct the struggle for the destruction of the socio-economic and political power of global capital (the commencement of the dissolution of its actual existence as a total historic complex). Indeed, for the time present, all conceptions and deliberations on the form of agency should be taken provisionally so as not to fall into the trap of speculation, positivism and dogmatism. The provisionality of all conceptions on this question of agency must be tested and re-tested against the developing situation of capital's structural crisis and the response of the proletariat to it. The conception of the 'Social Union' is no different in this regard and, accordingly, is subject to the overriding socio-economic and political criteria arising out of the relationship of the 'real movement' to the agencies of capital in its structural crisis.

However, what is certain is the need for a form of agency which will not simply conduct a political struggle to topple the state power of capital. It will also be structured and functional for the actual commencement of the re-organization of the whole socio-economic landscape ('social metabolism') beyond the capital relation. Notwithstanding this, the overturning of capital's nation state and global powers of capital (primarily in the politically and culturally most significant areas of the globe) becomes an absolute historical pre-requisite for the ensuing, long-term and unhindered objectives of socio-cultural transformation in which capital will be completely eradicated as a totalizing mode of control from the social metabolism itself.

Of course, this 'social form' of agency 'which defines itself through the expropriation of the expropriators', in all its specific detail and social complexity, can only be practically resolved and articulated in reality when the totality of the conditions necessary for its formation have emerged or, at least, are in the process of formation. Humanity only sets itself the solutions to problems where *the conditions* for such solutions have already arisen or are in the process of formation (paraphrasing Marx). Then, of course, a more concrete, detailed and definitive conception would be made possible and could be developed in close relation to these conditions of formation and the practical elaboration of the necessary forms of agency.

Historically, it may be argued that the most advanced form of agency which the proletariat has actually created under conditions of crisis is the workers' council. Mészáros refers to Lukács's analysis of workers' councils as examples of institutions which …

> in the situation **after the dictatorship** (emphasis SM) ought to overcome the bourgeois separation of legislative, executive and judiciary … and … in the struggle for power it is called upon to end the spatio-temporal fragmentation of the proletariat, and also to bring together economics and politics in the true unity of proletarian activity, and in this way to help reconcile the dialectical opposition of immediate interests and ultimate aim.[12]

Note the phrase '*in the situation **after the dictatorship***'. Is it not the work of this 'dictatorship' to 'overcome this bourgeois separation …'? How is it to be overcome only 'after the dictatorship'? So what is the purpose of this 'dictatorship'? Is not the actual temporal passing of this 'dictatorship' indicative that this 'bourgeois separation' has effectively been 'overcome' and, accordingly, the need for workers' councils has been transcended? In other words, they have already disappeared when Lukács asserts their need to 'overcome separations'? We shall leave readers to grapple with the paradox of this *apparent* (i.e. to the author) puzzle.

Nonetheless, the workers' council in this conception – taken from Lukács's influential work – is seen as a sort of 'one size fits all' or a 'Swiss Army Knife' of an institution in which it is not only central in organizing and prosecuting 'the struggle for power' but, it seems, is adaptable and sustainable enough to take us beyond capital. Mészáros contradicts this conception by asserting the need for 'institutions which must be restructured en route, through manifold transitions and mediations'.

With Mészáros, therefore, the workers' council, together with all the 'party trimmings', 'could not be considered a truly self-sustaining form, etc.'. There is a clear break here with the Lukács of *History and Class Consciousness*. This discrepancy can be largely explained, of course, by the qualitatively different historical conditions within which Lukács and Mészáros have developed their conceptions, times of cyclical crisis of displaceable contradictions and times of structural crisis in which the contradictions are becoming hemmed in, tending towards unresolvability and steadily intensifying, so that these root features are characterizing the different epochs and conceptions respectively.

In his critique of Lukács in *Beyond Capital*, Mészáros looks at Lukács's 'changing evaluation of the workers' councils' (see *Beyond Capital*, Section 9.2, p. 371 ff) and writes that he later dismissed ...

> the idea of self-management through the collective agency of Workers' Councils [...], without attempting to put anything historically concrete and institutionally safeguarded in the place of the criticised material complexes.[13]

and that Lukács fell into ...

> an idealist substitute for the necessary and feasible organs of participatory social control.[14]

Accordingly, Lukács himself, by falling into 'an idealist substitute', contradicts his earlier conception in *History and Class Consciousness* that workers' councils were essentially fit for the previously ascribed purpose.

It would be too hasty to completely dismiss workers' councils. However the axiomatic belief, especially within the sectarian left, for example, that workers' councils would always be the necessary organs of proletarian revolution now needs to be seriously questioned and re-evaluated. The formation of such bodies needs to be grasped historically just as we have, later in this text, re-appraised the 'vanguard party' within its historical context.[15]

The workers' council, of course, cannot be excluded as the first line of the offensive against the capitalist state but it cannot be axiomatically asserted as such. Referring to Lukács's description of workers' councils, Mészáros writes that it is an example of such an institution but 'only one example, however important it is in a strategic sense' (*Marx's Theory of Alienation*, p. 287). This 'one example' posited as atemporally axiomatic, however, under the emerged and intensifying conditions of capital's structural crisis and the altered occupational structure and social composition of the proletariat globally, must now be located historically as possibly the spent product of superseded times of '*conjunctural crises*'. It must not be simply and dogmatically re-articulated as a mantra to address the problems now confronting the proletariat arising out of capital's structural crisis.

Workers' councils were formed by the proletariat in times of intense crisis during the twentieth century and, not widely known, even in Japan after 1945.[16] However, this does not necessarily imply that they must always be formed as such. We have to bear in mind the changed global conditions and that these developments, in themselves, mediate the formation of future types of organizations for the 'socialist offensive'. Indeed, bearing in mind the altered global conditions, it may well be that the 'historical time' of the workers' council form has now passed and such new conditions now call out for a different type of proletarian organization. Once again, this is where a critique of Marx's conception of the proletariat must serve to inform the struggle for the necessary establishment of the 'new universal historic form' of proletarian revolutionary organization.

Were workers' councils, as we witnessed their structure and operation in the past, capable of starting to restructure the whole socio-economic landscape beyond capital in the menacing presence of the state power? Or were they simply and exclusively organs of political struggle against the same state power of capital? Were they the highest political expression of proletarian organization at the time? Were they the harbingers of a more comprehensive type of proletarian organization now made necessary by the deepening of capital's structural crisis? That is, were they exclusively creatures of the conjunctural crises of the capital system and not even *possibly* of its structural terminal crisis?

A form of agency is now required which can both commence the process of the restructuring of the social metabolism beyond capital – in the menacing and violent presence of the state power of capital – and can also, at the same time, prepare the proletariat for political mobilization against that state power, *to fight fire with fire*, to assert the power of the organizing and emancipating proletariat against that state power and work decidedly and unquestionably for its dissolution in every way possible and necessary.

Whatever form these agencies of revolution may take, a working conception of the historical tenure of such agencies would be required in order to adequately gauge the historical moment when they could be safely superseded (left behind) and replaced, or not, with higher forms. The prime consideration here, of course, would be any countervailing tendencies (threat) towards restoration of capitalism as the capital relation itself is being extinguished within the social metabolism. Or the danger of the re-introduction of elements which point backwards towards the capitalist epoch. *The imperative must be to drive the impetus of the social transformation forward beyond its prevailing stage to the next. To take society further beyond the age of capital. To look back and see it receding further and further into the abyss of historical time.*

Any intervening dogmatism and doctrinairism in terms of organization, under circumstances of revolutionary change, could only reflect the internal counter-pressures of the dying capital system. A 'this far but no further' brake on the process of going beyond capital. Hence, the vital importance to study and evaluate the real living historical process as it unfolds. To proclaim the institution of workers' councils as the only possible agency necessary for the proletarian struggle to overthrow the rule of capital is an example of this dogmatism and doctrinairism.

The experience of the history of proletarian struggle – in different parts of the world and at different times – does indeed reveal the workers' council form as a historical leitmotif of proletarian struggle, i.e. its spontaneous springing into existence and universal character, in times of intense class struggle. But how are we to approach this historical experience today in the present changed global conditions?

On pages 978–986 of *Beyond Capital* is a transcript of an interview which Mészáros gave to '*Marxism Today*' in April 1992. The last question in the interview raises the problem of how the differential rate of exploitation across the globe can serve as an impediment to the development of proletarian internationalism. Mészáros acknowledges this problem but also says that this is where ...

a critique of Marx has to be indicated, because the working class is fragmented, is divided, and there are so many contradictions.[17]

But if a critique of Marx is indicated here in relation to our conception of the proletariat, then does this not also simultaneously implicate and indicate a critique of the workers' council form as the traditional and most advanced form of proletarian organization of mobilization against the political power of capital? Moreover, does not such a critique also have implications for all those forms of agency and organization which the proletariat has formed and utilized over the past two centuries? Such a critique of the workers' council arises out of a critique of Marx's conception of the proletariat. For if there have been historically significant changes in the structure/nature of the proletariat itself since Marx developed his conception, then does this not indicate a critique of those organizations through which the class has traditionally conducted its struggles, be they defensive or offensive? Be they trade union or workers' councils or other forms?

Such a critique would inevitably relate the character of the workers' council form to past and superseded historical conditions within which it emerged and, specifically, to the character of the proletariat which formed these councils. And, moreover, consider its adequacy in terms of addressing the unfolding problems facing the proletariat today as capital's structural crisis deepens.

The addressing of this urgent question must be founded upon a comprehensive critique of Marx's conception of the proletariat in order to engender and inform a critique of the workers' council form and, of course, of trade unionism. In truth, the critique of these two organizational forms merely constitutes different sides of the same critique with roots in the critique of the selfsame, superseded historical conditions of their formation and development where the proletariat of Marx's day is contrasted with that of globalizing capital today. The change in historical conditions since Marx elaborated his conception of the proletariat now gravitates towards such a critique. The resulting conception can only be pivotal in informing perspectives and practical orientation on the question of revolutionary agency in the current global situation.

The workers' council form was a recurring product at different times and places (a political leitmotif) of the period of conjunctural, cyclical crises of the capital order. It was the most advanced form of organization created by the proletariat in struggle prior to the onset of the structural crisis of capital when the contradictions of the capital order were still displaceable. With the onset of capital's structural crisis and the relatively altered character of the proletariat itself, we need to ask questions about the adequacy of this form of organization. This is not to state categorically that the unfolding of the structural stage of capital's crisis will not produce workers' councils in different parts of the world. This may well happen. However, we need to raise the question of the 'adequacy' of the workers' council as a mode of revolutionary agency in the epoch of capital's structural crisis.

The 'Social Union' – which will be discussed in more detail later – constitutes the organizational framework which would bring together all those individuals, groups and organizations representing people being attacked by capital and its state power. It could unite industrial workers, the unemployed, benefits claimants, public sector workers, migrant workers, students, young and old, the homeless, community and campaign groups, small business holders, the 'professions', etc. Inclusiveness, mutual support and solidarity would be the watchwords of such an organization. The establishment and development of the democracy, structures, relations, etc., of this type of organization would arise out of the entry and participation of its various components as they bring their own experiences of struggle and organization into its midst. Only in this way could a rich political culture of participation be established and developed and a real non-sectarian, 'organically arisen' and sustainable form of revolutionary agency start to emerge and evolve. This contrasts, for example, with the 'Party-form' with its pre-established formal structures and 'constitution' which presents its pre-fabricated 'program and demands' to the 'masses' in the hope that it will attract a sufficient membership to make its constitution and program seem viable.

This 'organic constitution' of the 'Social Union' cannot be 'parachuted' into or imposed on the 'pluralities' from 'without' and 'from above' but must necessarily arise and crystallize out within the movement of the relations between these 'pluralities' so as to constitute an 'organizational framework' on the ground of the whole movement.

Notes and References

1 Mészáros, *Beyond Capital*, p. 699.
2 Ibid., p. 699.
3 Ibid., p. 703.
4 Ibid., p. 703.
5 Mészáros, *Beyond Capital*, p. 700.
6 Ibid., p. 699.
7 Ibid., pp. 700–701.
8 *Beyond Capital*, Part Four, Section IV, *Radical Politics and Transition to Socialism: Reflections on Marx's Centenary*, p. 941.
9 See Mészáros, *Beyond Capital*, Section 5.3, 'Women's Liberation: The Challenge of Substantive Equality', p. 187 ff.
10 The life and development of the object arises from the conflict of opposites within itself. Each object is the 'exponent' of this opposition. It is an identity that is a product of this opposition and yet, as a whole, it is qualitatively different and distinct from it. This is an example of what Hegel refers to as the '*identity of identity and difference*' in the 'Doctrine of Essence' in his *Logic*.

If we consider the object as a whole, each part of the whole develops only in relation to the movement of the whole and is connected to every other part through this whole movement. The parts are distinct from each other and from the whole only by virtue of their inseparable relation to it and to each other. Therefore, in the identity of the whole and the parts, each is distinct from the other. The movement of the whole conditions the relative movement of the parts which, in their turn, influence the whole movement. Each part has its own distinct characteristics whilst, at the same time, being continuous with and intrinsic to the life and development of the whole. In their interrelations, each part asserts its independence whilst reflecting and determining the whole movement i.e. it reveals its dependence simultaneously. Whole and parts mutually condition each other's movement. Their relation ... '*contains the independence of the sides and equally their transcendedness, and it contains both in one relation. The whole is the independent and the parts are only moments of this unity; but equally they too are the independent and their reflected unity (the whole – SM) is only a moment; and each is its independence just something relative to the other. Thus, this relation is itself immediate contradiction and cancels itself.* Hegel, *Science of Logic*, Vol. 2 (London: George Allen and Unwin, 1929), p. 144. Elaborating further, Hegel concludes that ... *'The whole and the parts therefore condition each other; [...] the whole is the condition of the parts, but also [...] is only in so far as it has the parts for presupposition'* (ibid., Vol. 2, p. 145).

The whole is qualitatively distinct from the parts. In the totality of its movement, the whole displays dependence upon, and yet its distinct independence from and conditioning of, the movement of the parts. The relationship between the whole and the parts is such that ... *'Whole and parts are indifferent to each other and have independent persistence, but also they are essentially related and constitute only one identity. The relation therefore is the antinomy that the one moment, in freeing itself from the other, immediately introduces the other'* (ibid., Vol. 2, p. 148).

Each side – the whole taken in opposition to the parts and vice versa – in repelling the other side from itself simultaneously relates itself to it in a process of identity with it. Each side, in asserting its independence, reveals its dependence and necessary connection to the other side. Each side can only exist in a state of unity with the other because they are in relation to each other as *discrete and opposed* moments in the continuity and identity of their relation. May, Shaun, 'Synopsis of Hegel's "Science of Logic"', *spmay.wordpress.com* <https://spmay.wordpress.com/synopsis-of-hegels-science-of-logic/> [Section 9].

11   Mészáros, *Beyond Capital*, p. 371.
12   Mészáros, *Marx's Theory of Alienation* (London: Merlin Press, 1975), p. 287. (Quote taken from *Geschichte und Klassenbewusstsein*, ed. cit. p. 93 [Berlin, 1923], translated by G. H. R. Parkinson.)
13   *Beyond Capital*, p. 375.
14   Ibid., p. 375.
15   On this question of vanguardism, see also Mészáros, *Beyond Capital*, p. 675 ff.
16   Moore, Joe, *The Other Japan: Conflict, Compromise, and Resistance since 1945* (Armonk, NY: M. E. Sharpe, 1997).
17   *Beyond Capital*, p. 986.

CHAPTER 11

From Trade Unions Towards the Formation of 'Social Unions'?

[i] The Struggle for Democracy within the Trade Unions

The struggle for democracy in the trade unions has always been a struggle against their control by the trade union hierarchy. The question of who controls the trade unions is primarily a *class* question. It is not simply a procedural or organizational consideration. The trade union hierarchy is the product of the class relations of the capitalist system and its very existence serves to perpetuate these relations. The bureaucratic relations of trade unionism are mediated by the class relations of bourgeois society. The trade union hierarchy – in the course of its origination and development under conditions of capitalist expansion – becomes the principal proxy of capital in the class movement of the proletariat. Historically, this has been its fundamental pro-capital role for which it has been amply rewarded.

The struggle for democracy within trade unionism is, accordingly, not simply a confrontation with its bureaucracy but is a collision with the mediating class relations founded on the existence and rule of capital. As a manifestation of the alien interests of capital in the workers' movement, the hierarchically structured relations within trade unionism confront trade unionized workers as steadfastly as does the capital relation itself in their workplace and its state power over society.

These outmoded structures are now, increasingly, serving a dual purpose. The maintenance of the privileged position of this top stratum (six-figure salaries, large pensions, perks, allocation of union properties, holidays and 'delegations' abroad, etc.) and, linked to this, acting as the disciplining proxy of capital in the workers' movement. The brick wall of bureaucratic control and inertia is an indication of the entrenched existence of separate, capital-mediated caste interests at the top of trade unionism.

How will the deepening structural crisis of capital impact these relations within trade unionism? It must generate emerging possibilities which point beyond the hierarchically structured traditional form; towards higher democratic objectives to be realized with the refoundation of a higher form of unionism. The other possibility is a continuing movement towards social vestigiality and extinction.

The question posited is, primarily, how to transform the trade unions into a higher form of agency of the proletariat, and that must, inevitably, bring members on a collision course with the whole current structure and organization of trade unionism as expressed in the conflict with the dominant bureaucratic form of rule of the top stratum.

We can envisage two scenarios here which, at root, can be resolved into either the continuing decline and extinction of trade unionism or its transformation into a higher form of agency of the proletariat in the age of capital's structural crisis. For its 'transformation', the following scenarios emerge ...

[a] the wholesale transformation of trade unionism into a higher form of agency – the 'Social Unions' – which will eclipse the 'trade union' form and give way to the higher, historically more adequate 'Social Union' form. This process of transformation will mean the actual supersedence (sublation) of trade unionism as a form of organization and its eclipse by the Social Union. The 'Social Union' would integrate within itself – as an essential aspect – the struggle for the class interests of the proletariat within the workplace. It would take on those functions – now radicalized – which trade unionism as a discrete form of organization previously and ostensibly did. But now within the broader scope, context and interests of the organization of the proletarian class as a whole. That is, trade unionism would now become superseded and re-posited as the 'workplace aspect' of Social Unionism or ...

[b] A 'revolution' within trade unionism itself which does not actually supersede trade unionism per se but actually posits it in a radicalized

form which will enable it to be used as a platform for the constitution of a higher form of Social Unionism. Within this higher form, it will be a centrally active, participatory, organically integrated and yet discrete part. In this way, trade unionism does not serve as the basis for its own self-supersedence into the higher 'Social Union' form. Rather, its current structures are democratically transformed so as to become an integrated yet discrete part of the higher form of unionism which it struggles to pioneer and establish. In this way, the continuation of trade unionism as a determinate form of organization would constitute itself as an intrinsic part of the pluralism of the Social Union, actively and directly articulating the interests of the workplace-based proletariat and serving as a sub-agency of the broader 'Social Union' in the workplace for the re-organization and restructuring of the 'workplace' beyond capital-based relations.

The fundamental distinction between the two scenarios lies in the discreteness and determinacy of trade unionism per se. In the first scenario, trade unionism itself is determinately *dissolved into Social Unionism* and ceases to exist as a separate form of organization of the proletariat. The activity of workplace-based workers becomes an integrated aspect of Social Unionism. In the second, trade unionism *retains its determinacy* but now within the overarching context of a broader Social Unionism. Its activity remains that of trade unionism per se but now as a related part of the broader Social Union movement.

The direction taken will, of course, be determined by the broad membership of the trade unions under the mediating influence of capital's deepening structural crisis. *However – and this must be emphasized – trade unionism (regardless of how 'radical' it is in organization, procedure and leadership) is historically outmoded as a discrete, separate, self-subsistent organization acting 'selfishly' and independently of a more broadly based, 'overarching', organization of the proletariat which articulates and expresses the interests of the class as a whole.* It can no longer survive as an isolated, self-subsistent 'island' (and as a form of organization more suited to past, dead 'defensive' conditions) in a 'sea' full of its non-unionized, 'drowning' brothers and sisters.

The trade union form – as an isolated, workplace-based organization simply, and putatively, representing the interests of employed workers only, regardless of form and how radical this form may be – has effectively reached the end of its historical road. It has, in this self-subsistent hierarchicalized form, entered the cul-de-sac of its own history. It has become funnelled into the 'bottleneck' of its own development as a result of the emergence, evolution and mediating influence of capital's unfolding structural crisis.

It is only in the sense of one or the other of the two above hypothesized scenarios that it will be possible for it to go beyond this 'bottleneck' and outmodedness and continue to play a progressive role in the struggle to move beyond the capital order towards socialism; to continue on a historically progressive trajectory. Needless to say, *without* its currently bureaucratized and hierarchically structured form of organization. If this latter form is maintained – in the face of capital's unfolding structural crisis – then it can only mean, in the long run, total submission to capital and its state power and the growing realization of a historic trend towards irreversible vestigiality followed by extinction.

When the capitalist media refers to the trade unions as 'dinosaurs', they know not of the import and significance of their term of castigation. For this media of capital, it is a term which denotes the necessary, inevitable and eternal triumph of capital over labour (TINA – There Is No Alternative). Whereas here, we may deploy it in order to denote the historic need for trade unionism, caught in the 'dead end of its history', to go beyond itself into a higher form of revolutionary agency of the proletariat for the epoch of capital's structural crisis.

Any possibility of a 'grassroots' movement within trade unionism realizing democratic objectives must, therefore, involve acknowledging the real existence of that which it is striving to overturn. There is a pressing need to recognize the 'constraints' and 'limitations' of the current 'state', structure and internal relations of the trade unions which serve to hamper the achievement of democratic objectives. Such 'constraints' must be recognized and faced as part of the conditions confronting us whilst still focusing on those possibilities which could enable democratic objectives and aspirations to be realized.

The current hierarchical relations within trade unionism – which actually serve to inhibit the realization of democratic objectives – will increasingly face ever-sharpening contradictions within the trade union body generated by capital's structural crisis. The response of this bureaucracy must gravitate increasingly and more comprehensively towards open alliance with capital and its state power since to do otherwise would actually serve to begin to posit the conditions for its own dissolution. In other words, the trade union hierarchies across the globe must become increasingly pro-capital and authoritarian with the worsening of this generalized structural crisis of capital.

The potential is emerging – with the intensification of capital's crisis – for trade unionism to serve as a point of departure for the 'new universal historic form' of proletarian organization which must either replace trade unionism (sublate it) or into which trade unionism must become integrated as a 'revolutionized' and active participant. This higher form of unionism – in order to be fit to deal with this developing crisis – needs to go beyond the currently self-subsistent and hierarchical form of organization of trade unionism and pass into a higher form in which a directly elective and participatory democracy is complimented by an integrated system of continuously revocable delegation, accountability and dismissability. This state of relations now becomes the necessary form of 'revolutionary democracy' as opposed to having officials and 'representatives' either elected 'once in a blue moon' or even appointed for life on featherbedded, six-figure salaries.

This perspective for changed form of organization must now be worked for within the trade union movement; to raise transitional proposals as capital's crisis deepens and becomes increasingly expressed in conflict within the body of trade unionism itself. In this sense, trade unionism contains the possibility of manifesting a very different historic role to its former one i.e. as the possibility of being the 'nursery' of a higher form of revolutionary agency.

It would be a mistake not to work within the trade unions – 'within the framework of existing institutions' (Mészáros) – and strategically inept to dismiss this vital work. A battle with the trade union hierarchy becomes more likely as the crisis within trade unionism deepens. Implicit in this conflict is the pressing need for more adequate strategies and forms of struggle against capital-in-crisis and its state power.

In a certain historical sense, the trade unions are 'finished'. But this does not dismiss them as containing the potential for the creation of a higher form of unionism. Trade unionism here displays contradictory tendencies. On the one hand, it is tied to the dead conditions of the past and, accordingly, in its isolated, exclusively workplace-based and self-subsistently bureaucratized and hierarchically structured forms, is outmoded. However, at the same time, the very crisis of capital itself posits within trade unionism the possibility of going beyond itself into a higher form or as an intrinsic, component part of such a form. It is important to acknowledge these contradictory tendencies within trade unionism which will undoubtedly sharpen as the structural crisis of capital unfolds in the course of this century.

But the so-called 'line of least resistance' cannot hold even with trade unionism bogged down in all its conservative traditions. Trade unionism will gradually decline into vestigiality or it must 'revolutionize' in going beyond this 'line'. *However, most certainly, if it tends irredeemably and irreversibly towards extinction, the proletariat will need to create forms of revolutionary agency which do not arise out of trade unionism per se but rather out of the organizational articulation of the mass struggles to come in the absence of trade unionism.* This cannot be dismissed. All conceptions and perspectives regarding the question of revolutionary agency are provisional and subject to the unfolding reality of the historical process. They are not *pronunciamento* and papal decree written on tablets of stone but are 'working conceptions' which must automatically preclude doctrinairism and the 'dead weight' of positivism.

The national state and global powers of capital have already declared a state of economic warfare on and against the life of the proletariat worldwide. This can only intensify – despite all pretensions towards a return to 'Old Labour' reformism with the election of Corbyn – because capital-in-crisis is driven by its own uncompromising logic of exploitation, profit and accumulation. Absolutely nothing must stand in the way of its untransgressable logic. The only historic force which is capable of transcending this logic of capital is the proletariat organized as revolutionary agency.

The notion of Corbyn's election being a 'blow against Blairism' is only legitimate if we consider the actual movement of hundreds of thousands which have brought Corbyn to power. A Corbyn government would find its limits determined by the unfolding conditions arising out of capital-in-crisis with any attempts to return to 'Old Labour' Keynesianism merely serving to sharpen the internal contradictions of this crisis. In truth, 'Neo-Blairism' – despite any socialist pretensions – would actually become the practical doctrine of such a government even if it repudiated it in words.

Can the trade unions pass over into a higher form of agency and incorporate themselves as a 'revolutionized', sub-agential, participatory part or a sublatively incorporated and transcended part of this higher form of agency? Or will they simply become historically vestigial and die away? They will not be able to take the former path and open out into a democratized, participatory component as they stand today i.e. as hierarchically structured, bureaucratically organized and defensively constituted organizations headed by a privileged caste.

It is because of the domination of this caste that any real organic links and organizational 'hybridizations' with the so-called 'social movements' (towards the formation and augmentation of any higher form of agency) will be severely curtailed and conditioned; limited and circumscribed according to the privileged interests of this labour caste. Such 'hybridizations' will only be established in the face of opposition to this bureaucratic caste. In spite of it and not because of it. As Mészáros clearly states ...

> as things stand today, labour as the antagonist of capital is forced to defend its interests not with one but both hands tied behind its back. One tied by forces openly hostile to labour and the other by its own reformist party and trade union leadership. The latter fulfil their special functions of personifications of capital within the labour movement itself in the service of total accommodation, and indeed capitulation, to the 'realistic' material imperatives of the system [...] Under these conditions the alternative facing the labour movement is either to resign itself to the acceptance of such constraints, or to take the necessary steps to untie its own hands, no matter how hard that course of action might be.[1]

[ii] The Case of UNITE's 'Community Membership' Initiative

The self-preserving 'blocking' function of the trade union hierarchy has been very clearly illustrated by a recent initiative in the UNITE union which is the largest trade union in Britain (about 1.42 million members, April 2016). The so-called 'community membership' scheme was launched in a blaze of publicity to recruit people from outside of the 'workplace' into this trade union. But this recruitment has taken place on the iniquitous basis that community members are barely afforded any rights at all. They are the 'second-class citizens' or 'poor relations' of UNITE without the full rights afforded to workplace-based members. Such forms of discrimination also apply to retired and unemployed members of UNITE who may have been lifetime members before retirement or unemployment.

The UNITE union rule book[2] has been amended to specifically exclude community members from a full, complete and democratic participation in the political life of the union. It precludes all community members from voting in virtually all ballots and elections and, of course, from holding any democratically mandated office in the union itself. Community members are excluded from nearly all the bodies of the union other than their local community member groups.

In perpetuating this iniquitous policy, the UNITE hierarchy is maintaining an outmoded system of differentiated rights between employed and non-employed members. Such manouevres and manipulations are an intrinsic part of the unavoidable conditions which confront us in relationship to the governance of the trade union movement today in 2017.

This bureaucratic exclusion from voting and actively participating in the full social and political life of the union means that, for the time being, any attempts at change within the union as a whole coming from the direction of the community membership is effectively blocked. The community member groups are expected to campaign on the basis of the union's policies and agenda and yet they are not given the full democratic rights of workplace-based members of the union. Only afforded a bare minimal concession, they cannot fully and democratically participate in the process of making decisions on, for example, the 'political fund' and affiliation to the Labour Party.

The union rule book of Unite has all manner of convoluted rules and bureaucratic imposition which explicitly or implicitly specify the limits of 'community membership'. Let's look at some of these superbly egalitarian clauses in the UNITE union rule book. Rule 3.3 refers to 'community membership' in which these particular members do not have ...

> an entitlement to vote in any ballot or election held by the Union other than an election to the office of General Secretary under rules 15 and 16 or any ballot or election in which all members must by statute be accorded an unconditional entitlement to vote. (page 4, Membership, UNITE rule book)

This rule effectively means that community members are precluded from voting in virtually all ballots and elections. Community members have only one solitary, occasional vote for the General Secretary every five years and, basically, that's it. It implies, according to the reading of the rules (see Rule 17, Branches, page 36), that community members cannot effectively constitute themselves as an active branch and elect branch officers because of the above Rule 3.3. Moreover, this applies according to 'Rule 17, Branches' (page 36), because 'branches' – it is explicitly stated – must be *workplace-based*.

Needless to say, because they are excluded from voting and actively participating in the full social and political life of the union, the hierarchy has very effectively put in place obstacles to any attempts at change coming from the direction of the community membership. It's rather like being given a membership card of the Women's Institute and then being told by its leader that the rules strictly state that you are not allowed to bake cakes. All 'Jerusalem' and no 'Jam'.

Rule 6.2 refers to eligibility to hold office in the union ...

> In order to be eligible to be a candidate for election to, or hold office on, the Executive Council and/or any committee, council, or other body of the Union provided for by these rules, the member in question must be an accountable representative of workers, with the exception of Area Activists Committees and Regional Political Committees as specified elsewhere in these rules. (page 9, Lay Office)

There appears to be an ambiguity or doubt about whether or not affiliated community member groups will be allowed to delegate such people to these committees (AACs and RPCs) by simple majority vote. If they do so, are they not contravening Rule 3.3, assuming that a vote to elect a delegate for these committees falls into the category of 'any ballot or election held by the Union'? Also Rule 6.2.1 ...

> Only members who are elected to represent workers will be eligible to participate in any body of the union, including any conferences, but with the exception of branch and workplace meetings (which all members can attend) and Area Activists Committees and Regional Political Committees as specified elsewhere in these Rules. (page 72, Appendix 1)

Community members are, therefore, according to this rule, excluded from all the bodies of the union other than their community member groups (which are not 'branches', according to the letter of Rule 17, and therefore where they cannot elect officers, according to rule) or the two committees specified. Notice the rule states 'can attend' and nothing about electing officers. And even here, community members cannot pass beyond the Regional Political Committees to positions on the National Political Committee because they are not 'accountable representatives of workers' as defined by Rule 6. Additionally, according to rule 3.3, community members will not be allowed to vote in any election or ballot on the AACs or RPCs.

Moreover, it appears that what is reinforced by 'Rule 17, Branches' is the *constitutional incapacity* of community members to effectively establish themselves as a branch with election of officers since *community members are not workplace-based*. The fact that they are not 'accountable representatives of workers' effectively excludes community members from holding office in the union and in the decision-making 'bodies of the union'.

The union bureaucracy has hobbled, from its inception, any real, full, active and democratic participation of 'community membership' in the full life of the union. The UNITE hierarchy effectively wants them as campaigning foot soldiers but without any substantial rights. All expectation and obligation but no rights.

Lurking underneath all the 'public relations' blurb and humbug – put out by UNITE to launch the initiative – is effectively instituted a form of internal apartheid within the union enshrined within the rule book in which community members are barely afforded any rights at all, except the undoubted privilege of being able to vote for 'The Big Cheese' once every five years. Community members are not afforded the full democratic rights of workplace-based members. The affiliated community groups are, in all but name, the outlying 'Bantustans' of UNITE.

This divisive practice of a differentiation of rights within trade unionism only serves to establish a discriminatory system of internal apartheid. And the way it has been structured means that the only hope, for the time being, for moving the trade union onto a new kind of unionism will have to come from its workplace-based membership. This division has been engineered to suit the caste interests of the UNITE bureaucracy. Prior to its launch, the status of 'community membership' was the subject of internal disputes within UNITE. The measures and rules put in place around this question clearly demonstrate – with an almost technical precision – the rule of a bureaucracy which is intensely aware of its own pecuniary and general caste interests.

The fact that UNITE has actually taken the steps (and trumpeted them in hype and publicity) to try to recruit people (the non-employed) from outside the workplace is a barely concealed acknowledgement that the trade unions are holed below the waterline and sinking fast. But giving the non-employed full and equal democratic rights (the same as employed members) is a different matter altogether. Such a measure would have implications and ramifications for the way in which the proletariat as a class actually organizes its trade unions and articulates its resistance to the rule of capital-in-crisis. It would posit the possibility where people could start to create the conditions for a totally new and different type of unionism. This is why the UNITE executive has ruled 'full and equal rights' absolutely out of the question.

A truly democratic and openly transparent move forward within the trade unions – recruiting people from outside the trade unions on a genuinely egalitarian basis – could form the embryonic, fertile ground for the emergence and growth of a higher form of unionism which could still, nevertheless, articulate the interests of members in the actual workplaces to a far greater extent and to a far higher degree of effectiveness than they are articulated at the moment with workplace-based trade unionism alone. It would involve the collaboration of the class as a whole within and outside the workplace. It would be a form of unionism (Social Unions) which would serve to undermine the historically privileged position of the top stratum of trade unionism and bring the whole class together within a new form of combative unionism.

In terms of structure, procedure and outlook, we need to ask what has fundamentally changed since Rosa Luxemburg wrote that ...

> The specialization of professional activity as trade-union leaders, as well as the naturally restricted horizon which is bound up with disconnected economic struggles in a peaceful period, leads only too easily, amongst trade-union officials, to bureaucratism and a certain narrowness of outlook ... There is first of all the overvaluation of the organization, which from a means has gradually been changed into an end in itself, a precious thing, to which the interests of the struggles should be subordinated. From this also comes that openly admitted need for peace which shrinks from great risks and presumed dangers to the stability of the trade unions, and further, the overvaluation of the trade-union method of struggle itself, its prospects and its successes.[3]

[iii] Transitional Proposals and a 'SUM' within and outside Trade Unionism?

A movement unaware that it has outlived its historical usefulness (that it is historically outmoded) is a movement in irreversible decline. It is sinking into the quicksands of historical time without any awareness of the need to pull itself out of the quagmire and return to a form of movement which is historically and politically adequate to address the demands imposed by the altered conditions of the new age of capital's structural crisis. A movement 'aware' of this 'outmodedness' is a different matter altogether.

The existence of the trade union bureaucracy – its privileges and self-serving system of control as a ruling caste within the workers' movement – is predicated on the continuation of the capital order. Its 'ideal' 'default' position is (and always has been) a reformable capitalism on the incontrovertible and unchallengeable basis of the rule of capital. The onrush of capital's structural crisis renders this position historically untenable. Under such conditions, capitalism ceases to be subject to any significant reformability in favour of the proletariat as a class. In fact, all previous reforms which preceded the structuralization of capital's crisis are now being reversed and erased in the attempts of capital and its state powers to counter the dynamic of this crisis.

All areas of the social metabolism which actively hinder or simply 'stand in the way' of this 'counter-dynamic' are now subject to being drawn into the orbit of the pre-eminent capitalist criterion: can surplus value be extracted, maximized and capital accumulated regardless of the most terrible costs to human beings or nature? The widespread appropriation and exploitation of any form of public provision for profit – along with the mass catastrophic and most disturbing forms of destruction of ecological habitats and nature's living creation – are the most salient categories which are being subject to this overriding criterion of the augmented reproduction of value.

The trade union hierarchy is a part of the whole problem because it is not in the existential interests of this ruling labour caste for this system of increasingly 'destructive reproduction of capital' to be challenged in order to create the conditions for its global supersedence. Within the trade unions – and outside – the evolving conditions of capital's deepening structural crisis point towards the need for an actual movement which can pioneer the 'new universal historic form' of proletarian organization to take on the capital system and bury it once and for all in the graveyard of history.

The proletariat has reached a historical cul-de-sac in terms of its present forms of organization and their associated consciousness. It continues, generally, with the old methods and mechanisms of struggle which are more suited to past, dead conditions: the strike (usually for no more than a couple of days), the demonstration, the parliamentary lobby, etc. But new strategies and tactics are now required in response to the altered conditions.

An example of this is the recent struggle of residents on the New Era estate in Hackney, London, who refused to vacate their rented homes to make way for the 'development' of luxury apartments by American property speculators Westbrook. They organized and simply refused to comply and can now remain in their homes for the foreseeable future. Westbrook was forced to cut its losses and sell the estate to a housing charity. These sections of the proletariat are indicating the way forward. To defend the interests of your communities, you have to go on the offensive against capital.

The only way to fully oppose capital-in-crisis today is to come together and organize collectively as a class and not simply as one narrow, workplace-based section of it. Trade Unionism in isolation and by itself is inadequate for this task. To begin to mobilize and organize the resistance to the destruction and devastation already taking place and rapidly worsening. This implies the need to work towards the establishment of new forms of agency which are adequate enough to build and spearhead resistance to the capital order itself.

Trade unions – in their present hierarchicalized organizational form and isolatedly self-subsistent mode of existence and operation – are not the type of organizations through which such total interests of the proletariat can be identified, consolidated and developed. Such an organization which brings many together – workers in production and service sectors, providers and users, etc. – on the basis of *this identity of social interest which is their common class interest* will require a leap forward in both organization and consciousness. Such an organization will be a Social Union and not a trade union.

The historical need for the organizational expression of this 'identity of interest' can be most clearly seen in the realm of the provision of public services where there is – and increasingly will be – a need to address the relations between service providers and users. The 'identity of interest' here, between service users and providers, needs to be articulated in practice through social and political organization.

One of the most insidious tactics deployed by capital and its print and broadcasting media in relation to public provision is to pit service users against service providers on strike as if their interests are inherently opposed and irreconcilable. It is the ancient divide and rule tactic applied within the new circumstances of the age of capital.

The 'new universal historic form' of proletarian organization must be structured in a way which politically articulates the identity of class interests between those who are providing and those who are using public provision. Indeed, in reality, 'providers' and 'users' are themselves, in one way or another, identical. The Social Union is a form of organization that can work and serve to overcome this *ersatz* antagonism which is encouraged by capitalist governments and their mouthpieces in the print and broadcasting media in order to divide the proletariat and put one section of the class against another. *Divide et Impera* was the watchword of the Roman imperium.

One strategy of moving towards the 'Social Union' form implicates a movement both within and outside trade unionism to fight for its realization. It would involve the initiation and development of a network of trade unionists within the trade unions (in liaison and networking with those individuals and organizations who support it outside the trade unions) to fight for the establishment of these higher Social Unions. For example, a 'Social Unions Movement' or 'Social Unions Network' ('SUM' or 'SUN') whose principal objective is the creation of these Social Unions. We could, perhaps, compare the objectives of such a movement with the way in which the UNITE hierarchy has approached its 'community membership' initiative involving the creation of a second-class category of members. For example, the political work of a SUM would be to organize and network within and outside the trade unions and propose, for example, the following transitional demands ...

> [a] The recruitment of people into the trade union movement from all areas of 'non-employment' i.e. from outside the workplace. For example, students, the unemployed, home-based individuals, etc.
> [b] An end to the discriminatory practice within the trade unions of different types of membership. The establishment of one single form of membership in which all members of the trade unions – employed or non-employed – have the same, full, equal, democratic rights. In order that every member can potentially or actually play a full role in the life of the union.
> [c] The creation of a sliding scale of membership subscriptions in which rights afforded to individual trade union members are not linked to the amount of the subscription fee paid out and such a fee is linked to the ability of individuals to pay. Fees to be waived in cases of proven need. For example, the unwaged, people on low incomes, students, etc., would pay a lower fee than those in full-time employment.
> [d] The initiation and elaboration of other demands considered to be productive to the development of a wider, more democratic, more inclusive and broader form

of unionism which represents the interests of a wider range and greater number of people i.e. articulates the interests of the class as a whole rather than simply its paid/salaried employed sections.

In Britain, demand [a] is already being carried through by some trade unions as we have seen with UNITE's community membership initiative but proposals [b] and [c] (without which [a] is rendered impotent and with which very profound changes and ramifications are implied for the way in which the proletariat actually organizes and articulates its resistance to the rule of capital-in-crisis) are absolutely out of the question as far as the trade union bureaucracy is concerned. It would mean the creation of the conditions for a higher form of unionism which could still, nevertheless, articulate the interests of members in the actual workplace to a far greater extent and to a far higher degree of effectiveness than they are articulated at the moment with current trade unionism per se. In line with the projection of the character of the Social Union, it would mean that all participants – employed or non-employed, organizations, affiliates, etc. – in the activities of the Social Union would have equal status with full and equal democratic rights for all.

The Social Union is a form of agency which would bring together producers and providers with consumers and users and locate its antagonist as the whole capital order itself and the state power which defends it. Such a type of organization would be of a fundamentally and qualitatively new typicality compared to previous defensive forms. It would constitute itself in response to the attacks taking place on the lives of millions by capital-in-crisis and its state power and would soon start to become the representative organ and organizational spearhead in the struggle against both capital within the social metabolism and its state power. Such a new type of broad-based, mass organization is becoming increasingly necessary with each passing day as the structural crisis of the capital order deepens. Trade unionism alone, in and by itself – and especially within its current bureaucratized structures and form of organization – is inadequate (historically outmoded) to deal with the maturing, unfolding crisis.

Fundamentally, the historic role of the Social Union – as an organization of struggle of and for the proletariat – would be directed towards mobilization against the predation of capital on the social body, the appropriation of its powers in the course of restructuring the social metabolism and the defence of these measures against the state power. And this, of course, would necessitate the development of new forms of struggle, new strategies and tactics not deployed widely before in the past because now we are operating under qualitatively and historically different conditions of struggle in the age of capital's structural crisis. The Social Union becomes the first line of offence against the capital order and its state power.

This is not to say that tactics from previous times like strikes, demonstrations, etc., are absolutely redundant. Quite the contrary. They would have a more important role but now within a totally different historical context where the intensity of struggle is heightening. There will be an increasing need to apply the strike weapon contingently and tactically when it is advantageous to the interests of the whole class and not if it undermines that interest in part or as a whole. The strike tactic would be elaborated alongside, and complementary to, the occupation and communal appropriation of threatened services, etc.

This crisis of the capital order today at the start of the twenty-first century is not a displaceable, conjunctural, cyclical crisis as we witnessed in the previous history of the capital order. It is intractably structural, enduring, broadening and deepening. The capital order – well beyond its 'prime' – now enters its period of breakdown and disintegration. The significance of this in terms of the way labour has traditionally organized is profound. It must bring in the deepest possible crisis for labour in regard to the forms within which it has traditionally organized and the strategies it has adopted in the past. The old forms will have to be 'thrown off' and replaced with radically new, offensive forms of organization in order to conduct the struggle against capital-in-crisis.

It must be stressed that there is nothing inevitable about this 'throwing off' actually taking place. History does not unfold according to a providential plan. Humans make their own history in response to the conditions which are confronting them. And if they do not make this absolutely necessary step – as an indispensable part of the historical process of ending the epoch of capital – a catastrophe of historically unprecedented proportions and magnitude awaits humanity in the forthcoming century.

It is not simply a case of 'waiting for the apples to ripen and drop from the tree'. If we proceed in that way, there will be neither tree nor apples remaining. The tree must be shaken with all our might, determination, vigour, audacity and ruthlessness. And only then will we be able to collect the fruit. The global capital order must be uprooted, cast into the furnace of history and replaced with a socialist society which can then proceed to evolve on its own self-created foundations based on common ownership and ecologically sustainable and planned management of the planet and its resources.

The wishful thinking of the salaried 'end of history' ideologues of capital is revealed in reality to be the complete sham that it is in thought. History is reaching a fork in the road. One road leads to a continuing and intensifying barbarism and mass destruction of humanity and nature. The other to socialism. The condition of global communist human life becomes the historical transcendence of capital and its state powers. This is the historic task facing the global proletariat itself. The proletariat (capital's structural antagonist) must now work towards the formation of the necessary initial forms of social and political agency which can actually commence the process of restructuring the socio-economic metabolism beyond the capital relation itself. That is, to commence the process of removing the capital relation itself from human society by making inroads into this domination by capital. But the commencement of this process will, indeed must, raise the opposition of the national state and global powers of capital itself. Implicit in this opposition is the dissolution of those state powers in order for the social horizon to be fully opened up, fully unhindered, so that this process of restructuring of society's landscape can be completed, fully consummated, by the necessary and evolving forms of revolutionary agency.

Marx divided his monumental study, *Capital*, into different interconnected parts. Volume 1, of the process of the production of capital; Volume 2, of the process of its circulation; and Volume 3, of capitalist production as a whole which assimilates and develops the content of the two previous volumes. Marx's study was left unfinished at his death. He planned further volumes on classes and the state, foreign trade and the world market, and further analyses of crises of the capital order.

The emergence, development and domination of capital, Marx reveals, is the foundation out of, and on, which the class relations of capitalist society develop and the state power becomes that of capital. i.e. the state power becomes the organized political power of capital. The capital order expands out of its 'homelands', out of this 'little corner of the Earth' (Marx was referring to Europe as the first capitalist region of the planet[4]) and becomes established as a global order; so-called 'globalization'. In the course of this process, global trade and the world market develop which leads necessarily onwards towards the structural crisis of the global capital order.

We are now living through the unfolding and maturation of this structural crisis. This calls for a fundamentally new type of unionism; a 'new universal historic form' of organization of the proletariat. A form which becomes an advance and development beyond mere trade unionism for the struggle against capital and its state power – to eradicate capital from the social metabolism – whilst also simultaneously being a return to a higher form of unionism as revolutionary agency.

Above all, what is required is a 'new universal historic form' which is capable of *offensively articulating* itself against the capital order on all levels – especially the economic and political level – and, if assaulted violently by the state power, is also capable of adopting and developing tactics and strategies of defence and offence against such state violence. The military implications of this would be inescapable.

[iv] The Social Union as the Revolutionary Democracy of the Class Movement of the Proletariat

The form of revolutionary agency implicit against the globality of the destructive manifestations of capital's crisis would undoubtedly bring together – vis-à-vis trade unionism – a greater diversity of proletarians into a single 'organizational framework'. It would possess a higher degree of historical concreteness in comparison to trade unionism. It would be more open, transparent and democratic than previous forms of agency and would operate to bring together proletarians who were previously separated from each other. For example, 'white' and 'blue collar', manual and professional, men and women, industrial and service sector worker, local and migrant worker, young and old, employed and jobless, students, the homeless, marginalized, environmentalists, etc. Its richer social composition (diversity-in-unity) would mean, necessarily and correspondingly, a far richer agenda of perspectives than trade unionism could ever elaborate. It would be orientated against the devastating effects of capital's crisis on the natural and cultural conditions of human life and articulating in struggle the need to defend and preserve these conditions for the future society.

It would, therefore, be a continuation and outgrowth of previous 'confrontational' activity. It would grow out of such struggles but it would also start to move towards the positing of organization which is qualitatively higher than mere 'mutual support', differentially expressing itself 'exponentially' as a qualitatively distinct whole from the mere 'sum of its component parts'. Through participation and the establishment of 'overarching' structures and procedures which arise 'organically' from within the relationships of the 'plurality' of participating parts, the coalition would develop into a new type of organized movement of the proletariat for the epoch of capital's structural crisis: a movement of Social Unions against the capital order worldwide.

We could, perhaps, envisage the seeds (embryonic elements) of the formation of such a movement through the creation of alliances between different organizations, campaigns and groups. There would be mutual support for the separate demands of each component of the coalition whilst, at the same time, pressing ahead on discussions and agreement on overarching demands to which all components of the alliance could subscribe. It may only start with a few groups/campaigns but as the benefits of this mutual support alliance were realized by each of the components working together as a whole, it would then possibly attract new groups and individuals to join or to 'crystallize' and 'condense' around it. A steady growth may see the transition from a mere alliance or coalition of groupings towards a larger, umbrella-type organization and then later, conditions permitting, towards a more-embracing, wider, 'organizational framework' in the form of a 'Social Union' against capital.

The conception that such organizations could only arise at *the zenith of crisis* needs to be treated with caution, circumspectly. And perhaps owes more in its approach to the ways in which workers' councils emerged rapidly in times of intense crisis throughout the twentieth century.

In the currently and indefinitely unfolding structural crisis situation as we see today (and not a cyclic, 'boom and bust', conjunctural one), the possibility of such new organizations emerging out of seemingly imperceptible shifts in conditions cannot be discounted. The qualitatively different (structural) character of capital's crisis means that previous parameters, criteria and 'models' – against which the possible emergence of workers' councils or Soviets were measured under 'conjunctural' conditions – can no longer be unconditionally applied to the emergence of new forms of revolutionary agency in the presently evolving epoch of capital-in-crisis. Of course, the more severe the manifestations of capital's structural crisis, the more likely are the conditions to be generated for the formation of Social Unions. But this is not to assert that such organizations cannot begin to come into being under more stable conditions of capital's structural crisis and start to prepare the grounds for their later development.

Alliances could be provisional at first but the advantage afforded to each member component by such a mutual support system of organization could attract more groups and individuals into a larger, more permanent cohesive totality. Each campaign would maintain its autonomy of action whilst, at the same time, receiving support from, and working to support, other component members and the growth of the coalition as a whole through its active participation. In this way, the coalition/alliance itself would, through participation and mutuality, start to develop into an organization which is qualitatively greater than and distinct from a mere sum of its component organizational parts. Such forms of 'sublated autonomy' would also simultaneously become intrinsic to a growing, unifying and cohesive interdependence.

The proletariat needs to establish and develop for itself forms of organization which can best articulate the interests of the proletariat as a whole class. To do this means to establish structures and forms of organization in which all participants see the organization as 'their own'. That is, a movement which would be organized and structured 'horizontally', democratically and consensually in which the democracy of the movement is organic, intrinsic, inalienable. This would be diametrically opposed to the 'Party' or 'Soviet bureaucratic' or the current 'trade union' type of centralized pyramidal structure which is 'vertical', hierarchical, superimposed on the proletariat with an arisen, alienated, detached and demarcated centre. In the structure of the Social Union, the 'centre' would be *totally subservient* to the democracy of the organization as a whole and not vice versa. *The 'centre' would be the 'servant' – not the 'master' – of the whole.*

In its pluralistic composition and activity, it would reflect both the immediate partial interests of its component parts and the long term aims and objectives ('reconciliation of immediate interest and long term aim') of the proletariat in its historic struggle to begin to restructure the socio-economic landscape beyond capital and to necessarily break the political power of capital. The structures and procedures of the organization would be based on, and decided through, a system of open and transparent democracy, election, recall, accountability and dismissability.

At this point, can we envisage the possible democratic structures and procedures of such an organization, of the Social Union as a determinate structure? How can the proletariat as a revolutionary class put in place measures and structures which ensure that the past mistakes, such as bureaucratic usurpation, etc., do not establish a foothold? What does 'democracy' actually mean for us as a class? The so-called 'democracy' of the capitalist class, of course, is not what we mean by democracy. How can we maintain, enrich and develop the continuity of our democracy in the period of transition with all its inevitable problems, contradictions, etc?

The fundamental principles of organization and internal procedure would have to be delegation, democracy and accountability. In the following context, to delegate would be understood to mean the assigning of responsibility and authority to a *subordinate* of the Social Union. It would not be the same as the appointment of a representative as, for example, in bureaucratized trade unions where the highly paid, elected-for-life general or regional secretary is the elected 'representative' of the union. The delegation we speak of here is something totally different. Indeed the complete inverse and opposite. *It would mean that those who are elected to the 'highest positions' in the union are those who are most subordinate and most accountable in their work.*

The size and complexity of the Social Union would necessitate delegation to its elected subordinates. The process of delegation would confer sufficient authority on delegates to enable them to make decisions in the absence of the assembly of the Social Union, i.e. discretion to act during intermittent periods. Obligations on delegates, therefore, would come with the rights and means to fulfill tasks decided by the union and the capacity of delegates to make decisions as its elected subordinates in the absence of the assembly. The decisions of the delegate would, of course, always be subject to approval or reprimand/reversal by the union at any time and point of recall.

Accordingly, through this democratic procedure, delegates would be given authority by, and remain accountable to, the Social Union as a whole. The decisions of the Social Union always standing higher than and superseding the decisions of the delegate. Any disputes are therefore ultimately decided by the democracy of the Social Union as a whole which is supreme.

The Social Union would decide by democratic process who it shall elect as delegates. It would work out and confirm by vote a process of nomination of candidates to be put forward for election by the assembly of the Social Union. The responsibilities and authority of delegates being generalized, circumscribed and understood by the union and the delegate. All delegates would be subject to a process of mandatory re-election annually, at least, in which the delegate can be re-affirmed or dismissed in his/her duties. Discretionary dismissal or re-election (re-affirmation) on recall at any time on majority vote of the Social Union at any given organizational level: local, regional, national, international.

The present trade union system where leading figures in the top stratum are elected by a one-off single vote of the membership or simply appointed (as in the British TUC) – and then effectively sit enthroned until pensioned off and are not subject to recall and dismissal at any time – would be abolished and replaced with a more democratic, ongoing system of revocable delegation.

An outline of the delegational process, for example, might be ...

1. Nomination of candidates
2. Election
3. Continuous monitoring of the appointee in his/her duties/role as delegate by the Social Union
4. Recall (procedure to be determined by the union)
5. Accountability process by means of a quorate assembly of the union
6. Dismissal and replacement by election or re-affirmation as delegate by the assembly

With the following possible democratic principles and procedures ...

1. Delegates to be elected by simple majority at a quorate assembly meeting of the union (whose number shall be determined by the union) and empowered to work for the Social Union in a specified capacity as determined by the union.
2. All delegates to be subject to recall at any time. The recall of delegates must afford a period of notice to the delegate so s/he has time to prepare a defence, if wishing to do so, against any charges made prior to the process proper of accountability of the Social Union assembly.
3. At the aforesaid assembly, the recalled delegate to be subjected to a process of accountability as determined by the Social Union.
4. The assembly of the union – by simple majority vote – to either dismiss the recalled delegate or re-affirm him/her in his/her position as delegate of the union.
5. New nominees for any vacant positions to be put forward as candidates and elected by simple majority vote at a quorate meeting, etc.

With the development and improvement of general information technology and internet communications over the past two decades, this process of delegational democracy would today be rendered easier, more accessible and participative than it would have been in the past, even the recent past.

In the transitional period, the social control of planning and centralization must be carried through democratically and not imposed bureaucratically from above. This is where the question of the form of agency is fundamental and critical. With the currently developing level of information technology and automation, the co-operation of producers would be facilitated and the collating of information regarding production levels, planning, etc., rendered easier than in previous times. This can all be carried through democratically without bureaucratic imposition. Delegation of such tasks on a regional and national level can, accordingly, fall within this democratic framework and remit.

The democracy and authority of the Social Union would be paramount. Procedures are established in order to serve as the basis for the Social Union to monitor the work of delegates and safeguard against the possibility of the rise of bureaucratic power and its imposition on the democracy of the union. This would constitute an attack by capital against the union and its movement as a whole. Accordingly, the activities of delegates would be subject on the whole to the democracy, decisions and will of the Social Union as a whole i.e. in the finality of matters, delegates would be serving as conduits for the decisions and activities of the Social Union. They would be its dismissable servants. Not its entrenched figureheads or masters.

The social power of the union – with this system of revocable delegational democracy – flows from the Social Union upwards to the elected delegates and always returns to that power base, arising out of its democracy, decisions and resolution. Therefore, all empowerment, authorization and disempowerment would necessarily reside with the Social Union as a whole, i.e. under its political control. The 'highest' body for each country (which would, at the same time, be the most subordinate body) would be the general national assembly of the Social Union which articulates and expresses the decision-making process of the union as a whole. The emphasis is to safeguard against the rise and entrenchment of bureaucratic imposition, power being usurped and concentrated in the hands of individuals/groups which cannot be shifted out of their positions and thereby flouting the open, transparent and popular democracy of the Social Union. *This must be avoided at all costs.*

The fundamental presupposition for the existence of the Social Union is the emergence and unfolding of capital's structural crisis and the union's ontological roots in a broad, proletarian class base to 'feed' it and hold it together. The Social Unions must be genuinely constituted as mass-orientated organizations in order to form the basis of the historic process of restructuring the social metabolism beyond capital.

The Social Union will start to address both the immediate tasks confronting the class under the prevailing conditions and those long term social objectives based on a grasp of the unfolding trajectory of the crisis of capital, a fusion or synthesis of both in its organization and work. For any organization to neglect or focus on one at the expense of the other is for it to either become 'lost' in the immediacy and particularity of the 'economism' of the moment or to abstractly divorce itself from the present day tasks confronting us as a class.

The actual addressing in practice of both immediate tasks and long-term objectives are not spatio-temporally separate but rather are embodied in one and the same forms of activity. Without the elaboration of 'long-term aims' (with a constant eye on what is coming into being as capital's crisis deepens), the Social Union will simply sink into and drown in the immediate tasks confronting it. But without addressing the 'immediate interests', it separates itself from the everyday concerns and struggles of the proletariat. The overall task will be to 'reconcile' (synthesize) both aspects and move forward on that basis with purposeful determination and ruthlessness against capital and its state power.

The Social Union cannot actually exist organizationally on the basis of long-term objectives and perspectives alone. It must be (and can only be) ultimately rooted in the vitality and driving force of the contradictions of the immediate. It cannot exist on the basis of the cult-ontology and methods of approach of the left-wing sect. Accordingly, any movement within trade unionism (for example, a 'SUM' or 'SUN') must carry with it this principle of the 'unity of the immediate and the mediate'; of what is directly confronting us today (how we proceed against it) and what is mediating its development as capital's historic crisis unfolds (how we organize for the restructuring of the whole socio-economic landscape currently governed by capital). In terms of where the proletariat is today, with its traditional trade union form and consciousness, this means, of course, bringing together what is actually done now in contemporary struggles – 'economistic' or otherwise – at this present stage in the unfolding of the capital's structural crisis, with the struggle for the required agency of revolution to go beyond the capital relation and its state power.

This 'synthesis' must be reflected in the way the Social Union is actually organized and proceeds in both its internal democracy and its mobilization against capital. To actually make this 'connection' means to participate in the present struggles (e.g. a strike, campaigns, etc.) not simply in order that they shall be successful but to participate in order to politically mediate the realization of long-term objectives.

The questions and worsening problems of the immediate situation confronting the proletariat can be truly addressed and resolved – under the conditions of the deepening crisis of the capital order – only by tactically developing the overall strategic perspective of the restructuring of the social metabolism beyond capital and the overthrow of its national state and global powers. The realization of long-term aims and the addressing of immediate tasks is inseparable from the question of agency. It is a question which cannot be left unanswered any longer as capital-in-crisis opens up its offensive against the proletariat and nature's creation. And against the full panoply of public provision which the proletariat has historically taken for granted but which is now starting to disappear into the whirlpool of capital's inexorable crisis-movement.

Notes and References

1 Mészáros, István, *Beyond Capital*, Section 18.4.7, p. 729 (London: Merlin Press, 1995).
2 Union rule book of UNITE. Effective from Rules Conference 2011 (updated by the Executive Council to December 2012) (Unite the Union, n.d.) <http://www.unitenow.co.uk/index.php/documents/documents/union-proceduresrules-and-policy-documents/206-rule-book-dec-2012/file> (Last accessed 2 November 2016).
3 Luxemburg, Rosa, 'The Mass Strike, the Political Party, and the Trade Unions'. In *The Essential Rosa Luxemburg*, edited by Helen Scott, pp. 105–182 (Chicago: Haymarket Books, 2008), p. 177.

4 '*The proper task of bourgeois society is the creation of the world market, at least in outline, and of the production based on that market. Since the world is round, the colonisation of California and Australia and the opening up of China and Japan would seem to have completed this process. For us, the difficult **question** is this: on the Continent revolution is imminent and will, moreover, instantly assume a socialist character. Will it not necessarily be **crushed** in this little corner of the earth, since the **movement** of bourgeois society is still, in the **ascendant** over a far greater area?*'

Karl Marx to Frederick Engels (8 October 1858), *Marx-Engels Collected Works, Volume 40* (London: Lawrence & Wishart, 1983), pp. 345–347 (bold denotes original emphasis by Marx).

CHAPTER 12

The Social Union as Revolutionary Agency against the Capital Order

[i] The Universality of Capital's Structural Crisis Drives the Conflict between the 'Social Unions' and 'Capital in Power'

As capital's crisis becomes more generalized and deepens, the social basis of the opposition to the manifestations of this crisis must inevitably widen, become augmented and diversify in its social composition. The structural crisis of capital must draw in an increasing number of people and more sections of the proletariat – in opposition to its manifestations – which before had escaped, or had remained relatively unaffected by, the unfolding effects of capital's crisis.

The growing intensification of the structural crisis of capital can only mean a historically unprecedented degree of destruction of the natural and cultural conditions of human existence itself. Increasingly, as each day passes, we witness on a global scale the horrendous effects on nature and humanity of the profit-driven activities arising out of capital's crisis. The wholesale destruction of natural habitats and their species for profit where advances made in biological science could actually enrich these habitats, the deaths of thousands of human beings every day from malnutrition in a world glutted with food and with the advanced technique required to produce food for all (according to UN figures, as a statistical average, one person dies every three seconds from malnutrition or a related condition),[1] millions condemned to an unfulfilling and mentally crippling existence in their daily lives, the predatory exploitation of the young, etc., are just a few of the broad categorizations which the development of capital's global crisis is creating and perpetuating. Its crisis is not exclusively economic or a crisis of the capital relation itself in isolation from the whole. It affects and is animating every single aspect of human life on the planet. Truly, a historical global storm of unprecedented, and previously unthought of, proportions is in the process of gathering.

Mass destruction of humanity and nature, social fragmentation, war and alienation in its multitudinous forms are interconnected consequences of the driving logic of the global trajectory of the capital order in crisis. *This developing process of the widespread destruction of humanity and nature can only be ended with the wholesale uprooting of the capital relation on a global scale and its historical negation as the fundamentally determining relation of the socio-economic metabolism.* To replace a society founded on the capital relation with one founded on the identification, cultivation and refinement of historically created human needs.

It is the deepening effects of this structural crisis of the capital system which motivate and drive the proletariat towards revolution, pushing it onwards under fire. If we, the proletariat, try to 'go on in the old way' we will become increasingly subject to the more profound, more brutal and barbaric effects of this intensifying crisis, becoming and being 'determined' in all aspects by these effects and tending to become as a class of paupers, beggars, low-wage slaves and vagabonds like the oppressed, downtrodden classes towards the latter end of the Roman period, of the colonate of late empire. This, of course, would not resolve the question for capital. Rather, it would intensify the whole crisis. What would arise subsequent to this is anybody's guesswork but catastrophic and horrific are words too mild to employ.

Human history is an 'open-ended' process. The 'fate' of humanity, insofar as it expresses the indwelling necessities and laws of development of capitalism, is an abstract metaphysic (the favourite preoccupation of 'the contemplative') when taken and deployed independently of the consciousness-mediated activities of real men and women. This means the real 'fate of humanity' resides in the hands of thinking-acting humanity itself. If this were otherwise, the maxims of the ancient Stoics would be incontrovertible. Human beings would be the mere 'playthings' of 'objective conditions' rather than being, simultaneously, their creations and creators.

Socialism is not the *inevitable outcome* of the development of capitalism. If that were the case, it would be the most pleasant of pleasant scenarios which would enable us all to sit back and wait for the appointed time of global capitalism's collapse. And then enter the remains of the proletariat to simply re-organize everything on socialist foundations. The benevolent spectre of the socialist future would then beckon humanity into its bosom only when fate had designated the appointed time. *En attendant* and fatalism would then replace revolutionary dialectics as the only legitimate *Zeitgeist* for all else would be futility in opposition. The 'wind bloweth where it listeth' would be the underlying *Leitmotif* and *Zeitgeist* of every social epoch.

In the present epoch, capital-in-crisis has not only created the conditions required for socialism but is also, at the same time, actively destroying those self-same conditions as a result of the playing out of its immanent nature. Capital's crisis must tend, undeniably, towards worsening phases. From a lengthy historical era of cyclical, conjunctural crises ('boom and bust' phases) towards an all-embracing, global structural crisis and onwards towards the intensification of the latter. And, inevitably, with all the worsening and crippling effects on the mode of life of the proletariat. It is the unfolding of this crisis-process which generates the conditions necessary for the emergence of organs of socialist revolution, for the necessary form of revolutionary agency of the proletariat; for the 'new universal historic form' of organization of the proletariat.

This is not to state that this form will inevitably come into existence under such conditions. Rather, the emergence and development of these crisis conditions continuously augments only the possibility of its birth and growth. It is, accordingly, this same crisis-process which would mediate and animate the subsequent actions of this agency once it had emerged to go forward and to resolve the crisis by the commencement of the process of going beyond the capital relation itself as the ground of the existence of capitalism and even of a period of 'post-capitalism'.

The principal political antagonist to the project of 'revolutionary agency' in this transitional period is, of course, the national state and global powers of capital. Powers which are constituted as state bureaucracies, police and armed forces, judiciary, prisons, and supplemented by the agencies of capital's media.

In relation to these powers – hovering menacingly above society – the default position of 'agency' – whilst not absolutely precluding the possibility of a 'peaceful transition' – would be a recognition of their violent and predatory character. These powers would – almost inevitably, to defend the class relations upon which they are founded – refuse to afford the proletariat a 'peaceful transition' to the new society. Accordingly, 'revolutionary agency' must organize for the defeat and dissolution of these national state and global powers of capital in order to open up and clear the horizon completely for the comprehensive elimination of capital from the social metabolism. *By peaceful means if possible. By means of war if necessary.*

The unfolding of capital's structural crisis is filling every channel, every tributary, capillary and cell of society, infusing itself and its effects into every aspect, without exception, of the life and relationships of society. No aspect is exempted, including the interpersonal, the moral and the aesthetic. *It is this universalizing crisis-process of capital which is increasingly making necessary the formation of fundamentally new types of organization (the 'new universal historic form' of proletarian organization) through which the proletariat can oppose the effects of this crisis and, ultimately, transcend the capital relation itself and its state powers and global agencies.* An essential role of these new organizations would be to defend the natural and socio-cultural conditions of the future human society which capital is destroying in the epoch of its structural crisis.

The very nature of this historic crisis, the widening of its extensive and especially the deepening of its intensive character, on a global scale, gives rise to the social need for such proletarian organizations *of a fundamentally new typicality* which, as society's representative bodies par excellence, can do no other but confront capital and bring these new bodies into direct conflict with the state power of capital itself as the historic representative of capital. The development of capital's structural crisis constitutes the historic ground for their social necessity, for their sociogenesis.

This defence of the natural and socio-cultural conditions of human life can only be realized if these novel organizations move onto an offensive trajectory to appropriate and re-direct the powers of capital in the midst of the latter's crisis. These organs ('Social Unions') would commence this process because they could do no other as the crisis and its effects worsen. It is, therefore, this crisis which would animate the taking over of capital's powers and the start, at the same time, of the re-structuring of the socio-economic metabolism towards a socialist one beyond capital.

This intensely political process would inevitably generate the most tenacious opposition from the state powers of capital and its global agencies. It is not that – in a mechanical, formalized, concatenated fashion – crisis must give birth to these agencies of revolution and then the conquest of state power must occur prior to the restructuring of the socio-economic metabolism. Rather, it is only in the compelled initiation ('imperative need' – Marx) and elaboration of struggle – by the proletariat through its agency ('Social Unions') in response to capital's intensifying crisis in the presence of its state power – that it can actually develop in the direction to expropriate, appropriate and deploy capital's powers in order to begin to resolve the crisis by pointing beyond capital. Moreover, only by engaging offensively with new strategies and tactics, can agency itself continuously re-create and develop itself in order to confront the changing circumstances which capital in power is directing at it.

The 'Social Union' is an organ for the actual restructuring of the socio-economic landscape beyond capital and for the taking over of capital's political powers for social refoundation in the presence of the state power of capital. It functions as a 'singularity' in which these different sides of the restructuring process constitute its co-ordinated activity as society's organizational mechanism to begin to move beyond the epoch of capital.

This, of course, would simultaneously bring on the conflict over who rules: the proletariat through its Social Unions *or* the state power of capital. Only when the state powers of capital are defeated – in the most significant regions of the planet and therefore as a global power – would the vista truly and fully open up for a complete, generalized, extensive and intensive restructuring of the socio-economic metabolism to go beyond the capital order itself. This would mean the continuation, growth and intensification of the very same process of transcending the capital relation which had commenced prior to the overthrow of these 'significant' state powers.

The organic process of restructuring can only become fully consummated when the political power of capital has been irreversibly defeated and consigned to the 'lumber room' of history. But this does not mean that this process cannot commence in the actual presence of capital and its state powers. Indeed, it must and can only commence in their presence.

Therefore, synchronously, (within the self-same historic spatio-temporality) revolutionary agency ('Social Unions') would not only begin to restructure the socio-economic landscape but also prepare politically to mobilize against the state power of capital which itself would be, under such conditions, actively engaged in and always preparing more counter measures. The antagonisms created between the activity of revolutionary agency and the reaction of the state power of capital over who rules would serve to accelerate the dynamic towards political revolution. In the course of the unfolding of such a dynamic, the historic tasks facing revolutionary agency would arise and be addressed in practice.

The quintessential tasks therefore facing revolutionary agency would be the elimination of the political power of capital – beginning with its state power – and an intensification of the invasion into and liquidation of the capital relation itself. This would include *the initiation of material alterations in its associated infrastructure*, in order to start to go beyond capital *in toto* towards communist human life, towards a truly human 'commonwealth'. For example, starting to break the grip of capitalist commodity production and the market by uncoupling production from exchange so that production is planned, restructured and re-directed towards distribution to meet social needs.

Revolution, of course, is a ruthless business which demands what is practically necessary in order to realize historic objectives, regardless of time and cost in the course of the prosecution of an unfolding global struggle against the capital order. A peaceful transition, if rendered possible by capital's compliance, is desirable but war would be necessary if capital violently refuses to submit, i.e. if a peaceful strategy fails as a result of the violent resistance of capital through the medium of its state power and its supporting agencies.

The unfolding of the structural crisis of the capital system – in contrast to the past cyclical, conjunctural crises of the system – can only manifest as a long drawn out, continuously deepening, determinate crisis-process in which different stages and phases of this crisis-process pass into higher ones with the emergence of qualitatively new, higher 'temporal determinations', material relations and characteristics as the crisis worsens. In other words, new determinate stages of this structural crisis must open up and unfold, characterized by phenomena and struggles which were previously unthinkable in the earlier phases of this crisis-process.

A simple analogy might be the start of a forest fire. Initially the fire might develop and spread relatively slowly and, to a certain extent, is containable by the authorities. But a sudden marked shift in conditions, for example very hot weather accompanied by high winds, would very rapidly transform the situation to the point where the containable fire becomes an uncontrollable firestorm. This latter stage becomes a determinately and qualitatively different stage of development of the forest fire compared to the initial containable phase. The deepening of the structural crisis of capital is creating the conditions for a global socio-economic 'firestorm', the likes of which human history has never witnessed before.

The structural crisis of the capital order – driven by the contradictions of its internal dynamics – therefore contains the possibility of arrivals at critical 'nodal points', where accumulated and continuously self-reinforcing alterations in the whole crisis-process create the conditions for 'leaps' in its whole qualitative nature (Hegel's conception of Measure (*Das Mass*) found in his *Logic*[2]). It is a question of 'degree' whereby an intractable, insoluble crisis passes beyond specific and previously 'normalized' parameters. Beyond these, a qualitative change ('transformation', a 'no return' point) sets in and the whole order degenerates into a distinctly new, higher qualitative phase of break-up and disintegration with the most profound consequences for humanity.

Humanity has witnessed such catastrophic 'phases' before in its history in different cultures and in different parts of the world. In Europe, the most obvious example that comes readily to mind is the fifty-year crisis of Roman economy in the third century CE which was rooted in the emergence and positing of the limits of the mode of production of the ancient world of Europe and the Mediterranean basin based on slave labour.[3] The post-crisis phase of the late third and fourth centuries was a fundamental shift away from the pre-crisis mode of production. The generalized form of labour altered from that of the 'slave' to that of the share-cropping 'colonus' and production became significantly more autarkic. The increasingly autarkic character of production intensified the conflict between the wealthy landowners on the conglomerated 'estates' – which were becoming more autonomous and independent of the Roman bureaucracy – and the state itself which was increasingly struggling to hold the remnants of empire together by means of heavy taxation through its 'Counts' ('tax-farmers') and the superexploitation of the populus. This final, post-crisis phase of development in Antiquity set the stage and contributing conditions for the later emergence of feudalism in western Europe.

The emergence and development of the new universal historic form of proletarian agency needs to be grasped not in terms of the historically experienced parameters and conditions of superseded, cyclical, 'boom and bust', conjunctural crises with their displaceable contradictions. On the contrary, this new form needs to be created and actively evolved in opposition to the capital relation itself in terms of its all-embracing, unfolding structural crisis. A crisis in which its contradictions are tending towards increasing non-displaceability, intensifying and playing themselves out in a seemingly unending series of 'discrete' crises, social explosions and cataclysmic events in the course of the unfolding 'continuum' of structural crisis as a whole.

We know that the dead weight of the capital order re-asserted itself and re-captured its equilibrium after the cyclical crises of the past but we are no longer speaking of such crises. So when István Mészáros writes that ...

> as history amply testifies, at the first sign of 'recovery', politics is pushed back into its traditional role of helping to sustain and enforce the given socio-economic determinations.[4]

we have to note, circumspectly, that 'as history amply testifies', it is a testament of past crises, and not of the now developing structural one. In past crises, 'radical politics ... accelerated its own demise ... by defining its own scope in terms of limited economic targets ... etc.' dictated by the capital order in crisis. This order re-trenched itself 'at the first sign of recovery' with the aid of 'politics ... in its traditional role'. But previous crises were not structural. 'Recovery' would have a different connotation within this 'structuralized' context as would the response of 'politics in its traditional role' even if those 'politics' still had 'the legs' to come to the rescue. We cannot discount the possibility that the socio-economic and political landscape coming into being as the present century opens up may be unrecognizable compared to what it is now and that 'politics in its traditional role' may have effectively disappeared under the impact of unfolding events.

The maturation of a structural crisis must give rise to a qualitatively new situation between the contending classes which surpasses the character of the determinations and relations which emerged under the conditions of the old, displaceable crises. Thus, in relation to the deepening of capital's structural crisis, it may be that the presently available 'testimony of history' – in regard to the application of the lessons of the historical experience of conjunctural crises to the situation of the unfolding structural crisis – needs to be employed with all due prudence and qualification. This 'testimony' may well turn out to be as useful for this purpose as employing copper wiring for computers which have been designed to receive fibre optic cables.

The 'radical restructuring of politics itself'[5] is therefore understood here to mean the establishment of the historically necessary form of revolutionary agency which will actually commence the process of appropriating capital's powers and begin to restructure and re-organize the entire socio-economic landscape in favour of socialism. This 'mass-oriented', 'radical restructuring of politics' – grounded in and arising out of the maturing of capital's structural crisis – is therefore intrinsic to this appropriation and re-organization. It not only 'arises out' of structural crisis but simultaneously 'returns into' it in order to resolve it and pass beyond the epoch of capital.

The agency of revolution arising in the process of this 'radical restructuring' – to begin and continue with the whole process of the transcendence of the capital relation – must fuse itself with the proletariat as a whole in the closest organic relationship 'from which subsequent material and political demands would emanate'. In other words, it must 'fuse the power of political decision-making with the social base from which it has been alienated for so long'.

History furnishes an important lesson here. In the Soviet system, this 'power of political decision making' remained 'alienated from the social base'. Without such a transfer of political power to 'the sphere of mass self-activity', defeat becomes, according to Mészáros, a 'self-imposed certainty'. This transfer therefore becomes a necessary condition for breaking the resistance of the state power of capital to these actions and negating it in the ensuing struggles.

The Soviet system was socialist in name only. According to Mészáros, the Soviet system was a 'post-capitalist capital system' so that capital maintained its pre-dominance as the fundamental determining parameter and 'mode of control of the social metabolism'. Not, however, in the same sense as we see under capitalism itself in which capital is the organically intrinsic and dominating social relationship of production and distribution. We need to critically review this conception of a 'post-capitalist capital system' because, quite clearly, the Soviet system was not a 'capital system' in the same sense and mode in which we understand it, for example, in Europe, the United States or Japan. This conception of the Soviet system as being a 'capital system' informs the conception that ...

> the real target of emancipatory transformation is the complete eradication of capital as a totalizing mode of control from the social reproductive metabolism itself, and not simply the displacement of the capitalists as the historically specific 'personifications of capital'.[6]

This process of 'complete eradication' is ...

> not conceivable without the painful enterprise of an all-embracing material restructuring of society's productive and distributive intercourse. And the latter in its turn involves the practical establishment of the necessary forms of material mediation through which capital's eradication from the social metabolic process becomes feasible in due course.[6]

Hence, this process of 'complete eradication' means the complete extensive and intensive restructuring of the way in which the whole social metabolism is reproduced. This can only involve the creation and development of forms of social agency – that must be mutable according to the demands and requirements of altering conditions and circumstances – which are capable of pursuing the trajectory of moving humanity beyond the capital relation and consummating the process of its 'eradication' from society's landscape.

[ii] Long Term Objectives: From Free-Market to Market-Free Zones

The agency of revolution will need to move towards the establishment of a system of production based on *directly socialized labour* in order to move away as rapidly as possible from capitalist commodity production. To undermine commodity production and exchange. Computer technology (e.g. electronic card systems, digitalization, high-speed computers and transfers, etc.) would now make this process easier to establish and develop.

Capitalist commodity production is based on private, concrete labour becoming abstract, general, social labour only through the exchange of the products of private labour. This private labour receives the stamp of social labour only through exchange and thereby is only *indirectly socialized labour as mediated through exchange*.

This exchange is an essential, inalienable mediation in capitalist commodity production as a whole. This indirectly socialized character of labour under capital necessitates the dichotomy between money and commodities. Private labour can only become stamped and recognized as social labour through the mediation of exchange at which point the products of private labour assert their character as commodities and the realization of their values in the form of money as universal equivalent (the market system).[7] *Socialism is based on directly socialized labour* which is the antithesis of its indirect, exchange-mediated form under capitalist commodity production.

Implicit here is the negation of the commodity as historic form and therefore of money itself. A system of highly developed, directly socialized labour has, increasingly, no need for money in order to mediate its reproduction because the commodity-form is becoming extinguished. This was the case in the communes of prehistory before the rise of exchange and can be so again (a return to the old but at a higher stage of development).

Progressively stripping the product of labour of its commodity-form, on the one hand, and the initiation and development of directly socialized productive labour in the period of transition, on the other hand, are inseparable moments of the same historical process. Hence (a) the need to rapidly establish – conditions permitting – a system of production and distribution arising out of directly socialized labour and (b) the creation of a universal system of accountancy of labour-time which now becomes easier with the use of electronic and computer technologies, etc.

Marx writes of the point of metamorphosis of the commodity into money (C – M) as the *'salto mortale of the commodity'*. A point of high vulnerability (literally 'deadly leap', a 'weak link in the chain' or 'Achilles Heel') for capital in the process of its circulation. The point at which the product of private labour receives the stamp of acceptability of general social labour. At this point, capital is not only susceptible to the fluctuations and vicissitudes of the market but also to social actions such as mass consumer boycotts. Severing the nexus here serves to disrupt capital in the whole process of its circulation. It severs the link between the production of use-value and the realization of value in circulation i.e. it dis-assembles the necessary relation between the production of use value and the market realization of value and therefore facilitates the disruption of the capital relation itself. Sever the nexus which serves to integrate and maintain the two sides (production and circulation) of the process of reproduction of capital as a whole, and the process as a totality starts to break down and disintegrate. Deprive capital of the essential metamorphosis into the money-form and the cyclical process of the reproduction of capital starts to break down and perish. To do this, we must develop social practices and corresponding forms of organization which dis-establish (strip) the product of labour of its commodity-capital form and disrupts the process of the circulation and accumulation of capital. This would serve to undermine dependency on the global market and facilitate its dissolution.

The transition to a system of immediately (directly) socialized labour is the fundamental, mediating ground for eliminating the process of capitalist commodity production. *'On the basis of commodity production, labour becomes social labour only as a result of the universal alienation of individual kinds of labour'* (Marx). The irreversible establishment and development of production based on directly socialized labour implies the end of capitalist commodity production and therefore the termination of its mediation by the money form because ...

it would be impossible for a specific commodity ... to confront other commodities as the incarnation of universal labour and exchange-value would not be turned into price; but neither would use-value be turned into exchange value and the product into a commodity, and thus the very basis of bourgeois production would be abolished.[8]

Private labour only becomes social labour indirectly (taking the money form) through commodity exchange. Directly socialized labour circumvents ('short-circuits') this mediation and, by doing so, represents the negation of capitalist commodity production. The creation of social relations founded on directly socialized labour must therefore eliminate those relations founded on the 'universal alienation of individual kinds of labour'. The negation of the commodity-form is, accordingly, the negation of the universal form of value, of money, per se.[9]

In the epoch of capital, the taproot of all forms of alienation – including 'secondary' and 'tertiary' forms such as we encounter in interpersonal relations – is constituted by the historic process whereby wage labour itself continuously re-creates capital (as condition for its own existence) and, in so doing, creates and erects above itself a 'hostile power confronting itself and of its own making'. Analogously, in religion, mankind bows down and worships its own creation.

This process cannot take place, of course, without the augmentation of value (valorisation, production of surplus value) which then becomes capitalized in accumulation. Herein the intrinsic, inalienable nature of capital is realized: self-augmenting value. The real source of valorisation (i.e. labour time performed beyond that required to reproduce the value of labour power) is concealed in the production process. The most fetishistic and highest form of this 'concealment' becomes expressed in the apparent 'money-breeding' character of money capital ($M - M'$) which Marx analyses in Volume 3 of *Capital*.

When accumulated wealth ceases to confront the producers as the alien property of others (capitalist class, state property, etc.) and is appropriated, developed and controlled by the producers themselves, then the presentation of wealth in personified forms will cease. Capital itself must be eliminated but also capital or property as 'state property' and positively replaced by the self-managing and self-directing activity of the associated producers. For if the means of production and distribution continue to confront the producers as 'state property', this itself denotes that the producers have still not become disentangled from relations of alienation in which the state still stands as an 'extra-social' or 'suprasocial' body.[10]

A direct accountancy and calculation of labour-time must remain *in the initial post-capitalist stages* as an unavoidable legacy from capitalist production. But it takes place, progressively and increasingly, as an accountancy of directly socialized labour in order to plan and extend production, distribution and the development of human culture in general.

This accountancy and allocation of labour-time ceases to present itself disguised in fetishistic commodity and money forms. Labour-time is calculated as a means to producing a definite quantity of use-values and for catering for the social needs of people generally. Later, with the dissolution of the state power, human beings organize themselves in their activities and alter these activities according to their developing needs without the presence of alien bodies and structures confronting them and directing their activities over and against their human interests. These measures, of course, characterize the early phases of the transition period. Beyond these phases lies the actual transcendence of account keeping itself on the basis of the expenditure of labour time. Then free time (not labour time) becomes the real measure of wealth.

Exchange is absolutely fundamental to the continued existence of commodity production. We must move as quickly as possible to the elimination of exchange and its replacement with a universal system of accounted distribution founded upon the socialist principles of need, quality, human welfare, ecological considerations and sustainability, etc. A socialist accountancy of labour time directed towards the realization of these needs. The uncoupling of production and distribution from exchange will serve to undermine commodity production itself. It will facilitate the move from free-market zones to market-free zones.

The abolition, or rather phasing out, of capitalist exchange which involves *'opposing the products of different forms of labour with each other on the basis of equality'* necessarily means the phasing out of the market system. Under capitalist commodity production, the products of private labour only become commodities at that point when they enter circulation and receive the stamp of social general labour in their exchange relations with other commodities. This is the point at which ...

> the equalisation of the most different kinds of labour can be the result only of an abstraction from their inequalities, or reducing them to their common denomination, viz., the expenditure of human labour-power or human labour in the abstract ... only exchange brings about this reduction.[11]

Human labour as specific quantum of labour in the abstract must then manifest its quantity in the 'objective form' of a given equivalent of use-values. For example, five cars for fifty sheets of machine-compressible steel sheets, mediated by money, etc. Hence Marx's conception of a social relation appearing as a relationship between things, etc. Furthermore, the diremption of the commodity-form into use value and value is the mirror replication of the antithetical character of the labour (in the epoch of capital) which produces it, i.e. labour which is simultaneously 'useful labour' and 'value creating'.[12]

The different forms of 'useful labour' constitute the panorama which is the division of labour. Accordingly, the exchange of labour activities will serve, in the initial phases of the directly socialized labour process, to facilitate the breakdown of this division of labour and to enrich the skills and life of the human individual. The development of these labour-exchange activities becomes mutual, reciprocal accommodations of socially useful, directly socialized productive labour. The evolution of these exchanges creates the medium for the interrelationships and enrichment of human culture in its diverse forms and aspects – technical, scientific, artistic, aesthetic, etc. This will serve to initiate the transcendence of the division of labour within the places of production and within society as a whole.

The division of labour under capitalism engenders the 'crippled' human generations of the time of its historic existence. From this basis of alienation, men and women must proceed to transcend the division of labour and hence there is a need to recognize the highly problematic nature of this movement. It is these 'crippled' generations which must commence the historic process of 'undoing' all this 'crippling' (the 'uncrippling' of humanity) of the 'generations of revolution' and in the process create new generations free of all of it.

Humanity can only start to transform itself by starting to transform its conditions of life and it can only commence this momentous and enduring process from where it really stands at the prevailing stage of development. Humanity can only use itself as, and struggle with, the material which it itself finds available and at hand which it has inherited from the history of capitalist society. In moving forward from the proletarian of the twenty-first-century global capital order towards the human being of the 'true realm of freedom', it commences with all the conflicts and problems which are presented as the legacy of this final order of class society.

[iii] On Means and Ends in the Revolutionary Strategy of Agency

In so far as the long term objectives and immediate aims of revolutionary agency, in its historically modifying or altering forms, constitute its most essential dual purpose, the means to achieving these ends must be simultaneously determined by both immediate aims and long term objectives. This is the true, broad historical dialectical consideration of the question of the relationship between 'ends and means' in the elaboration of revolutionary strategy.

To posit the notion that all revolutionary strategy and activity must be determined solely by one or the other – by long term objective or immediate aim – is itself, therefore, a strategically debilitating metaphysic. It reduces the question to a formal, ahistorical consideration which fails to address these intrinsically dual aspects of revolutionary agency regardless of any persisting or altering forms in the course of the period of transition.

For at any given stage in the transition, both these aims will be the 'business' of agency which will, therefore and necessarily, determine its activity ('means') according to the requirements of both ends which are simultaneously and mediatively determining this activity of revolutionary agency in the transitional period. Any conception which insists on the subordination of revolutionary strategy to either long term objectives *or* immediate aim is a metaphysical recipe for defeat. It is effectively to propose that the revolutionary class fights with 'one arm tied behind its back'.

Revolution is an unfolding process (incorporating different stages and phases in its overall development) in which ends and means are continuously becoming transformed into each other. The means adopted at any given stage in that process are determined not simply by long term aims but by antecedent process which has produced them and by the actually existent conditions of struggle confronting the revolutionary class organized in any given, specific form of agency.

No form of struggle, change of strategy or deployment of tactics is automatically excluded when what is at stake is the achievement of the immediate aim and the bringing of the realization of long term objectives one step closer on the road of struggle in the transitional period between the epoch of capital and the 'true realm of freedom'. All possible and necessary 'means' – which serve the interests of the proletariat as democratically determined by itself as an organized class within the participatory process of its historically specific form of revolutionary agency – must remain 'on the table' of agency's revolutionary strategy in order that the revolution is *fully armed* to achieve both immediate and long term objectives. To exclude anything which, in the long or short term, may become incontrovertibly necessary to deploy in order to further developing aims in the unfolding period of transition is a gross political and strategic error. All means must remain 'on the table' which does not necessarily mean or imply that they would be deployed. But they must be there in order to be deployed when possible and if necessary to defeat the forces of capital.

Whether the 'end' is 'immediately confronting' or mediating our activities 'at a future distance', the 'means' is indeed 'justified' if it serves to realize those ends on the basis of decisions arrived at by the ongoing democracy of revolutionary agency. The question of the political relationship between 'means and ends' in revolutionary strategy can therefore only be resolved in the 'revolutionary practice' of agency itself ('practical critical activity') and cannot be subject to *restricting transcendental moral paradigms* and ethical considerations which could, very easily and readily, merely serve to place shackles on the arms and legs of revolution.

The 'ends and means' of the Stalinist regimes are often used to illustrate opposition to the principle that 'the end justifies the means'. But these regimes were adopting means which were serving to realize, preserve and develop ends that ran contrary to the historic interests of the proletariat. They were not socialist ends as such. In this regard, the specific character of the means deployed were related to the ends which were posited. Mass murder of millions, deportations, Gulags, state oppression of the proletariat and the rest were not serving the interests of the international proletariat but serving those of international capital. The actual measured use of internment camps, for example, is not necessarily excluded as part of an overall revolutionary strategy against global capital today. Stalin used them to break the revolutionary opposition to his regime. Not to break the rule of capital and its state power. The question of 'means and ends' must be related to the specific tasks in hand in real situations and conflicts. It must not be subject to the moral criteria of metaphysics and ethical considerations divorced from the realities of such situations.

Here, in agency's struggle to supersede the epoch of capital, the means would be serving a different purpose altogether. Revolution is not a narrative (recount) and agreement between 'parties'. It is the forceful dispossession of one class by another and the imposition of the rule of the revolutionary class over the former ruling class and its agencies by all those means which the organizations of the revolutionary class considers possible, necessary and expedient.

These methods are not necessarily inconsonant with the revolutionary, open, transparent democracy of the proletarian class organized in its determinate forms of agency as the revolutionary class. To assert that revolutionary violence and terror is inconsonant with (contradicts) the 'freedom' and 'democracy' of the revolutionary movement effectively means that the period of transition (which will inevitably be 'turbulent') must limit itself in its methods of struggle and must preclude automatically certain tactics and strategies which may be required and advantageous under certain conditions of struggle.

In the very nature of the initial phases of struggle against capital, its state powers and global agencies, the methods of revolutionary struggle adopted and elaborated are furnished and conditioned by the nature of the opposition of capital itself, the 'enemy within' as a class and its state power. In the very nature of such a situation, the process of the practical realization of immediate aims must contradict the long term aims of the revolutionary transition period. For example, the major aims of creating a world without class, state, war and violence. But war, revolutionary violence and terror are unlikely to be dispensable in the initial phases of the period of transition because capital and its state powers will almost inevitably put up political and military resistance to revolutionary change.

The period of transition is not a period of 'freedom' but rather governed by what Marx refers to as 'natural necessity'. Only as this period of 'natural necessity' is gradually transcended, does the 'true realm of freedom' (Appendix I) start to come into being. 'Freedom' as such ceases to be driven by 'external necessity' – as it is in the transitional period – and becomes a humanly internalized 'real inward necessity which is identical with freedom' in the unfolding 'true realm of freedom'.

In order to move from the realm of capital to that of the 'true realm of freedom', human beings will be compelled ('external necessity') to engage in activities which are not (and can never be) those of the men and women of the 'true realm'. The people of the transition period cannot miraculously furnish themselves with the consciousness, affectations, 'human culture' and sensibilities of the people of the later realm but can only proceed on the basis of the conditions prevailing as the outcome of their own history conditioned by the legacies of capitalist society. Only when capital and its various state and other agencies are irreversibly eliminated from the social landscape, will humanity be able to commence and consummate the process of 'turning swords into ploughshares'. For the simple fact that 'swords' will no longer be required by people in their relations with each other whereas 'ploughshares' will.

The means which are required to put an end to the epoch of capital will be generated and presented by the nature of that epoch. To assert that the means deployed (to put an end to the epoch of capital) must be consonant with the nature of the long term communist ends to which social revolution is tending is, of course, a completely ahistorical 'separation and divorcement' – in theory and activity – from the tasks confronting the proletariat in the epoch of capital's structural crisis. It amounts to a demand to address the practical questions and problems of the current epoch with forms of consciousness-mediated activity which belong to and will characterize the men and women of later epochs.

Opposition to the capital order and its state powers implies determination by capital-in-crisis in both organization and in the means which such organizations adopt in order to prosecute the struggle against capital. Revolutionary agency adopts and develops means and ends which it does not find arising self-subsistently and independently within the determinations of its own life process but rather finds them confronting itself outside of itself in its dialectical relations to the capital order which is protected by state violence, intimidation, deceit and subterfuge. Revolutionary agency itself is not its own end but merely a transient means (instrumentality) to the realization of immediate and long term ends.

Of course, the dialectic of means and ends operates within the life of agency as a determinate formation but here we are referring ontologically and epistemologically to the actual source of agency's overall movement as an organ of class struggle. *The internal 'teleology' of the organizational form of revolutionary agency finds its principal and real impulse and life 'external' to itself in the unfolding structural crisis of the global capital order.* This is why 'means' in revolutionary strategy cannot be isolated from its determination by the historical whole within which agency finds itself temporally lodged. And, moreover, in the initial phases of struggle against the capital order, the means adopted by revolutionary agency against it in struggle necessarily contradict projected long term objectives such as we find in Marx's seminal *Economic and Philosophical Manuscripts of 1844* (Paris Manuscripts).

The path to these long term ends can only be constructed by means of an endless succession of temporally conditioned means which lead to it. The realization of each end by the required means then posits the material conditions for the development of new means for the realization of higher ends. This may be an example of the 'spurious infinite' for Hegel but it is a matter of life and death for humanity as a whole.

This endlessly unfolding dialectical relationship between changing means and ends (in which each is, historically, always becoming continuously transformed into the other) is the actual evolution of succeeding phases and aspects in the historical realization of longer term goals and each belongs wholly to the other. And these means adopted in real, living struggle are determined by an endless array and complexity of specific circumstances which compel their adoption and deployment to realize specific ends along the way. It is politically foolish and artless to think that the means deployed – in the long, drawn out, historic process of the revolutionary transcendence of a whole epoch – can be subject to any constricting, overriding criteria when the need to drive forward the revolutionary process in specific circumstances of struggle may require the use of expediently determined means. Such means may contradict these 'constricting criteria' or any conceptions of a 'socialist moral uprightness'. And they are very likely to be inconsonant with the humanly refined sensibilities of those human beings of a later, far-distant age of classlessness where alienation is irreversibly and asymptotically tending towards its 'vanishing point' in an unfolding 'true realm of freedom'.

The historically immediate ends (which are part of the developing process of the realization of long term objectives) are presented to agency by 'force of circumstance' which must then condition and decide the means of their realization. It is not a question of positing an 'ideal' which has to be realized but rather of addressing in practice the real 'forces of circumstances' which drive forward agency in the struggle against capital for the realization of ends which necessarily arises out of these very circumstances. The derivation of the necessary means which animate purpose and the realization of the socially necessary ends are imposed by, and under, the unfolding temporality of specific circumstance. They are not taken from a cookbook of human history and then applied according to the instructions of recipe. The means adopted become the revolutionary instruments for the transition from the pressing situation of 'force of circumstance' to the realized end.

Strategy and tactics can only be actively determined and developed according to, and in response to, the specific social and cultural conditions which differentially prevail in any given part of the globe. But this does not disregard the growing uniformity and homogeneity of socio-economic conditions with capitalist globalization and, implicitly, the need for a new universal historic form of proletarian organization to replace the trade union form. There is no choice in that confronting matter because the class movement of the proletariat cannot step outside of these differentiations in historical conditions in different parts of the world.

For example, how trade unionized workers or 'social movements' struggle against the theocratic capitalist state in Iran is conditioned by circumstances differing from those in Britain. And the real experts on this are those engaged in struggle and who know how to orientate according to the specificity of conditions. For example, how does the proletariat as a class in Iran orientate itself in regard to these questions of agency, with all the traditions, Shia Islam, etc., in that land and how does the proletariat in Britain address the same basic questions with its differing class traditions, history, etc.? These are not peripheral 'inessential' questions but are intrinsic to the totality of the determination.

[iv] By Peaceful Means if Possible

The principal objective of revolutionary agency is the transcendence of capital; its removal from the process of the reproduction of the social metabolism. The existence of the state power of capital is predicated on its role in maintaining capital as the dominant social relation of this reproductive process. Inevitably, as the agency of revolution commences the process of eradicating capital from the social metabolism, this must bring it into collision with the state power of capital.

Is this state power going to stand to one side and let the historical basis of its existence be pulled from underneath it and let itself be dismantled without resisting this restructuring of the socio-economic landscape? Is the transition to the new socialist society to be carried through by peaceful means or by force of arms? How do we address this pivotal question?

Let us consider a situation in which this question is having to be addressed in the heat of the real living struggle. Increasingly, as capital's crisis deepens, we must witness a polarization between the conflicting interests of capital – as embodied in its state power – and those of the revolutionary class. We know that this state power is a violent organization of 'armed bodies of men' (Engels) which stands guard – in all its 'capacities' arising out of the experience of centuries of rule – over the interests of capital against the 'social body'. We cannot, therefore, discount for one single moment that this state power will not move onto the offensive – political and military – and endeavour to crush the agency of revolution. This is our 'default' position which we must always carry with us and therefore prepare for in words and deeds.

However, our provisional position (which is essentially tactical) must also admit the possibility of a peaceful transition no matter how remote this possibility. Accordingly, for political purposes, we must articulate the conception of a peaceful transition to the new society if, and only if, we are permitted to make such a transition by this state power. Such a peaceful transition would, of course, involve the dismantling and the dissolution of this state power in the course of this transition. If this state power does not permit such a transition and openly or covertly goes onto the offensive against us, then we would have no other option but to mobilize for war against that state power; that is, to deploy mass force of arms towards its break up and dissolution. As an intrinsic part of an overall strategy to break this state power, revolutionary agency will have to determine tactically that point beyond which the struggle has passed which has rendered a peaceful transition impossible and now requires the deployment of armed force to topple this state power.

The provisional utilization of the bourgeois parliamentary system is a question which also needs to be addressed at this point. According to an old fable, the Labour Party was created by the trade unions in order to 'represent the interests of labour in parliament'. Ultimately, of course, the historical interests of labour are not representable through institutions of the capitalist state. Elementary theoretical principles as well as the most cruel and bitter experience is testimony to this ultimate unrepresentability (for example, Chile, September 1973). By implication, the transcendence of the political power of capital will mean, eventually, the dissolution of the parliaments and national assemblies of the capitalist order and their replacement with higher forms of popular democratic assembly. On this question, Mészáros writes that …

Parliament, in particular, has been the target of many a justified criticism, and up to the present time there is no satisfactory socialist theory as to what to do with it beyond the conquest of power ...[13]

Is this question of 'what to do with it beyond the conquest of power' really a theoretical question? Or is it more of a strategic question? Parliament is an institution of the capitalist state and, although it can be utilized by the proletariat in its struggle for socialism, that character will not fundamentally alter in conditions of crisis. What will the historical effect be on parliamentarism with the transfer of power to the organs of revolution? It will be the pronouncement of a death sentence on it.

The transfer of power to the agency of revolution will necessarily render parliament obsolete as an outmoded bourgeois institution. Whether such a transfer takes place through parliament itself (which would probably precipitate a massive political crisis and conflict between the state organs of the bourgeois class and the newly established organs of the proletariat; a dual power situation) *or* the parliamentary system itself will have become so discredited and outmoded prior to this transfer that it will simply be 'left behind' in the wake of events, would be a temporally determined strategic question to be addressed by the organs of revolution.

When the time is judged to be right, the organized proletariat will know how to discard it as a necessary, transient act in the unfolding of an overall revolutionary strategy. This is where posing 'what to do with it after the conquest of power' as a theoretical question is itself a theoretical misarticulation and illegitimation of the matter. It is essentially a revolutionary strategic question and not a theoretical question which theory and experience has already resolved. *The proletariat in revolution – not parliaments, national assemblies or nation-states – is 'sovereign'.*

The proletariat needs to develop organs of 'socialist offensive' and revolution which rival the parliamentary system in its legislative, judicial and executive capacities and powers so that parliament itself can and must be abolished as soon as is politically feasible; it remains in existence only in so far as it is politically necessary and expedient.

For example, we do not call for its abolition whilst we are using it to further the aims of socialism but once the pursuit of those aims have been irreversibly transferred to the organizations of transition, and we are confident that it is no longer of any use, then it effectively becomes politically and culturally vestigial; the parliamentary system becomes redundant and can be safely left behind.

Parliament in England, and later Britain, was always historically associated with the bourgeoisie. First as a regally appointed chamber of consultation in which the nascent bourgeois class in the feudal order could make its representations to the crown and the crown could issue its directives to the 'commons'; secondly as a organization through which the revolutionary bourgeoisie could organize and conduct its struggle for supremacy against the nobility and church, and later against the crown itself and thirdly, as a means of the 'commons' asserting that won supremacy over the crown in a 'constitutional arrangement'. Perhaps its final and, historically, most useful (revolutionary?) function will be as a means to abolish the rule of the bourgeois class itself once and for all?

Mészáros also refers to a possibly very lengthy 'intermediary stage' which 'retains at least some important features of the inherited parliamentary framework while the long-drawn-out process of radical restructuring is accomplished on the required comprehensive scale'.[14] What 'important features of the inherited parliamentary framework' would this 'intermediary stage' retain? Surely, one of the earliest casualties of the actualization of the 'socialist offensive' and the 'long-drawn-out process of radical restructuring' would be the whole bourgeois parliamentary system itself in the wake of the unfolding of the 'necessary political restructuring'? Why would any of these 'important features' hang around in the course of the unfolding of the 'process of radical restructuring'? Surely an important aspect of that very 'process of restructuring' would be to put parliamentarism behind us as quickly as possible?

Also – and this is historically related to the role of parliamentarism – that Marx in a speech in September 1872[15] mentions the possibility of working people 'achieving their goal by peaceful means'. Of course, it would be dogmatic to assert the absolute impossibility of a peaceful transition. However, over 140 years of experience of how the capitalist state proceeds in crises gravitates against Marx's temporally conditioned 'aside' not to mention the bloody history of the ascendancy and consolidation of the rule of the bourgeois class in England and elsewhere over a period of five centuries.

It would be folly in the extreme to proceed on the basis of the presupposition that the guardians of the capital order would cave in without a fight. To err on the side of caution is therefore to presuppose a 'stormy transition'. Standing on guard behind capital's 'veneer-thin' so-called and self-styled 'democratic' institutions of government and state lies the axeman and executioners. This so-called 'democracy' is only a relatively recent phenomenon. A cursory inspection of English history will show that the executioners were always kept busy. The nineteenth and the first half of the twentieth century was, of course, a century of slavery under the brutal yoke of British colonialism for countless millions across the globe. The 'peace' of colonialism was equivalent to a murderous rampage of exploitation and capital accumulation.

Parliament is a form of political rule of capital – not the only one – which can be put aside if necessary and wheeled back out at the convenience of the capitalist state when the storm of a crisis passes. The Chilean state murdered thousands of socialists and trade unionists in 1973 and subsequently – when it was expedient to do so – restored the parliamentary farce as a façade to supposedly legitimize its re-found 'democratic credentials'.

However, what we are experiencing today is a crisis in the whole traditional system of political governance of the bourgeois order; a crisis arising out of and mediated by the structural crisis of capital. This starts to generate trends in the ruling class which see the parliamentary system as an obstacle which could possibly be discarded rather than a traditional institution of rule which must be conserved. It also becomes a deceitful institutional means of imposing 'authoritarian' rule by means of the parliamentary 'back door', that is, through the imposition of draconian legislation on society which has passed through the normal parliamentary mechanisms and is therefore afforded the stamp of 'bourgeois political legitimacy'. The movement from the 'reading and stages' of a 'Bill' to 'Royal Assent' is equally, if not more, effective as the 'Jackboot' and 'Baton' in imposing draconian laws on the people of the land.

Sometimes the personifications of the state power of capital are indiscreet enough to 'give us the truth, the whole truth and nothing but the truth'. In a recent comment (in response to the election of Jeremy Corbyn as leader of the British Labour Party in September 2015) by a serving British Army General – who was courageous and valiant enough to hide behind the anonymity of Ministry of Defence 'windbreaks' and the capitalist media – a threat was made that an elected Corbyn government could invite 'mutiny' from the armed forces. The unnamed General 'gallantly served' in Ulster in the bloody imperialist war against the Republican movement and its supporting communities. More incontrovertible 'evidence' of the possibilities of a 'peaceful transition' beyond the capital order.[16]

Historical experience (as well as theoretical development) has qualified Marx's 'aside' (raised in the speech in Amsterdam in 1872). Quite the contrary – whilst not totally discounting the possibility of 'peaceful transitions' and proceeding tactically and strategically with this in mind and with the utmost caution – we must expect storm after storm before we can even see 'dry land', never mind set foot on it.

The capitalist states and their globally organized formations and agencies have to be pursued across the face of the planet, run down and destroyed by all means available and necessary with an absolute determination and ruthlessness if the social revolution to take humankind beyond capital is to succeed. And this is why any conceptions about 'peaceful transitions' need to be regarded with the highest possible degree of provisionality and scepticism.

Needless to say, the outcome of any class struggle never depends on force alone. Regardless of to what degree this is central in the struggle. This is as much the case in a situation of open military conflict. The outcome is a function of the operation of a complex of mediations as the struggle takes its course and those 'factors' which motivate to victory. Logistical considerations are just as important as, if not more important than, strategy and tactics and, indeed, are an intrinsic part of the overall strategic approach to struggle.

A cursory glance into the history of military affairs demonstrates that, generally, force alone was never sufficient by itself to win through. In fact, many victories were actually won against overwhelming odds when military force was heavily weighted against the eventual victors (For example, Caesar at Alesia and Cromwell at Dunbar). Such victories also depended on insight, intelligence, moral and spiritual motivation as well as brilliant tactical applications of manpower, resources and forces amongst other factors at the disposal of the winning side. In war, it is the strategic and tactical operation, application and articulation of the totality of available instruments and resources under the prevailing conditions which determine the eventual outcome of a struggle and not simply one aspect of this totality, no matter how central it may appear to be located within the scheme or order of the given situation. Von Clausewitz taught us this – amongst other things – almost two centuries ago.[17] We can all cite examples in human history where the 'odds' stacked against a protagonist did not prevent it winning through in the end.

If the 'guard dogs' of capital do not allow us to enter the garden peacefully in order to cultivate it, then we will have no other option but to use forced entry. In the course of deploying such measures, these state structures and powers of capital will have to be forcefully destroyed or transferred rather than being peacefully dismantled. To paraphrase Trotsky (*The Transitional Programme*[18]): *If the state power refuses to disarm peacefully then it will have to be forcibly disarmed. And, in order to disarm this state power of capital, the revolutionary class and its agency must arm.*

This state power – which has ruled in Britain in one form or another for about 500 years – has a bloody and violent history and equally monstrous feudal pre-history. This history informs us, undoubtedly, that the ruling class under threat has historically, at least as a last resort, always deployed force to defend its interests. It had, under such conditions, everything to lose if it had simply let the challenging class march in and take power. A cursory amble through the class struggle in England over the last millenium demonstrates the truth of this general conception.

And this is precisely why we must never lose sight of the presupposition that an armed transition will, in all probability, be necessary whilst not precluding absolutely the possibility of a peaceful transition. And then, of course, there are the global powers of capital against the proletarian class. The coming revolution will, necessarily, be an unfolding global affair and not simply 'in one country', not a Stalinist monstrosity as we witnessed in the Soviet system.

In his 1872 preface to the *Manifesto of the Communist Party*, Marx – referring to the defeat of the Paris Commune of 1871 – wrote that …

'*One thing especially was proved by the Commune, viz., that the working class cannot simply lay hold of the ready-made state machinery and wield it for its own purposes*'.

The state power of capital must be broken and dismantled. It is the highest political expression of the rule of capital. It is one thing to use it, conditionally and provisionally, for our 'own purposes' when required and possible but it is something else altogether to leave it in place once it is no longer necessary to use it.

The root problem to address is the existence of capital itself as the cube root of capitalism and the foundation upon which its state power rests. As long as capitalist commodity production maintains its presence in the reproduction of the social metabolism, this state power is implicitly (if not actually) present. It maintains its ghostly (spectral) presence (haunts society) even if it has been overthrown as long as the capital relation and the commodity-form linger.

The eradication of capitalist commodity production is the revolutionary act of humanity revolutionizing itself, of transforming itself in the process of transforming its actual conditions of life beyond the epoch of global capital. The struggles of the proletariat through its agencies of revolution to make the transition from the realm of capital to that of the 'true realm of freedom' will rouse, disinter and bring to life all the ghosts and demons of capital's past. All these and more will be directed against revolutionary agency in capital's attempts to defeat it. It would invite disaster to posit a 'peaceful transition' as presupposition when the history of the capital system reveals that it has arisen and held sway by means of extreme oppression, violence and blood.

[v] Restructuring the 'Social Metabolism' beyond Capital

The establishment and development of the initial forms of proletarian revolutionary agency are necessarily and intrinsically connected to the co-temporality (synchronous character) of the commencement of the restructuring of the 'social metabolism', on the one hand, and the onset of political revolution against the state power of capital, on the other. It is the unfolding of the structural crisis-process of capital which generates the conditions necessary for the emergence of the necessary forms of agency of socialist revolution, for the revolutionary 'agency' of and for the proletariat.

This is not to state categorically that they will *inevitably* come into existence under such conditions. Rather, the emergence and development of these crisis conditions continuously augments only the *possibility* of their birth and growth. Only beyond a certain point – when all the necessary conditions, including 'subjective', for its existence are assembled – does the required form of agency come into being.

The unfolding of the totality of these conditions arrives at a point where the possibility of this higher form of agency becomes transformed into its historic actuality. It is, accordingly, this same crisis-process which would mediate and animate the subsequent actions of this agency once it had emerged to go forward and to resolve the crisis by the commencement of the restructuring process of going beyond capital. The specifically orientated and self-directed activities of the proletariat are intrinsic to these 'necessary conditions'. These 'necessary conditions' do not emerge independently – as an inevitable 'objective' *fait accompli* – of this consciousness-directed activity. The latter is intrinsic to the formation of the former.

The commencement of the process of appropriating the powers of capital and the restructuring of the socio-economic landscape can only, indeed must, commence in the obstructing and violent presence of the state power of the capital order. This implies a form of revolutionary agency which is endowed with all the requisite strategic and tactical capacity and flexibility and an enduring tenacity in terms of the initiation and elaboration of struggle against this state power itself.

Whatever the nature of those organizations which are predominant in commencing the struggle to break the socio-economic power of capital (to 'restructure the social metabolism'), such institutions will have to, sooner or later, take on a directly political role in the revolutionary struggle against the state power of capital itself.

Can it be any other way? Can the proletariat, in the epoch of capital's structural crisis, overthrow the state power of capital prior to the struggle to restructure the social metabolism? On what material grounds would it thereby carry out such an overthrow without simultaneously moving onto a trajectory of 'restructuring' within the presence of capital's state power?

Otherwise how will the proletariat move to revolution in an age when the continued existence of the capital relation is destroying all the natural and cultural conditions necessary for the new society? There has to be actual, existentially animating material grounds for the destruction of the state power of capital. In the inverted, topsy-turvy world of the left-wing sect, the overthrow of the state power must proceed prior to this restructuring. For the sect, one can only follow on from the other. They fail to grasp the basic lessons of the work done by Marx and Engels in the 1840s. This approach of the sectarian groups also feeds into their 'vanguardist' self-importance as the 'revolutionary party supplied to, and required and ready to lead, the masses'.

The activity of revolutionary agency in the process of restructuring and re-organization of the social metabolism would constitute the grounds for such an overthrow of the state power of capital by actually making inroads into eliminating the capital relation and appropriating its social infrastructure. This would inevitably start to shift the ground from under the feet of the capitalist state.

In other words, without the initiation of the struggle by agency to make such changes, there could be no material grounds established for the overthrow of the capitalist state itself. Thus, the struggle to 'radically restructure' the social metabolism and the struggle to overthrow the capitalist state are inseparable 'moments' and must commence together. The initiation of the struggle to go beyond capital is co-temporal with the political revolution to break the state power of the capital order, occurring within an identical historic temporo-spatiality.

[vi] Restructuring and the Economic Parameters of the Capital Order

Because the structural crisis of the capital order presents itself to society in its appearance as a shifting or even temporary, displaceable crisis of economy, the proletariat initially seeks answers to its problems in economic measures, 'leaving their social causes intact'. The outcome is a defining of economic solutions by the proletariat in the terms of the social parameters of the capital order itself, so that the 'restructuring potential of revolutionary politics' is buried under 'narrowly defined economic tasks' within the established framework and parameters of the capital system (Syriza in Greece, Corbyn in Britain, Podemos in Spain, etc.). The capital system can, by such measures, be unwittingly stabilized …

> Times of major economic crisis always open up a sizeable breach in the established order which no longer succeeds in delivering the goods that served as its unquestioned justification. Such breaches may be enlarged, in the service of social restructuring, or indeed filled in for shorter or longer duration, in the interest of capital's continued survival, depending on the general historical circumstances and on the relation of forces in the political and social arena … only a radical political initiative can move into the breach.[19]

Moreover, unless the appropriate measures are adopted – and does this not imply the existence of the requisite strategies and tactics of struggle and 'appropriate' form of agency? For example, *its absence* in the Syriza movement in Greece – then the 'measures adopted to fill it' can serve to temporarily stabilize the capital order rather than undermine it. The dead weight of the capital order, its socio-economic structures, institutions and traditions of political inertia tend to re-trench themselves out of their temporary instability once a given phase of the unfolding structural crisis has passed over its peak.

Accordingly, it is not simply the role of any future revolutionary agency to stick to 'limited economic targets' (immediate tasks). It must initiate a struggle to actually begin the offensive process of restructuring the socio-economic metabolism. The measures adopted must actually start to make inroads into the social infrastructure of capital and into the capital relation itself. Such an 'invasion' must take place even in the obstructing presence of the state power of capital, as it casts its menacing shadow over the organized proletariat itself.

For example, if, under such conditions, the proletariat merely seeks to improve its wages and employment terms or repeal anti-labour legislation, etc., within the 'economic parameters' of capital – after years of denudation of those conditions – rather than also fighting to completely alter the actual social relations within which the denudation of those wages and terms has actually taken place, then its actions serve to re-trench those social relations which arise out of the rule of capital rather than negate them.

Given the expedience of favourable conditions, capital can readily make a tactical retreat on the economic front in the full knowledge that the overall social parameters of its existence are preserved. If agency remains within the parameters of the old exploitative framework rather than attempting to dissolve that framework and establish relations which point beyond capital, then 'radical politics rapidly invites its own negation – shortening rather than prolonging the favourable "moment" of transformation so that any economic gains or concessions made do not necessarily serve to prolong the historical moment of radical politics' (Mészáros).

Rather they tend to serve to relieve the 'most pressing crisis symptoms' and therefore serve to reinforce the old conditions (the 'old reproductive mechanism shaken by the crisis'). The 'first sign of recovery' serves to facilitate – 'sustain and enforce' – the re-trenchment of the old conditions by means of inertia, political reaction and the re-positing of the 'line of least resistance'. The ensuing 'claimed 'recovery' itself' is used as ideological justification for a return to the old ways 'in harmony with the dominant institutional framework'.[20] The opportunistic and 'economistic' 'twists and turns' of the Syriza movement in Greece has very clearly exemplified this process of the actions of its so-called 'radical politics' serving to 're-trench' the 'old ways'.

Such 'economic measures' are therefore effectively dictated by the ruling order in crisis. These would be measures through which agency is essentially defining its aims merely in relation to and in terms of the dominant, prevailing socio-economic order in crisis. And this is precisely what the leadership of Syriza in Greece has done, causing consternation, turmoil, splits and even disillusionment within that movement. We can expect the same approach with other 'left' or 'radical' movements across Europe and elsewhere unless their consciousness-mediated activity is animated by the absolute imperative to go beyond the parameters of the capital system itself.

The initiation of a struggle to radically alter the social relations in the workplace of a transnational corporation by bringing it into communal ownership, for example, is a struggle to go beyond the determining parameters of the prevailing socio-economic order. A workplace struggle to realize such an objective constitutes a measure adopted by the organized proletariat which points beyond the age of capital; measures which will generate the most tenacious resistance from capital and its state power.

What the proletariat actually does with these appropriated powers is absolutely critical for what unfolds subsequently: reaction or the opening out of the horizon of revolution. *The only way revolutionary agency can maintain its influence in the deepening crisis and accelerate the momentum of initiated changes is by relentlessly pressing ahead with further measures of restructuring the socio-economic landscape and the continuation of the transfer of the powers and institutions of decision-making into the broad movement of the proletariat itself.* Only in this way, by such defensible offensive changes – however minor or major they may be – can the activities of revolutionary agency point beyond capital and not serve to re-trench it.

If they point beyond capital, they serve to augment, to accelerate and perpetuate the whole revolutionary dynamic which has, thereby, already commenced in the face of opposition from the capitalist state. The skirmishes and collisions between the capitalist state and the young organs of revolution must then inevitably start to turn into, take on the direct, immediate form and expression of a struggle for power, a life and death struggle in which the capitalist state fights to defend the old conditions and the organized proletariat to transcend them and establish conditions for the transcendence of the age of capital proper by breaking its state power.

At all costs, what is fundamental is not to 'revitalize capital' but to point beyond it by means of a complete radical restructuring of powers and decision-making to initiate and sustain such measures. And herein lies the essential character of the relationship between revolutionary agency ('radical politics'), on the one hand, and the proletariat (the 'social body') as a whole, on the other.

It is, accordingly, a question of establishing a form of agency which will not simply and exclusively define its objectives and adopt 'narrow economic' measures within the terms and parameters of the capital order but, on the contrary, in terms which challenge and point beyond that order rather than patching or shoring it up. The Corbyn victory in the Labour Party leadership contest in Britain in 2015 augurs such a 'shoring up', Keynesian-style, regardless and in spite of the inspirational mass movement behind Corbyn's victory.

The relationship between agency ('radical politics') and proletarian class ('the social body') must be such that the developed forms of agency are capable of transferring ...

> at the height of the crisis its aspirations – in the form of effective powers of decision-making at all levels and in all areas, including the economy – to the social body itself from which subsequent material and political demands would emanate. This is the only way in which radical politics could sustain its own line of strategy, instead of militating against it.[21]

This is a critical observation for this whole question of agency concerning the relationship between the agency of revolution and the proletariat as a whole. In order to safeguard gains made and give impetus and momentum to the unfolding revolutionary process, it would be necessary for revolutionary agency to become the agency of this transfer of powers 'to the social body'. Only in this way does it actually become and exist as the revolutionary agency of and for the proletariat in the struggle to transcend the capital epoch.

Implicitly, the actual transfer of 'effective powers of decision-making at all levels and in all areas' takes place through the activity of the agency of revolution which also implies a deeply organic relationship between this agency and the proletariat as a whole. Without this organic relationship there can be no transfer and 'intercommuning' between form of agency and proletarian class.

This vital consideration remains a fundamental part of the whole question of agency to be addressed. The development of the conception, and practical articulation, of agency must therefore grapple with the specific character of this 'organic relationship' between agency and proletariat as a whole under the real, unfolding social crisis conditions within which the formation and development of agency ('Social Unions') is taking place.

Clearly, the emergence and development of capital's structural crisis demands, increasingly, a direct challenge to the rule of capital itself in both realms of production and 'public provision'. The question of 'occupation and appropriation' and the mobilization of people for maintaining this appropriation as communal property, as part of a 'commonwealth', becomes tactically necessary as part of an overall strategy to eliminate the capital relation. This is where the development of the perspective of the 'Social Union' comes into play.

In a *personal observation* of the organizational form of the 'mass street demonstration' (involving thousands, sometimes hundreds of thousands and millions as was the case of the popular demonstrations against Blair's war in Iraq in 2003), I was struck by the richness and diversity of its social and political composition. What came to mind – as a 'preliminary notion' so to speak – was a sort of mobile 'Social Union', something embryonic which was fluid and had not yet 'crystallized' or structured out into a determinate organizational form for appropriating and re-organizing the socio-economic metabolism on new foundations through the progressive elimination of the capital relation from the social landscape.

The interchangeability ('intermorphing') of the political form of the mass popular street demonstration with the 'overarching' determinately established organizational structure (strategically incorporating the 'occupation and appropriation' tactic and 'socially palisading' these communal appropriations) of the 'Social Union' came to mind as part of an overall strategy for the conquest of power (implying the dissolution of the state power of capital) and the uprooting of the capital relation, i.e. for socio-political revolution.

Such occupation and 'offensive to defend' (the 'social palisade') appropriation effectively becomes a means for taking over the powers of the capitalist state itself. Not only in the provision of social service and welfare. But in all areas of the socio-economic landscape which are fundamental for the defence and development of human culture beyond capital. With occupation and appropriation and its conscious political defence by means of the newly arisen form of agency (Social Unions), the proletariat, can start to take control of the historical process and determine its future direction thenceforth.

This strategy of 'society's offensive' against capital is stating unequivocally that we appropriate these 'means of and for the reproduction and development of human culture' as communal property. We will not accept their closure, mothballing or destruction or their transfer into the grasp of finance capital. And, on the contrary, we remove them from that grasp. We hold them out of the way of the grasp of self-valorising value and its state power by deploying and advancing the triangulated strategy of determinately 'organized Social Union' – 'occupation and appropriation' – 'mass street mobilization and demonstration'. *'Unheard-of combinations of circumstances demand unheard-of rules.'*[22]

Accordingly, forms of defence of these communal appropriations would need to be established and developed; a sort of social and political palisading of them, so that attempts to re-establish control by capital's state power could be adequately opposed and defeated through mobilization of the Social Unions.

Such communal appropriations would constitute themselves collectively and progressively as a sort of 'state of internal secession' from the capital order. Of course, not geographical secession in the manner of a national or ethnic region breaking away from a larger entity but rather an internal social and political secession, palisaded and defended by all means necessary which, again, is where the conception of Social Unions reappears. With Social Unions and the mass street movement as the mobilizing and intermorphing 'offensive to defend' forces, such occupations and appropriations would become a growing declaration of independence from the economic orbit and polity of the capital order.

Therefore, what is at stake here is the appropriation of the powers of capital which is equivalent to the disempowering of capital's state power. This must provoke reaction from this power because it opens up the capital relation itself to the vulnerability of breach and dissolution. Strategically and tactically, the priority at this stage is to defend all communal appropriation in the face of the mobilization and resistance by the state power that defends the rule of capital. Perspectives, strategies and tactics will be altered and developed according to the changing conditions of the struggle against the capital order.

And for all this, the proletariat must develop, elaborate and be animated by new, more offensive strategies and tactics of struggle against capital. Its general mode of struggle must switch from 'defensive' to 'offensive'. The conception of a tri-faceted movement of revolutionary agency would involve:

[a] the Social Union as the overarching, determinate form of agency, positively established organizational structure.
[b] occupation and appropriation tactics as a method of struggle, fundamental and intrinsic to the activity of the Social Union and its struggle against capital and its defending state power.
[c] the mass and, if necessary, offensive street demonstration deployed as a palisading method for the defence and entrenchment of occupation and appropriation of the infrastructure and powers of capital. Potentially, this offensive tactic of struggle, has implications for possible military mobilization and organization.

The 'intermorphing' of a, b and c into each other would constitute the different interconnected and intermediating sides of the fundamental, unified structure of the offensive dynamic of revolutionary agency against the capital order.

The 'mass street demonstration' is rich and varied in terms of its social and political composition. It articulates a wide variety of demands which are not necessarily directly related to the major demand of such demonstrations. On their own – as analysed previously – such individual demands would be supported by 'liberals' in general but when they combine into the 'programme' of an overarching form of agency, they start to challenge the capital order itself.

Such mass street demonstrations are a kind of mobile 'Social Union'. They are 'Social Unions' in embryo which are not, as yet, established as a determinate, overarching organizational form for appropriating and re-organizing the socio-economic metabolism on the basis of new socialist foundations. The interchangeability ('intermorphing') of the political form of the mass street demonstration with the organizational form of the Social Union and vice versa becomes politically articulated here as part of an overall strategy for the conquest of power and the uprooting of the capital relation, that is, for political and social revolution.

[vii] Restructuring and the State Power of Capital

Although it is necessary that the battle to 'materially restructure' commences prior to the overthrow of the state power of capital, it is, at the same time, totally unfeasible that the momentum of this restructuring could be maintained and sustained so as to go totally beyond capital without that overthrow. Only when the capitalist state is well and truly dissolved and replaced with the transient state power of the proletariat, at least in politically significant parts of the globe, does the global horizon truly start to open out for the unhindered and full consummation of this 'material restructuring' of the social metabolism beyond capital.

However, it is vital to emphasize that it is not simply a question of overthrowing the political power of capital in the form of its state, critical as that is in order to open up an unfettered and unhindered historical horizon for the consummation of the restructuring of the social metabolism. The actual restructuring of the social fabric and landscape which capital-in-crisis itself is now in the process of devastating will have to begin prior to the overthrow of this state power. However, this restructuring can only be fully consummated after the overthrow of the major centres of that state power across the globe. And, in particular, we will not be able to fully and comprehensively embark on the historic process of this 'full consummation' until the state power of capital in the United States of America is well and truly broken.[23] The widest possible social horizon will not be fully opened up for restructuring until the major national state and global powers of capital have been defeated and dissolved.

The 'conquest of state power' – the appropriation of political power by the proletariat for the continuation of this restructuring process – therefore commences in the struggle to appropriate and restructure the whole socio-economic ground on which that power is founded, disempowering capital of the ownership and control of society's landscape. Who owns, organizes, controls and runs this ground and determines its future development? Capital with its state powers or the proletariat with its agency of revolution?

Implicitly, what would arise is a 'dual power' situation (whose character is not simply 'political' but also 'socio-economic') animated by the arrival of capital's structural crisis at the point where the proletariat is actively forced to take such invasive socio-economic measures against capital. It is at this critical point where the commencement of the transfer of capital's powers becomes necessary in order to develop and consummate the initiated process of material restructuring.

Consider a situation where the conflict between the proletariat and the state has reached such a point that there is, effectively, such a duality of power emerging. The depth of the crisis is animating the whole situation. The capitalist state still has an effective counter-revolutionary coherence of organization intact and is struggling by various means to hold on to its rule over society. And yet the proletariat has coherently organized itself into mass socio-political bodies ('Social Unions') and is endeavouring, at the same time, to assert its rule over society and, as a result, employing various methods and coming into open conflict with the capitalist state.

It is at this point, whilst the capitalist state still retains a degree of effective coherence and is still struggling to hold on to power, that the proletariat is already, at the same time, fighting to point the way beyond capital by initiating socio-economic changes and using its organs of revolution to develop, sustain and defend these changes. So already, at this stage, the process of disempowering the capitalist state has already begun whilst the capitalist state is still in power.

The state power of capital will resist and fight to re-impose control over any areas which have been taken over and are being subject to 'restructure' by the Social Unions, i.e. by a process of re-organization which differs fundamentally from the old way of management under the appointees of capital and its state. So, in a certain sense, we have here the beginnings of the 'material restructuring' prior to the overthrow of capital's state power. However, and this needs to be stressed, these initial beginnings to 'materially restructure' are tentative, conditional, and not built on solid foundations because the oppressive shadow of capital's rule still looms over the proletariat in the form of its state. As soon as this tentative, highly conditional and insecure process of restructuring commences in the presence of this state power, the capitalist state itself must prepare to act with the totality of its forces because it senses its social ground shifting and disappearing from under its feet. Control of this socio-economic ground is the foundation of its very existence.

This is the point of 'do or die' because the proletariat cannot go on and sustain its changes under fire without the fullest mobilization of the socio-economic and political forces of its Social Unions. It must act or go under. And the state power of capital cannot re-establish its control and 'law and order' without continuing to resort to martial measures until it has achieved its objectives of crushing 'rebellion'. Such would be the dynamic established if the Social Unions start to take control of areas of the socio-economic landscape which capital has always taken for granted to be its very own untrespassable ('sacrosanct', inviolable) ground.

Herein, under such conditions, lies the absolutely fundamental importance of the unity and coherence of proletarian organization. What does 'pluralism' actually mean under such conditions, without a unifying, participatory coherence and co-ordination of action, without a determinately established, overarching, positive form of agency, when the state is launching a full scale, and very likely military assault against the proletariat fighting to lay down the conditions and foundations for the new society?

Even when the state power of capital is 'overthrown', the 'power' of capital itself remains just by its continued presence and by that of commodity production or its remnants in the social metabolism. And this can generate reactionary and restorationist trends in its favour until social revolution eradicates commodity production completely from the social metabolism.

The termination of the state power of capital does not automatically and immediately bring in its wake the elimination of capital from the socio-economic landscape. Indeed, it is only when and where the state per se is in the final phase of 'withering away' (i.e. society is finally dispensing with the state once and for all and becoming free of it) that humanity will have arrived at the final stage of disentangling itself from the legacies of bourgeois relations.

The state power – in its changing historical forms – is the guardian of the prevailing class relations. It is the organized instrument for the rule of one class over the whole of society but, primarily, over that ruling class's historically antagonistic class. The 'state' per se as a transhistorical formation only finally passes through the hour glass of human history with the termination of these relations. This point marks the beginning of a global communist human life mediating its own development on its own self-created and self-reproducing foundations.

Thus, whilst capital retains political power in any politically significant part of the globe, there will be a need for forms of proletarian agency, and this implies – no matter how transient or mutable – 'state' organization in one form or another. For the movement towards communism, it is the social character of that state which is crucial and not the fact that it remains a form of the 'state' as such.

The elimination of the capital relation from the social landscape cannot be fully realizable in the obstructing and violent presence of the state power of capital, that is, whilst it remains firmly entrenched on the historical scene. How does the proletariat proceed to a stage where the 'material restructuring of society's productive and distributive intercourse' opens out onto an unobstructed historical horizon in the presence of the nation state and global powers of capital?

Given the necessary conditions and the formation of the required organs of revolution, it is both feasible, and indeed necessary, that the appropriation of capital's powers and the commencement of this 'restructuring' of the socio-economic metabolism actually begins in the presence of the state power of capital. However, once this process of restructuring has begun, it would be totally unfeasible that it could continue apace without the defeat and break up of these same national state powers globally in the most politically significant regions of the planet.

Socialist theory has not, as yet, put forward a comprehensive conception of how the whole social metabolism can be globally and 'materially restructured' without the supersedence of the political powers of globalizing capital. Or at least in their most significant domains. The various struggles, in that they must strive to defend the natural and socio-cultural conditions of human life which are necessary for the development of the future society, must become oriented towards the formation of the necessary forms of agency which start to address this question of 'material restructuring' in actual historical practice.

The dissolution of the national state and global powers of capital is a pre-condition for the emergence of this 'unobstructed horizon'. But – to pose the fundamental historical problematic caught within which the proletariat now finds itself – the destructive and most devastating reproduction of capital continues apace as its crisis unfolds. The growth of opposition movements to the destructive manifestations of this crisis has already begun. However, they engage without a common 'organizational framework' which would multiply the power of their struggles and give them collectively a socialist character. In order to halt the havoc being wreaked by the crisis of the capital order, the implication is that the process of destruction of the state power of capital must start co-temporally with the appropriation of capital's powers and the beginnings of restructuring whilst the 'horizon' is still 'obstructed' by the existence of this state power. This is where the question of the character of agency is absolutely fundamental and comes into its own.

In these initial stages, the organs of revolution must, under such conditions, articulate themselves in their multiple functionality – socio-economic, political, logistical and other aspects. But to establish an optimal degree of freedom to 'completely restructure' in the continued presence of the state power of capital is another, totally and qualitatively different, question altogether. For the determinate positing of this degree of action implies the historical roadblock of the state power of capital has been broken up and dispersed in its critically and historically significant areas of the globe. Thus, although it is absolutely vital to stress that ...

> The principal impediment for embarking on the realization of the socialist project, and the strategic lever that must be firmly held in order to break the vicious circle of capital's organic system, is not the repressive power of the state – which can be overthrown under favourable conditions – but the defensive or offensive posture of labour towards capital.[24]

it is likewise crucial to stress that from where the proletariat stands now in terms of its organization, the primary pre-occupation and focus must be on the formation of the adequate forms of agency which can begin the process of appropriating capital's powers. It must do this in order to 'restructure' the social metabolism and, at the same time, step onto the political road of the dissolution of the state power of capital (as a 'principal impediment' to this full and unhindered 'restructuring') under those 'favourable conditions'.

And yet what is asserted here by Mészáros[25] is surely one of the most vital lessons, i.e. that history has already witnessed post-capitalist societies emerging after breaking the power of the capitalist state but labour did not fully and completely break the power of capital by transcending it globally either as a governing social relation of production and/or as a 'mode of metabolic control'. Rather, that social and political power of capital remained transmitted, according to Mészáros – as a 'mode of metabolic control' – through the bureaucratized structures of the Soviet state confronting the proletariat as alien bodies. The continuing presence of this power provided the ground for the ongoing process of capitalist restorations in Russia, China and Eastern Europe. Such trends have also started to emerge and are gaining momentum in 'revolutionary' Cuba.

Accordingly, the most urgent and concrete tasks at hand are to address the question of those forms of 'material mediation' (agency) through which the struggle to appropriate capital's powers, restructure the socio-economic landscape and break the political power of capital will be conducted in the course of the unfolding structural crisis. And this most definitely implicates new, offensive forms of struggle against capital and its state power. The question of these new, offensive forms of struggle and that of the creation of the higher form of agency (the new 'universal historic form' to replace the trade union form) are not two distinct questions but merely two, inseparable aspects of the same urgent question.

Under conditions of the deepening crisis of the capital order, the proletariat can only work towards the formation of the initial, necessary forms of revolutionary agency which actually commence the process of restructuring the socio-economic metabolism beyond the capital relation itself. That is, to commence the process of removing the capital relation itself from human society by making inroads into its universal domination. But the commencement of this process must raise the opposition of the state power of capital itself. Implicit in this opposition is the dissolution of that state power in order for the historical horizon to be fully opened up, fully unhindered, so that this process of the restructuring of society's landscape can be completed, fully consummated, by the necessary and evolving forms of revolutionary agency. Completing the historic task of eliminating capital from the social metabolism as whole on a global scale means that world perspectives and strategies will have to be developed as the situation unfolds and demands their elaboration, i.e. the actual unfolding of capital's crisis-process itself will necessitate the initiation and development of these global perspectives and strategies. This will require courage, audacity, determination and sometimes ruthlessness on the part of agency. Capital and its major state powers globally will try to muster any and every resource at its disposal to try to defeat agency's perspectives. 'Ethical' and 'human' considerations will not be a guiding paradigm in its counter-revolutionary strategy and actions.

[viii] Necessary Mutability of the Forms of Revolutionary Agency

The alteration, adaptation or modification of the agency of revolution or even its complete replacement by qualitatively distinct, new forms of organization ('not dependent on the negated object') which are more adequate for changes or transformations in conditions ('restructuring en route') will be decided by 'mass activity' and prosecuted through the 'agency' of the masses according to the conditions prevailing at the time. The constant 'self-criticism' to which revolutions subject themselves must therefore necessarily involve this constant possibility of the 'restructuring en route' of the forms of agency themselves. The 'criticism' involved is the real practical-conscious, revolutionary criticism which provides for, and actually organizes, the real process of this material restructuring 'en route' as conditions alter.

The capacity of people to proceed with these ongoing processes of organizational restructuring and the supersedence of older, outmoded forms of agency – when the time comes to move on – illustrates that it is they who are 'in charge' and not an aloof party machine or conservative, ossified state structures like bureaucratized 'Soviets'. For such ossified structures are themselves the historically superseded testimony (post 1989) that social interests had risen, congealed and crystallized out into state formations that opposed the historic interests of the proletariat and stood ruling over it as refractory, alien bodies.

These selfsame bodies have become instrumental as agencies for the restoration of capitalism in the so-called 'really existent socialist' societies of the Soviet Union, Eastern Europe and China. As far back as the early 1970s, in relation to the sustainability of the forms of revolutionary agency, Mészáros wrote that ...

> no socialist strategy can hope to succeed unless its general principles of orientation are adequately translated into socio-historically specific, dynamic and flexible, instruments and institutions capable of restructuring the whole of society, in accordance with the constantly changing realities of world-situation.[26]

and on the next page ...

> It is, therefore, inconceivable to achieve this radical restructuring of society in one sweep, however broad and elemental it might be. One can realistically set out only from the available instruments and institutions which must be restructured en route, through manifold transitions and mediations. To pretend otherwise is nothing but dangerous, self-disarming 'maximalism' which in reality turns out to be not only 'minimalism' but, more often than not, also directly responsible for disarray and defeat.

What we have presented here is a conception of institutions of transition which are not only 'socio-historically specific' and 'dynamic and flexible' but, furthermore, must not become ossified but always be liable to 'restructuring en route' according to the 'changing realities of world-situation'.

We set out 'only from the available instruments and institutions' (the importance of this 'setting out only from ...' must be emphasized) and proceed, proteus-like, to develop the forms of organization necessary for the transition according to the arising and disappearing demands and conditions of the 'world-situation'. The demands of changing global conditions (specifically the varying degrees of resistance of capital and its state powers) modulate the alterations and re-affirmations in the forms of agency in the course of the transition in which the capital relation is being eradicated from the 'social metabolic process'.

The question of the operation of a single fixed 'institution' being capable of tackling the constantly changing demands arising out of the unfolding period of transition is raised here. The danger that such an institution could clamp the fetters on this process of transition needs to be addressed. The dangers of 'institutionalization' thereby raises the possibility of the re-creation and re-trenchment of alienated structures, confronting the revolutionary class as organizational expressions of the continued existence and dominance of capital. The dangers of 'institutionalization'[27] imply the entrenchment of structures which stand in opposition to further development so that, for example, such structures – if posited as *the* institutions of transition – start to turn into their opposite. They become institutions of stasis and constituted as historical 'roadblocks'.

The bureaucratization of the Soviets in the Russian Revolution very clearly exemplifies this re-positing of alien social structures. They became organs of state power exercised above and over the proletariat i.e. organs through which the party machine and state bureaucracy transmitted its power and dominance over the proletariat. Hence the importance to guard against this in the development of 'institutions' i.e. against the re-trenchment of alienated structures which confront the producers as 'hostile powers of their own making'. Such a re-trenchment would become a prelude to the restoration of the state power of capital. The course of development after 1989 in the Soviet system and elsewhere is the real historic testament to this overall conception.

Thus, implicitly, it must not be any 'external' (alienated) body or organization which is in charge of the products of human labour and their distribution but rather the 'associated producers' themselves. It is the associated and organized producers themselves – in their *directly socialized labour* – who must make the 'democratic decisions from below' in regard to the reproduction and distribution of their products.

They make the 'democratic decisions from below' as to the distribution of the surplus according to the need to accumulate (technical development and innovation), transfer to a collective fund for public provision, workers' education/training, private consumption, etc.

Once the surplus is out of the hands of the producers themselves and appropriated/controlled by an alien body/organization then all the old 'muck of ages' has an even greater potential to re-establish itself (the Soviet Union, China, etc.). Those who appropriate and control the distribution of the surplus invariably generate and consolidate power structures for self-serving interest and privilege which stand in alien, hostile opposition to those whose labour has produced the surplus unless, of course, appropriation and control over production and distribution is by the associated producers themselves.

There can be no 'external separation of powers' as there was, for example, between party and soviets, in the Russian Revolution. The 'Social Union' is not, therefore, merely a 'political' body like a party which 'leads' the struggle against the state power of the capital order through the organization of a military struggle and war. Rather it constitutes itself as a socio-cultural singularity in which socio-economic, cultural, political and other roles and functions would arise out of it as demanded by the changing conditions and development of the struggle to put an end to the age of capital.

A practical-conscious conception of the point of termination (or appropriate condition-dependent modification of its structures, etc.) of the historical tenure of any specific form of agency would be arrived at by that form of agency through an evaluation of altered circumstances. Primarily, whether or not these altered circumstances demand its modification or politically safe supersedence, and whether this is politically expedient for the further onward transition to a society beyond the capital relation.

Men and women will have to adequately gauge the historical moment when a given form of agency can be safely left behind – because its existence is no longer socially necessary – and replaced without any actual or latent threat of the restoration of the political power of capital. If humanity continues to be caught in the revolutionary process of eliminating capital from the social landscape, this will, of course, remain the primary political consideration.

The initially arising, new higher universal historic form of proletarian organization which will constitute itself in opposition to the rule of capital must itself be a mass movement for socio-cultural transformation which has become established as a determinate and coherent 'organizational framework' prior to the overthrow of the capitalist state. And yet, simultaneously, it must be the active, flexible organ of political revolution capable of negating the state power of capital.

Moreover, it does not and must not preclude an inherent capacity for self-restructuring itself and this must apply to all forms of agency 'en route' in the course of pushing society's landscape beyond the capital relation as already mentioned. This self-restructuring function must, necessarily in response to altering social conditions, itself be 'structured' into all forms of agency and primed for operation. The reactionary and counter-revolutionary dangers of not intrinsically including such a democratic mechanism into all forms of agency are obvious. It is agency's own internal, built-in mechanism of historical obsolescence which becomes activated when it is necessary to alter its structures or, indeed, completely abolish them to be replaced by a higher form of agency more suited to altered socio-historical circumstances.

The agency of proletarian socialist revolution is, therefore, not simply characterized as an inflexible, static political agency. It is, necessarily, a multi-functionalized and historically mutable type of organization. Its character embodies and expresses the social, economic and cultural tasks which history spurs it on to realize as well as, simultaneously, its obvious and intensely political tasks.

The agency of revolution does not simply bear a political character but an essentially socio-cultural one out of which its political nature arises in the course of the drawn-out struggle against capital and its national state and global powers. It must combine these variety of functions – socio-economic, political, etc. – into a singularity of organization and activity. It moves and fights as a single, multi-functional organism with the actual and/or latent availability, dispensation and operation of its different functions according to the altering demands of changing conditions.

It can produce and withdraw, create, supersede and re-create, alter or discard 'en route', etc., in the course of the transition period, any function or weapon as required. And it contains within itself – and this is critically important against the possibilities of bureaucratic usurpation and imposition – those democratic mechanisms which permit its self-dissolution into higher forms of agency, if necessary, in order to push society continuously onwards beyond the age of capital and towards the 'true realm of freedom'.

Notes and References

1 *'In 2007, the United Nations said that on average, around 25,000 people die every day due to hunger or hunger-related causes. This means, every three and a half seconds one person dies. Children are dying most often.'*
   Asmaa Al-Hameli, 'How many people die each minute from starvation?' *Factchecking Injustice Facts* <https://factcheckinginjusticefacts.wordpress.com/2012/01/16/asmaa-al-hameli/> (Last accessed 6 November 2016).
   On average, *'1 child dies every 4 seconds. The silent killers are poverty, hunger, easily preventable diseases and illnesses, and other related causes. Despite the scale of this daily/ongoing catastrophe, it rarely manages to achieve, much less sustain, prime-time, headline coverage.'*
   Shah, Anup, 'Today, around 21,000 children died around the world', *Global Issues. Social, Political, Economic and Environmental Issues That Affect Us All* <http://www.globalissues.org/article/715/today-21000-children-died-around-the-world> (Last accessed 6 November 2016).

2 Hegel, G. W. F., *Logic, Part One of the Encyclopaedia of the Philosophical Sciences* (Oxford: Clarendon, Oxford University Press, 1975), pp. 157–161, Chapter VII, 'The Doctrine of Being'.

3 *'For some two centuries, the tranquil magnificence of the urban civilization of the Roman Empire concealed the underlying limits and strains of the productive basis on which it rested. For, unlike the feudal economy which succeeded it, the slave mode of production of Antiquity possessed no natural, internal mechanism of self-reproduction, because its labour-force could never be homeostatically stabilized within the system ...'*
   Anderson, Perry, *Passages from Antiquity to Feudalism* (London: NLB, 1974), pp. 76–103, Chapter 4, 'Rome'.
   See also G. E. M. de Ste Croix, *The Class Struggle in the Ancient Greek World from the Archaic Age to the Arab Conquests* (Ithaca, NY: Cornell University Press, 1981).
   Chapter IV, subsection (iii) *From Slave to Colonus*, p. 226 ff.
   Chapter VIII, *The 'Decline and Fall' of the Roman Empire: An Explanation*, p. 453 ff.

4 Mészáros, *Beyond Capital*, p. 950.
5 Ibid., p. 951.
6 Ibid., p. 369.

7   'Objects of utility become commodities only because they are the products of the private labour of individuals who work independently of each other. [...]; so that their character as values has already to be taken into consideration during production.'
   Marx, Karl, *Capital. A Critique of Political Economy*, Vol. 1, translated by Ben Fowkes (London: Penguin Books in association with New Left Review, 1976), pp. 165–166, Chapter 1, Section 4, 'The Fetishism of the Commodity and its Secret'.

8   Marx, *A Contribution to the Critique of Political Economy* (Moscow: Progress Publishers, 1977), pp. 84–86.

9   'The question why money does not itself directly represent labour-time, so that a piece of paper may represent, for instance, x hours labour, comes down simply to the question why, on the basis of commodity production, the products of labour must take the form of commodities. [...] Owen never made the mistake of presupposing the production of commodities, while, at the same time, by juggling with money, trying to circumvent the necessary conditions of that form of production.'
   Marx, Karl, *Capital. A Critique of Political Economy*, Vol. 1, translated by Ben Fowkes (London: Penguin Books in association with New Left Review, 1976), pp. 188–189, Chapter 3, 'Money, or the Circulation of Commodities' [Footnote 1].
   Only within the post-capitalist, socialist transitional phase does and can money 'directly represent labour-time' as 'time chit'. In the epoch of capital (capitalist commodity production), it does so only *indirectly*. [SM]

10 'If the labouring producer pays himself his own wages and if his product does not at first assume the 'shape' of other people's revenue from which savings are made and then paid back by these people to the labourer, it is necessary that the labourer be in possession of his conditions of production [...]. In order that his wages and consequently the labour fund can confront him as alien capital, these conditions of production must have been lost to him and have assumed the shape of alien property. [...] Once this separation exists, this process (the process of the real generation of capital – SM) does indeed take place and it continues and extends, since the surplus labour of the worker always confronts him as the revenue of others, through the saving of which alone wealth can be accumulated and the scale of production extended.'
   Marx, Karl, *Theories of Surplus Value, Part 3*, translated by Jack Cohen and S. W. Ryazanskaya, edited by S. W. Ryazanskaya and Richard Dixon (London: Lawrence & Wishart, 1972), pp. 412–422, Chapter 24, 'Richard Jones'.

   'Accumulated stock becomes capital only because of this personification.' Marx, Karl, *Theories of Surplus Value, Part 3*, translated by Jack Cohen and S. W. Ryazanskaya, edited by S. W. Ryazanskaya and Richard Dixon (London: Lawrence & Wishart, 1972), p. 427, Chapter 24.

11 Marx, *Value: Studies by Karl Marx* (London: New Park Publications, 1976), pp. 5–6.
12 '*If we proceed further, and compare the process of creating value with the labour process, we find that the latter consists in the useful labour which produces use-values. [....] Whether it was already contained in the means of production, or has just been added by the action of labour-power, that labour (labour as 'creator' and 'substance' of value – SM) counts only according to its duration. It amounts to so many hours, or days, etc.'*
    Marx, Karl, *Capital. A Critique of Political Economy*, Vol. 1, translated by Ben Fowkes (London: Penguin Books in association with New Left Review, 1976), pp. 302–303, Chapter 7, 'The Labour Process and the Valorisation Process'.
13 Mészáros, *Beyond Capital*, pp. 678–679.
14 Ibid., p. 679.
15 Marx, Karl, 'On the Hague Congress. A Correspondent's Report of a Speech Made at a Meeting in Amsterdam on September 8th, 1872'. In *Marx-Engels Col-lected Works, Volume 23, 1871–1874*, pp. 254–256, 254 (London: Lawrence & Wishart, 1988).
16 Mortimer, Caroline, 'British Army "could stage mutiny under Corbyn", says senior serving general', *The Independent* (20 September 2015) <http://www.independent.co.uk/news/uk/politics/british-army-could-stage-mutiny-under corbyn-says-senior-serving-general-10509742.html> (Last accessed 3 November 2016).
17 Von Clausewitz, Carl, *On War*, edited and translated by Michael Howard and Peter Paret (Princeton, NJ: Princeton University Press, 1989).
18 '"*Disarmament?*" *– But the entire question revolves around who will disarm whom. The only disarmament which can avert or end war is the disarmament of the bourgeoisie by the workers. But to disarm the bourgeoisie, the workers must arm themselves.'*
    Trotsky, Leon, *The Transitional Program. The Death Agony of Capitalism and the Tasks of the Fourth International* (1938) <https://www.marxists.org/archive/ trotsky/1938/tp/> (Last accessed 4 November 2016), Section: 'The Struggle against Imperialism and War'.
19 Mészáros, *Beyond Capital*, p. 949.
20 Ibid., p. 950.
21 Ibid., p. 951.
22 Brontë, Charlotte, *Jane Eyre* (New York: Dover Publications, 2011), p. 130.
23 '*In fact I am paradoxically convinced that the future of socialism will be decided in the United States, however pessimistic this may sound. I try to hint at this in the last section of "The Power of Ideology" where I discuss the problem of universality.*

Socialism either can assert itself universally and in such a way that it embraces all those areas, including the most developed capitalist areas of the world, or it won't succeed.'

Mészáros, 'Marxism Today: An Interview with István Mészáros', interview with Chris Arthur and Joseph McCarney, *Monthly Review* Vol. 44, No. 11 (April 1993). Reply to the question: 'What do you think of the current state of Marxist philosophy?'.

24 *Beyond Capital*, p. 790.
25 Ibid., p. 790.
26 Mészáros, *Marx's Theory of Alienation* (London: Merlin Press, 4th Edn, 1975), p. 287.
27 Mészáros, *Marx's Theory of Alienation*, p. 286.

PART IV

The Question of Revolutionary Agency in the Twentieth Century

CHAPTER 13

Lenin and the Question of Revolutionary Agency

[i] Lenin's Ahistorical 'Appeal to the Model Character of the Russian Revolution'

What are the lessons of the Russian Revolution – and the subsequent path it took – for us today in regard to the question of revolutionary agency? This chapter attempts to address this most fundamental of questions. Can we actually draw out lessons from this period in order to inform us in our work on agency today? How and why must the form of agency today differ from that which animated the Russian Revolution at the start of the last century?

If we study the highly differentiated conditions of capitalist development in different parts of the globe at the beginning of the last century, we can contrast this highly differentiated and polarized state to the growing uniformity of the socio-economic conditions of capital's rule in the different parts of the world in the epoch of its structural crisis today. This is a highly important consideration which impacts on the uniformity and degree of similarity and relatedness of the character of revolutionary agency in the different regions of the globe.

At the time Lenin was organizing in the first two decades of the last century, the more mature socio-economic conditions in other parts of the world were not necessarily conducive to Lenin's conception of agency and required different forms of agency even at that time.

Increasingly, today, we see a growing uniformity of conditions in different regions of the planet with the intensifying process of globalizing capital. The domination of globalizing capital in the national economies, state powers which articulate and defend the interests of capital, the proletariat as the overwhelmingly majority class in national populations, the trade union form as the persisting, general yet declining political organization of the proletariat, a diminishing peasantry in the 'new' capitalist centres such as China and India, the development of technique with globalization and local developments, the integration of communication systems globally through the internet, satellites and other technologies, the profit-driven services provided to the local populus, etc., are some of the major features of this growing uniformity and homogeneity of conditions within the indisputable historico-cultural differentiations within and between regions of the planet.

Life in all the major (and most 'minor') 'world cities' – in terms of the above and more – displays a growing uniformity and homogeneity in its socio-economic character as a result of the integrative processes being driven by structural-crisis mediated capitalist globalization. And this growing homogeneity is taking place despite the real social, economic and cultural divisions which exist within and between the proletariat in different regions of the planet. The major cities of the planet have become 'cities of the global empire of capital': 'cities of empire'.

This tendency towards a greater degree of uniformity and homogeneity of historical conditions across the globe (and, critically, the increasing homogeneity and uniformity of the proletariat as a global class) compared to those existent at the commencement of the twentieth century is highly significant for the question of the development and character of revolutionary agency. It implies and points towards the creation by the proletariat of a 'new universal historic form' of proletarian organization of a fundamentally new typicality across the globe to replace the trade union form and to address the problems arising and evolving out of capital's structural crisis. To move forward to terminate the epoch of the capital order.

This development of capital into its 'globalizing stage' forms the ontological basis for eclipsing the conception that at the time of Lenin and Trotsky – which is contrary to the uniformity of their 'model' conception of agency – different forms of agency were actually necessitated by widely differing conditions in different parts of the world. Now the tendency towards socio-economic uniformity, homogeneity and integration brought on by capitalist globalization points towards the establishment, development and co-ordinated activity of forms of 'revolutionary agency' in different parts of the world which are of a single universal type. This is engendered by the integrating power and character of the historic process of the globalization of capital itself as it continues to unfold.

This implies that each specific 'form of agency' for each country/region – in terms of its structure and organization – emerges as a 'concrete universal'; the particular expression – according to the specific, prevailing cultural conditions in each area of the globe – of the 'new universal historic form'. The unfolding socio-economic, homogeneous yet differentiated cultural conditions elicit the form of revolutionary agency in each region of the globe, constituting itself as a particular form of the 'new universal historic' type of organization replacing the trade union form. This universalizing and integrative process facilitates the co-operation and co-ordination of the activities of the proletariat in different regions of the planet as it struggles to end the epoch of capital globally. Just as the trade union form (a 'concrete universal' for the former, 'non-structural' epoch of capital's rule) arose independently in different parts of the world as a direct organizational response of workers to the general conditions of their exploitation in the workplace by capital, so the uniformity of social conditions being generated and propagated by globalizing capital-in-structural-crisis generates the conditions for the emergence of the 'new universal historic form' of proletarian revolutionary agency. Those aspects which differentiate the universal form of revolutionary agency in its various particularities and uniqueness of organizational expression must arise 'organically' out the prevailing localized historical conditions of time and place and not be transposed from and imposed as a 'template' from historically 'external' conditions. However, with the driving process of the global homogenization and integration of conditions engendered by globalizing capital's extension and intensification, the form of agency in each area of the world must reflect and articulate, simultaneously, both global universal and localized particular conditions.

To proceed on the basis of a historically divorced template of a form of agency arising necessarily out of the conditions in another age, time and place, is an 'ideological' way of proceeding in matters of revolutionary agency today. The agency of revolution must arise 'organically' (as it did in Tsarist Russia) out of 'already existing material conditions'[1] and not be ahistorically imposed by abstracting from the forms of agency of 'dead conditions' now superseded which barely resembled existent ones in advanced capitalist countries even at the time of the origination of the form of agency in the Russian Revolution.

After the Russian Revolution, this emulation of the 'Leninist model' took place everywhere. It was totally inconsonant, at variance, with the historical conditions which existed in Western Europe, even Japan and certainly the United States at that time. It was an ideologically mediated organizational error of historic proportions and, we need to consider, was perhaps an animating factor in the defeats of the proletarian class movements of the twentieth century.

All forms of revolutionary agency are historically conditioned and are most certainly not transcendent of place or time. The 'truth' (outcome) of the consideration here (namely how Lenin and Trotsky after 1917 approached the whole question of agency) gravitates around the conception which regarded the continuation of the 'orienting framework' of the 'model' of the Russian Revolution (with all the paternalistic 'vanguardist' accoutrement) as historically valid in parts of the world where conditions were totally unsuited to it at the time of the Russian Revolution never mind today.

Both Lenin and Trotsky maintained this 'orienting framework', this 'model' which was carried over from the Russian Revolution into and within the later Internationals (where it became axiomatic or 'rule'). And, of course, all the sundry 'Leninist' and 'Trotskyist' groupings and sects that came later adopted it. These groups raised it to scriptural status as one of the commandments or sacred pillars of so-called 'Leninist' party organization.[2] A dogmatic example today of the haunting and debilitating presence of this 'orienting framework' are the pre-occupations of the left groups with the 'democratic centralist *Party* form'.[3]

The form of proletarian organization given impetus by the events of the Russian Revolution and used in the attempt to conduct the struggle against capital was – through its universal adoption within the Comintern in 1920 – divorced from the real conditions of life of the proletariat in many parts of the world, especially the capitalist homelands of Europe and

North America. Trotsky was still insisting on the need for a Bolshevist-Leninist type party in 1937[4] for the Western European proletariat without any reference whatsoever to the markedly different historical conditions of the life of this more advanced section of the proletariat compared to the Russian proletariat at the turn of the century. The content of his absolutized 'democratic centralist *Party* form' conception was flexible and relative but he never openly acknowledged that the Party-form itself may be inappropriate under certain historical conditions. The 'spirit' became subsumed under the 'letter'.

As with Lukács, and with an 'indeterminate validity' (Mészáros), Trotsky turned *'Lenin's historically defined proposition into a general methodological principle'*.[5] The most we can say here about Lenin's conception of agency was that it was historically specific to the conditions under which it originated and developed and very soon revealed its limitations and its potential for deformation and adaptation to the needs of reaction and bureaucracy in the post-revolutionary epoch in Russia: 'Lenin created the apparatus. The apparatus created Stalin' (Trotsky).

And, of course, its complete inadequacy as the guiding framework of revolutionary agency and organization in the most advanced capitalist countries of the time onwards. Mészáros alludes to this for the altered conditions today when he writes ...

> The objective potentialities of the socialist offensive are inherent in the structural crisis of capital itself, as we shall see in a moment. Now the point is to stress a major contradiction: the absence of adequate political instruments that could turn this potentiality **into reality**. Furthermore, what makes things worse in this respect is that the self-awareness of the organizations concerned is still dominated by past mythologies, depicting the Leninist party, for instance, as the institution of strategic offensive **par excellence**. (emphasis IM)[6]

The 'Leninist', 'vanguard-type party' (as 'mythologized' by the 'organizations concerned') is rendered unnecessary today as a result of the radically altered conditions of struggle of the proletariat at the beginning of the twenty-first century. There is a need to develop forms of revolutionary agency which arise organically out of the specific nature of these new mediating, globalized conditions. Furthermore, in two startling criticisms of Lenin's position on 'party organization' and the 'model character of the Russian Revolution', Mészáros writes that ...

> the advocacy of the clandestine form of party organization as the universally valid guarantor of the correct ideology and strategy, to be applied also in Germany and elsewhere in the West, and later his (i.e. Lenin's – SM) direct ideological appeal to the model character of the Russian revolution, had their insuperable dilemmas. Once the strategic orientation of 'socialism in one country' prevailed in Russia after Lenin's death with dogmatic finality, the general line of the Third International – which continued to insist on the model character of Soviet developments – was in fact a contradiction in terms as far as the prospects of development for a genuine international socialist movement were concerned. It was therefore not in the least surprising that the Third International should come to the sorry end which it eventually reached[7]

and that ...

> the adoption by the Third International of the perspectives according to which the Russian revolution and its aftermath represented the 'near and immediate future' of even the capitalistically most advanced countries cannot be dissociated from Lenin.[8]

Implicitly, both Lenin and Trotsky 'ideologically' articulated a form of revolutionary agency – which arose in the historically specific and localized conditions of the Russian Revolution – as 'model' and historically necessary for the prevailing conditions of the most advanced capitalist regions (Western Europe, United States and Japan) of their time from 1920 to 1940. Today, the 'revolutionary groups' still adhere to *their* 'democratic centralist form' as the form of 'revolutionary agency' 'necessary' in the age of globalizing capital.

Lenin position (which became more pronounced after 1917) was indeed 'ideological'. In what sense? The form of revolutionary agency must arise organically within those same historical conditions which it is meant to address in the course of its activity. If the form is taken from markedly different conditions of a different historical time and place and imposed on the more socially advanced conditions, this amounts to an 'ideological' misappropriation and mis-deployment of the old conception of agency which was suited to the more 'backward' historical conditions.

Lenin's 'appeal to the model character of the Russian Revolution' was an example of such an 'ideological imposition'. The 'forms' in the Russian Revolution were taken as a 'template' for those conditions in the more advanced capitalist regions. In the course of such a 'deployment' outside of its grounding and superseded historical conditions of origination, the 'templated' conception itself is emptied of its historical content and significance, i.e. of any real, *organic* relationship to those historical conditions within which it arose and, moreover and critically, into which it has been ideologically grafted. It becomes the ideologically imposed dogma of organization.

Lenin, and Trotsky, after 1917, both moved towards an 'ideological' conception of revolutionary agency by 'appealing to the model character of the Russian Revolution' as the 'near and immediate future of even the capitalistically most advanced countries'. In doing this, the ideological concept arrived at – as the outcome of the experience of the form of agency in the Russian Revolution – served to divorce the necessary and specific form of agency from the historical conditions within which it actually germinates and grows, i.e. within the specific historical conditions giving birth to the necessary form and for which it is most suited and adequate in the struggle against capital in that particular part of the world. This became clear in the work and programmes of both the Third International and later in Trotsky's Fourth International within which the dogma of the 'democratic centralist Party form' was continued as the 'alpha and omega' of organization. It demonstrated that both Lenin and Trotsky, post 1917, had lost contact with Marx's approach in this particular regard. Many years before, Marx and Engels had concluded that ...

> The premises from which we begin are not arbitrary ones, not dogmas, but real premises from which abstraction can only be made in the imagination. They are the real individuals, their activity and the material conditions under which they live, both those which they find already existing and those produced by their activity. These premises can thus be verified in a purely empirical way.[9]

To adequately address the question of revolutionary agency today presupposes that the necessary and historically adequate form of organization of agency cannot be ahistorically imposed like a 'template' on existent conditions. Rather it must arise organically and be intrinsically related and intertwined with these unfolding historical conditions. This means that any past conceptions – which reflected the form of organization of revolutionary struggle in a previous time, place or epoch – must be subject to a critique on the basis of existent conditions, their specific character and on the changes which have taken place since the old forms disappeared. If ideologically imported from outside of the prevailing, socio-historically and specific conditions of its necessary creation, the form of revolutionary agency cannot be historically adequate to function as the required form of agency necessary to go beyond these specific conditions in social revolution.

Accordingly, it assumes a supersedence in both theory and practice of the ideological pre-occupation with forms of agency which were more suited to the past, dead conditions of a society which had only relatively recently witnessed the abolition of serfdom (1861) and had only just started to establish the foundations of a modern capitalist system in its major urban centres.

The organizational needs of the proletariat and their practical articulation in the age of capital's structural crisis are, accordingly, increasingly hindered the more that thought ceases to move beyond this *ideological realm*. The theory of organization becomes increasingly 'ideological' the more it ceases to continuously re-fresh itself anew as a result of changes and shifts in socio-historical conditions. It begins to get bogged down in dogma and continues to wade around in the dead conceptual refuse of past, historically superseded forms of organization.

The conception of the 'need' for a 'democratic centralist revolutionary party' in the diminishing left-wing sectarian groups today is a lucid example of this dogmatization and 'conceptual refuse of history'. It is the *ideological* appropriation of a 'need' by these groups within historical conditions which necessitate different forms of agency and stand as the negating ground of such a 'need'. In this respect, it becomes, as Engels writes, an '*occupation with thoughts as with independent entities, developing independently and subject only to their own laws*'.[10] and, indeed, can be characterized as a form of '*false consciousness*'.[11] 'Marxists' possessed by a 'false consciousness'. Like men (and they are, strangely, mostly male) presently haunted by the ghosts of past, dead, spent conditions, the organizational forms created by which are identified as those now necessary for the currently deepening conditions of capital's structural crisis.

The conception of the 'democratic centralist party form' has been subjected to this *ideological fate* since its imposition as statute at the second congress of the Third International in 1920. Its organizational precepts have been located as an 'entity' – an inalienable principle of proletarian revolutionary organization – 'developing independently' and regardless of any radically divergent shifts in 'material life conditions' outside of those of the Russian Revolution in the first decades of the last century.

If the subject, *on the one hand*, does not make *the connection between the negation* of those historically specific conditions within which a particular form of thought and organization *necessarily* emerged and developed in order to address confronting tasks at the time *and, on the other hand*, the consequential requirement to move beyond those particular, historically conditioned and limited thought-forms (with its profound significance in terms of organization and revolutionary agency), then the continuing persistence of these thought-forms takes on an *ideological* and *outmoded* character, divorced from the newly posited conditions, without any *real connection* to them. It means that the subject persists in operating with the 'insubstantial ghosts' of the past rather than with the activity-engendering 'substantial shadows' of the living present.

Such an ideological thought-process makes it impossible to address the urgent questions of revolutionary agency today as the structural crisis of the global capital order opens up and worsens. It renders the notion of the 'democratic centralist *Party* form' as applied to the more advanced capitalist regions at the time of the Russian Revolution, and subsequently, to be a form of 'false consciousness'. Of course, it was not such a form at the time Lenin was writing *What is to be Done?* but by 1920 – as presented for assimilation and articulation by the national sections in the Comintern – it had indeed become so.

This raises a further question: was it *unrelated and accidental* that the two decades of 'Leninist agency' (1919 to 1940) also coincided with the worst defeats for the international proletariat in the twentieth century? Could not the actual ahistorically and ideologically imposed and advocated form of agency – using and 'appealing to the *model* character of the Russian

Revolution' – have mediated, partially at least, the series of defeats for the proletariat throughout these two decades? As if the proletariat in the major capitalist regions was employing a form of agency which was organizationally unsuited to the prevailing conditions at the time? Did Lenin's method of approaching the question of agency actually alter after 1917 in so far as he abstracted and ideologized the experience of the Russian Revolution, projecting and positing it as a 'model' or 'template' for different and varying conditions of the capitalist system around the globe?

We need to ask ourselves if the 'democratic centralist *Party* form' is the necessary form of revolutionary agency today in the epoch of capital's structural crisis. Moreover, if it would be folly to deny the possibility that 'trade union consciousness' and so-called 'spontaneity' cannot develop into a higher form of agency and begin to evolve a 'communist consciousness' on a mass scale. Only the ever-diminishing 'vanguardist' groups today would give an affirmative 'yes' to the former question and most certainly 'deny the possibility' in the latter consideration.

[ii] From the Temporally Conditioned Strategy of Lenin's *What is to be Done?* in 1901 to the Ideologically Posited Internationalized Statutes of the *Comintern* in 1920

Lenin's conception in *What is to be Done?* was a remarkable piece of strategical and tactical thinking – to inform real activity and organization – which was rendered necessary by the conditions confronting the young Russian proletariat and socialist revolutionaries at the start of the last century in Tsarist Russia. Adopting an approach to revolutionary agency, at that time in Russia, which was more suited for the historically 'more mature' bourgeois 'democracies' – where the proletariat had established and was developing more democratic rights – would have been disastrous with the likely consequence being the wholesale destruction of Lenin's organization under the repressive conditions of the time. The strategy and tactics Lenin adopted and developed made possible the actual formation of revolutionary organization. This would not have been possible – or not have maintained itself – under the conditions of the time if any other strategy had been elaborated.

The strategy Lenin initiated and developed arose directly from the historical conditions within which he was working. We are now living under radically altered historical conditions at the start of the century of capital's deepening structural crisis.

In Russia, Lenin necessarily orientated his political activity in close and direct relation to these conditions of struggle of his time under Tsarism as we must today in our time under the prevailing conditions at the beginning of the twenty-first century. And who wouldn't proceed accordingly today? Except the 'vanguardist' sects and cults, many of which have elevated *What is to be Done?* to the status of a Vedic dogma or mantra.

If Lenin had derived his conception of agency from Marx's work in the International Workingmen's Association (IWMA), thirty years earlier, this itself would have been 'ideological' and totally inappropriate for the conditions of Tsarist oppression facing Lenin and his fellow revolutionaries.

Marx's conception presupposed a historically more advanced, more 'mature' proletariat than was found in Tsarist Russia in 1900 at the time. Marx did not exclude the possibility of socialist revolution in 'backward' lands but he was presupposing a more 'mature' stage of development of the capitalist system within which a successful international struggle for socialism could be opened up and developed. This constitutes the historical and theoretical basis for the explicit or implicit aspects of his conception of the character of the proletariat as a revolutionary class and of revolutionary agency. This can be studied in detail in the documents of the IWMA (First International) and in his work on the Paris Commune of 1871.

We must not forget that the IWMA was essentially a movement of the most advanced sections of the global proletariat in Europe and the United States. The Russian proletariat was in its infancy when Marx and others were forming and attempting to build the IWMA within the ranks of these most advanced sections. The immature nature of the Russian proletariat gave the early class movement in Russia, at this time, a petit-bourgeois, *Narodnichestvo* character. We need to explain Marx's conception in contrast to that of Lenin by taking into account the differential character of the conditions within which they were working. They were radically different and Lenin clearly appreciated the simple truth of this matter when he wrote *What is to be Done?* in 1901.

We need to consider the prevailing conditions of persecution, clandestinity, arrest, execution, exile, etc., at the time *What is to be Done?* was written and published (1901/02). Only in the light of, and within, these prevailing conditions can its content and historical significance be located. Certainly not 'outside' of them. These conditions were primary determinants which informed the type of political organization necessary to conduct the struggle against the Tsarist state machine and capital in Russia at this particular stage at the start of the twentieth century. As Lenin himself very clearly stated, the text was written and developed essentially as a tactical/strategical (and not axiomatically) document informing political organization under very definite, specific, historical conditions which we saw in Tsarist Russia at this time. This was Lenin's conception at the time in 1901/02. And, indeed, his conception actually altered soon afterwards. In September, 1907, Lenin wrote that ...

> The basic mistake made by people who polemicise with What is to be Done? at the present time is that they tear this production completely out of specific historical context, out of a specific and by now long-past period in the development of our party ... What Is To Be Done? is a summary of Iskra tactics and Iskra organizational policy in 1901 and 1902. Precisely a 'summary', no more and no less.[12]

Two years earlier – in his draft resolution for the Third Party Congress – he had written ...

> Under conditions of political freedom, our party can and will be built entirely on the elective principle. Under the autocracy this is impracticable for the collective thousands that make up the party.[13]

Later on in November 1905 in his article *The Reorganization of the Party*, he argued that ...

> The conditions in which our Party is functioning are changing radically. Freedom of assembly, of association and the press has been captured ... We, the representatives

of revolutionary Social Democracy, the supporters of the 'Majority' [Bolsheviks], have repeatedly said that complete democratization of the Party was impossible in conditions of secret work, and that in such conditions the 'elective principle' was a mere phrase. And experience has confirmed our words ... But we Bolsheviks have always recognized that in new conditions, when political liberties were acquired, it would be essential to adopt the elective principle.[14]

The completely 'non-ideological spirit' of Lenin in *What is to be Done?* was to orientate the development of revolutionary organization in relation to the prevailing, mediating conditions under which he was working. His conception of agency at the time – and its real, practical articulation in terms of organization – arose necessarily out of his approach to these confronting conditions. It was an adequate organizational response to these conditions which took place within the medium of historically backward conditions of capitalist development incorporating a numerically small and immature proletariat relative to the more advanced capitalist regions of Europe and North America.

However, the form of organization necessarily developed under these conditions – whilst being an adequate response to them – could only be taken as adequate for these specific conditions. And this is not what actually took place throughout the twentieth century. The work of the Third and Fourth Internationals was testimony to the transposition of this 'orienting framework' beyond those historically specific conditions in which it was made necessary. The historically conditioned form of revolutionary agency specific to and arising out of the backward conditions of Tsarist Russia was taken as a 'model'. It was then unrealistically and metaphysically re-located to where it had not grown organically out of the specifically existent historical conditions of capital's rule in the more advanced regions of capitalist development across the globe.

In Section 10.2.2 of *Beyond Capital* (pp. 394–396), Mészáros discusses Lenin's approach on the question of agency in '*opting for an organization of professional revolutionaries who can operate under the conditions of strict secrecy*' rather than '*the creation of a mass political organization*'. He then proceeds to show why such a model would now be '*hopelessly inadequate*' under the present conditions at the start of the twenty-first century, the century of capitalist globalization. And, specifically and vitally, on how the so-called *'from outside'* can become the *'from above'*.[15]

The Soviets established by the Russian Proletariat in 1905 (like the Paris Commune of 1871) sprang from its self-organization and self-activity in the struggle against the ruling conditions of the day. These bodies were not the creations of the Bolsheviks or the Mensheviks. But Lenin and the Bolsheviks adopted a specifically 'vanguardist' relationship with and to the Soviets. A relationship which contained an approach to the self-organizing activity of the proletariat as an activity to be located within the 'revolutionary gravity' and 'orbit' of Bolshevism itself.

What arose in Lenin's and others' conceptions – under the pressing conditions of the time – was that the Soviets were the 'spontaneous' products of the class movement which could only become 'truly revolutionary' if the Bolsheviks were at their helm. In and for themselves, they could not be 'revolutionary' without such 'intervention'. This served to validate any explicit or implicit conceptions of 'vanguardism' and of 'bringing revolutionary consciousness from the outside into the masses' so that the whole relationship of Lenin's party with the class in Russia at the time operated within the enclosing orbit of this relationship.

In Marx's conception, the centre of 'revolutionary gravity' is located within the self-organizing activity of the proletarian class itself so the 'emancipation of the proletariat must be the act of the proletariat itself'.[16] And this difference in conception, of course, arises out of the different historical conditions within which Lenin and Marx lived and were working.

The Bolsheviks – under threat from many sides from 1917 – located the centre of 'revolutionary gravity' (and more decidedly and prominently after 1917) within their own 'Party' body rather than it being centred within the revolutionary self-activity of the proletariat itself as with Marx's conception in his IWMA work. The rule of the 'Party' constituted itself as a fertile ground for the rise of a place-hunting, careerist bureaucratic elite. It was the unfavourable conditions of struggle and the economic devastation after the civil war that formed this ground for the increasingly authoritarian and centralized structuring of Lenin's party and the state power. As Trotsky was later to write in his notebooks in the 1930s: *'Lenin created the apparatus. The apparatus created Stalin'* (see Note 20).

Moreover, the social composition and ontological 'immaturity' of the proletariat in Russia at the time actually served to hinder opposition to the growing trends of bureaucratic dictatorship of which Stalin became the figurehead and personification. This contrasts with the character of the proletariat today in the age of globalizing capital and differentially impacts on the nature of the forms of revolutionary agency required today in contrast to those in Lenin's day.

Lenin's 'dictatorship of the proletariat' turned against the proletariat itself, at which point its whole character altered and became the rule of a tyrannical clique which actually served the interests of the international capitalist system by acting as a conservative brake on genuine socialist revolution across the world. This ruling caste – in the course of establishing its rule over Russian society – identified and distinguished its own interests as a caste from that of the historic interests of the proletariat as a class. This is a lesson of history (from the Russian Revolution) which we take with us not only into the struggles to come but, more specifically, in regard to the question of the creation of the necessary and evolving forms of revolutionary agency with which capital's deepening structural crisis will inevitably and increasingly continue to confront us.

En passant, the emergence of bureaucratic dictatorship after 1917 is a phenomenon which anarchism continues to point to as a vindication of its abstract conception that the 'state is the ultimate enemy' regardless of its form. This anarchist position, in actual practice, merely serves to re-invite what it purports to eradicate. In its opposition to the transitory state power of the proletariat, it merely serves to re-introduce the capital relation and its political powers.

Lenin's shifting conception of revolutionary agency – according to the changes taking place in Russia between 1900 and 1923 – was fundamentally influential throughout the twentieth century and even today. But the 'model' conception of the need for a 'democratic centralist Party' – outside of specifically Russian conditions in this period and supposedly adaptable to the most advanced capitalist countries – was taken out of the historical conditions within which it was generated and made necessary. Attempts were then made (primarily through the work of the Comintern) to graft the conception into different conditions in Europe and in other parts of the world where its 'necessity' was not grounded in the social conditions of these more advanced capitalist formations. Lenin's initial conception – which he clearly stated was a 'summary of *Iskra* tactics and no more' – was developed in the conditions of struggle in Tsarist Russia at the beginning of the twentieth century. But beyond that, in the more advanced capitalist countries, its relevance was questionable to say the least. In relation to the *modus operandi* of the 'Party form', Lenin moves away from the 'clandestine' to the 'elective' mode after 1902. However, the fundamental conception of the 'democratic centralist Party' structure remains.

The fact that it was necessary in the conditions of Tsarist Russia did not render it necessary (an organizational pre-requisite) for other parts of the capitalist world at the time where more advanced conditions prevailed. But Lenin's 'democratic centralist Party' conception distilled over into the work of the Third and Fourth Internationals where it took the ideological form of organizational statute. Even at the beginning of the twentieth century, the conditions in Russia were 'worlds away' from those in capitalist Western Europe and the United States. And this means these more mature conditions were not necessarily conducive to Lenin's conception of agency and required different forms of agency *even at that time*.

Lenin's conception shifted from the historically limited, temporally conditioned and strategically and tactically mobile before 1917 towards an increasingly, fully posited, fixed ideological and 'internationalized' conception after 1917. By the time we reach the second congress of the Comintern in 1920, the precept of the 'democratic centralist Party' form had become incorporated into the work and programmes of the different national sections of the Third International, albeit with opposition from some sections and trends within the International.

The 'democratic centralist Party' form of organization now became an incantation to which revolutionaries worldwide should dance in their organization. Its 'historically conditioned and limited' content had become transformed into its opposite. The 'democratic centralist Party-form' (which, in its 'clandestine' mode – by Lenin's own admission in 1907- was historically relative to very specific circumstances and largely 'tactical' in this mode) now became ideologically posited as a dogma to which all national sections must conform in their organizational structure in order to satisfy the criteria of admission to the Comintern. All national sections were to follow this line if they were to be admitted to the Third International.[17] And all under the direction of Lenin and Trotsky from 1920 onwards. This was imposed on the different national sections through the so-called '21 conditions' (formulated in the Summer of 1920) as a *sine qua non* for admission to the Third International. The Dutch, so-called 'Left Communist', Pannekoek criticized this Bolshevik approach as 'a doctrine of the revolutionary minority'.[18]

The implication in Pannekoek's article that the Bolsheviks 'whipped up the masses' into revolution is, of course, far from the truth of the history of the Russian Revolution. And it was a misconception to refer to the Bolsheviks as 'New Blanquists' when we consider the prevailing conditions at the time in the first two decades of the twentieth century in Russia. However, Pannekoek's implicit assertion that Lenin and the Bolsheviks were 'modelling' the experiences of the Russian Revolution – and then were metaphysically extrapolating and imposing them on the struggles of the proletariat in the more advanced conditions existing in the United States, Europe and Japan at the time – is a consideration that cannot be ignored in the light of the history of the twentieth century. Indeed, it may be asserted that Lenin's position, in this respect, was a radical departure from the historical dialectics of Marx.[19]

The adoption of this 'model' of agency by the Third International (to be followed by all national sections) was an intrinsic part of Lenin's 'direct ideological appeal to the model character of the Russian revolution'. The politically most significant national sections were those where historical conditions prevailed that did not remotely resemble those of Tsarist Russia at the start of the twentieth century. The imposition of the leading agency-form mediating the Russian Revolution into Comintern statute actually meant that national sections could not employ the necessary degree of freedom of movement and political flexibility which was required to develop the form of revolutionary agency which was more suited to the conditions within which they were active in the most advanced capitalist regions of the planet.

The widely differing historical conditions in different parts of the world necessitated greater flexibility and modulation in relation to the form of revolutionary agency. Such differences were politically represented in the various national sections of the Comintern from 1919 to 1923. The precepts for admission to the Comintern were pre-established and imposed rather than leaving the question of the form of organization to the different national sections according to the differences in the stages of capitalist development with their specific, localized socio-economic and historical conditions.

Lenin's perspective – under the impact of events from 1917 to 1923 – on the form of revolutionary organization became ossified in relation to the differentiated conditions in different parts of the world. The political organizations of the proletariat in the major, politically significant, capitalist countries were not under the intense internal and external pressures of the infant revolution in Russia after 1917. The socio-economic and political conditions of their activity as class organizations did not remotely resemble those within which the numerically small Russian proletariat and the Bolsheviks were active. This 'ossifying tendency' in Lenin's conception on agency after 1917 – in combination with 'his direct ideological appeal to the model character of the Russian revolution' – later served to provide Stalin and the 'apparatus' with the political feed and justification for its brutal dictatorship over the Russian proletariat.[20]

Lenin's closing approach to the conception of revolutionary agency – in the last five years of his life – ran counter to his earlier propositions regarding the need for flexibility in regard to the form of organization based on 'real material conditions'. This was both a theoretical and a political mistake. It was wrong in 1920 and wrong in Trotsky's Fourth International in 1938; it is most certainly wrong now at the start of this twenty-first century – a time of globalizing capital in its growing structural crisis. In this sense, Lenin's conception of agency became the victim of the dialectic rather than its master, moving from the historically limited and temporally conditioned in 1901 to the ideologically posited for all sections of the Comintern according to the '21 Conditions' for membership in 1920.

Today, in the age of capital's deepening structural crisis, it would be a mistake of historic proportions to 'dance to the tune' of conceptions of agency which were more suited to totally different and past conditions of struggle.

[iii] The 'Intelligentsia', the 'Origin Myth' of Socialism and 'Consciousness from the Outside'

Lenin – at the termination of the nineteenth century when the capital order was at least a century behind its maturing structural crisis – writes, unequivocally, that ...

> Class political consciousness can be brought to the workers only from without; that is, only from outside the economic struggle, from outside the sphere of relations between workers and employers. The sphere from which alone it is possible to obtain this knowledge is the sphere of relationships (of all classes and strata) to the state and the government, the sphere of the interrelations between all classes.[21]

Later we read that 'the history of all countries shows that the working class, exclusively by its own efforts, is able to develop only trade-union consciousness' and that the theory of socialism was the creation of the 'educated representatives of the propertied classes'; the 'bourgeois intelligentsia' within which category Lenin locates both Marx and Engels. All this, of course, resonates with Kautsky's famous article in *Die Neue Zeit*, regarding the 'bourgeois intellectual' origins of 'modern socialism', in which he writes ...

> it was in the minds of individual members of this stratum that modern socialism originated, and it was they who communicated it to the more intellectually developed proletarians who, in their turn, introduce it into the proletarian class struggle where conditions allow that to be done. Thus, socialist consciousness is something introduced into the proletarian class struggle from without [von Aussen Hineingetragenes] and not something that arose within it spontaneously [urwüchsig].[22]

Kautsky's conception here is highly abstract. A metaphysic which runs contrary to the basic conceptions of materialist dialectics. It renders, implicitly, the proletariat as a passive receptacle. And the intelligentsia as the subjective progenitor and active agent of introducing socialism to the proletariat. Under the life conditions of a historically immature proletariat in Tsarist Russia, it was entirely feasible that such a conception could take root amongst revolutionaries and the conception of 'consciousness delivered from the outside' find fertile ground for germination and growth.

Philosophically, and especially in terms of a historical epistemology, it is highly formalistic and akin to a 'reverse food chain' approach and conception applied to the development of 'socialist consciousness'. It implicates hierarchy and an almost priestly approach to the proletariat in which socialism originates in the heads of the so-called bourgeois intelligentsia in order for it to be passed down – through a series of social connections and mediations – to the politically and intellectually starving proletariat who are awaiting, in their servitude, a revelatory message of emancipation from on high.

Kautsky's notion of the genealogy of 'modern socialism' has a pseudo-religious resonance: the founders of the religion ('individual members of this stratum') as the source and emanators of 'the divine message' and, by means of a devoted refraction through their apostles ('intellectually developed proletarians'), the massed congregation of followers ('proletarian class struggle') come to see the 'light'. As Mike Cole writes, this is a conception in which ...

> The working class could only arrive at the necessary consciousness and thereby the unity necessary for social revolution by understanding the full historical implications of its role in production and its capacity for **abolishing class society**. This body of theory could not come from the working class but only 'from the outside, from bourgeois intellectuals' (ibid.). This perspective rests on a particular ontological presupposition: that there is an 'outside' of capital's social universe. It assumes that a group of people – bourgeois intellectuals – can exist socially **qua** intellectuals outside of, and beyond, capital. This needs some justification and, as it stands, appears to present the bourgeois intellectual who dons the revolutionary cloak as a feral, Romantic figure. Moishe Postone (1996), for example, has argued that there is no 'outside' of capital's social universe; there is no 'wild'. Capitalist society is a form of **totality** and totalizing of human existence, which incorporates all that it encounters. It has to be imploded from **within**. (emphasis Mike Cole)[23]

Accordingly, this conception of 'consciousness from the outside' is deeply problematic on both ontological and epistemological grounds. The primordial source of the 'emancipation of the working class' is not the 'working class itself' but rather is presented as the 'bourgeois intellectual' who comes shining forth from the depths of the 'transcendent realm' outside of capital's kingdom – donning *'the revolutionary cloak as a feral, Romantic figure'* – as an indispensable *demiourgos* 'bringer of light' to the masses. Philosophically, the Hegelian, and even Platonic, connotations can be discerned in such a figure. In the beginning was the word. And the word was with ... the 'bourgeois intellectual'.

The conception of the origins of 'modern socialism' in the 'minds of the bourgeois intelligentsia' virtually confers the status of an 'origin myth' or 'foundation myth' which leads directly on to the path towards the political justification of the notion of 'consciousness from the outside'. In the same way that 'foundation myths' in general serve to support and justify the established relations and structures of that whose 'origins' are being described in the narrative of the 'mythology'.

Of course, it is *completely inadequate* to assert that socialism, as a theory of social development, was simply the product of the most 'advanced minds' of the bourgeois intelligentsia. Both Marx and Engels and their 'utopian' predecessors were born, reared and educated as part of the life of the bourgeois class, that is, under the social and intellectual conditions of this class. In this sense, *in their intellectually formative years*, the term 'bourgeois intellectual' is valid.

However, Marx himself – as he got to work in the 1840s – moved away very rapidly from, and actually ceased to be part of, the 'bourgeois intelligentsia' to which Kautsky refers. Marx the 'bourgeois intellectual' of 1840 (age 22) – by process of development through the 1840s – had ceased to be a 'bourgeois intellectual' well before 1848 in the year of the publication of the *Manifesto*. Marx – in the process of becoming 'Marx' – is no longer part of this stratum but has become a communist revolutionary. One cannot be a 'bourgeois intellectual' and a communist revolutionary at the same time; on a question of determinacy, 'one cannot be a whitewasher and a chimney sweep at the same time' (Hegel). Marx, of course, started out as a radical 'bourgeois intellectual' in his youth but this is different to asserting that *'class political consciousness can be brought to the workers only from without'*.

This is not, of course, to assert that Marx personally did not retain certain cultural sensibilities of his class of origin. But to assert that Marx the communist revolutionary was a part of the 'bourgeois intelligentsia' from the mid-1840s onwards is actually incorrect. We must suspect that Marx himself would have replied with an appropriate retort if others had addressed him directly as a 'bourgeois intellectual'. Were Kautsky, Lenin and Trotsky all 'bourgeois intellectuals' when they 'brought socialist theory' into the 'ranks' of the 'more intellectually developed proletarians'? No, of course not.

'Bourgeois intelligentsia' does not simply imply that an individual is an intellectual who originates socially from the bourgeois class. The term 'bourgeois' in the expression denotes *class outlook*. It is entirely feasible today for somebody of proletarian origins to be part of this intelligentsia and for someone who originates from the bourgeois class and its intellectual circles to make the transition to become a revolutionary. The term intrinsically implies that the conceptions which an individual develops actually *articulate and represent* the historical interests of the bourgeois class. And, of course, this was not the case with Marx whose life's work articulated the interests of the proletariat.

Under the prevailing conditions of nineteenth-century capitalism in Europe, the *individual human agents* of the *theory* of socialism could not possibly have originated from the proletarian class. They could only have come from a class which had the leisure and time and all the latest discoveries in human thought and technique at its disposal. But that is different from asserting that 'it was in the minds of individual members of this stratum that modern socialism originated'.

The theory of socialism is, *more concretely*, the product of the development of *bourgeois culture as a whole* and not simply the creation of the bourgeoisie or its intelligentsia *abstractly identified* as such. It was the *necessary* creation of the development of bourgeois *culture* as a whole and that, of course, is an entirely different matter from it being the creation of the 'bourgeois intelligentsia' or 'bourgeois class' as we find asserted in Kautsky. Or even simply being the creation of Marx and Engels. Its leading creative thinkers were the sons and daughters of the bourgeois class. But it is historically incorrect and *unduly abstract historically* to assert that the theory of socialism was the creation of the bourgeois class (from which its leading agents originated) or of its intelligentsia.

The actually existent and sharpening contradictions of the capitalist system itself point towards socialist society as its successor. On this historical ground alone, the 'theory of socialism' finds deep ontological roots independently of the 'minds of individual members' of the bourgeois intelligentsia. Hence, the historic origination and development of socialist theory has *a manifold causality* in the history of bourgeois culture. This has implications for Kautsky's view of the origins of socialist theory growing out of the 'minds of the individual members' of the bourgeois intelligentsia and the proletariat then being 'seeded' with its conceptions as a result of dispersal from the 'intellectual tree of socialist theory'. The religious undertones are almost audible.

The historically immature conditions under which the Bolsheviks were working provided fertile ground for conceptions of 'consciousness from the outside' to take root. It would be simplistic to assert that Lenin merely adopted Kautsky's concept without a comprehensive consideration of the historical conditions within and under which the Bolsheviks were active. When conceptions are suited to specific historical conditions – even though they may have originated outside of those conditions – it is sometimes expedient to adopt and employ them ideologically and politically if they serve the interests of a class in struggle against the old order. We have seen this done in the course of revolt and revolution throughout history.

We are forced to consider the origins of the 'delivery of revolutionary consciousness from outside the class movement' by a centralized party of revolutionaries within historical conditions where a very young and small proletariat had very recently, in historical terms, just appeared on the scene. And where all its struggles and opposition to capital and the Tsarist regime were being subjected to the most brutal forms of oppression and persecution.

However, to assert that Lenin completely lifted the inspiration for his party structure and organization from Kautsky would be to discount these overwhelmingly determining conditions. The fact that Lenin was 'under the influence' of Kautsky on this question does not exclude the primary determination of these animating conditions on this question of organization itself. However, in a certain sense, the conditions in Russia at the time were ideal for Lenin to be 'under the influence' of Kautsky despite the fact that Kautsky himself, paradoxically, lived, worked and wrote in one of the more advanced or advancing capitalist countries of the time.

Today, at the commencement of the twenty-first century, it is the proletariat, incorporating its most class conscious sections educated and schooled in Marx, which now stands as the inheritor of the theory of socialism. It is the proletariat globally – both theoretically and in terms of a 'practical consciousness' – which takes on the historic role and responsibility of carrying forward the struggle to put an end to the age of capital. The tendency towards the emergence of socialist thinkers within the proletariat will become strengthened and more coherently expressed as the crisis of the capitalist order unfolds and deepens over the coming century.

Whereas the conception of 'consciousness from the outside', in relation to the question of agency, possessed a certain degree of legitimacy under *Tsarist Russian* conditions incorporating an historically immature proletariat at the start of the last century, today this conception is totally and absolutely outmoded. Implicitly, it makes all the left-wing 'vanguardist' sects and grouplets today irrelevant and redundant with it. Many have already disappeared or dissolved and more are in deep crisis of one kind or another.

Notes and References

1 Here, at this point, we need to acknowledge that the historical process is a *totality of unfolding historical conditions, actualities and possibilities* which dialectically embodies both the object and the subject of history inextricably bound into and constituting this totality of conditions. Marx's conception of 'practical consciousness' is central here (*Theses on Feuerbach*).

   It is very easy, theoretically, by ignoring the content – explicit or implicit – of Marx's *Theses*, to bury the subject of history under a smothering avalanche of 'objective conditions'. So much so that this active subject (relegated to a mere respondent) can be almost written out of the historical process itself by a 'vulgarizing' and 'objectivist' 'Marxism' which locates the question of agency *'in the form of the object'* and not as *'sensuous human practice'*, not as 'activity' itself, not 'subjectively'. Then the historical 'dialectic' becomes a one-way street (and therefore not dialectic at all) in which the subject 'responds' to 'objective conditions' but does not actively create the very conditions to which humanity 'responds'. The conception in Marx that humanity is both the creation and active creator of its own history loses its dialectical content and significance as a result of this metaphysical separation of the subject and the object of history.

2   'The inner structure of the Fourth International is based on the principles of *democratic centralism*: full freedom in discussion, complete unity in action.'
    Trotsky, Leon, *The Transitional Program. The Death Agony of Capitalism and the Tasks of the Fourth International* (1938). Section: 'Under the Banner of the Fourth International!' <https://www.marxists.org/archive/trotsky/1938/tp/> (Last accessed 4 November 2016).

3   A specific example here of such a *pronunciamento* is the 'Constitution' of the 'Leninist' sect known as the *Communist Party of Great Britain* (CPGB) which publishes the almost predictably and prosaically named *Weekly Worker* newspaper: '*Communists operate according to the principles of democratic centralism. Through ongoing debate we seek to achieve unity in action and a common world outlook. As long as they support agreed actions, members have the right to speak openly and form temporary or permanent factions.*'
    This grouplet denies, in its section 'What We Fight For', that it is a 'confessional sect' unlike all the other 'many so-called "parties" on the left' which the CPGB implicitly 'labels' as such.
    Communist Party of Great Britain (CPGB), 'What we fight for' (CPGB, 2015) <http://cpgb.org.uk/pages/what-we-fight-for/> (Last accessed 2 November 2016).

4   Trotsky, Leon, 'On Democratic Centralism and the Regime (1937)', from a US *Internal Bulletin* (December 1937) <https://www.marxists.org/archive/trotsky/1937/xx/democent.htm> (Last accessed 4 November 2016).

5   Mészáros, *Beyond Capital*, p. 393.

6   Mészáros, *Beyond Capital*, p. 675, Section 18.1.2, first paragraph.

7   Mészáros, *Beyond Capital*, Chapter 7, 'From the Closed Horizon of Hegel's "World Spirit" to Predicating the Imperative of Socialist Emancipation', Section 7.3.2, p. 318.

8   Mészáros, *Beyond Capital*, Notes to Part Two, 'Material Mediation and Transition', p. 500.

9   Engels, Frederick, and Karl Marx, 'The German Ideology'. In *Marx-Engels Collected Works, Volume 5, 1845–1847*, pp. 19–581, 31 (London: Lawrence & Wishart, 1976), 'Premises of the Materialist Conception of History'.

10 Engels, Frederick, 'Ludwig Feuerbach and the End of Classical German Philosophy'. In *Marx-Engels Selected Works*, p. 618 (London: Lawrence & Wishart, 1973).

11   Frederick Engels to Franz Mehring (14 July 1893). In *Marx-Engels Selected Works in One Volume*, p. 690 (London: Lawrence & Wishart, 1973).
12   Lenin, Vladimir I., 'Preface to the Collection Twelve Years'. In *Lenin Collected Works, Volume 13*, pp. 94–113, 102 (Moscow: Progress Publishers, 1972).
13   Lenin, Vladimir I., 'Draft Resolutions for the Third Congress of the R. S. D. L. P'. In *Lenin Collected Works, Volume 8*, pp. 191–196, 196 (Moscow: Progress Publishers, 1965).
14   Lenin, Vladimir I., 'The Reorganization of the Party'. In *Lenin Collected Works, 10*, pp. 29–39, 29–30, 32 (Moscow: Progress Publishers, 1965), Part I.
15   'For after the revolution, when the party holds the reins of power and social control, there can be no such thing any longer as plain "from outside". The so-called *from outside* – vis-à-vis the masses of workers – becomes simultaneously also the hierarchically self-perpetuating *from above*' (Mészáros, *Beyond Capital*, p. 395). Mészáros argues, in paragraphs 3 and 4 (pp. 394–395, *Beyond Capital*), that to maintain 'from the outside' as the 'orienting framework' now becomes 'inadequate' 'in 1968'. But it was actually 'inadequate' at the first congress of the Third International and later with Trotsky's now defunct Fourth International. It is undoubtedly 'inadequate' today and beyond.

Marx's conception that 'the emancipation of the working classes must be conquered by the working classes themselves'* makes no mention of the need for 'revolutionary consciousness' to be imported from outside (Kautsky's article in *Die Neue Zeit*, 1901–1902, XX, I, No. 3, p. 79) or being 'exported' into the proletariat by the bourgeois intelligentsia as a distinct social layer.

  *Marx, Karl, 'Provisional Rules'. In *The First International and After. Political Writings. Volume 3*, edited by David Fernbach, pp. 82–84, 82 (London: Penguin Books in association with New Left Review, 1974).
16   A fundamental question – which may appear mundane to some but surely is truly critical for the foreseeable future, because it impacts directly on the question of revolutionary agency – is, therefore, 'what does it mean to be an intrinsic, integrated, organic part of the class movement of the proletariat itself today?' What it means to be *not* such a part of it is very clearly illustrated by the activities of the left-wing sectarian grouplets. Marx wrote (in *Capital* and in the *Grundrisse*) of the Jews living 'in the pores' of Polish society and the 'trading peoples living in the pores of the ancient world'. What did he actually mean by this statement? Did being in these 'pores' make the Jews an intrinsic, organic part of that society or were they merely in a 'semi-detached' state with it through being in its 'pores'? The Jews were traders in feudal Poland and those who lived exclusively by trade in Antiquity were the exception, not the norm. What is the

character of the relationship of the left-wing sectarian groups, for example, to the class movement of the proletariat as a whole?

'Living in the pores' of this movement seems an apt description of the relationship between these groups and the class movement. Are these groups an intrinsic, organic part of the class movement of the proletariat? The answer is 'no' in the sense that 'they live in its pores' in a semi-detached relation with it in order to serve their own sectarian requirements. Just as the Jews did in feudal society and the 'trading peoples' did in the ancient world where the agricultural production of use-values for subsistence was the social 'norm' and trade was the consequence of dealing in unrequired surpluses which could be exchanged for other useful products. Agricultural production in Antiquity wholly and specifically for exchange is not generalized. Production in agriculture is more or less subsistent and autarkic. This 'agricultural production for exchange' only emerges later and systematically with capitalist agriculture.

17   The famous '21 Theses' as conditions for the admission to the Comintern. Thesis 12 states: '*The parties belonging to the Communist International must be built on the basis of the principle of democratic centralism. In the present epoch of acute civil war the communist party will only be able to fulfil its duty if it is organized in as centralist a manner as possible, if iron discipline reigns within it and if the party centre, sustained by the confidence of the party membership, is endowed with the fullest rights and authority and the most far-reaching powers.*'

Second World Congress of the Communist International, Petrograd, 19 July to 7 August 1920, *Minutes of the Second World Congress of the Communist International, Petrograd, July 19 to August 7, 1920* (2 Vols), translated by Robert A. Archer (London: New Park Publications, 1977) <https://www.marxists.org/history/international/comintern/2nd-congress/index.htm> (Last accessed 6 November 2016). This particular quotation accessible at <https://www.marxists.org/history/international/comintern/2nd-congress/ch07.htm> (Last accessed 6 November 2016).

18   Pannekoek, Anton, *The New Blanquism*. Published originally in *Der Kommunist* (Bremen), No. 27 (1920) <https://www.marxists.org/archive/pannekoe/1920/blanquism.htm> (Last accessed 2 November 2016).

I make no apologies for reproducing this passage from Pannekoek's article in full.

'*We are by no means fanatics of democracy, we have no superstitious respect for majority decision nor do we render homage to the belief that everything the majority does is for the best and must succeed. Action is crucial, activity overpowers mass inertia. Where power enters as a factor, we want to use and apply it. If, nonetheless, we firmly reject the doctrine of the revolutionary minority, this is just for the reason* that it must lead to a mere semblance of power, to merely apparent victories, and thus to serious defeats. It could be applicable in a country where the apathy of the masses is a characteristic of their class situation, such as, for instance, in a country with a peasant majority, who do not see anything outside of their villages and turn their backs on national politics; there, an active proletarian minority of the population could conquer state power. But if this tactic has never been attempted or recommended in Russia, it should be all the more surprising were it to be recommended for the western European countries, where the situation is very different.

It is therefore correct to emphasize that the process of the revolution will be much slower and more difficult in Western Europe, because the bourgeoisie is much more powerful here than in Russia. But in what does this power consist? Does it consist of control over the state apparatus? The bourgeoisie already lost this control on one occasion. Does it consist of numerical superiority? The bourgeoisie confronts an overwhelming number of workers. Does it consist of the power of command over production? Or the power of money? In Germany, these things hardly mean anything anymore. The roots of capital's power are much more deeply set. They lie in the reign of bourgeois culture over the population as a whole, as well as over the proletariat. Over the span of one hundred years of the bourgeois era, the spiritual life of the bourgeoisie has soaked into all of society, and has created a spiritual structure and discipline which, by way of thousands of channels, penetrated and dominated the masses. This will have to be gradually purged from the proletariat through a long and tenacious struggle.

First, the liberal and Christian ideology was fought by social democratic enlightenment. But it is precisely the Social Democracy which shows how profoundly rooted and how adaptable capital's spiritual rule over the masses actually is: it seemed to spiritually free the masses and to unify them in a new proletarian world-view, and now it is demonstrated that this organization created by the masses themselves has been fully converted to the side of the bourgeoisie and prevents their revolution. It is thus the case that the resistance which must be overcome by the proletariat alone in the old bourgeois countries is infinitely greater in its immense scale than in the new countries of Eastern Europe, where bourgeois culture of any kind is lacking and where a communal tradition favors the revolution. Respect for the bourgeois legal order is deeply ingrained in the masses, and becomes visible in the fear inspired by the outcry over terrorism, in the belief in all the lies, in the hesitancy to undertake the necessary measures. Bourgeois ethics are deeply ingrained in the ethics of the masses, which confuses them with noble words, which disorients them with its hypocrisy, which mocks them with its clever deceitfulness. The old bourgeois individualism is deeply ingrained in their blood, so that today they think they can win everything with one furious assault and tomorrow they recoil before the enormity of the task.

This does not mean that victory is not possible here: the proletariat also has vast untapped resources; the revolution here will take place on a much greater scale. Nor does this mean that revolutionary expropriation must be postponed to a distant future: circumstances could somehow compel the masses to take power into their hands at any time, despite all the spiritual impediments, which can then only be overcome later, within a subsequent process of struggle. But this does mean that the revolution is not possible as a result of the actions of a resolute minority. Everything the latter does is done to seize a hostile power in the hands of the bourgeoisie, rather than on behalf of the revolution. In this social environment the revolutionary party is not embedded among the masses, who look on with indifference – or so it seems; everything which may appear to be an apparently apathetic stance towards communist propaganda is capable of turning into an instrument of the counterrevolution thanks to the power of capitalist-bourgeois ideology. While one part of the proletariat, upon whom crucial struggles rely, is paralyzed, passive, and rendered indecisive by the old ideology, the more backwards elements, whose passivity is expected, become a force for the bourgeoisie.

The history of the Munich Council Republic is a rich example of all these distinct tendencies. In the capitalist countries with a spiritually powerful bourgeois culture, any deviation in the direction of a Blanquist tactic is consequently doomed and must be condemned. The doctrine of the revolutionary minority, of the Communist Party dictatorship (Parteidiktatur), is a sign of the underestimation of the enemy's power, and of the underestimation of the necessary work of propaganda, which must lead to the most serious setbacks. The revolution can only issue from the masses, and it is only through the masses that it is carried out. The Communist Party has forgotten this simple truth and, with the insufficient forces of a revolutionary minority, it wants to do what only the class can do, in such a way that the consequence will be defeat, which will set back the cause of the world revolution for a long time, at the cost of the most painful sacrifices.'

19 'Each step in the development of the bourgeoisie was accompanied by a corresponding political advance of that class. An oppressed class under the sway of the feudal nobility, an armed and self-governing association in the medieval commune: here independent urban republic (as in Italy and Germany); there taxable "third estate" of the monarchy (as in France); afterwards, in the period of manufacturing proper, serving either the semi-feudal or the absolute monarchy as a counterpoise against the nobility, and, in fact, cornerstone of the great monarchies in general, the bourgeoisie has at last, since the establishment of Modern Industry and of the world market, conquered for itself, in the modern representative State, exclusive political sway. The executive of the modern state is but a committee for managing the common affairs of the whole bourgeoisie.'

Engels, Frederick, and Karl Marx, 'Manifesto of the Communist Party'. In *Marx-Engels Selected Works, Volume One*, translated by Samuel Moore in cooperation with Frederick Engels, pp. 98–137 (Moscow: Progress Publishers, 1969), Chapter 1, 'Bourgeois and Proletarians'.

In the history of the rise of the bourgeois class, its forms of social and political organization altered and developed (in order to articulate its interests as a class) according to changes taking place in the historical conditions of its life activity. Why must the forms of political organization of the proletariat be exempted from the inner laws of such a historical dialectic? Is political organization embalmed in aspic regardless of changing conditions? Is the 'trade union' or 'Party-form' the only form of organization through which the proletariat *must necessarily* prosecute its struggle against the capital order and by means of which it will go on to put an end to that order?

20 '*Lenin created the apparatus. The apparatus created Stalin.*' Trotsky, Leon, *Trotsky's Notebooks, 1933–35. Writings on Lenin, Dialectics, and Evolutionism*, translated by Philip Pomper (New York: Columbia University Press, 1986), p. 86, 'Second Notebook'.

21 Lenin, Vladimir I., 'What is to be Done? Burning Questions of our Movement'. In *Lenin Collected Works, Volume 5*, pp. 347–530 (Moscow: Foreign Languages Publishing House, 1961), Section E, 'The Working Class as Vanguard Fighter for Democracy', Part III, 'Trade-Unionist Politics and Social democratic Politics'.

22 Karl Kautsky, *Die Neue Zeit*, XX, I, No. 3 (1901–1902), p. 79.

23 Cole, M., *Marxism and Educational Theory: Origins and Issues* (London and New York: Routledge, 2008), p. 73.

CHAPTER 14

Trotsky's *Transitional Programme*, the 'Bolshevist-Leninist' Approach to Trade Unionism and the Demise of the Sectarian Politics of the 'Revolutionary Left'

The immature, 'non-structural' crisis-conditions before 1940 – within which international capital was able to attenuate the intensity of its contradictions by means of Stalin's counter-revolution, the defeat of various struggles against it in Europe and across the world, 'New Deal' measures and the preparation for world war – informed Trotsky's conception of the relationship between the 'revolutionary Bolshevist-Leninist vanguard' and trade unionism.

His conception of the future of trade unionism was directly related to his vanguardist outlook which viewed the 'banner of the Fourth International' as that of the 'approaching victory' of the proletariat. This outlook was bereft of any possibility that trade unionism could itself enter a period of decline and move towards outmode as the contradictions of the capital order matured and sharpened into a qualitatively new type of crisis differing from all previous crises. That is, that the traditional, universal historic form of proletarian organization itself could reach an historic impasse as the conditions of capital's rule changed into structural crisis, regardless of 'vanguards' in its leadership or not.

Trotsky advanced the formulaic conception that only if the trade unions were under the leadership of the 'vanguard' could they serve a revolutionary function in the struggle for socialism. Less than eighty years after Trotsky wrote the *Transitional Programme* (1938)[1] we are witnessing trade unionism – in its traditional mode of organizational self-subsistence – in a cul-de-sac of history. The need to put Trotsky's work through the fine sieve of theoretical-historical analysis asserts itself in order to identify any aspects which are worth taking forward into the twenty-first century and, by implication, leaving behind on the roadside of history those aspects which are no longer relevant. For example, if we study the section in *The Transitional Programme* titled 'Trade Unions in the Transitional Epoch', parts of this section read like tracts from a bygone age.

Trotsky contrasts the 'powerful growth of trade unionism' in his time with the 'preaching' of 'ultra-left doctrinaires' who were stating that the trade unions had 'outlived their usefulness'. What would he be writing today in relation to the 'powerful' decline of trade unionism? Would 'outlived their usefulness' receive the same dismissive response and labelling of 'ultra-left doctrinaire'?

The principle of participation of socialists within the trade unions remains; it is indeed 'sectarian' and 'doctrinaire' to walk away from them because they are the mass organizations of the proletariat. But Trotsky – following on from Lenin – co-opted the 'model of the Russian revolution' in his whole approach to the trade unions. They were viewed as organizations which had to be 'won' to his Fourth International so that even here we see the advocacy of 'supplying' a revolutionary party to the organized proletariat.

The same advocacy of today's left-wing sects is rooted in Lenin's and Trotsky's approach to the question of the relationship between the 'vanguard' and the mass worker organizations. The *a priori* trajectory is one of 'finding a path' to the trade unions in order to encompass them within the 'gravity' of the 'revolutionary orbit' of the 'Party' rather than working as an intrinsic, inseparable part of their self-organizing and self-directing activity towards the formation of new types of organization for emancipation.

The long shadow of the 'model character' of the Russian Revolution casts itself over the whole outlook of Trotsky in the *Transitional Programme*. He is clearly deploying it as a historical point of reference (historical template, 'rough guide' or 'metaphysical measure') against which to elaborate and put forward a 'programme' for revolution in the more advanced countries.

Nearly two decades earlier – in full agreement with Lenin – he had supported the thesis that all sections of the *Comintern* must be organized on the basis of the 'democratic centralist Party form' developed by the

'Bolshevik-Leninists' in relation to the historically specific circumstances of the Russian Revolution. And, as we have analysed earlier, this was a mistake which not only departed from Marx's *approach* but actually contradicted it.

Trotsky insisted that trade unions 'cannot offer a finished revolutionary program' (note the word 'finished' here) and 'in consequence, they cannot replace the party'. How dogmatic was that? In themselves, of course, the trade unions as they stand today (and did in the 1930s) are/were not historically structured to constitute themselves as a revolutionary movement. But today can we dismiss the possibility that the growth of a movement within trade unionism (and in its pluralistic relations with other organizations and movements) may constitute the basis for developments in organization leading to a higher form of 'revolutionary agency'?

Of course, Trotsky was writing in the 1930s in the wake and legacies of the Russian Revolution but the *pronunciamento* here still appears staggeringly dogmatic today. The Soviets were viewed by Trotsky as the perennial social (class) basis of the revolutionary activity of 'the Party' which is likewise identified as the indispensably active 'agent of revolution'. The absence of 'national revolutionary sections' of the 'vanguard party' in any country is, accordingly, the absence of the necessary revolutionary 'agency'. Consequentially, what flows from such a 'grave' state of affairs is that revolution is, at best, doomed to defeat, if possible at all.

He is, of course, correct when he writes that the trade unions organize only a minority of the proletariat (and today this is even more so, of course, with the decline of trade unionism) and a genuinely revolutionary movement must embrace all the major sections of the proletariat. And, moreover, as hierarchically structured organizations formed historically within the system of bourgeois relations, they tend to 'compromise' with the capitalist regime and actually prepare for surrender and defeat.

However, even the 'renewal of the top leadership' with 'militant leaders' of the trade unions today would not fundamentally alter their downwards historic trajectory into a deeper outmodedness and the consequentially and increasingly corporatist relationship with capital and its state power. Moreover, even the much sought after 'independent militant organizations corresponding more closely to the tasks of mass struggle' would very readily reveal their ineffectiveness in the face of global capital's intensifying structural crisis if trade unionism remained in a state of social and political self-subsistence as it does today in the currently hierarchically structured forms.

The fundamental question which is confronting the proletariat today is not simply 'breaking *with* the conservative apparatus of the trade unions'. Rather, it is more a question of actually *breaking the whole apparatus of the trade union form*. Burying it. And, in this sense, Trotsky is correct when he asserts that 'trade unions are not ends in themselves; they are but means along the road to proletarian revolution'.

The notes which make up Trotsky's *Trade Unions in the Epoch of Imperialist Decay*[2] were found in the drawer of his desk after his assassination in 1940. In these notes, he recognizes the increasingly 'corporatist' character of trade unionism; its 'growing together with the state power' …

> The trade unions of our time can either serve as secondary instruments of imperialist capitalism for the subordination and disciplining of workers and for obstructing the revolution, or, on the contrary, the trade unions can become the instruments of the revolutionary movement of the proletariat.

This is insightful and remains valid today. The emphasis is on 'instruments' of the revolutionary movement. But what happens in an epoch where the nature of capital's crisis actually undermines the historic legitimacy of trade unions themselves i.e. not only their *relative approach* to capitalist exploitation but *absolutely* in terms of their structure and *modus operandi*, regardless of how radical they are in their democracy and leadership? When the character of capital's crisis has become altered to such a degree that it renders self-subsistent trade unionism historically outmoded and obsolete? In other words, the only legitimate role which is left for them to play lies in the initiation and development of a fundamentally altered form of the proletarian class movement into which they become incorporated or superseded (sublated).

Today, as the twenty-first century unfolds, the future of the trade unions is already sealed. It is merely a question of the form of that fate. Either trade unionism will continue to act as the proxy of capital, slowly decline, atrophy and terminate, at best, as a workers' provident association possibly bound to no strike agreements or it will constitute itself as a platform for ('refoundation') the organization of a higher form of Social Unionism which brings the whole proletarian class together both inside and outside the workplace. The final paragraph of the sections from Trotsky's notes reads ...

> As a matter of fact, the independence of trade unions in the class sense, in their relations to the bourgeois state can, in the present conditions, be assured only by a completely revolutionary leadership, that is, the leadership of the Fourth International. This leadership, naturally, must and can be rational and assure the unions the maximum of democracy conceivable under the present concrete conditions. But without the political leadership of the Fourth International the independence of the trade unions is impossible.

But even with so-called 'revolutionaries' leading the trade unions in the age of capital's structural crisis, the four-decade trajectory of decline would continue if there were not a fundamental political re-orientation towards the proletariat as a whole. Not simply in terms of perspectives but, more critically, in regard to the organization of a form of agency which must and can only be of a radically new typicality which brings together the proletariat as a whole and not simply that part which is employed by capital in production and distribution or in its various state and other agencies.

It is really not a matter for any self-appointed and self-proclaimed 'revolutionary leadership' to 'assure' ('rationally' or otherwise) the proletariat – trade unionized or otherwise – of a 'maximum of democracy' under any conditions. Rather the creation of its democracy is the work and function of the self-organizing, self-directing and self-emancipating activity of the proletarian class in movement against capital. The roots of the approach of the left-wing sects are clearly identifiable in Trotsky's final sentence of this document. Of course, in terms of its specific relevance then and today, the Fourth International was/is not remotely capable of guaranteeing any such thing as the 'independence of the trade unions'. Under the evolving and worsening conditions of capital's structural crisis, its sundry sects and grouplets can no longer 'guarantee' their own existence.

The period of capitalist expansion and accumulation subsequent to 1945 and the development of the structural crisis of capital since the 1970s has effectively 'pulled the rug' from underneath such a remote possibility. And the socio-economic relations of this period do, indeed, as mediating ground, largely explain the trajectory which the totally ineffective Fourth International has taken into an endless series of divisions, splits and fragmentations resulting in more squabbling sects and grouplets than there are languages in the Babel of Earth. The approach to an analysis and understanding of the trajectory which the Fourth International has taken since its foundation in the 1930s can only be based on the principles of the materialist conception of history. Hence the real conditions of its demise must be sought in the actual material socio-historical evolution over the past eighty years.

Trotsky, in *The Transitional Programme* (written in 1938), stated unequivocally that 'mankind's productive forces stagnate'. And, at the time, it was true to assert that they were 'stagnating' *relatively* under the pre-war conditions of the 'Great Depression' of the 1930s. This notion itself informs the whole conception in his programme. But what we have witnessed, contrary to Trotsky's assertion and implied projection, since the publication of this document, is a tremendous development of these productive forces. In fact, to a degree that, in the past, we may have considered impossible within the framework of capitalist relations of production and distribution. But, critically, this acceleration in the development of the forces of production has actually served to bring in the epoch of capital's structural crisis.

Computerization, automation, robotics, pioneering developments in electronics, nanotechnology, biotechnology, etc., and the interfacing of technologies (e.g. computer-aided design, computer-controlled manufacture, biotechnology, etc.) has increased the productivity of labour on the whole to such a high degree that on the basis of the further development of this technology alone, socialism is not only entirely possible but revealing, with each passing year, to be absolutely necessary for its further development. Trotsky's prognosis (implicating his method of approach to the historical process), and especially in his perspectives for the Fourth International, was hopelessly misplaced.

In his interview with Kingsley Martin (editor of *The New Statesman*) in 1937, Trotsky argued that the Fourth International would be a massive force in the class movement globally within five years.[3] How 'wide of the mark' was that? No room for the doubts embryonic in possibilities. Whatever happened to the powers of 'the prophet outcast'?

The history of the Fourth International since its foundation in 1938 has been a history of sectarianism, sub-division, splits, splinters and fragmentation. Why? Were these splits simply founded on ideological differences? What were the mediating, post-war socio-economic grounds after 1945? These divisions and fragmentations took place in a time of the expansion and accumulation of capital, not in a time of deepening structural crisis. What were the mediating links between this 'root ontology' of displaced contradictions and global expansion of the capital order and the 'causalities' mediating the dissolution and disintegration of Trotsky's International?

The political legacies of all the infighting, generated hostility and 'pique' remain. As anyone who still has contact with the 'groups' will know. The term 'Trotskyist' – regardless of Stalinist calumny and smear – has become synonymous with squabbling grouplets and internecine self-destruction. Despite this, various attempts have been made at 'regroupment', all of which have failed dismally, ending in the usual recriminations, identification of new enemies and augmented bitterness. This regroupment 'strategy' is merely a desperate response to and manifestation of the continuing disintegration and disappearance of the 'revolutionary' sects. Any 'regroupment' serves to replicate the characteristics of sect politics in a newly clustered form.

The Fourth International has achieved nothing and is now in an advanced state of decay and dissolution. For all intents and purposes, Trotsky's International is extinct. But was it ever viable? A tiny number of Fourth Internationalists remain who still adhere dogmatically and doctrinally to the *Transitional Programme* written in 1938.

Invariably, we observe, amongst them, the re-assertment of the principle of 'supplying a party and programme' to the proletariat which renders the whole scenario immediately null and void. All attempts at regroupment by the *class rootless* sects are doomed because they are attempts at 'supplying' a party to the proletarian class rather than being the emergence of organization which actually arises out of the historic struggle of the broad proletarian class movement. Only in this way will a legitimate organization grow out of the life of the class and be actually *rooted* in it. The regroupment of the sectarian left-wing groups becomes a case of 'more of the same but slightly larger' as a prelude to its almost inevitable disintegration, fragmentation and dissolution.

Any regroupment of the sects will merely serve to give sectarianism re-birth in new form by returning the assorted devotees to a new but higher form of the life of sect politics. A thorough critique of regroupment strategy – based on the unfolding and development of the historical conditions mediating the existence of left-wing sectarianism in the last century – is required. These sundry attempts at regroupment are merely a reflex response of the sects to their own abysmal state and demise. They are the last dying gasps and death rattles of these grouplets. Any regroupment will simply be a regroupment of the sectarian groups with others and their members will follow the same internecine practices in such a regroupment. Sectarianism 'writ larger'. It is the transmogrification of the concept of 'consciousness from the outside' which was more suited to the conditions of Tsarist Russia and Ochrana persecution but not to the conditions we are living through and organizing under today at the start of the twenty-first century with globalized capital-in-crisis.

Such a regroupment is bogus and cannot be sustained. It is the activity of the grouplets within their own self-created orbits and cannot stand regardless of how many times (and how large the result) they seek to overcome their 'Babelesque' multitude of differences in such faux regroupments. The form of revolutionary agency must arise organically within the whole class movement of the class itself in response to the deepening of capital's structural crisis.

In regard and opposition to such organically arisen relations, the *vanguardist sect* seeks to substitute its programme for the movement as a whole. Each one strives to impose *its* programme on and manipulate the class movement for its own advancement, rather than self-dissolving into that movement to enrich it.

Marx himself wrote of the 'socialist sectarianism' of his time and recommended that its practitioners left it behind and integrated themselves with the class movement as a whole rather than trying to preach to it from their various pulpits. In every twist and turn of the class movement for the last seventy years, we have witnessed literally hundreds of left-wing sects and groups 'parachuting in from on high' into the class movement with their fully formed programmes, paper-selling, doctrines and revelations – like divine visitations from the Platonic realm of the Universals – attempting to convert the 'unenlightened masses' to their particular and exclusively enlightening brand of sect politics. Preaching to the proletariat from various pulpits, as we see with the left-wing sects and cults, is a worse than useless 'intervention'. Marx himself asserted many years ago that the 'emancipation of the working class must be the act of the working class itself'.

Sectarianism was an ongoing problem in the International Workingmen's Association (IWMA) which Marx had to address.[4] Marx himself sought to address the *religious character* of sect politics in his differences with Ferdinand Lassalle who was a leading figure in the German workers' movement at the time. His words on Lassalle still have a resonance when we observe sect politics today. In his criticism of Lassalle in Germany in the 1860s, Marx wrote, in a letter to Schweitzer, that ...

> he gave his agitation from the very beginning the character of a religious sect, as does every man who claims to have in his pocket a panacea for the suffering masses. In fact, every sect is religious. Furthermore, precisely because he was a founder of a sect, he denied any natural connection with the earlier movement in Germany or abroad. He fell into the same error as Proudhon, of not seeking the real basis for his agitation in the actual elements of the class movement, but of trying to prescribe the course of the movement according to a certain doctrinaire recipe. [...] You yourself have had personal experience of the contradictions between a sectarian and a class movement. The sect seeks its raison d'être and point of honour not in what it has in common with the class movement but in the particular shibboleth which distinguishes it from the class movement.

Later in the letter Marx writes, in regard to Lassalle's group, that ...

> The dissolution of the General Association of German Workers gave you the opportunity to accomplish a great step forward and to declare, if it were necessary, that a new stage of development had been reached and that the sectarian movement was now ready to merge into the class movement and to completely abandon its separation. As far as its true aims were concerned, the sect, like all earlier working class sects, would bring them as an enriching element into the general movement. Instead you have in fact demanded of the class movement that it subordinate itself to a particular sectarian movement. Those who are not your friends have concluded from this that you are trying under all circumstances to preserve your 'own workers' movement'.

And in relation to Lassalle's position regarding the structure and organization of trade unions, Marx writes that ...

> As for the draft of the rules, I regard it as fundamentally misguided and I think I have as much experience as any contemporary in the field of trade unions. Without going into details here I would only remark that the centralist organization, no matter how valuable it may be for secret societies and sectarian movements, contradicts the essence of trade unions. Even if it were possible – and I declare quite frankly that it is not – it would not be necessary, least of all in Germany. There, where the worker is subject to bureaucratic discipline from his infancy and believes in officialdom and higher authority, it is above all a question of teaching him to walk by himself.[5]

A constant re-evaluation of the living tendencies and trajectories of development of a movement, class relations, relation to state, etc., – i.e. a grasp of the real, living forces and dialectics of the whole situation – is always necessary in order to adequately and productively contribute to the development of the class movement. This movement is constantly changing according to the unfolding conditions of the development of capital's crisis and, accordingly, so must the 'evaluation' and 'contributions' as such.

It is one thing to be an organic and intrinsically participating part of the class movement and 'contributing' as such but it is quite something else being in distinct separation from it in a sect of one's own, dictating to it and expecting the class movement to *'subordinate itself to a particular sectarian movement'*. Implicit in Marx's letter to Schweitzer is this difference between, on the one hand, participating and being involved in the broad mass movement of the proletariat in a non-sectarian, contributory mode of working and, on the other hand, preaching, intervening, pointing to the 'validity' of the 'scripture' of the sect and fishing around for new members in it in a sectarian way. This way of proceeding substitutes the sect and its programme for the proletarian class movement itself as a whole.

To work in a non-sectarian way means to participate in order to unconditionally further the interests and emancipation of the proletariat as a class. It does not mean doing this in order to further the interests of the sect independently of the whole movement. Neither does it mean substituting the 'programme' or interests of the sect or grouplet for the historical interests of the proletariat or even identifying the two. It does not mean merely using the class movement as a fishing ground for recruitment and augmentation of the membership of the sect. The sect always identifies its own dogma or, as Marx writes, its own *'particular shibboleth'* with the interests of the class movement as a whole. In contrast to this, Marx wrote, in relation to the First International, that ...

> it is the business of the International Workingmen's Association to combine and generalize the spontaneous movements of the working classes, but not to dictate or impose any doctrinary system whatever.[6]

The International Workingmen's Association ...

> has not been hatched by a sect or a theory. It is the spontaneous growth of the proletarian movement, which itself is the offspring of the natural and irrepressible tendencies of modern society.[7]

and that ...

> the emancipation of the working classes must be conquered by the working classes themselves.[8]

Of course, this does not mean that there is no debate, and even struggle, within the broad class movement as to inform direction of change, tactics, strategy, etc., as new situations unfold and conditions change. Without this, there can be no development or advance. *It cannot simply be a case of 'the wind bloweth where it listeth'*. The direction of the movement is determined in struggle against capital and its state power and that struggle simultaneously generates internal diremption, disagreement, even open conflict, as regards alterations in direction.

In other words, the conflict between the class movement and capital is 'determinatively reflexive' so that it necessarily creates conflicts within that movement itself which need to be resolved in order to move forwards in the unfolding struggle against capital and its state power. It is not participation per se in the mode of a sect 'living in its pores' but rather a participation of socialists in the class movement which is constituted as an intrinsic organic part of it and not as a sect or cult in semi-detached relationship to it. Not in its 'pores' but in its 'body'. The sect is 'uninvolved' as such because it maintains itself *essentially* in a relationship of separation and discreteness to the movement whilst simultaneously presenting the *appearance* of 'involvement'.

For the sect, of course, its methods of working actually mean being 'involved' and being 'an intrinsic part of it'. But these methods – whilst giving the appearance of a non-sectarian involvement and identity of interests between sect and movement – actually contradict and foreclose an unconditional involvement. Ultimately, as a presupposition of its very existence, the sect always places its own interests before that of the movement. It then proceeds to seek to identify these sectarian interests precisely with that of the whole class movement.

The sect does not participate in order to unconditionally develop the whole movement (for it cannot do this without undermining and denying its own paltry existence) but rather its participation *is conditional on its own development*. The function of the lines of news sheet and paper sellers to be found at any large demonstration or march is to recruit people into the various 'vanguardist' groups. The sect maintains its separation from the 'real movement' and distinguishes itself from it by its particular 'shibboleth' as it does from all the other sects and grouplets. The newspaper is the written manifestation of this 'shibboleth' which isolates the sect and divides it off from all the others.

The sect is ('we are') 'over here' and the 'real movement' of the class is 'over there' and the former only engages in its separation and distinction from the latter on its own terms and not those of the class movement. This is a fundamental and inalienable principle of approach of the left-wing sect to the class movement of the proletariat.

The left-wing sect demands *'of the class movement that it subordinate itself to the particular sectarian movement'* according to its *'particular shibboleth which distinguishes it from the class movement'* and thereby *'to prescribe the course of the movement according to a certain doctrinaire recipe'*.[9] A more perfect characterization of the operation of the contemporary left-wing groups (under the names of so-called 'parties', 'leagues', 'movements', 'workers' 'this and that', etc.) could not have been written today in 2017.

The left-wing sectarian groups perpetuate and continuously return to forms of activity which have never really 'touched' the rule of capital over the past seventy years. Changes in conditions (the emergence and development of the structural crisis of capital and the end of the Stalinist systems worldwide) are shifting the anchoring and mediating grounds for their actual existence. They have 'lived in the pores' of the class movement (parasitically fed on it) for the previous seventy years. Their sectarian character precludes them from truly being an intrinsic part of the life and development of that movement. Alterations in the global circumstances of capital's rule now demand a radically changed trajectory of this class movement as a whole. And this must mean the pronouncement of an irreversible death-sentence on the sects and not, as many of them are hoping, the basis for one of them to become the 'vanguard party' of a revolutionary movement.

The expansionary phase of capitalist accumulation and development (after the mass destruction of production, infrastructure and human beings in the course of the 'Great Depression' of the 1930s and the subsequent second imperialist world war) from 1945 onwards enabled the capitalist system to displace its internal contradictions prior to the onset of capital's structural crisis in the 1970s. *This 'Keynesian' expansionary phase was only made possible on the grounds of this mass destruction of capital and people.*

Under the presently unfolding conditions of capital's structural crisis, a 'Bretton Woods' type programme and consensus would simply serve to aggravate this structural crisis of the global capital order.[10] The stratum in the labour and trade union bureaucracy – Corbyn and his supporters in the trade unions – who now advocate the re-articulation of such a policy for the twenty-first century merely reveal their complete ignorance of the intrinsic and intractable character of capital's terminal crisis in the reproduction of its actual structure under the new conditions of the 'globalized' epoch. Moreover, this advocacy of a return to the 'good old days' actually reflects the entrenched caste interests of this ruling layer in the labour movement. The only alternative is a move against and beyond capital. But this would dissolve the grounding relations from underneath its privileges as a labour caste.

It is within the development of these post-war conditions – inclusive of the period of the Stalinist political domination of the international workers' movement and its influence on the so-called 'national liberation struggle' (Appendix III) – that the grounds for the existence of the left-wing sectarian vanguardist ('Trotskyist', 'Leninist', 'Maoist', etc.) groups must be located. The emergence of the global crisis of capital inevitably shifts the socio-economic and political ground from underneath the existence of these groups. Rather than facilitating their growth, the unfolding of this crisis will actually serve to break them up and is already doing so.

In order to understand both the origins and character of these groups, there is a need to investigate the actual historical conditions which gave rise to and nourished left-wing sectarianism in the last century. It rested on these conditions which developed after the second imperialist world war but also pre-dated them in the wake of the rise of the conservatism of the hierarchically governed Soviet system.

The age of the cyclical, conjunctural crisis is over. And this hastens the demise of the sect politics of the so-called revolutionary left. A rationalistic and exclusively polemical approach to left-wing sectarianism indicates a misappropriation of its actual character. For no amount of 'rationally opposing' argument will make it disappear whilst grounding historical conditions continue to mediate its existence. Such an approach means that any analysis simply gets drawn into the *ideological* orbits and prisons of these groups. The sectarianism of the left is not a form of politically counter-productive activity to be 'argued out of existence'. We observe a similar approach with Richard Dawkins and others who try to do the same *rationalistically* with religion.[11]

Rather, the sect politics of the left must be explained according to the historical conditions within which it arose. Only in the process of struggle by the whole class movement against capital and its state power – and by creating class organizations of a fundamentally new and historically higher typicality – will the conditions be created for its historical transcendence. We need to study the historical conditions which created these sects and groups and how changes in conditions are shifting the ground from underneath their very existence today as capital's structural crisis deepens and intensifies.

Accordingly, the real roots and secret of left-wing sect politics will not be found in their various ideological positionings but in the actual historical conditions which fed and mediated their emergence and evolution in the last seventy years or so. It is important to relate left sectarianism – its differentiation in organization and ideology – to these changing conditions, inclusive of the 'progressive' and 'retrogressive' legacies of the Russian Revolution.

Trade union militancy – which served to deliver improvements in working conditions and wages in the post-war period – was the ontological basis *within the proletarian class movement* for the continuing existence of sect politics. But this form of militancy itself was only possible and could realize specific goals and advances under, and because of, the conditions of post-war capitalist expansion and accumulation. These relations constituted the socio-economic basis, over the past seventy years, for the left-wing sects to be able to attach themselves to the trade unions. That is, to 'live in the pores' of this non-sectarian movement.

The activities of the 'revolutionary' sects were therefore facilitated by the unfolding scenario of a post-war expanding capital system which provided the ideal socio-economic conditions for conspiratorial organization and the self-serving machinations and manipulations of sect politics. Today, with the decline of the trade unions, and especially the growing moribundity of the trades union councils movement, the trajectory of the sectarian groups is increasingly and desperately downwards. Herein lies the source of the various attempts at 'regroupment'.

The advent and development of capital's structural crisis erodes the ground from underneath these politically parasitic relations. With trade unionism sinking deeper into its 'twilight period', the crisis of labour organization ushered in by capital's structural crisis within trade unionism itself begins to cease to provide fertile conditions for the residence of the left-wing sects. The crisis of proletarian organization simultaneously posits the dynamic for the decline and disintegration of these groups. The declining host can no longer provide a nutritious medium for the parasite living and seeking to propagate itself in its pores. The 'death agony' of the sect politics of the 'revolutionary left' commences and unfolds.

The existence of these groups was nourished by the post-war decades of Keynesian expansion of the capital order into the 1970s. Ontologically, of course, this must mean that they did have a real relationship with the 'material life conditions' and the 'real motive forces' animating the evolution of this period. However, politically and theoretically in terms of perspectives and the class interests of the proletariat itself throughout this period, they were indeed 'out-of-touch' with the character of the period, living out the existence of solitary grouplets seeking to communicate with the host body.

This 'body' (trade unionism), in historic retrospect, had no real need of them and more or less could ignore them throughout the whole period. At best, they were deployed as a subsidiary propagandist means of furthering the aims of strikes. They were, in the terms of the socio-economic requirements of millions of workers at the time, actually divorced from the conditions of struggle of this period of capitalist expansion. Today, they are even more politically divorced and isolated from the altered conditions of capitalist globalization and its maturing structural crisis which has rendered them 'more a hindrance than a help'.

The structural crisis of globalizing capital will not catch up with their 'conception' because this unfolding reality has left it behind decades ago. The truth of the matter being, of course, not that 'their day will come' but that their conceptions never held any historical validity whatsoever: 'their day never was'. The historic content of the practices and conceptions of the sects were, taken collectively, the practices and conceptions that 'never were' in terms of any historic validity, adequacy or relevance for the class movement of the proletariat as a whole. Today, those that remain in ever-diminishing number and membership are dominated by bureaucratism, ideology and, increasingly, internal crises (often involving the physical, emotional and/or even sexual abuse of members) of one form or another which reflect the decay and degeneration of the epoch.

Trade unionism itself has now reached its own historic impasse. Its outmodedness becomes more evident with each passing day in the era of globalizing capital-in-crisis. Trotsky – in founding the Fourth International – sought to extrapolate and apply the forms of proletarian organization operative in the Russian Revolution to the more advanced capitalist regions of Europe and North America. It was a political mistake then which has attained the status of a pseudo-religious dogma today as articulated by the outlooks and practices of the various 'Trotskyist' grouplets.

The agency of revolutionary transformation does not necessarily and inevitably involve the internal relationship between 'party and class' (next chapter). This relationship was appropriate for the conditions of Tsarist

Russia. The formula of 'Class + Party = Revolution' is not a transhistorical formula (a mantra) suitable for all times and places and under all conditions.

The Transitional Programme was a creation presupposed on the expectation that the Fourth International would be a 'mass organization within years' and the 'banner of the approaching victory of the proletariat'. It set a path in advance for the proletariat in an unfolding, developing situation which was forever throwing up new situations, conflicts (including a new imperialist war shortly after its creation), demands and ambiguities which could not be adequately addressed by such a programme.

Proceeding on the basis of *The Transitional Programme* today (as some grouplets still do) becomes fidelity to the word, taken out of the context of its historical locus, which contradicts the spirit of Marx's historical dialectics. This way of proceeding in revolutionary politics constitutes the basis out of which the elements of dogmatism arise and crystallize. And then we have a doctrine made out of a set of mantras and incantations which is absolutely unfit for anything vaguely 'revolutionary'. This is the practice today of the various left-wing sectarian groups.

The fundamental voluntaristic error which all 'suppliers of a revolutionary programme' (as a part of 'supplying a vanguard revolutionary party') make is the *overlooking* of the ontological pre-requisite in which revolutionary ideas only grip and animate the lives of millions of people when these ideas are consonant with their real living experiences and when they actually address their needs which arise out of this collective experience.

Today, it is vital to view Trotsky's *Transitional Programme* as a historically superseded document which, on critical appraisal, may furnish some lessons and considerations for future struggle. And as a historically temporal programme of the day. Marx's work was and is subject to the same historical dialectic. For example, in 1847 in his *Poverty of Philosophy*, Marx was still referring to the 'value of labour'. According to Engels' preface to the first German edition,[12] Marx 'still speaks of *labour* as a commodity, of the purchase and sale of labour, instead of *labour power*'. By the time we reach *Capital* this 'error' had been resolved. Marx had traversed and resolved the critically important and fundamental difference between 'labour' and 'labour power' in the period between the publication of the *Poverty* and that of *Capital.*

Notes and References

1   Trotsky, Leon, *The Transitional Program. The Death Agony of Capitalism and the Tasks of the Fourth International* (1938) <https://www.marxists.org/archive/trotsky/1938/tp/> (Last accessed 4 November 2016).
2   Trotsky, Leon, *Trade Unions in the Epoch of Imperialist Decay* (1940) <https://www.marxists.org/archive/trotsky/1940/xx/tu.htm> (Last accessed 4 November 2016).
3   '"I tell you," he said, "that in three to five years from now the Fourth International will be a great force in the world." The Trotskyist trials in Russia had not convinced the workers abroad, had shown Stalin in his true light, and had dealt a great blow at the Third International. In any case, Stalin's policy was forcing the Second and Third Internationals to come together; this was the beginning of its end. The Fourth International must develop in any case. In war its development would be very rapid.'
    Martin, Kingsley, 'Trotsky in Mexico' (10 April 1937), *The New Statesman* (29 January 2007) <http://www.newstatesman.com/society/2007/01/trotsky-mexico-russia-trial> (Last accessed 3 November 2016).
    The Fourth International never became that 'great force in the world'. If workers were 'convinced' about Stalin's 'true light', it did not move them into the orbit of Trotsky's International because any possible real, material grounds for such a movement had become attenuated with the rise of Stalinism under the impact of the Russian Revolution's isolation and 'socialism in one country', major defeats for the proletariat in different parts of the world, and Stalinism's counter-revolutionary role as the proxy of capital and its major state powers in the workers' movement internationally. The capital system was still decades away from the emergence of its structural crisis.
    Using, implicitly, the 'model example' of the development of the Bolshevik Party during the First World War, Trotsky expected the development of the Fourth International to be 'very rapid' during the course of the next world war. It did not rise any higher than a paltry, isolated group existence which rapidly fragmented into a Babel of squabbling sects each with its very own self-identifying 'shibboleth' which distinguished each one from its 'Trotskyist' competitors. Truly, and even comically, like the fragmentations we have observed historically in religious doctrines. This disintegration commenced almost immediately after the founding conference of the Fourth International.
4   For example, see Engels, Frederick, and Karl Marx, 'The Alleged Splits in the International'. In *The First International and After. Political Writings. Volume 3*,

edited by David Fernbach, pp. 260, 272–314, 298 ff (London: Penguin Books in association with New Left Review, 1974).

5   Karl Marx to Johann Baptist von Schweitzer (13 October 1868). In *Marx-Engels Collected Works, Volume 43* (London: Lawrence & Wishart, 1988), p. 132.

6   Marx, Karl, 'Instructions for Delegates to the Geneva Congress'. In *The First International and After. Political Writings. Volume 3*, edited by David Fernbach, pp. 85–94 (London: Penguin Books in association with New Left Review, 1974), p. 90.

7   Marx, Karl, 'Report to the Brussels Congress'. In *The First International and After. Political Writings. Volume 3*, edited by David Fernbach, pp. 94–99, 99 (London: Penguin Books in association with New Left Review, 1974).

8   Marx, Karl, 'Provisional Rules'. In *The First International and After. Political Writings. Volume 3*, edited by David Fernbach, pp. 82–84, 82 (London: Penguin Books in association with New Left Review, 1974).

9   It is vital to question everything in the clear light of activity itself and in an appraisal of the results of activity. Interrogation in regard to all forms of so-called 'authority' is a necessary consequence. And, indeed, it is vital not to be afraid to express differences directly to 'authority' itself when this is required. '*Doubt everything*' (Marx) ['De omnibus dubitandum', attributed to French philosopher René Descartes].

'When Engels and I first joined the secret communist society, we did so only on condition that anything conducive to a superstitious belief in authority be eliminated from the Rules. (Lassalle subsequently operated in the reverse direction.)'

Karl Marx to Wilhelm Blos (10 November 1877). In *Marx-Engels Collected Works, Volume 45* (London: Lawrence & Wishart, 1991), p. 288.

10 See Section 14.7.2, Mészáros, *Beyond Capital*.

11 Richard Dawkins was Professor of Public Understanding of Science at the University of Oxford. His rationalistic approach to religion is exemplified in his book *The God Delusion* (New York: Bantam Books, 2006). The whole approach of Dawkins to religion in general is rationalistic in the sense that he explicitly or implicitly advocates the 'power of argument', technology and science in overcoming it. In doing so, he fails to 'see the wood for the trees'; he fails to grasp that religion in its various forms in different cultures always emerges and evolves on the grounding basis of very definite socio-historical relations. These relations are the 'soil' on and within which religious thought and sentiment is nourished and grows. Only by their supersedence in the course of historical development, is the ground removed for the actual existence of religion in its many forms.

12 Marx, Karl, *The Poverty of Philosophy* (London: Martin Lawrence, n. d.), p. 21. Preface of Frederick Engels to the First German Edition (dated 23 October 1884).

CHAPTER 15

A Critique of 'Vanguardism' and the 'Party-Form'

The formulation today that 'the revolution' cannot be 'made' without 'the revolutionary vanguard' is not valid globally and never was sustainable in the more advanced capitalist countries in the twentieth century. Under the evolving global, structural crisis-conditions of capital's rule today, the outmodedness of trade unionism as a form of proletarian organization brings in its wake – with the necessity and inevitability of the operation of a natural law – the crisis, implosion and dissolution of the left-wing sectarian, vanguardist groups. The historic impasse reached by trade unionism under conditions of capital's deepening structural crisis – and the resulting outmodedness – means the 'end of the road' for the assorted vanguardist groups. Moreover, it raises the question of the sustainability of the 'Party-form' in general as a form of agency for the proletariat's revolutionary struggle against the capital order. The 'Party-form' is understood here as an explicitly, exclusively and wholly political organization which is not fully and organically integrated with the socio-economically restructuring functions of agency. 'Party' as a separate political body from these restructuring functions of agency and, in the dialectical sense of the word, is 'external' to these same functions.

Lenin and Trotsky did the proletariat in the more advanced capitalist countries the greatest disservice when they insisted on the 'democratic centralist Party-form' (at the founding conferences of the Third International) as the historically necessary form for the organization of the revolutionary agency of the proletariat. Trotsky stayed with it 'unto death'. Their insistence was, once again, *lucidly ideological*. And today, the spellbound sectarian groups have kept it 'alive' as a cryogenically frozen corpse. They remain stuck and lost in the shadow-world of the *ideological*.

And why? Because the ideological loop in which they remain caught (and whose existence was nourished by the decades of post-war Keynesian expansion of the capital order into the 1970s) has no real, living contact with the 'material life conditions' and 'real motive forces' (Engels) of the developing social ontology of globalizing capital's structural crisis today. That is, they are divorced theoretically and politically from the altered conditions of capitalist globalization and its maturing structural crisis.

'Living in the pores' of the class movement has led them down the path of degeneration and is pushing the sects further out beyond contact with these crisis-conditions. They are all effectively disappearing whilst trying to hang on 'for grim death' by employing various strategies such as 'regroupment' or 'entryism'. Gerry Healy's ultra-sectarian and internally abusive Workers Revolutionary Party in 1985 was the first major 'Trotskyist' casualty of the developing structural crisis of the capital order – mediated by the events and defeat of the miners' strike in 1984–1985 – but others have followed and will continue to do so.

Subjectively, the ideologically thinking individual does not grasp his thinking as 'ideological'. This form of thinking serves and operates to conceal its own ideological nature: *ideological* thought cannot grasp its own *ideological* nature simply because it is *ideological*. If Lenin had realized that his 'appeal to the model character of the Russian Revolution' was indeed *ideological*, would he have continued to make that 'appeal'? Would he not have 'corrected himself'?

A 'breakthrough' and 're-evaluation' in Lenin's thought and practice (an intrinsic aspect of the 'active side' so to speak to which Marx refers in the *Theses on Feuerbach*) would have been required in this respect. And, in its ideological character, this side of thought remains unconscious of its own ideological nature: the ideologically thinking individual remains unconscious of the ideological nature of this side of his own thought. Ideology cannot grasp its own nature.

In regard to the varying socio-economic conditions in different parts of the globe at the time of the Russian Revolution – and the advised and proclaimed necessary 'democratic centralist Party-form' organizational response to those spectrum of conditions by the proletariat – the Bolsheviks had their feet, partly at least after 1917, rooted and impeded in the 'boggy ground' of the *ideological*.

This ideological approach of the sectarian groups has been instrumental in the universal practice amongst them of 'supplying a revolutionary party' to the proletarian class. It is the transference and transposition of the concept of 'consciousness from the outside' which was more suited to the conditions of Tsarist Russia and Ochrana persecution at the beginning of the twentieth century but not to the conditions socialists are working under today at the start of the twenty-first century with globalizing capital-in-crisis.

This 'supplying' (sometimes euphemistically referred to, and trumpeted, as 'Party building' by the sects) is symptomatic of the relationship of these left groups to the class movement as a whole. Marx, in both the *Grundrisse* and *Capital*,[1] referred to the trading peoples of Antiquity as 'living in the pores' of its ancient societies *primarily* based on subsistence agriculture. He also used the same figure of speech ('living in the pores' or 'on the margins') to describe the life of the Jews in medieval Polish society. The same term can be applied to the commercial activities of the Jews in medieval Europe as a whole but not universally to their life in ancient societies.[2]

To further deploy this metaphor, we may assert that the left-wing sectarian groups have always 'lived in the pores' of the class movement of the proletariat. In a semi-detached relation to the whole movement. This principal mediating relation is intrinsic as to why their political relation to the class movement has always taken on a sectarian character. To be an intrinsic part of this movement means not 'living in its pores'. Not dictating to it and expecting it to dance to the formulations of programme and *pronunciamento*. It means a fully integrated immersion of socialists within the 'real movement' itself so that all conceptions and perspectives arise and develop within, and animate the life of, that class movement without ever separating out from it as confronting determinations and, thereby, not separating out of organic relation within it. This 'organic relation and connection' mean that newly arisen conceptions and perspectives arise within the 'real living movement' itself and not within the isolated perambulations of sect politics.

Any attempt at 'supplying a Party' to the class – as opposed to a 'party' being a form of organization which actually arises organically out of the historic struggle of the proletarian class – is doomed to fail. Only by 'arising organically' – out of the struggles of the proletariat 'within the existing framework' of the mass class organizations of the proletariat – will a legitimate organization of the class (form of agency of revolution) become established. This is because it will be intrinsically and *essentially* rooted in these struggles and arise out of them as a development of their real life-process. Such a movement of revolution – which articulates the interests of the whole class, is transparent in organization, internal relations and procedure – is the direct antithesis of the conspiratorial, inauthentic, *ersatz* politics of the sect. Such a movement, which is a development of the 'real movement', becomes imbued with the necessary degree of revolutionary democracy. Its mass, universal, democratic character cannot be 'supplied from the outside'. It must arise organically out of the struggles of the 'real movement' as it articulates the 'imperative needs' of the proletariat as a class.

Trade unionism remains the *currently dominant* form of organization of the proletariat across the globe (the traditional 'universal historic form'). This is where the proletariat 'is located' at the historical moment in terms of its organization and consciousness. It remains with it despite its decline and degeneration.

The hierarchical structure of trade unionism now confronts the proletariat as a retarding force in the development of the articulation of its class interests and requisite form of consciousness. In relation to these structures, and on 'agency', only the proletarian class itself can and will discuss, decide and move to resolve these questions in the course of the coming struggles and development of its organization. Such questions will not be decided by the proclamations of the sectarian groups (self-appointed 'vanguards') followed by their attempted impositions on the class movement. This class movement – responding in struggle and organizationally to the widening and intensification of capital's structural crisis – will repudiate and reject such methods and attempts to control and strait-jacket it. It requires the greatest possible degree of flexibility not simply in terms of its perspectives, strategy and tactics. Moreover, critically, in terms of the nature of its organization, it must be always subject to proteus-type alterations and transformations in order to adequately address changes in the conditions of the class struggle itself as capital's structural crisis unfolds in the coming century.

The 'Party-form' itself – regardless of its class character, structure, mode of administration, *modus operandi* and *modus vivendi*, etc. (and more specifically, the *'democratic centralist Party-form'*) – is a historically determined and conditioned political form (as were the Soviets). It represents and articulates class interests according to the historical conditions within which it arises and develops.

This, of course, means or implies that different class interests do not necessarily require their expression in the organizational form of different *political parties*. It does not mean that under different conditions, such interests cannot be articulated by forms other than the 'Party-form'. Unless, of course, by 'political party' we mean something other than 'Party'. That is, party with an upper case 'P' as opposed to the lower case 'p'.

The fundamental organizational question facing the proletariat today in the age of capital's structural crisis is not whether this or that type of Party is required or not. The question that truly needs to be addressed is **the whole character of the proletarian class movement itself** *which, as it stands, is totally inadequate to deal with the worsening crisis and is now very clearly manifesting its historically outmoded character in relation to the tasks which are confronting the proletariat today* **as a class** *as capital's structural crisis inevitably worsens in the course of the unfolding of the twenty-first century.*

Every closure of a factory or plant leaving thousands jobless, the mass terminations of thousands into structural unemployment which we are increasingly seeing in all sectors of capitalist economy, every assault on public provision leaving millions without adequate social, health and educational services, growing beggary, homelessness and destitution, every destruction of any aspect of the planet's ecosystem threatening human survival (and the survival of the whole of nature's wondrous and majestic living creation) and every further step towards the termination of democratic and political rights by the state power of capital, reveals that the response of the proletarian class movement (specifically trade unionism) reflects an approach which is more suited to historical conditions which have already passed through the hour glass of history. The approach of the 'old forms' is to use the same methods (or even altered methods which have become accommodated and compromised to the new conditions) where they have ceased to be productive of the pursuance and realization of any general class interests of the proletariat and of any subsidiary 'economistic' objectives within and outside the workplace.

The general response to capital's assaults on both the employed and unemployed has become either verbal or written protest, demonstrations, lobbying of government and parliament, using channels in the capitalist media to complain, working within the Labour Party (the traditional party of allegiance of the proletariat) and, very infrequently, the strike weapon which today is usually no more than a one-day strike or a series of strikes punctuated at certain points over a given period of time. Methods associated with past conditions of expansion of the capital system but 'toned down' for the age of capital's structural crisis.

All these are methods which were relatively adequate – in combination with longer, more intense militant struggles – to secure gains in wages and conditions or defend those already established in a period of economic expansion and capital accumulation. However, today, they are, in 2017, absolutely inadequate to address in practice the confronting conditions and problems being generated and reproduced by the qualitatively different character of capital's crisis. *What has very clearly become posited is the conflict between the historic demands being placed on the proletariat arising out of the structural-crisis conditions of capital's existence and rule, on the one hand, and the antiquated methods of struggle associated with the traditional form of class organization by means of which the proletariat has always struggled to defend or fight for its class interests, on the other. Hence the conception of the proletarian class movement being 'stuck in a bottleneck' of history. This posited relation remains 'silent and unacknowledged' to millions of trade unionized workers and socialists and to the countless millions outside of any form of proletarian organization whatsoever such as the sick and disabled, unemployed, destitute, homeless and casualized/precarized, etc., at the mercy of capital-in-crisis and its increasingly authoritarian state power. However, there is a 'general sense' – or even 'malaise' – amongst millions that the old ways of struggle no longer 'work' and that 'something new' is required.*

What is truly required – in order to practically address this question of revolutionary agency – is a fundamental alteration in the *trajectory of class organization towards a new form* and not another farcical regroupment with this or that individual/grouplet calling for a 'new Party', etc. In other words, the class movement must start on the basis of its current organization (inside and outside the trade unions, etc.) and its level of consciousness in order to move forward towards a requisite form of agency for the epoch of capital in structural crisis. It needs to proceed in terms of a perspective for the need for a mass organization of the whole class (not simply its trade unionized part) based upon a developing class conception of mass democracy.

It must be a form of agency that increasingly becomes capable of actually restructuring the whole social metabolism as well as carrying through associated political struggles against the agencies of capital – principally its state powers – to their necessary conclusion and consummation by any means which it considers possible and necessary. Only in the course of initiating and building such a movement will the proletariat become capable of forging and developing itself as a 'party' of social transformation. And in this mighty historic process, capable of making and articulating in practice the necessary decisions to move against and beyond the capital order.

In other words, socialists need to envisage the possibility that *the agency of revolution itself will be identical with 'the party' of the class without the need for some separated, distinct, even 'alien', political 'Party' within itself, within its own political body and hovering above and over it. The mass revolutionary agency of the class itself will become the 'party' and the 'party' will be this agency of revolution.* The maturing crisis of organization for the proletariat – which arises directly out of capital's structural crisis – contains implications for the historic tenability of the traditional 'Party-form' itself.

Vanguardism – ideologically and dogmatically in thrall to the events of the Russian Revolution – remains locked into the conception of the 'need for a revolutionary party'. The historical experience of this revolution is metaphysically extrapolated and imposed like an ideological shroud on and over living experience and unfolding events. It merely serves to suffocate the understanding and organizational articulation of this real experience today in terms of the need for the 'new universal historic form'.

The form of agency ideologically advocated by vanguardism today is more or less identical to a form of agency which arose specifically under profoundly different historical conditions at another time and place. The new structural crisis-conditions of capital now unfolding foreclose the realization of vanguardism's ahistorical conception for the tasks confronting the proletariat in the epoch of this qualitatively higher form of capital's crisis. This vanguardist outlook of sect politics is the *actual divorcement* of the consideration of the urgent question of revolutionary agency from the totality of conditions of capital-in-structural-crisis which now confronts the proletariat. The ghosts of dead organization grip and enchant the 'Marxists'.

The 'dead empty shell' of the 'democratic centralist Party-form' of the 'old conditions' of 'another place and time' becomes ideologically and presuppositionally preserved, and awaiting, in historical aspic, in the expectation that the evolving conditions will sooner or later engender a movement which is suited to fill it. The form of revolutionary agency is historically specific to the conditions within which it arises in order to meet and articulate the historic needs of the revolutionary class. Its form is not transhistorical beyond time and place. To propose otherwise is the ahistorical, metaphysical deposition of a historically and politically useless mantra which runs contrary to Marx's historical dialectics.

This is not to infer that the agency of revolution will not possibly contain 'Parties', groups, tendencies, etc. The trade unions, for example, have always had members of such groupings *but their existence as trade unions has not been conditional on the existence of such groupings within them*. Rather, quite the contrary. Vanguardism has always lived a parasitic existence within the host. We would, perhaps, need to continuously struggle to maintain and reaffirm the identity and integrity of the organized agency of revolution against the influence of sectarian centrifugal forces and elements whose activities are tending to fragment and disintegrate it. In this regard, such forces would serve as conscious or unconscious proxies within the agency of revolution facilitating the disruption of any coherent struggle against the capital order in crisis.

But how would such vanguardist 'Parties', sects, groups, etc., (which substitute their 'programmes' and 'party literature' for the self-activity of the proletariat itself) actually survive (if they are still around at the time) and for how long under such conditions? Or even establish themselves at all in the ongoing internal democratic conditions under which the revolutionary agency would be actually operating? These 'Parties' can only subsist in the absence of any real, open discussion and democratic election, recall, accountability and dismissal, etc. Under such conditions of intensifying conditions of capital's crisis, what future could such 'Parties' possibly have except a greater degree of political marginalization? *Incidentally, when the proletariat as a class becomes truly conscious in practice of its real class interests, it never becomes (and simply is unable to become) a prisoner of, or reduce itself to, dogmatic, sectarian, inflexible thinking or to any formal political movement which works on this basis.*

Who or what decides what are the 'interests of the proletarian class' at any point or phase in the transitional period? Once again, this returns us to the crucial and historically precedent question of agency. Are these 'interests' decided 'from above' or 'from the outside' by a party elite or bureaucratic stratum substituting themselves for the class or are they decided through democratic procedure and process by the class organized in the most democratic forms of agency that are possible at the time?

The agency of revolution will, of course, necessarily have a 'political expression' but what is crucial is the *character of the relationship* of this 'expression' to agency as a totality. This 'expression' would have to be totally and politically subordinate to the ongoing and unfolding democracy of the operation of the agency of revolution as a whole. For it to be posited as an alien structure within and distinct from the whole would itself indicate its conservative and retrogressive character. Indeed, its *bourgeois* class character. The appropriate, inalienable safeguards and limitations would necessarily have to be put in place to prevent the emergence of bureaucratic structures, usurpation, imposition, etc.

The democracy of the movement would be paramount and transparent. We would not be able to make the transition to the new society without the highest and most transparent forms of democracy in the revolutionary agency of the proletariat. This would constitute an intrinsic aspect of what Marx refers to as the need for the proletariat to 'win the battle for democracy'.[3]

The self-organizing, self-directing proletariat in the mode of revolutionary agency as being identical to the 'party form' is a different matter to agency being mediated by an 'external' 'Party-form' and the latter as distinct ('alien') from agency in its separation and *contra mundum* modality. When Marx used the term *'Communist Party'* in the *'Manifesto'*, he was not employing that term *formalistically*. He did not mean that 'The Party' is the necessary form of agency which is required under all conditions and at all times.

The age of the 'Parties' may be over despite the possibility that history still has many in store to spew forth and to no avail. But, apparently, not over for vanguardism. The implicit or explicit position of the 'Party Men' is that the experience of revolutionary struggle of another age teaches us that the Bolsheviks 'did it' with a 'democratic centralist Party'. Accordingly – metaphysically disregarding the real historical conditions of each period and sinking into the crass vulgarity of a mechanistic utilitarianism – if it 'worked for them' in 1917 then it should 'work for us' in the coming century of globalizing capital-in-crisis. The attempt to squeeze the 'toothpaste' (content) of the totality of current conditions back into the empty, flattened plastic tube of the 'Revolutionary Party' form is the self-referential (and self-reverential) and self-justificatory ideology of the left-wing vanguardist sect.

It is the advocacy and attempted *ideological* imposition of a previously necessary but today *dead form* as the form of agency through which the proletariat is to prosecute its struggle today against globalized capital and its state powers. It amounts to the burial of revolutionary transformation; the imprisonment of the revolutionary content of living struggle under the unfolding conditions of capital's structural crisis within an *ideological* tomb. Not a burial of the dead but an interment of the living. This is why the vanguardist groups have entered their 'death agony' and the unfolding and intensifying conditions of capital's structural crisis are pushing them further into it.

The liturgical insistence on the need for a 'Revolutionary Party' form – supposedly emulating that of Lenin's Bolshevik Party – is an ideological presupposition and dogma of these groups. The epigones of Lenin and Trotsky have substituted the letter for the spirit; they have become the undertakers of the spirit of Lenin rather than its inheritors and warriors. The 'Party Men' calling for a 'new socialist Party' or to build the 'revolutionary Party' are politically and ideologically haunted; they are in the grip of the ghosts of past, dead conditions. Ghosts which can only be exorcized in the course of the actual experience and lessons of real living struggles against the capital order in the presently unfolding epoch of its structural crisis. The late socialist thinker, Cyril Smith, touched on this when he wrote ...

> If the working class is going to develop that 'communist consciousness on a mass scale', which is the essence of Marx's notion of revolution, we must stop trying to reconcile Bolshevism with Marx's conception of 'mass communist consciousness'. The two are diametrically opposed. That is why it is so vital that we tear ourselves away from the idea that Lenin's work gave us a 'model' for all revolutionary activity. Lenin's idea of forms of party organization changed with the political context in which he fought. But that is not the basic issue. These changes themselves were decided by 'the Vanguard Party', always lagging behind the changes in the class movement. It is neither a matter of correcting Lenin's 'mistakes', nor of deciding whether 'Lenin planted the seeds of Stalinism'.[4]

Smith correctly insists here that *Lenin's idea of forms of party organization changed with the political context in which he fought.* However Lenin, nevertheless, had a 'pocketed' 'centralist' 'default' conception to which he and Trotsky return ideologically after 1917 in their work in the Comintern and Fourth International. Under the historical conditions in Russia at the time within which both Lenin and Trotsky were fighting, there was a certain political legitimacy for this constant re-affirmation. However, it was not universally justifiable, and applicable, within the differentiated international context in Lenin's time and is certainly not valid today with regard to the form of proletarian agency necessary in the age of capitalist globalization.

This 'vanguardist' way of approaching the question of agency today by the left-wing groups is the self-serving 'cart before the horse' rhetoric of the sect. If we study the incredibly rich and seminal work of Marx and Engels in the 1840s – specifically *The Holy Family, The German Ideology* and the groundbreaking *Theses on Feuerbach* – we can see very clearly that this 'vanguardist' position is completely at odds with their materialist conception of historical development.

People only really start to change the totality of the conditions of their life – and thereby themselves in the process of doing this – under the impact, weight and influence of real material changes actually taking place in these conditions. The beginnings of such a movement towards socialist revolution cannot take place without forms of real social-material mediation actually motivating people or even *demanding* that they take such and such a road. People do, indeed, tend to take the 'line of least resistance' until that position is no longer possible or tenable and people must then start to fight to go beyond the old, defensive ways of struggle and organization.

Such changes – arising directly out of the crisis of the old conditions and materially impacting peoples lives, often in the most intimate ways – begin to impress on people the need for real material changes in their mode of life and this tends to bring on the emergence and development of changes in the way people organize in opposition to the ruling order. Inevitably, arising out of such material changes, political conceptions and perspectives start to develop. 'Imperative need' (Marx) is the driving force of social revolution.

This is precisely what the unfolding of capital's crisis is doing globally today. People are, in a certain sense, already 'experimenting' with new ways of struggle, new ways of opposing capital in contrast to the traditional forms and strategies. These real developments, full of contradiction, are the source of alterations and 'leaps' in consciousness. These developments and their internal conflicts are the source of the origination and development of what Marx refers to as the necessary 'alteration of men on a mass scale' and the growth on a 'mass scale of this communist consciousness'. But these 'alterations' ...

> can only take place in a practical movement, a revolution; this revolution is necessary, therefore, not only because the ruling class cannot be overthrown in any other way, but also because the class overthrowing it can only in a revolution succeed in ridding itself of all the muck of ages and become fitted to found society anew.[5]

It is, therefore, the actual unfolding of capital's global structural crisis which is generating new ways of 'dealing' with this crisis on the part of the proletariat globally. The development of this crisis-process is actually serving to promote changes in 'mass consciousness'.

Vanguardism, however, remains convinced that it is still possible and necessary to import this 'consciousness from the outside' (or rather, more correctly, 'export' it from 'the outside into the interior of the class movement') by selling papers, leafletting, etc., regardless of alterations and shifts in historical conditions. This conception of 'consciousness from the outside' contains its own inherent dangers. It can, under unfavourably changing circumstances, according to Mészáros, very readily become consciousness 'from above' with all the hierarchical organizational implications in accompaniment.[6] But alterations in the direction of a 'mass communist consciousness' can only really come about as a result of the *activity of millions* in response to real material changes taking place in their social relations and mode of life. The dynamic of revolution will only start to become determinately established when people in their multitudes actually start to take matters into their own hands, independently of the state power of capital, and under the impact of capital's currently unfolding structural crisis.

The ontologically and epistemologically flawed conception of 'consciousness from the outside' mediates vanguardism's notion of the need for political transformation to precede socio-cultural transformation in which the latter necessarily and mechanically must follow only when the former has actually taken place. This is tediously repeated as a fundamental presupposition in the activities of the various vanguardist grouplets. Indeed, it is fundamental to their very existence and *modus operandi* as a self-justifying principle of this existence. To merely suggest that we can and must build a movement that starts to move onto the road of going against and beyond the capital relation itself – in the violent presence of the state power of capital – is immediately dismissed by such 'vanguards' as 'idealism' or 'unrealistic', etc.

In the vanguardist politics of the left-wing groups, the beginnings of social transformation (transition to socialism) are predicated on a previously completed, successful political revolution. According to the pronouncements of their leaders, the state must be toppled first in political revolution and then, and only then, can the proletariat proceed with the transition to socialism.

This vanguardist conception of the 'transition to socialism' is always contrasted with the actual historical genesis and development of the capitalist mode of production. Capitalism, it is asserted, developed slowly and embryonically 'within the womb' of feudalism and was then born onto the historical scene in a series of political and social upheavals and revolutions in opposition to the social relations and structures of the feudal order. Then follows the oft-repeated thesis that socialism does not arise out of capitalism in the same way that capitalism arose out of feudalism. Self-evidently, since the transition taking place is between two different modes of production. However – and this is the nub of the question – the left-wing sects use this to falsely imply that only when a 'revolutionary party' has been built and the state power of capital overthrown by this party leading the proletariat, can the transition to socialism take place. This is the self-referential and self-justifying vein of the vanguardist group.

In the documents of the First International, Marx writes of 'the emancipation of the proletariat being the act of the proletariat itself'.[7] He does not add that the emancipation of the proletariat will depend on the formation and delivery of a 'vanguard' from 'outside' or otherwise. His *implicit* conception of the proletariat in his work for the International Workingmen's Association (IWMA) was that of the existence of a *globalized* proletariat and not that of a backward, semi-feudal country. His conception of socialist revolution and international agency presupposes the globalized rule of capital and its various state and global powers which we see today.

'Bolshevism' was merely a historically specific form of 'Marxism' which arose under the Tsarist conditions of capital's (largely 'foreign' capital) rule in Russia. Under the present circumstances of capital's rule, it would be folly (historically and politically inadequate) to suggest that the theory and practice of 'Bolshevism' is the necessary form of revolutionary agency of the epoch. Such an assertion is, in truth, a move away from the animating spirit of Marx's historical dialectics and the substitution of the jaded letter for his method of approach. To equate 'Bolshevism' with 'Marxism' today – without the necessary distinctions and divergences which historical development has introduced and imposed over the course of the last hundred years – constitutes the formulation of a normative conception against which all 'deviations' are measured and compared. It is a conception of socialism and agency which divorces the urgent question of revolutionary agency today from the real, existent conditions of the rule of global capital-in-crisis and the changing nature of the proletariat globally as the twenty-first century unfolds.

The 'revolutionary left' has fixed its conception of revolutionary agency in the mode of a *mathematical invariant* which must remain unaltered when the historical context has changed and become transformed beyond the conditions within which this 'invariant' arose. Capital now dominates a changing proletariat under altered global conditions but the 'necessary and adequate' form of agency continues to be identified by the 'revolutionaries' as that which was required for the conditions of another time and place which have been superseded and left behind by a century of development.

Both Lenin and Trotsky *ideologized* the 'democratic centralist' form of party organization after 1917 in their work in the Third and Fourth Internationals. The fact that vanguardism today continues to dance to this ideology demonstrates how far it is from Marx and his life work as well as from a critical grasp of the relationship between required form of revolutionary organization today and the prevailing yet changing conditions of capital's rule in the age of its structural crisis. For these vanguardist sects, Trotsky and Lenin on 'democratic centralist' organization have become dogma; part of an organizational ritual and liturgical formula for the so-called 'Leninist' party. One of the 'sacred pillars' of Leninism. They have ossified the 'democratic centralist Party' form into scriptural status which runs counter to the actual spirit of dialectics. They have taken it as an unassailable manual of 'Party organization' for all times and all places. In the spirit of a trained mechanic using a car repair manual valid for a given model of car. Lenin and Trotsky were both in error to *ideologize* it as they did.[8] They identified and raised a form of organization – that was historically specific to time and place – to the status of an eternal structuring principle of organization.

It is a characteristic of vanguardism to constantly point to what Lenin or Trotsky did and said, etc., and then rationalistically extrapolate and/or 'recontextualize' this and seek to graft it onto conditions today. A profound mistake. An error which is beyond stupidity. The substitution of the letter for the spirit. It is not so much that the 'democratic centralist Party form' itself must always be historically valid under all conditions of capital's rule but rather the more general, crass, ahistorical, metaphysical and *undialectical assumption that the 'Party-form' per se must be transcendent of all historical conditions of capital's rule* as the necessary form of revolutionary agency of the proletariat to move against and go beyond the capital order. Such a conception is a complete abandonment of dialectical thinking and leaves the contemporary proletariat as a class 'in the lurch of history'.

Mészáros briefly looks at the *'self-defensively closed structure of the Vanguard Party'* and reveals its historical roots in the police state conditions of Tsarist autocracy. He compares this Vanguardism with *'Marx's original idea of producing communist consciousness on a mass scale – with its necessary implication of an inherently open organizational structure'* which gives the *'measure of the fundamental difference between a defensive and an offensive posture'.*

The form of revolutionary organization of Lenin's party – necessary for the conditions of struggle in his time – were *'mythologized'* and then – by Trotsky in the Fourth International and by others after 1945 – used as the organizational point of departure for the various 'revolutionary' sects and groups. But the organization of Lenin's party was developed in totally different conditions to those emerging and developing subsequently after 1945. And to even assert that increasing capitalist state authoritarianism today, with the deepening of capital's crisis, may necessitate a return to Lenin's type of organization is itself a misconception of the nature of the current 'globalized' epoch of capital and of the altered character of the proletariat as a 'globalized' class. Moreover, it is a misunderstanding of the nature of revolutionary agency required today under different technical and social conditions of capital's existence and rule. The age of *nom de plume* revolutionary politics is over.

An important, retrospectival consideration which today can serve to inform our understanding of the degeneration of the Russian Revolution (and subsequent developments in the twentieth century) is the fact that the capitalist system had not started to enter its period of structural crisis in the first half of the twentieth century. It only entered this period in the final quarter. Capitalist commodity production still contained the potential for further accumulation and expansion and this, in itself, must have mediated and reinforced those tendencies checking the further development of world socialist revolution.

The key to comprehensively understanding the past is located in the historical conditions and relations of the present. Hindsight becomes a necessary corrective to any misplaced conceptions and perspectives of this superseded past. The resulting retrospective – incorporated into a 'new political foresight' and perspective – then serves to inform the emergence and development of the 'practical consciousness' of the class movement against capital and its national state and global powers.

In the course of the unfolding of the twentieth century, conditions had not reached a stage globally where capital no longer had the potential and means of displacing its accumulated contradictions. The internal dynamic of its contradictions had not become 'hemmed in' as a result of the tendencies of development of its own inherent nature leading to the structural character of its terminal crisis. *It is inherent in the capital relation that its development necessarily leads towards structural crisis.* Mészáros, in *Beyond Capital*, does not 'discover' this but merely draws out theoretically, and identifies empirically, from a study of globalizing capital's trajectory and its social manifestations, what is *actually implicit* in Marx. In this sense, 'living perception' becomes consonant with the historic implications of Marx's scientific theory.

The degeneration of the Russian Revolution cast an 'ideological shadow' across the class movement of the proletariat internationally as the twentieth century unfolded. This 'shadow' continued to 'grip' or 'shroud' the class movement because the 'sun had not yet set' on the capitalist order. The emergence of globalizing capital's structural crisis is the 'setting of the sun' on that order. As capital's structural crisis deepens, the first revolutionary breach in any politically significant geographical region of capital's rule will undoubtedly create a global earthquake for the whole capitalist system. Its repercussions will be felt across the whole capitalist world because – unlike at the time of the Russian Revolution – capitalism as a more integrated global system in a state of intensifying structural crisis will be more vulnerable and more subject to such an 'historic earthquake' and its cultural and political aftershocks.

The Russian Revolution could be contained ('encircled') as a loss (not as an irreversible 'write off' but as a potentially recoverable domain) for capitalism in an epoch where capital still had the capacity to re-adjust and regain its global equilibrium and momentum. But such a 'reaffirmation out of a partial negation' as took place for capital after the Russian Revolution must become increasingly more difficult as the twenty-first century unfolds. Compared to the Russian Revolution a century ago, such a revolutionary breach in any major capitalist country will have profoundly revolutionary effects on the class movement of the proletariat across the globe.

The conception of the need for the vanguardist, democratic centralist Party-form could only be sustained throughout the twentieth century precisely because the conditions for global socialist revolution had *not* matured. The conception of organization founded on the Party-form was fed and sustained by the conditions of capital's expansion throughout the twentieth century and – connected with and nurtured by this continuing expansion – the ideological legacies of the Russian Revolution. This was reflected in the 'ideological appropriation' of the Party-form taken from the Russian Revolution as *the required form* of revolutionary agency par excellence in the course of the twentieth century. The *direct historic necessity* for revolution could not arise out of capital's conjunctural crisis-phases in this period. Structural crisis only starts to emerge in the final quarter of the twentieth century.

In other words, this 'appropriation' was an unconscious articulation and expression in organization of the simple historical truth that the global conditions for a series of successful socialist revolutions in the major capitalist regions – driven by the 'self-organization' and 'self-emancipating activity' of the proletariat – across the globe had not come to the historically required stage of maturity. This only emerges with capital's unfolding structural crisis where its inner contradictions tend to sharpen to the point of non-displaceability. Only as this stage opens up and develops, is the proletariat then truly driven onwards towards self-direction, self-organization and self-emancipatory activity in the form of the creation and evolution of the 'new universal historic form of proletarian revolutionary organization'.

Such a self-directing, self-organizing, self-emancipating, mass class movement of the proletariat was inconceivable in the twentieth century as a result of the immature conditions. These conditions simultaneously formed the mediating basis for the degeneration of the Russian Revolution and served to sustain the 'Party-form' in the various 'movements' around the world in the wake of the Russian Revolution. In other words, the ideologically adopted 'model' of the Russian Revolution expressed the global historic immaturity of these conditions for global revolution which had not throughout the twentieth century passed over into the stage of structural crisis for the capital order. Lenin himself was unaware of this when he ideologically advocated the 'model of the Russian Revolution' as the 'near and immediate future of even the capitalistically most advanced countries'

Only with the emergence of capital's structural crisis globally are the conditions now being assembled for the opening up of a general offensive against capital and its political powers and the prosecution of a series of successful, concatenated socialist revolutions across the globe. In this sense, all the previous four *Internationals* can be situated within a historical locus of ontologically 'unripe' conditions. 'False starts' of history in the previous two centuries. Of course, all the *Internationals* were formed under the mediating impetus of changing conditions. However, in the sense that the capital relation had not in the previous two centuries – under these conditions of the formation of these *Internationals* – entered its period of terminal and intractable crisis but still contained the potential for further global development, these *Internationals* were effectively attempts to 'erect tent cities in an overpowering hurricane wind'.

Herein lies the historically real, underlying, anchoring causality on the basis of which an understanding of why all four *Internationals* have 'failed' can be elaborated. They 'failed' because the capital order as a total global system of social reproduction had not reached its 'endpoint' of structural crisis and still had room for expansion and further development. As a system, it was not fatally weakened to the point where the proletariat was 'no longer willing to live in the old ways, and the ruling class could no longer rule in the old ways'. These inexhausted conditions of further capitalist development (expansion and accumulation) were the 'best' and 'harshest' 'critics' of the *Internationals*. The series of defeats for the proletariat throughout the twentieth century were rooted within – but not exclusively determined by – this causal potential for the further development of capitalism (regardless of wars, 'turndowns' and cyclical economic crises) throughout the last century.

The social democratic labour bureaucracy, the ruling caste of the Soviet system and 'Communist Party' hierarchies in and out of power across the world all functioned on the basis of their self-preservatory relationship with the capital system. Implicitly, the opening up of an offensive against the capital order will bring the conservative character of any vestiges of these hierarchies (notably in their trade union forms) into sharp relief and set them up for dissolution. The simple truth that capital did not enter its period of structural crisis until the final quarter of the twentieth century served to mediate the various defeats in the international workers' movement.

These defeats, moreover, reciprocally attenuated any offensive against capital and helped to maintain it as a coherent global system of production and distribution. 'Reformism' and 'socialism in one country' were the major ideological exponents of these relations in the workers' movement internationally. Moreover, Trotsky's conception of the 'historical crisis of mankind' being reducible to 'the crisis of revolutionary leadership' also fell victim to these inexhausted conditions and relations of capital's rule. Ditto the Fourth International as an organizational initiative.

Stalinism was the major anti-communist force in the world labour movement. The Soviet Union, as the 'homeland' of Stalinism, has now collapsed. This barrier of Stalinism has been removed but it has simultaneously left behind an anti-communist ideological legacy. Millions of people across the globe mistakenly – but conveniently and expeditiously for capital, its powers and ideologues – equate communism with Stalinism and Maoism.

The contradictory outcome of the fall of Stalinism is very clear here: the barrier is now down and the road ahead is now open but, at the same time, we are having to deal with the counter-revolutionary ideological legacies of Maoism and Stalinism. This collapse therefore expresses itself in contradictory form. But the younger (post 1989) generation, and those to follow, are becoming increasingly 'distant' from it chronologically. Moreover, they are not imbued with all the conservatism of hierarchically structured trade unionism, labour organization and practice in its current moribund structure. This has been demonstrated in the 'Momentum' movement supporting Corbyn which is hundreds of thousands of mainly young people.

Of course, ideology is 'powerful' but it can never be stronger than radical alterations and transformations in material conditions. At most, it can temporarily serve to 'put the brakes' on the consequences and mediating effects of these altered conditions until its conflict with them necessitates its transformation or complete supersedence. In the end, it is the character of changing conditions (inclusive of ideological changes) which will move people and re-orientate them in struggle. If an ideological legacy contradicts their experiences of living reality, then it will be put to one side, or altered itself so that it is consonant with this new reality or even discarded completely by throwing it into the all-consuming furnace of history.

Notes and References

1. Marx, Karl, *Capital. A Critique of Political Economy*, Vol. 1, translated by Ben Fowkes (London: Penguin Books in association with New Left Review, 1976), p. 172, 'The Fetishism of the Commodity and its Secret'.
    Marx, Karl, *Grundrisse. Foundations of the Critique of Political Economy (Rough Draft)*, translated by Martin Nicolaus (London: Penguin Books in association with New Left Review, 1973), p. 253, 487, Notebook II, Notebook V.
    'The peasant and the lord during the Middle Ages are not producers of merchandise ... It is true that they exchange their surpluses on occasion, but exchange is for them something fundamentally alien, an exception. Thus, neither the lord nor peasant generally possesses large sums of money. The greatest part of their wealth consists of use values, of wheat, cattle, etc. ... Circulation of merchandise, circulation of money-capital, and money economy in general are fundamentally alien to this form of society. Capital lives, according to the clear expression of Marx, in the pores of this society. It is into these pores that the Jew penetrated.'
    Bauer, Otto, *Die Nationalitätenfrage und die Sozialdemokratie* (Vienna: Ignaz Brand, 1907), p. 367.
2. Leon, Abraham, *The Jewish Question: A Marxist Interpretation* (New York: Pathfinder Press, 1971).
3. 'The first step in the revolution by the working class is to raise the proletariat to the position of ruling class to win the battle of democracy.'
    Engels, Frederick, and Karl Marx, 'Manifesto of the Communist Party'. In *Marx-Engels Selected Works, Volume One*, translated by Samuel Moore in cooperation with Frederick Engels, pp. 98–137 (Moscow: Progress Publishers, 1969), Chapter 2, 'Proletarians and Communists'.
4. Smith, Cyril, *Mészáros on Lenin*. A Contribution by Cyril Smith to the International Socialist Forum Seminar on 'Beyond Capital' by István Mészáros (28 June 1998) <https://www.marxists.org/reference/archive/smith-cyril/works/articles/meszaros.htm> (Last accessed 4 November 2016).

5 Engels, Frederick, and Karl Marx, 'The German Ideology'. In *Marx-Engels Collected Works, Volume 5, 1845–1847*, pp. 19–581 (London: Lawrence & Wishart, 1976), pp. 52–53.
6 Mészáros, István, *Beyond Capital: Towards a Theory of Transition* (London: Merlin Press, 1995), pp. 394–396, Section 10.2.2.
7 Marx, 'Provisional Rules'. In *The First International and After. Political Writings. Volume 3*, edited by David Fernbach, pp. 82–84, 82 (London: Penguin Books in association with New Left Review, 1974).
8 In this regard, see the documents of the Third International 1919–1922 and, of course, those of the Fourth International. For example, '12. *Parties belonging to the Communist International must be based on the principle of democratic centralism. In the present epoch of acute civil war the Communist Party will be able to fulfil its duty only if its organization is as centralized as possible, if iron discipline prevails, and if the party centre, upheld by the confidence of the party membership, has strength and authority and is equipped with the most comprehensive powers.*'

Degras, Jane (ed.), 'Conditions of Admission to the Communist International Approved by the Second Comintern Congress, 6 August, 1920'. In *The Communist International: 1919–1943 Documents. Volume 1 1919–1922*, pp. 166–172, 171 (Oxford: Oxford University Press, 1956), Condition 12.

'*Democracy and centralism do not at all find themselves in an invariable ratio to one another. Everything depends on the concrete circumstances, on the political situation in the country, on the strength of the party and its experience, on the general level of its members, on the authority the leadership has succeeded in winning. Before a conference, when the problem is one of formulating a political line for the next period, democracy triumphs over centralism.*

When the problem is political action, centralism subordinates democracy to itself. Democracy again asserts its rights when the party feels the need to examine critically its own actions. The equilibrium between democracy and centralism establishes itself in the actual struggle, at moments it is violated and then again re-established.' Trotsky, Leon, 'On Democratic Centralism and the Regime (1937)', from a US *Internal Bulletin* (December 1937), prior to the formation of the Socialist Workers Party in the United States <https://www.marxists.org/archive/trotsky/1937/xx/democent.htm> (Last accessed 4 November 2016).
9 Mészáros, *Beyond Capital*, p. 675.

Appendices

APPENDIX I

Marx's Realms: Capital, Natural Necessity, True Realm of Freedom

1. Hegel, Marx and 'Freedom and Necessity'

Written more than twenty years after the seminal Paris Manuscripts and embracing and sublating within itself the content of those manuscripts and all the subsequent theoretical development, the third volume of *Capital* represents the highest point of development of Marx's critique of political economy. Without a detailed study of this text, no truly coherent discussion of the onset, in the 1970s, and the unfolding of the structural crisis of capital can be evolved. Accordingly, a study of *Capital* as a whole is a presupposition for such discussion.

A re-read of any of Marx's writings always invites one on a new journey of discovery. Just when we thought we knew the 'ins and outs' of a work, we find that there is always more to unearth and dig out. A new reading brings out new aspects, reveals new channels and fissures which we overlooked before, and this augments and enriches our overall conception. Just when we start to think the mine has been exhausted, new seams are discovered.

We know essentially what we are fighting against but what are we fighting for? What are we fighting to establish? This article focuses on Marx's concepts of the 'realm of natural necessity' and the 'true realm of freedom' found in his third volume of *Capital*.

What follows is a lengthy quote from Volume 3 with which we will work and to which we may refer back and return as and when required ...

> Surplus labour in some form must always remain, as labour beyond the extent of given needs. It is just that in the capitalist, as in the slave system, etc., it has an antagonistic form and its obverse side is pure idleness on the part of one section of society. A

certain quantum of surplus labour is required as insurance against accidents and for the progressive extension of the reproduction process that is needed to keep pace with the development of needs and the progress of population. It is one of the civilizing aspects of capital that it extorts this surplus labour in a manner and in conditions that are more advantageous to social relations and to the creation of elements for a new and higher formation than was the case under the earlier forms of slavery, serfdom, etc. Thus on the one hand it leads towards a stage at which compulsion and the monopolization of social development (with its material and intellectual advantages) by one section of society at the expense of another disappears; on the other hand it creates the material means and the nucleus for relations that permit this surplus labour to be combined, in a higher form of society, with a greater reduction of the overall time devoted to material labour. For, according to the development of labour productivity, surplus labour can be great when the total working day is short and relatively small when the total working day is long. If the necessary labour-time is 3 hours and surplus labour also 3 hours, the total working day is 6 hours and the rate of surplus labour 100 per cent. If the necessary labour is 9 hours and the surplus labour 3 hours, the total working day is 12 hours and the rate of surplus labour only 33 1/3 per cent. It then depends on the productivity of labour how much use-value is produced in a given time, and also therefore in a given surplus labour-time. The real wealth of society and the possibility of a constant expansion of its reproduction process does not depend on the length of surplus labour but rather on its productivity and on the more or less plentiful conditions of production in which it is performed.

The realm of freedom really begins only where labour determined by necessity and external expediency ends; it lies by its very nature beyond the sphere of material production proper. Just as the savage must wrestle with nature to satisfy his needs, to maintain and reproduce his life, so must civilised man, and he must do so in all forms of society and under all possible modes of production. This realm of natural necessity expands with his development, because his needs do too; but the productive forces to satisfy these expand at the same time. Freedom, in this sphere, can consist only in this, that socialized man, the associated producers, govern the human metabolism with nature in a rational way, bringing it under their collective control instead of being dominated by it as a blind power; accomplishing it with the least expenditure of energy and in conditions most worthy and appropriate for their human nature. But this always remains a realm of necessity. The true realm of freedom, the development of human powers as an end in itself, begins beyond it, though it can only flourish with this realm of necessity as its basis. The reduction of the working day is the basic prerequisite.[1]

Realm of necessity? realm of freedom? In the very nature of things, any realm of necessity must be intermediated by a given degree of freedom and any realm of freedom intermediated by relations of necessity of a given nature and order. It is the actual, historically established, real, specific, character of social relations within and through which humanity lives which determine and denote the stage of living development at which the relationship between necessity and freedom has arrived.

Hegel teaches us that ...

> A freedom involving no necessity, and mere necessity without freedom, are abstract and in this way untrue formulae of thought. Freedom is no blank indeterminateness: essentially concrete, and unvaryingly self-determinate, it is so far at the same time necessary. Necessity, again, in the ordinary acceptation of the term in popular philosophy, means determination from without only – as in finite mechanics, where a body moves only when it is struck by another body, and moves in the direction communicated to it by the impact. This however is a merely external necessity, not the real inward necessity which is identical with freedom.[2]

It is this 'real inward necessity which is identical with freedom' which Marx is articulating when he writes of the 'true realm of freedom'. As Hegel demonstrated, necessity and freedom, in their dialectics, are mutually engendering, relating, negating and reaffirming sides of each other. They are *'not independently real'* and *'to abstract and isolate either conception is to make it false'*[3,4] (*Zusatz*, §§157–158).

Hegel contrasts this conception of a necessity which is inseparable from freedom with 'necessity immediate or abstract' in which it is walled off from 'abstract freedom' in a state of 'rigid externality'. For Hegel, neither necessity nor freedom can have subsistence independently of each other, have 'no independent reality'. To think so is the work of the 'understanding' (*Verstand*), 'formal', 'unspeculative', 'metaphysics'. In Hegel's formal exposition in his *Logic*, the separation of necessity and freedom – their 'externality' to each other – is transcended by demonstrating that ...

> the members, linked to one another, are not really foreign to each other, but only elements of one whole, each of them, in its connection with the other, being, as it were, at home, and combining with itself. In this way necessity is transfigured into freedom – not the freedom that consists in abstract negation, but freedom concrete and positive. From which we may learn what a mistake it is to regard freedom and necessity as mutually exclusive. Necessity indeed, qua necessity, is far from being

> freedom: yet freedom presupposes necessity, and contains it as an unsubstantial element in itself.[4] (Zusatz, *§158*)

Therefore, in Hegel's exposition in his *Logic*, necessity and freedom are not 'external' or 'foreign' to each other but contain each in the other. The mechanistic conception of necessity is the absolute negation of freedom and vice versa so that they are 'mutually exclusive'. But in Hegel's dialectical conception 'freedom presupposes necessity' and holds it as an 'element in itself'[4] (*Zusatz*, §158).

In Marx's 'true realm of freedom', the activity of the human individual is that of a social individual (as opposed to the private individual of class society) which is lived necessarily as a 'free mediation' in the life of the commune as whole. The social form of necessity in this realm ceases to bear the same compulsive 'external' character as it does in the 'realms of capital and natural necessity' which precede it. The 'necessity' of the 'true realm of freedom' is the 'truth' of the previous form of 'external' necessity. It emerges as the actualization and development of what is found latent within the antecedent realm. It is the outcome of the inherent tendencies which have emerged in this antecedent 'realm of natural necessity'.

It is a necessity which is no longer 'external' and compulsive but of a totally different, higher order altogether. It is the character of this higher order of necessity to 'suspend its presupposition' – that is, to transcend the previously compulsive 'external' form – and, in so doing, creates itself as the very ground, the presupposition of itself. It posits itself as a higher, humanly internalized, form of necessity which is a 'real inward necessity which is identical with freedom'. And in this lies the human freedom of this realm. The 'free mediation' of each becomes the necessary condition for the 'free mediation' of all and vice versa. This 'free mediation' of each and all in the commune of the 'true realm' is not psychosocially internalized by the individual or society as a whole as driving 'compulsion', as a 'must be so and so', etc.

This 'true realm of freedom' creates a fundamentally different kind of individual as compared to the type we find in bourgeois society. In his foreword to Marx's *Grundrisse*, Martin Nicolaus writes ...

> Finally, instead of 'species-being', the **Grundrisse** speaks of two very broadly and generally defined types of human individuality. The first is the 'private individual', meaning the individual as private proprietor, both as owner of the means of production and as 'owner' of the commodity, labour power; the individual within the exchange relation. The abolition of the relations of private property is the abolition of the conditions which produce and reproduce this kind of individual. The place of this type is taken by the **social individual**, the individual of classless society, a personality type which is not less, but rather more, developed as an individual because of its direct social nature. As opposed to the empty, impoverished, restricted individuality of capitalist society, the new human being displays an all-sided, full, rich development of needs and capacities, and is universal in character and development.[5]

This all-round development and cultivation of 'social individuality' to which Nicolaus refers becomes an *inner social necessity for the individual* as the transition is made from the post-capitalist 'realm of natural necessity' towards the capital-free 'true realm of freedom'.

This 'cultivation' does not, of course, take the form of an oppressively coercive social imposition on the individual where the individual is 'compelled' to become 'cultivated' (Hegel's 'external necessity'). Rather, it springs directly – 'unforced' and 'spontaneously' – from the actual nature of human relationships in the commune where all forms of oppressive coercion have been transcended and the life of the individual is not subject to the social compulsion which characterizes human relations in bourgeois society and, to a lesser degree, in the post-capitalist 'realm of natural necessity'.

The individual becomes 'developed' as a 'social individual' in order to live a fully developed and integrated human life with his/her fellow men and women. This development of the social individual does not take place under the weight of any 'external' coercion or expediency, of any 'external necessity' which is internalized as a 'compulsion'. The social relations of the 'true realm' are not identified as 'other' or 'alien' as bourgeois relations are to the 'private individual' of bourgeois society in his/her 'asocial sociability'.

They become internalized – without 'compulsion' or 'otherness' – as direct manifestations of who s/he is as a human being simply because these communal relations *are* 'her or him' in immediate social form just as s/he *is* the direct, 'disestranged', individual expression of them. The individual, under such conditions, remains the spontaneous yet actively creating creation of the 'ensemble of social relations'. Born into this 'true realm', s/he becomes developed as a directly socialized, intrinsic, increasingly 'disestranged' and 'disestranging' 'cultivated' part of the life of society (Hegel's 'real inward necessity which is identical with freedom'). The historical persistence, down the ages, of 'asocial sociability' (Mészáros) starts to lose its grip on humanity and recede into the abyss of time.

2. Realm of Global Capital

The development of capital itself creates the historic grounds for a higher form of human individuality ...

> Capital's ceaseless striving towards the general form of wealth drives labour beyond the limits of its natural paltriness [Naturbedürftigkeit], and thus creates the material elements for the development of the rich individuality which is as all-sided in its production as in its consumption, and whose labour also therefore appears no longer as labour, but as the full development of activity itself, in which natural necessity in its direct form has disappeared; because a historically created need has taken the place of the natural one. This is why capital is productive; i.e. an essential relation for the development of the social productive forces. It ceases to exist as such only where the development of these productive forces themselves encounters its barrier in capital itself.[6]

These 'historically created needs' superseding (sublating) 'natural needs' – to which Marx refers here – does not, obviously, mean that human beings will not require and need to satisfy all the basic, transhistorical, material presuppositions which it has required down the ages in order to survive: eating, clothing, shelter, etc., resulting from and mediating its activities.

It means, rather, that humanity does not engage in these activities in order to *simply satisfy* these needs solely as 'natural ones', *merely* to eat, clothe, keep warm, etc. The 'historically created needs' are the *sublation* of these 'natural needs' because their satisfaction ceases to be merely material but becomes simultaneously, in this supersedence, the satisfaction of a socially created, and therefore historically created, need. Needs and their satisfaction are not simply 'physical' or 'natural' but with humanity become 'socio-historical' and 'cultural'.

In the ages beyond capital, humanity does not simply 'socially satisfy' but creates new, higher and distinct needs compared to those under capitalism; the whole structure of human need alters so its identification, cultivation, refinement and development become a primary pre-occupation of humanity beyond the epoch of capital. Work itself and its development becomes a 'vital need'.

In this regard, Marx makes a distinction between a 'natural need' and a 'necessary ('vital') need' which is historically created and contains subsumed and sublated within itself 'natural need'. However, insofar as all needs are created, located and satisfied socially, ultimately all human needs are satisfied within and through specific socio-historical relations and this, in itself, makes such needs 'social' as opposed to 'merely natural' or 'merely physical'. The social mode within which needs are satisfied alters the character of needs from 'mere natural' to social and therefore historically created needs. In this sense, all human needs are socio-historically created and developed. The dominant criterion here in the determination of need is not 'survival' but 'humanization' and this becomes increasingly so in the epochs beyond the capital relation; not the 'crude need' of the epochs of private property but the 'rich human needs and capacities' of their historical negation.

The historic genesis and development of capital creates the material basis for this eclipsing of 'crude need' by this 'richness of needs' and this is why it is *'an essential relation for the development of the social productive forces. It ceases to exist as such only where the development of these productive forces themselves encounters its barrier in capital itself'*.[6]

The 'true realm of freedom' emerges out of the 'realm of necessity' which stands as the historic presupposition and ground of this higher realm of freedom. This transitory period of 'necessity' therefore mediates the movement from the relations of bourgeois society to those of this 'true realm'. Globally, the evolution of the capital relation into its stage of structural crisis destructively posits this 'barrier in capital itself' which is an inherent tendency of its own historic development.

The fundamental distinction between this transient period of 'necessity' and that of the previous capitalist epoch lies in *the associated producers holding and working the means of production in common to produce a directly social product and their labour therefore takes the form of directly socialized labour in contrast to the form it takes in capitalist commodity production.* However, only as the 'true realm of freedom' unfolds does *'labour [...] appear no longer as labour, but as the full development of activity itself, in which natural necessity in its direct form has disappeared; because a historically created need has taken the place of the natural one'*. Where 'labour no longer appears as labour' but rather as the *'full development of activity itself'*, then the transition period of 'natural necessity' has been superseded into and replaced by the 'true realm of freedom'.

Under the rule of capital, private concrete labour receives the stamp of general abstract, social labour *indirectly* (mediatively) only by its products taking the form of commodities and their values being realized on the market. Objects of utility ...

> become commodities only because they are the products of the labour of private individuals who work independently of each other. The sum total of the labour of all these private individuals forms the aggregate labour of society. Since the producers do not come into social contact until they exchange the products of their labour, the specific social characteristics of their private labours appear only within this exchange. In other words, the labour of the private individual manifests itself as an element of the total labour of society only through the relations which the act of exchange establishes between the products, and, through their mediation, between the producers. To the producers, therefore, the social relations between their private labours appear as what they are, i.e. they do not appear as direct social relations between persons in their work, but rather as material [dinglich] relations between persons and social relations between things. It is only by being exchanged that the products of labour acquire a socially uniform objectivity as values, which is distinct from their sensuously varied objectivity as articles of utility. This division of the product of labour into a useful thing and a thing possessing value appears in practice only when exchange has already acquired a sufficient extension and importance to allow useful things to be produced for the purpose of being exchanged, so that their character as values has already to be taken into consideration during production.[7]

Exchange itself becomes a fundamentally inalienable relation in, and condition for, the reproduction and accumulation of capital. Exchange is a historical presupposition for the origination of capital in its first historically posited forms (commodity and money forms). It therefore precedes capital in all its forms and later develops with commodity production and capitalist commodity production.

During the transition period, there will be a growing need to develop measures to transcend exchange relations and replace them completely with a universal system of accounted production and distribution in which the identification and refinement of needs, quality, human and nature's welfare and ecological sustainability are the primary considerations. A 'socialist accountancy' (of labour required for production and distribution) prevails in the 'realm of necessity' which, in the long term, becomes transcended within the unfolding 'realm of freedom' in which *disposable time* – not value as a manifestation of labour time – becomes the measure of wealth. Thus, in the first phase of communism (realm of natural necessity) ...

> even after the capitalist mode of production is abolished, though social production remains, the determination of value still prevails in the sense that the regulation of labour-time and the distribution of social labour among various production groups becomes more essential than ever, as well as the keeping of accounts on this.[8]

Humanity must continue with a system of social accountancy based on the determination of value in both production and distribution. Labour-time and its social distribution amongst the different sectors, in this transitional period, remain regulated according to the criterion of value on the basis of which social accountancy takes place in this period.

This 'determination of value still prevails' within the 'realm of natural necessity' but becomes transcended as the 'true realm of freedom' emerges and unfolds out of this antecedent 'realm of necessity'. Of course, it does not 'prevail' in the sense of the determination of value of products in exchange i.e. as commodities. But rather in the sense, as Marx writes, of the distribution and regulation of labour time in order to serve and meet social needs. The regulation of labour time becomes a transitory but necessary form of social accountancy. Here, therefore, labour time remains the measure of wealth and is only replaced by disposable time as the measure of wealth as the 'true realm of freedom' emerges and unfolds.

In the 'deep time' of communism the distinction itself between necessary and surplus labour will actually disappear to be replaced by forms of human labour in which ...

> labour [...] appears no longer as labour, but as the full development of activity itself, in which natural necessity in its direct form has disappeared; because a historically created need has taken the place of the natural one.⁹

'Activity' then becomes a 'vital need' for human beings in that this 'activity' will be the direct, increasingly de-alienated, social expression of the human freedom which prevails.

This 'true realm of freedom' contains its own mediating necessity which is identical with human freedom i.e. necessity and freedom become internal to each other. Social relations in which necessity is 'external' to freedom (and vice versa) – and therefore *manifest as compulsion* in social relations and within the realm of the psychology of the individual – start to disappear in the course of the transition to this 'true realm of freedom' within which such relations become extinguished.

Surplus labour (surplus product) remains but humanity's relationship with it will be utterly different *('Surplus labour in some form must always remain, as labour beyond the extent of given needs')*.¹ Humanity will not acknowledge it and relate to it as 'surplus' just as humanity will not acknowledge and relate to its life as a 'communist human life' even though, ontologically, it will be daily deepening this communist existence.

In the first phase of communism, therefore, labour time remains the measure of wealth. It is the animating criterion against which the wealth of society continues to be measured. In this sense, it is a legacy of capitalist commodity production but this 'determination of value' in the 'realm of necessity' does not mediate relations in this realm in the same way as it does in the realm of capital in which value is the principal underlying relation.

In this first phase of communist development, *'the relations of men in their social production do not manifest themselves as 'values' of 'things'.* However, at the same time, *'the determination of value still prevails in the sense that the regulation of labour-time and the distribution of social labour among various production groups becomes more essential than ever'*. Thus, accordingly, the need for an accountancy of labour time remains. This, of course, is the complete opposite (since it is consciously planned) to the 'regulation' and exchange of labour time which takes place under the market system of capitalism with all its inhuman consequences. Under capitalism ...

> as values, commodities are social magnitudes, that is to say, something absolutely different from their 'properties' as 'things'. As values, they constitute only relations of men in their productive activity. Value indeed 'implies exchanges', but exchanges are exchanges of things between men, exchanges which in no way affect the things as such. A thing retains the same 'properties' whether it be owned by A or by B. In actual fact, the concept 'value' presupposes 'exchanges' of the products. Where labour is communal, the relations of men in their social production do not manifest themselves as 'values' of 'things'. Exchange of products as commodities is a method of exchanging labour, [it demonstrates] the dependence of the labour of each upon the labour of the others [and corresponds to] a certain mode of social labour or social production.[10]

The process of the objectification of human labour – i.e. the specifically human form of movement, form of energy which is human labour transforming nature into socially utilizable products – takes place historically under different, evolving social relations of production. The process evolves *socially* as the application of this human energy in order to transform nature into socially useful products. Humanity objectifies this 'essential power' in the labour process in order to wrest its needs from nature by transforming nature in the course of its relationship with it.

Labour – in the broadest sense of the word – is this transhistorically enduring, intrinsically human, indispensable 'mediation' in the relation between humanity and nature. We must note, at this point, that labour (in the broadest sense of the term as human productive activity) was the creative ontological basis for, and operative principle within, the evolutionary transformation of ancestral animal primates (through different stages in the lineages over millions of years) into humans.

Marx revealed that it is only under certain historically derived social relations of production that this process of objectification takes alienated forms. This is the positive, forward-looking, moment in his analysis. Namely, that the process of objectification is not inherently a process of alienation but rather takes a specific alien form under capitalism as a function of the character and reproduction of capital. In the epoch of the rule of capital, the social ...

> effects of things as materialised aspects of the labour process are attributed to them in capital, in their personification, their independence in respect of labour. They would cease to have these effects if they were to cease to confront labour in this alienated form.[11]

The capitalist class is the collective social representation of the capital relation just as the proletariat is that of wage-labour. The capital relation is wage-labour's own creation which stands in opposition to it. The class of capitalists, as the collective social representation of capital, is the secondary, alien expression of this antagonistic relationship which is maintained and regulated politically by capital's state power as the highest political expression of its rule in the social metabolism.

In contradistinction, Hegel *ahistorically* and *absolutely identifies* (this is a *formal* moment in the content of Hegel's conception) the process of objectification of human labour energy with its alienation. For Hegel, the realm of the 'Absolute Idea' and religion is the only sphere in which the problem of the transcendence of human alienation can be addressed and resolved. *Objectification* is, in Hegel, *ultimately thinking's own creation identical with alienation itself* which can only be overcome in thought 'returning out of this alienation into itself' as the Notion, Absolute Idea, etc.

Hegel's position here is essentially the same as that of classical bourgeois political economy. Marx notes in the *Grundrisse* that ...

> The bourgeois economists are so much cooped up within the notions belonging to a specific historic stage of social development that the necessity of the objectification of the powers of social labour appears to them as inseparable from their alienation vis-à-vis living labour. But with the suspension of the immediate character of living labour, as merely individual, or as general merely internally or merely externally,[12] with the positing of the activity of individuals as immediately general or social activity, the objective moments of production are stripped of this form of alienation; they are thereby posited as property, as the organic social body within which the individuals reproduce themselves as individuals, but as social individuals. The conditions which allow them to exist in this way in the reproduction of their life, in their productive life's process, have been posited only by the historic economic process itself, both

the objective and the subjective conditions, which are only the two distinct forms of the same conditions.

The worker's propertylessness, and the ownership of living labour by objectified labour, or the appropriation of alien labour by capital – both merely expressions of the same relation from opposite poles – are fundamental conditions of the bourgeois mode of production, in no way accidents irrelevant to it.[13]

Once the labour process takes this open, communal form, it transcends the *alienated need* for private, concrete labour to take the *salto mortale* into the realm of social, abstract labour through the mediation of exchange. It takes the unmediated form of 'immediately general or social activity' so that the products of this labour process are posited immediately as 'communal property'. Implicitly, the whole character of human individuality starts to alter and reproduce itself differentially *from that* of the private individual owner of the commodity labour-power *to that* of the social individual of the new relations of the commune.

Labour power as a commodity, and the proletarian as its personified salesman, is the creation of the historical development of the capital relation and not engendered as an eternal 'law of nature'. This condition of the propertyless producer class as sellers of the commodity of labour power is intrinsic to the very existence of capital itself which drives the producers to create a magnitude of value which is always greater than the magnitude required to reproduce this labour power. Without this forced extraction of surplus labour there could be no surplus value, no profit (amongst its other forms) and no accumulation of capital. Accordingly, no capital (self-valorising value) per se.

Hegel's conception of human alienation flows from his idealist position which necessarily locates the supersedence of alienation in the realm of a theism rather than understanding that *theistic practice is itself a socio-historical product of the evolution of alienated humanity*. Implicitly, Hegel's conception is that alienation can only be overcome in thought itself or rather by thought establishing some form of determinate 'objective' relationship with social being. Herein is posited the theistic character of Hegel's outlook which was critiqued by Marx in *The Holy Family* and *The German Ideology* i.e. in his critique of Left Hegelianism.

Marx locates the overcoming of alienation in the elaboration of a revolutionary practice wherein the prevailing forms of alienation are grasped as integral products of the character of social relations in bourgeois society. Marx understands the determinate tendency towards the transcendence of alienation as only becoming fully and comprehensively realized in communism. The theistic roots of Hegel's system are clearly exposed in his idealist analysis of alienation which ultimately finds itself trapped in the circularity of a theological cul-de-sac.

Thus, for Hegel, alienation can only be transcended within thought as the *demiurgos* of social relations. For Marx, it is these relations which must be transformed (revolutionized) in real practice in order to create the social conditions for the transcendence of alienation which is, by its very nature, an enduring, unfolding, historical process.

Herein lies the major difference between the perspective of Hegel and that of Marx on the question of alienation. The final refuge, arising out of Hegel's conception, is that the Christian religion is the only arena within which alienation can be transcended as a manifestation of his specific, theological form of idealism.

The objectification of human labour (transforming nature into useful creations) is an absolute material relation running through the history of all previous societies. Where capitalism is the dominant mode of production, this objectification takes the form of the continual and necessary reproduction of capital which stands opposing the producers as a hostile social relation. Labour power itself becomes a commodity which the producer is forced to sell to the owners of capital in order to survive. The producers become alienated from their own activity and the results of this activity. In the capital-wage labour relation, the exercise of this 'essential power' (labour power) is alienated and belongs to the capitalist as part of his capital (variable capital).

In this relation of alienation, the estrangement of the wage worker from others and from self (from 'his own essential species-being', Marx, Paris Manuscripts of 1844) comes to its fullest, most complete realization with the global dominance of capital. With the historical genesis, establishment and global domination of the capital relation, the producer class (the proletariat) becomes comprehensively *'opposed by a hostile power of its own making, so that it defeats its own purpose'* in the act of continuously reproducing this relation.[14]

The labour process only ceases to take alien form once it divests itself of its historic operation within the conditions of the reproduction of capital. Wage labour engenders its opposite in the form of capital which then necessarily enslaves the former as a pre-condition and presupposition for its own existence. Wage labour becomes the necessary presupposition for the existence of capital and thus, in so doing, mediates the perpetuation of its own historical existence as long as the capital relation continues as the dominant relationship of production and distribution.

Labour is that form of human energy which creates value but, in the epoch of capitalist commodity production, it only does so under those historical conditions created and reproduced by capital in order to serve the constant augmentation of its value (valorisation) and accumulation. Under different conditions this form of human energy can serve different ends where the labour process ceases to serve the needs of capital.

Under the conditions of the domination of capital, the human source of this labour-energy is compelled to alienate it. The potentiated form of this energy – labour power – is a commodity. It becomes a 'component' (variable capital) in the composition of the total value of capital with all its dehumanizing consequences for the labourer. The labourer is wage-labour personified for the capitalist who is capital personified for the labourer. The labourer is a personified source of surplus value and the capitalist is the personification of the capital relation. The wage-worker – alienated from self, from others, from his activity and its product – experiences the exercising of this 'essential power', and himself, merely as an object of use (*objet d'emploi*) for self and others. Labour is not lived as an intrinsic, meaningful part of life (as the 'full development of activity') but merely as a painful and alienating means towards its version in the epoch of capital. For the worker, 'life' commences after labour, as Marx writes in *Wage Labour and Capital* (1847), 'at table, in the tavern, in bed'. Who would dispute the enduring truth of this latter conception, today, in 2017?

During the epoch of capital, the *'general social form of labour appears as the property of a thing'* so that *'social relations between men ... assume for them the fantastic form of a relation between things'* resulting in *'the action of objects which rule the producers instead of being ruled by them'* (Marx, Vol. 1, *Capital*). In Marx's conception, the capitalist mode of production presents itself, *appears as*, a 'natural' rather than a 'socio-historical' formation. The relations reproduced by capital serve as the historical source of nebulous notions of an eternal 'human nature'. But this 'eternal nature' is merely the 'ensemble' of the temporal and transient characteristics of bourgeois social relations which serves to ideologically justify the existing capitalist order itself. The continuously reproduced 'predicament' of 'asocial sociability' is a direct manifestation and ingredient of these relations. However, as Mészáros writes ...

> 'Asocial sociability' is the historical predicament of human beings only under determinate social and economic circumstances, and not their absolute ontological predestination. As self-mediating beings, and not genus-individuals, they are not only the sufferers of the antagonistic conditions of asocial sociability but also their makers. Yet, what is historically created by human beings – even if in its origins under the conditions of structurally embedded social antagonisms – can be also historically altered and ultimately consigned to the past. But the necessary precondition of success in that respect is that the social individuals should engage in the task of overcoming the antagonisms in question through the institution of a radically different and historically viable social order: the only conceivable way in which deep-seated structural antagonisms can be superseded.[15]

People are not only the creations but also the creators of these circumstances and can 'uncreate' them in the course of further development by the restrucuring of society's landscape and the establishment of relations which embody and express the transcendence of those circumstances which gave rise to 'asocial sociability'.

Intrinsic to these circumstances is the world market which is viewed as a 'natural' rather than understood as a *social* relation created by humanity at a particular stage (epoch) in the history of human society. Likewise, capital is not a 'thing of nature' but a determinate social relation of production originating and developing in the course of a specific historical period in the evolution of humanity's productive forces.

Societies without markets, capital and the commodity form have existed in previous epochs and can be re-created by humanity given the formation of the required forms of mutable and flexible agency to drive the whole process against and beyond the capital epoch. And not simply beyond capital, but also transcending the commodity-form itself.

In the circulation of commodities, the labour time incorporated into products in the course of their production appears as a material property of the commodity, i.e. value appears as a 'thing' rather than as a social relation between producers. Money itself (as universal expression of value) is ...

> an objectified relation between persons; ... it is objectified exchange value, and exchange value is nothing more than a mutual relation between people's productive activities.

Money ...

> can have a social property only because individuals have alienated their own social relationship from themselves so that it takes the form of a thing.[16]

Marx, in Volume 1 of *Capital*, analogizes the fetishism of commodities with the *'mist-enveloped regions of the religious world'* revealing that in the world of religion *'the productions of the human brain appear as independent beings endowed with life'* which enter *'into relation with both one another and the human race'.*[17] In this *'religious reflex of the real world'* (ibid., p. 84) *'man is governed by the products of his own brain'* (ibid., p. 582) just as in the fetishism of commodities he is governed by the productions of his own hand.

Capital confronts humanity as an alien power yet produced by humanity. The capitalist mode of production presents itself as a 'natural' rather than a 'socio-historical' formation. It is true that commodities are 'things' in so far as their material use-values are inseparable from their existence as commodities. However, in the age of capital, a produced thing cannot be made available as use-value (as socially useful) without simultaneously being a commodity and as realized value as such. It is not its concrete 'thinghood' as a specific material use-value which is fundamental for capital. What, *a priori*, animates and determines the movement of capital globally is rather the character of commodities as embodiments of *'socially necessary general labour, utterly indifferent to any particular content'*.[18]

3. A Note on Human Individuality in the Epoch of Capital

The social relations of the capitalist epoch are mediated by a social division of labour which corresponds to the prevailing stage of development of its technical productive forces. The *'enslaving subordination of the individual to the division of labour'* (Marx, *Critique of the Gotha Programme* [London: Lawrence & Wishart, 1973], p. 320) creates psychosocial conditions under capitalism within which humans are limited in their development of an all-round, multifaceted, multi-skilled personality which enables the individual to participate in all spheres of human activity and life. Marx observes that ...

> If circumstances in which the individual lives allow him only the one-sided development of one quality at the expense of all the rest, if they give him the material and time to develop only that one quality, then this individual achieves only a one-sided crippled development. No moral preaching avails here. And the manner in which this one pre-eminently favoured quality develops depends again, on the one hand, on the material available for its development and, on the other hand, on the degree and manner in which the other qualities are suppressed.
>
> Precisely because thought, for example, is the thought of a particular definite individual, it remains his definite thought, determined by his individuality and the conditions in which he lives ... In the case of an individual, for example, whose life embraces a wide circle of varied activities and practical relations to the world, and who, therefore, lives a many-sided life, thought has the same character of universality as every other manifestation in his life ... From the outset it is always a factor in the total life of the individual, one which disappears and is reproduced as required.[19]

The development of a many-sided human personality – which is not 'one-sided' and 'crippled' – is dependent on the actual existence of social conditions and relations which provide the social and material ground for such a development. An all-rounded, many-sided, multifaceted development of the capacities of human individuals is therefore only possible in a society which furnishes such conditions. Capitalism is not such a society. Quite the contrary. It 'cripples' the human being and personality.

The determinations of the human personality and interpersonal relationships in the age of capital derive from the general character of its exploitative social relations. The development of the individual human being is located within the conditions prevailing in the given society. Whether an individual develops one-sidedly ('crippled') or in a many-sided and richly multifaceted way therefore ...

> depends not on consciousness, but on being; not on thought, but on life; it depends on the individual's empirical development and manifestations of life, which in turn depends on the conditions obtaining in the world.[20]

Likewise, whether an individual is 'satisfied' or 'dissatisfied' with *his or her* life – or with 'life' in general – 'depends on the conditions obtaining in the world'. Ultimately it is rooted in the character of these conditions so that ...

> Dissatisfaction with oneself is either dissatisfaction with oneself within the framework of a definite condition which determines the whole personality e.g. dissatisfaction with oneself as a worker, or it is moral dissatisfaction. In the first case, therefore, it is simultaneously and mainly dissatisfaction with the existing relations; in the second case – an ideological expression of these relations themselves, which does not at all go beyond them, but belongs wholly to them.[21]

The transformation of social relations by humanity simultaneously brings about the transformation of the transformer, of the human agent of and for this transformation (Marx, *Theses on Feuerbach*). The transcendence of the capital relation is the complete transformation of humanity in nature and therefore the total transformation of the relationships between human individuals i.e. of human individuality as the 'ensemble of social relations' (Marx, Thesis VI, *Theses on Feuerbach*).

The 'true realm of freedom' becomes established as the resolution of the conflict between the 'external necessity' and its necessarily associated 'freedom' found within the post-capitalist 'realm of natural necessity'. We are given an indication of the arrival of this time for the whole of humanity by Marx when we read, in the Paris Manuscripts of 1844, of the characterization of communism ...

> as the positive transcendence of private property as human self-estrangement, and therefore as the real appropriation of the human essence by and for man; communism therefore as the complete return of man to himself as a social (i.e. human) being – a return accomplished consciously and embracing the entire wealth of previous development. This communism, as fully developed naturalism, equals humanism, and as fully

> developed humanism equals naturalism; it is the genuine resolution of the conflict between man and nature and between man and man – the true resolution of the strife between existence and essence, between objectification and self-confirmation, between freedom and necessity, between the individual and the species. Communism is the riddle of history solved, and it knows itself to be this solution.[22]

The development of production and distribution founded on capital creates the conditions and possibilities for the transcendence of the division of labour under communal production. In relation to the labour process itself ...

> large-scale industry, through its very catastrophes, makes the recognition of variation of labour and hence of the fitness of the worker for a maximum number of different kinds of labour into a question of life and death. This possibility of varying labour must become a general law of social production, and the existing relations must be adapted to permit its realization in practice. That monstrosity, the disposable working population held in reserve, in misery, for the changing requirements of capitalist exploitation, must be replaced by the individual man who is absolutely available for the different kinds of labour required of him; the partially developed individual, who is merely the bearer of one specialised, social function, must be replaced by the totally developed individual, for whom the different social functions are different modes of activity he takes up in turn.[23]

The evolution of capitalist economy itself multiplies the variety of different types of concrete labour and '*makes the recognition of variation of labour and hence of the fitness of the worker for a maximum number of different kinds of labour into a question of life and death*'. But the possibility of effortlessly moving around and engaging in different types of work can only become fully expressed in a post-capitalist epoch where human need, and not the requirements of capital, is the governing social criterion in the labour process. The worker of restricted capacities of the capital order is supplanted by the multi-skilled and multi-capacitated individual of communal production relations so that '*the partially developed individual, who is merely the bearer of one specialised, social function, must be replaced by the totally developed individual, for whom the different social functions are different modes of activity he takes up in turn*'.

However, nonetheless, large-scale industry '*in its capitalist form reproduces the old division of labour with its ossified particularities*' (ibid., p. 617).

The requirements of capital itself increasingly turn the specialized worker into one who must be prepared and able to readily adapt and change his mode of labour in order to meet the demands of capital. However, the capital system continuously re-posits 'the old division of labour with its ossified particularities'.

Beyond the age of capital lies the development of a rich and multifaceted human individuality in which the division of labour is becoming transcended with the emergence of the 'totally developed individual' (social individual) replacing the 'partially developed individual' (private individual, owner of capital or of the commodity of labour-power) of bourgeois society.

The division of labour becomes increasingly unnecessary as the realm of capital is transcended. The social division of labour under capitalism is a necessity for this system based on commodity production, exchange and the reproduction of capital. As, of course, is the technical division of labour whilst capital continues to exist as the dominant social relationship of production and distribution. Exchange is as intrinsically necessary to this process as production and distribution in the realm of capital. This, of course, does not apply in those stages of communist society beyond the epoch of capital and beyond the initial stages of socialist society dominated by social compulsion driven by 'natural necessity'.

Critically, the very existence of commodity production and exchange, on the one hand, and the division of labour within the workplace and society, on the other, are organically connected. In the long term – in the course of the irreversible establishment and evolution of a global socialist life – one cannot continue to subsist in the absence of the other; they exist and are bound together as dialectically intermediated sides of a single social relation.

The 'development' of global capital (its increasingly more destructive reproduction as a social relation in structural crisis) is now actually starting to erode and destroy the required natural and cultural conditions for the future socialist society. This is what gives rise to the urgency of revolutionary change in the present epoch and, specifically, to the driving necessity for new forms of revolutionary agency.

All the time the capital system continues, and its crisis unfolds and deepens in the twenty-first century, it actually undermines the necessary conditions required to build the future human society. It makes its realization more difficult and problematic, in one sense, whilst intensifying the urgency for the establishment of forms of revolutionary agency which can move forward towards its negation, in the other. In destroying the necessary natural and cultural conditions for socialism, it simultaneously starts to posit the dynamic and pressing social need to oppose and move beyond the capital order.

4. Moving Against and Beyond Capital: Realm of Natural Necessity and True Realm of Freedom

A developed, post-capital system of production and distribution based on common ownership and the co-operation of the associated producers is one which does not involve or require the exchange of the products of labour. The labour of the individual is instantaneously and immediately *directly socialized labour* and, therefore, does not require the mediation of exchange to make it 'a component of the total labour' of society. Labour-time ceases to manifest as 'value' in the products of labour and, moreover, 'value' (as the *social existence* of the products of labour as opposed to their *material existence* as use values) is no longer presented as a 'material characteristic' of these things (commodity fetishism). As humanity begins to develop beyond the realm of global capital ...

> within the cooperative society based on common ownership of the means of production, the producers do not exchange their products; similarly, the labour spent on the products no longer appears as the value of these products, possessed by them as a material characteristic, for now, in contrast to capitalist society, individual pieces of labour are no longer merely indirectly, but directly, a component part of the total labour.[24]

In this 'cooperative society, based on the common ownership of the means of production' on a global basis ...

The communal character of production would make the product into a communal, general product from the outset. The exchange which originally takes place in production – which would not be an exchange of exchange values but of activities, determined by communal needs and communal purposes – would from the outset include the participation of the individual in the communal world of products.[25] On the basis of exchange values, labour is posited as general only through exchange. But on this foundation it would be posited as such before exchange; i.e. the exchange of products would in no way be the medium by which the participation of the individual in general production is mediated. Mediation must, of course, take place. In the first case, which proceeds from the independent production of individuals – no matter how much these independent productions determine and modify each other post festum through their interrelations – mediation takes place through the exchange of commodities, through exchange value and through money; all these are expressions of one and the same relation. In the second case, the presupposition is itself mediated; i.e. a communal production, communality, is presupposed as the basis of production. The labour of the individual is posited from the outset as social labour. Thus, whatever the particular material form of the product he creates or helps to create, what he has bought with his labour is not a specific and particular product, but rather a specific share of the communal production. He therefore has no particular product to exchange. His product is not an exchange value. The product does not first have to be transposed into a particular form in order to attain a general character for the individual. Instead of a division of labour, such as is necessarily created with the exchange of exchange values, there would take place an organization of labour whose consequence would be the participation of the individual in communal production. In the first case the social character of production is posited only post festum with the elevation of products to exchange values and the exchange of these exchange values. In the second case the social character of production is presupposed, and participation in the world of products, in consumption, is not mediated by the exchange of mutually independent labours or products of labour. It is mediated, rather, by the social conditions of production within which the individual is active. Those who want to make the labour of the individual directly into money (i.e. his product as well), into realized exchange value, want therefore to determine that labour directly as general labour, i.e. to negate precisely the conditions under which it must be made into money and exchange values, and under which it depends on private exchange. This demand can be satisfied only under conditions where it can no longer be raised. Labour on the basis of exchange values presupposes, precisely, that neither the labour of the individual nor his product are directly general; that the product attains this form only by passing through an objective mediation, by means of a form of money distinct from itself.

On the basis of communal production, the determination of time remains, of course, essential. The less time the society requires to produce wheat, cattle, etc., the more time it wins for other production, material or mental. Just as in the case of an individual, the multiplicity of its development, its enjoyment and its activity depends on economization of time. Economy of time, to this all economy ultimately reduces itself. Society likewise has to distribute its time in a purposeful way, in order to achieve a production adequate to its overall needs; just as the individual has to distribute his time correctly in order to achieve knowledge in proper proportions or in order to satisfy the various demands on his activity. Thus, economy of time, along with the planned distribution of labour time among the various branches of production, remains the first economic law on the basis of communal production. It becomes law, there, to an even higher degree.[26]

In the spontaneously arisen communes of prehistory, before the rise of class societies, the product of the labour of the individual was immediately the property of the whole of the commune. The actual nature of the social relations of the early tribal and clan formations meant that labour could not be private labour and manifest itself as exchange-value.

The exchange of products disappears post-capital because labour is posited immediately as general social labour. There is no need for the 'leap' (*salto mortale*) in exchange from concrete private labour to that stamped with the 'passport' of general social labour. Production and distribution – in becoming stripped of exchange relations – start to shake themselves free of the market system. The associated producers do not require the exchange of products as an indispensable element in order to participate in production. The individual producer – in participating in communal production – shares in the total product of communal production. All products, in their individualized forms, are instantaneously communal products as opposed to private ones. Consumption itself – as 'participation in the world of products' – is not dependent on their exchange but rather determined by the communal 'conditions of production within which the individual is active'.

But if this form of 'objective mediation' eventually becomes superseded (with labour becoming 'immediately, general socialized') then so does the need for money per se in the long run. If exchange becomes unnecessary, then money itself must follow the same path into extinction.

Time management remains in communal production in order to organize the different spheres of production and to increasingly broaden the arena of 'free time' within which higher forms of 'free activity' and 'creativity' can take place. This latter sphere becomes wider as 'compulsion' increasingly loses its grip in the area of direct material production.

Here, in this lengthy latter passage, Marx's description remains within the sphere of 'natural necessity' – a post-capitalist age which has not, as yet, passed over into the 'true realm of freedom'. Its 'social necessity' continues to be 'external' and hence an epoch where 'labour determined by necessity and external expediency' still dominates. As this period matures, a new dynamic sets in which points the way towards the 'true realm' because once the associated producers ...

> have appropriated their own surplus labour – and disposable time thereby ceases to have an antithetical existence – then, on one side, necessary labour time will be measured by the needs of the social individual, and, on the other, the development of the power of social production will grow so rapidly that, even though production is now calculated for the wealth of all, disposable time will grow for all. For real wealth is the developed productive power of all individuals. The measure of wealth is then not any longer, in any way, labour time, but rather disposable time.[27]

And then, as a matter of course ...

> The theft of alien labour time, on which the present wealth is based, appears a miserable foundation in face of this new one, created by large scale industry itself. As soon as labour in the direct form has ceased to be the great well-spring of wealth, labour time ceases and must cease to be its measure, and hence exchange value [must cease to be the measure] of use value. The surplus labour of the mass has ceased to be the condition for the development of general wealth, just as the non-labour of the few, for the development of the general powers of the human head. With that, production based on exchange value breaks down, and the direct, material production process is stripped of the form of penury and antithesis. The free development of individualities, and hence not the reduction of necessary labour time so as to posit surplus labour, but rather the general reduction of the necessary labour of society to a minimum, which then corresponds to the artistic, scientific, etc., development of the individuals in the time set free, and with the means created, for all of them.[28]

Marx's understanding of the relationship between necessity and freedom informs us in his understanding of the 'true realm of freedom'. Within this realm – beyond that realm of 'natural necessity within which labour remains under the compulsion of external expediency' – the whole social character of human activity changes. It truly represents a *social qualitative break* in the history of human activity. From being a compulsive and repulsive activity, labour – imposed as an external, alien necessity in previous class societies – becomes posited and developed simultaneously as both means and end in itself. 'Activity' (no longer 'appearing as 'labour' as such') becomes necessarily intrinsic, 'internal', to the development of human freedom itself, a 'vital need' in itself, so that *'the realm of freedom really begins only where labour determined by necessity and external expediency ends'*.[29] In other words, human activity ceases to take place under compulsive, repulsive, alien coercion as we see under capital and, obligatorily, as required in the first phases of post-capitalist society. The motto of this first phase of communism in terms of labour can only be: 'We *must* all work together as one communality in order to create the future for all'.

Labour itself is *not inherently* repulsive, coerced activity. It is so only as a result of being imposed or imposable, that is, only when performed within the context of specific, antagonistic social relations and under the historical conditions corresponding to them. To ideologically assert this coercive, repulsive character of labour as an 'eternal feature' of human existence is itself an ideological manifestation of its *actual* repulsive and coercive character in the epoch of capital.

Within the 'realm of natural necessity', labour remains subject to this 'necessity and external expediency'. Work retains its character as 'a means of keeping alive'.[30] 'Work' (labour ceasing to be 'labour' as such determined by 'external expediency') as enjoyable human 'activity' only becomes 'a vital need' [ibid.] in the 'true realm of freedom'. Here, within this realm, it ceases to bear this compulsory character driven by an external and alien necessity as imposed in previous epochs in the course of the realization of 'mundane considerations'. Accordingly, it loses its character as 'work' or 'labour' which it possessed in the epoch of capital and the early stages of post-capitalist society. In the life-process of the commune, the distinction between 'labour' and other forms of activity becomes progressively subject to a resolution and supersedence into 'human activity' which, as a rich totality of differentiated, interconnected forms, ceases to bear a compulsory, coerced character.

Within the period of development of the 'realm of natural necessity' itself, labour becomes posited simultaneously as labour-for-self and labour-for-others (and vice versa) and as directly social labour unmediated by the commodity-form. This communal relation, therefore, is a self-objectification (self-realization, self-actualization) which is simultaneously the realization of the needs of others (objectification-for-others, actualization-of-and-for others). In the commune, self-actualization can only be distinctly individual on inseparable condition that it is actualization of and for the whole commune and therefore expresses the intimate identity of the individual and the social. This has profound implications for the evolution of the human personality involving the transcendence of the opposition between the 'ego' (who I am internally) and the 'persona' (how I present myself to the world of people). Likewise, because this relation is 'organically social', the activity of the social totality which is the life-process of the commune is simultaneously the direct realization of the needs of the individual and the individual's self-actualization. The activity of the individual is simultaneously posited as communal activity ('human togetherness') and this latter activity of the freely associated social individuals is the activity of the individuals in their collectivity and the realization of the needs of the human individual.

This communal activity is that of the freely associated social individuals. The establishment of such relations must itself create the conditions necessary for, and mediating, the psychological transformation of humanity. The social pre-conditions for the psychological transformation of humanity become established and evolve in the post-capital age of 'globalized' humanity.

When Marx writes that within the 'true realm of freedom' the 'development of human activity becomes an end in itself', he is merely asserting a 'genuine resolution' of the opposition between means and ends (as of that between freedom and necessity) and that 'human activity as an end in itself' is the living truth and manifestation of this 'genuine resolution'. That human beings will find satisfaction in activity which contains a humanly internalized necessity (not as an alien-imposed 'external necessity' or 'expediency'); a necessity which is identical to the free active mediation of the individuals in the commune. Activity as both creative self-realization and creatively realizing the needs of each and all so that self-fulfillment is simultaneously the fulfillment of others and vice versa. Activity, of course, continues to be determined by its objectives and therefore locates ...

> its measure from the outside, through the aim to be attained and the obstacles to be overcome in attaining it. But [...] this overcoming of obstacles is in itself a liberating activity – and that, further, the external aims become stripped of the semblance of merely external natural urgencies, and become posited as aims which the individual himself posits – hence as self-realization, objectification of the subject, hence real freedom, whose action is, precisely, labour.[31]

Labour retains a coercive character in the post-capitalist transitional phase but not in the same degree or in the same coercive mode as its does under capital. Under capital as *'external forced labour'* and in the transitional phase in a form in which labour *'has not yet created the subjective and objective conditions for itself in which labour becomes attractive work, the individual's self-realization'.* Marx asserts that the precondition and historic presupposition for this free activity is the ...

> 'social character' of production and at that stage when and where the labour process 'is of a scientific character and at the same time general character, not merely human exertion as a specifically harnessed natural force, but exertion as subject, which appears in the production process not in a merely natural, spontaneous form, but as an activity regulating all the forces of nature'. (Ibid., p. 612)

Communal coercion ('we *must* all work together for the benefit of all') in the labour process in the initial stages is the historic motor which drives the transition beyond the realm of capital and projects humanity towards the true realm of freedom. In the process of doing this, it simultaneously supersedes this period of transition as a realm of natural necessity. Marx refers to the passing of this transitional period when he writes ...

> In a more advanced phase of communist society, when the enslaving subjugation of individuals to the division of labour, and thereby the antithesis between intellectual and physical labour, have disappeared; when labour is no longer just a means of keeping alive but has itself become a vital need; when the all-round development of individuals has also increased their productive powers and all the springs of cooperative wealth flow more abundantly – only then can society wholly cross the narrow

horizon of bourgeois right and inscribe on its banner: From each according to his abilities, to each according to his needs![32]

'Work' becomes a 'vital need' and intrinsic to the self-development, self-fulfilment and self-realization of the social individual in the life of the commune. 'Work' (activity) as human creativity is enjoyment of activity as the *intrinsically human* and the exercise and development of this essential human power stripped and divested of its alienated historical form found in the epoch of capital. The actual distinction between 'work' and 'not work' becomes superseded as does that between necessary and surplus labour despite the need for the provision of a surplus within the 'true realm' (*Critique of the Gotha Programme*, ibid.).

Labour must manifest subjectively (psychosocially) as a form of compulsion where the activity of the producers remains determined by external expediency. Activity as such still retains its coercive character. Therefore, in the initial post-capitalist phases – which remain a realm of natural necessity but to a lesser degree compared to the epoch of capital – the labour process continues to exhibit compulsory traits in common with labour in previous but surpassed epochs. And this despite the general character of labour being directly socialized labour. In this regard, the labour of the individual remains subject to the direction of the whole community through its communal assemblies. These 'assemblies' must still retain a certain a degree of 'otherness' in the mind of the individual; a preserved yet transcendable moment of alienation carried over from the capital epoch. But the power of the assembly expresses the power of the whole commune *devoid of established antagonistic class forms*. The individual is directed by the whole and, insofar as s/he is an intrinsic part of this whole yet distinct from it, is both self-directing and directing of it.

Whilst labour remains under a compulsion, everybody who is capable of work *must* work in order to contribute to the communal fund and, in the course of this collective labour, prepare the way for the higher stages of communist society to be established and developed in the 'true realm of freedom' ...

> If everybody has to work, if the contradiction between those who have to work too much and those who are idlers disappears – and this would in any case be the result

of capital ceasing to exist, of the product ceasing to provide a title to alien surplus labour – and if, in addition, the development of the productive forces brought about by capitalism is taken into account, society will produce the necessary abundance in six hours, [producing] more than it does now in twelve, and, moreover, all will have six hours of 'disposable time', that is, real wealth; time which will not be absorbed in direct productive labour, but will be available for enjoyment, for leisure, thus giving scope for free activity and development. Time is scope for the development of man's faculties, etc.[33]

Labour itself only takes a coercive, compulsory, repulsive form when it is subject to an external, alien necessity i.e. when it remains imprisoned within its wage-form either as money in the epoch of capital or later – as transient form – as money and then time-chit within the immediacy of the post-capitalist 'realm of natural necessity'.

Within this latter realm, of course, it does not bear the same degree of compulsion as in the former capital realm since within the movement of this realm beyond the capital epoch, it is already beginning to divest itself of this compulsory alienated character as it becomes posited and developed as directly socialized labour. The positing of the labour process as a directly socialized process – the negation of the historical form of the labour process under capital – is a signpost of history pointing towards the new epoch of human freedom beyond compulsion. Within the realm of natural necessity, the growth in the productivity of communal labour will always mean an increased availability of free time. But within this realm ...

> Labour-time, even if exchange-value is eliminated, always remains the creative substance of wealth and the measure of the cost of its production. But free time, disposable time, is wealth itself, partly for the enjoyment of the product, partly for free activity which – unlike labour – is not dominated by the pressure of an extraneous purpose which must be fulfilled, and fulfilment of which is regarded as a natural necessity or a social duty, according to one's inclination.
>
> It is self-evident that if labour-time is reduced to a normal length and, furthermore, labour is no longer performed for someone else, but for myself, and, at the same time, the social contradictions between master and men, etc., being abolished, it acquires a quite different, a free character, it becomes real social labour, and finally the basis of disposable time – the labour of a man who has also disposable time, must be of a much higher quality than that of the beast of burden.[34]

Then, according to Marx ...

> Free time – which is both idle time and time for higher activity – has naturally transformed its possessor into a different subject, and he then enters into the direct production process as this different subject. This process is then both discipline, as regards the human being in the process of becoming; and, at the same time, practice [Ausübung], experimental science, materially creative and objectifying science, as regards the human being who has become, in whose head exists the accumulated knowledge of society. For both, in so far as labour requires practical use of the hands and free bodily movement, as in agriculture, at the same time exercise.[35]

Accordingly, this availability of 'disposal time' for both rest and activity actually transforms the character of the individual's relationship with production itself because it alters the character of the individual. Moreover, not only is the individual in a determinate relationship with the labour process which is the source of his/her human development but the individual is scientifically and technically participating in, and contributing to the evolution of, the labour process as 'materially creative and objectifying science', 'experimental science'. The creative activity of the social individual becomes intrinsic to the creation of the conditions of his/her own social existence and 'free mediation' within the commune. Simultaneously, this activity and relation becomes the source of the formation and development of the creative individual (creator) in his/her life-process in the commune.

The 'necessity and external expediency' to which Marx refers in Volume 3 of *Capital* only ends when humanity has entered what he refers to as the 'true realm of freedom'. Within this realm, communist humanity is developing as a unified, whole, self-mediating being beyond class relations (has left them behind) and on the basis of the continuously self-reproduced foundations of this higher realm of freedom.

Herein the condition for the development of each becomes the condition for the development of all and vice versa. Work becomes a 'vital' inner need of the social individual in the course of a full participation in the life of the commune. In the course of doing so, fully developing his or her capacities and the capacities of others.

Within this higher realm of freedom, the creation, development and refinement of historically posited human needs have superseded (*aufhebung*, sublated) natural needs. This is the freedom which 'lies beyond the sphere of actual material production', that is, beyond this 'sphere' designated as a separate and distinct sphere of human activity bound by the operative principle of 'external' and expedient compulsory need.

'Production' itself ceases to be divided off from communal life – ceases to operate as a sub-division of that life – and is no longer internalized by humanity as a distinct activity from other forms of activity as it is under capital and in the realm of natural necessity. Activity becomes simultaneously productive, scientific, artistic, aesthetic, etc. Activity takes on this rich, multifaceted character. This is the enrichment and cultivation of the social individual – work as a 'vital need' and 'end in itself' – which serves to address, meet and develop the historically created needs of all …

> It will be seen how in place of the wealth and poverty of political economy comes the rich human being and the rich human need. The rich human being is simultaneously the human being in need of a totality of human manifestations of life – the man in whom his own realization exists as an inner necessity, as need.[36]

The individual of the 'wealth and poverty of political economy' becomes superseded by the 'rich' human individual of 'rich human need' who is *'in need of a totality of human manifestations of life – the man in whom his own realization exists as an inner necessity, as need'*.

The 'internalized' fully humanized necessity (which is identical to freedom) found in the higher realm of freedom is the direct opposite of the 'external' necessity operative in previous epochs, including in that of the initial stages of global post-capitalist society. The transcendence of this previously operative alien necessity – imposed and coercive in nature – posits the higher and simultaneously internalized and socialized form which is identical to a forever expanding and developing human freedom. This form of necessity within this higher realm of human freedom is not registered in the human subject as 'compulsion' as such because it ceases to be imposed 'from without' as external and alien.

Accordingly, on a psychological level, the subject does not (*and does not have to*) internalize it as 'a necessity of life'. The subject does not internalize it as an alien demand because it becomes a fully humanized expression of the subject's increasingly deepening, de-alienating life process as a free social individual.

In the epoch of capital, the producers internalize, as compulsion, the alien demands of capital. In this higher movement of the human freedom of the commune, this internalization of alien demands becomes transcended. Labour itself ('dominated by the pressure of extraneous purpose which must be fulfilled') becomes 'free activity' expressed in an intensely rich aggregation of human activity in the 'true realm of freedom'.

Labour becomes divested of its coercive, expedient character as an imposed 'necessity'. It ceases to be 'labour' as such and becomes increasingly supplanted by the free, multifaceted, enriching activity of human beings living in classless communion. But this higher movement is also the transformation of humanity's productive activity itself. The transformation of the subject is simultaneously the transformation of humanity's relationship with nature ...

> Man himself is the basis of his material production, as of any other production that he carries on. All circumstances, therefore, which affect man, the subject of production, more or less modify all his functions and activities, and therefore too his functions and activities as the creator of material wealth, of commodities. In this respect it can in fact be shown that all human relations and functions, however and in whatever form they may appear, influence material production and have a more or less decisive influence on it.[37]

All alterations in social circumstances which alter the human personality (embodied within 'human relations and functions') simultaneously alter humanity's relationship with nature. This influences the nature of production itself because humanity as subject is the self-mediating basis of its activity in nature.

These changes, accordingly, have repercussions for all human 'functions and activities' at the deepest possible levels in terms of both structure and content, including the psychological and interpersonal. Eventually, as the 'deep time' of communism unfolds, this can only mean the emergence of a universal human personality type to which present-day 'bourgeois humanity' could not possibly relate or even recognize as 'human'.

In as much as we do not 'feel the need' to metabolize our food at the cellular level, humanity in this realm of freedom will not feel compelled to engage in 'activity' as such in its many and varied, richly multifaceted forms. It will be as natural as a healthy body digesting its food to engage in this wealth of activities which will distinguish the 'social individual' from the 'private individual' of previous epochs. Such activities (objectification) – divested of their alien forms – become a 'vital need'. A historically created human need unmotivated by any external or alien necessity.

The freedom of this realm forever deepens in degree. An abstractly metaphysical, absolute human freedom is not a point at which humanity will arrive in some distant future within this realm. It is always a state which actually mediates the human life of this realm which humanity is forever expanding and deepening in the activity of its life-process. Humanity – in the movement of this dialectic of the absolute and the relative – is always becoming 'more free' within this 'realm of freedom'.

In this regard, this interminable process – to use a mathematical analogy – can be said to be 'asymptotic'. And this asymptoticality is found expressed in Marcuse's 'instinctual root of freedom' in which the social relations and institutions created by man must be made specifically by man in order to accommodate them to this 'instinctual root'. That is, to facilitate and encourage its growth, its continuous expression and eternal onward evolution. To allow for the free and unconditional development of the higher form of human sensibility which arises out of revolution and the creation of the new life in the commune ...

> The Subject of a socialist society must be the Subject of a new sensibility. There is such a thing as an instinctual root of freedom in the individual itself, and if this instinctual root cannot grow, the new society will not be free, no matter what institutions it will provide. [...] The socialist society as a qualitatively different society would be the achievement of men and women who have liberated themselves from the material and intellectual culture of class society, and who are free to develop a language, art and science responding to and projecting a free society.
>
> Let us not forget that domination and exploitation perpetuate themselves not only in the institutions of class society, but also in the instincts and drives and aspirations shaped by class society, also in that which the people, that is to say the managed and administered people, love, hate, strive for, find beautiful, pleasurable and so on. Class society is not only in the material production, it is not only in the cultural

production and reproduction, it is also in the mind and body of the subjects and objects of the system.[38]

The commune will educate the individual in all areas of human culture – in technique, science, literature, art, etc. – and provide access to all its different spheres. This, in itself, will create the cultural preconditions for the flourishing of the human personality and intellect in the commune where the identification, refinement and realization of the needs of each and every individual will be the governing principle of social relationships. It is only within the commune that each individual has …

> the means of cultivating his gifts in all directions; hence personal freedom becomes possible only within the community. In previous substitutes for the community, in the state, etc., personal freedom has existed only for the individuals who developed under the conditions of the ruling class, and only insofar as they were individuals of this class. The illusory community in which individuals have up till now combined always took on an independent existence in relation to them, and since it was the combination of one class over against another, it was at the same time for the oppressed class not only a completely illusory community, but a new fetter as well. In the real community the individuals obtain their freedom in and through their association.[39]

The identification, meeting, cultivation, refinement of the comprehensive needs of human beings become socially and unconditionally guaranteed. This 'unconditional guarantee' arises out of the nature of human relationships within the commune itself. The state forms and systems of exploitative social control of bourgeois society become unnecessary and disappear. Consequentially, those forms of human behaviour, forms of thinking and ideology which are the outcome of, and correspond to, the exploitative relations of bourgeois society vanish. The social exploitation of man by man disappears.

Those characteristics of interpersonal relationships which grow out of the various forms of exploitation in bourgeois society must also perish. The disappearance of old and the emergence of new characteristics of the evolving human personality will – as in previous epochs – be related to and specific to the altering stages of the commune and the conditions therein. In this regard, Marx reminds us that …

> In order to examine the connection between spiritual production and material production it is above all necessary to grasp the latter itself not as a general category but in definite historical form. Thus for example different kinds of spiritual production correspond to the capitalist mode of production and to the mode of production of the Middle Ages. If material production itself is not conceived in its specific historical form, it is impossible to understand what is specific in the spiritual production corresponding to it and the reciprocal influence of one on the other.[40]

The 'different kinds of spiritual production' correspond to and are related to the different, specific epochs in the history of society. Hence *'if material production itself is not conceived in its specific historical form, it is impossible to understand what is specific in the spiritual production corresponding to it and the reciprocal influence of one on the other*. This must apply no less in the evolution of the commune as in previous epochs.

The exploitative forms of social control and coercion are a necessary feature of bourgeois society. They find their consummate expression in the form of the capitalist state; the state of and for capital. The state – in whatever form – always represents the interests of a ruling caste or class. It is the product of the developing class antagonisms of societies. It embodies and articulates the politically organized rule of one class over another or others.

With the dissolution of class society in communism, the state begins to wither away. The state is a product of socio-historical development which, *ab initio*, becomes necessary as the prehistoric 'primitive communism' of clan and tribal societies is abolished with the progressive differentiation of society into opposed classes. It becomes socially unnecessary as the transition to global classless society takes place since there are no class interests to defend in this society. The character of this return (negated negation) to classless social relations no longer gives rise to or necessitates the existence of the state. In this regard, a return to a state of statelessness takes place but at a higher stage of development which sublatively incorporates the wealth of all the antecedent socio-historical development of previous class societies.

Lenin, for example, uses the existence or non-existence of the state as a criterion for the existence or non-existence of a free human society; a society of free human beings. Thus, he asserts, somewhat formally, that *so long as the state exists there is no freedom. When there is freedom, there will be no state.*[41]

We say 'formally' because 'freedom' is not, as such, an absolute, unchanging state to be reached once and for all. It is, rather, more a state of being for humanity to continuously expand and deepen to wider and more profound states of existence once the fundamental pre-conditions for such a development have been established in a classless, stateless, global human life.

The very *notion of freedom* can no longer have social grounds for existence in such a society. When the state perishes, notions of freedom vanish with it. The hankering after 'freedom' is a manifestation of enslavement. A truly free human being can have no concept of freedom since such notions are the products of the human relations of class societies. Accordingly, a truly free human being can have no awareness of being 'free'. Humanity in the commune will see itself as 'free' no more than it will see itself as 'communist'. This is simply because it will truly be free and be continuously developing this 'realm of freedom' to ever greater degrees of freedom.

In the transition to a global, stateless, classless society, the forms of human consciousness corresponding to this period of transition will continue to reflect a disappearing connection to and with bourgeois society. This will show that society – in this transitional phase – has not completely disentangled itself from the various legacies of this form of class society.

Human society will not have re-founded and re-developed itself as an association of free human beings as long as the historical umbilical cord connecting society to the social legacies of bourgeois society – and the human memory of them – has not been completely severed. At such a stage, the legacies of the relations of bourgeois society would continue to exert their diminishing influence. These 'lingering' influences will continue to bind humanity (psychologically at least) to the forms of social antagonism of the past. Under these conditions, the thinking and feeling, and the behaviour and interpersonal relationships of people will continue to be conditioned by the legacies of the exploitative relations of the class societies of the past until the new society firmly and irreversibly establishes itself and starts to evolve on the basis of its own self-created and self-reproducing foundations.

The tendency towards the transcendence of alienation only becomes fully and comprehensively realized and operative in the commune when the objectification in the labour process itself ceases to take alienated form and expression. That is, when the *'process of objectification appearing as a process of alienation from the standpoint of labour and as appropriation of alien labour from the standpoint of capital'* (Marx, *Grundrisse*) comes to an irreversible end. Necessarily, the true unfolding of this tendency must lie beyond the realm of capital. The elimination of capital from the whole social metabolism is only the historical introduction to the real, determinate positing of this tendency towards the transcendence of alienation.

In a certain sense, the whole of previous human history has been a process of the *perfecting* of human alienation. From the very dawn of human existence, the alienated character of religious thinking represents *'from the outset consciousness of the transcendental arising from actually existing forces'* (Marx, *The German Ideology*). The global transition to communist life represents the reversal of that tendency wherein an antithetical process of 'de-alienation' commences. The unfolding of this process tends towards the transcendence of alienation in all its forms. These various forms start to vanish, to cease to mediate human relations and, therefore, humanity's relationship with nature. As Marx notes ...

> although at first the development of the capacities of the human species takes place at the cost of the majority of human individuals and even classes, in the end it breaks through this contradiction and coincides with the development of the individual; the higher development of individuality is thus only achieved by a historical process during which individuals are sacrificed, for the interests of the species in the human kingdom, as in the animal and plant kingdoms, always assert themselves at the cost of the interests of individuals, because these interests of the species coincide only with the interests of certain individuals, and it is this coincidence which constitutes the strength of these privileged individuals.[42]

The development of human society and the capacities of human beings contains a 'long, painful' transhistorical phase in which different forms of class society eclipse and succeed one another. This means that this progression in social development always takes place at the expense of the oppressed classes. The 'flag of human progress' becomes identified with and flown by the ruling class of the day and the system which its existence and rule expresses. However, eventually, social development reaches a stage which creates the necessary conditions for the supersedence of these antithetical relations of social evolution. This stage posits the conditions which provide the basis for the universal development of the associated individuals. Hereafter, the development of these human capacities 'coincide with the development of the individual' and the social interests of the individual. Hence *'the higher development of individuality is thus only achieved by a historical process during which individuals are sacrificed'*. The progress of humanity as a whole is asserted at the expense of the countless millions of the different, oppressed classes in the course of the unfolding of the historical process itself. The 'progress of humanity', in any particular epoch, coincides with the interests of the newly emerging ruling class to be as it *ascends* historically and *subsequently develops* 'its system' as the negation of the previously established social formation. During such periods of 'progress', the interests of humanity, as a socially evolving species, coincide with the interests of these emerging and 'revolutionary' classes. The driving force of this historical progression is embodied and expressed in the development of these classes and in their ideological and spiritual productions and articulations. Only as these stages of social development enter their periods of decline, decay and disintegration, does this historically progressive sheen (the *'belle époque'* of the prevailing mode of production) start to wear thin and flake off. The historically progressive role of these ruling classes becomes transformed into its opposite. The historical process must once again identify and develop the requisite forms of agency of the new 'revolutionary' class. The 'old order' must be uprooted and destroyed in order to move forward to the new epoch. This outmoded state of affairs is put through the transforming fire of revolutionary change.

The onward evolution of human life in the commune necessarily implies a complete transformation in interpersonal relations. This must mean a transformation in the very nature, *psychological* structure and forms within which the human personality itself unfolds and expresses itself. This development within the human personality will represent a qualitative break with the antecedent forms of the human personality types of bourgeois society and, moreover, *transhistorically* with the personality types in general of all previous class societies based on private property.

In an evolving society which has passed beyond the realm of capital, the human personality will undoubtedly 'mellow' and interpersonal relations be of a higher, more creative and gentler order. In so doing, these alterations will mediate and influence the collective relationship of humanity with nature. The violence and brutality against people and animals (and the destruction of ecosystems and habitats is primarily a capital-in-crisis mediated destruction) which we witness daily in the epoch of capital will become consigned to past ages. The age of mansuetudinous human beings will come into being and deepen in intensity as the 'true realm of freedom' evolves globally.

Notes and References

1   Marx, Karl, *Capital. A Critique of Political Economy*, Vol. 3, translated by David Fernbach (London: Penguin Books in Association with New Left Review, 1981), pp. 958–959, Chapter 48, 'The Trinity Formula'.

A comparison of this passage in the Penguin edition with the Lawrence & Wishart version may be appropriate since it reveals differences and nuances in translation, etc. For example, in the Penguin edition, *'It is one of the civilizing aspects of capital that it extorts this surplus labour in a manner and in conditions that are more advantageous to social relations and to the creation of elements for a new and higher formation than was the case under the earlier forms of slavery, serfdom, etc.'* is translated in the Lawrence & Wishart edition as *'It is one of the civilising aspects of capital that it enforces this surplus-labour in a manner and under conditions which are more advantageous to the development of the productive forces, social relations, and the creation of the elements for a new and higher form than under the preceding forms of slavery, serfdom, etc.'*

Marx, Karl, *Capital. A Critique of Political Economy*, Vol. 3 (London: Lawrence & Wishart, 1974), p. 819.

As we can see, *'the development of the productive forces'* is missing in the Penguin edition or has been inserted in the Lawrence &Wishart edition. Generally speaking, if we compare the volumes of the two editions, we find all manner of omissions, errors, insertions, inconsistencies, divergences and disagreements, etc., on translations, meaning, etc., and even the simple insertion or omission of words which changes, or at least significantly modifies, the whole meaning of the original. In one section, in Volume 2, the word 'buyer' is given where only 'vendor' or 'seller' gives sense and meaning to the sentence. The editions are replete with such examples. A reading of *Capital* must therefore also mean

watching out for the mistakes in translation, typography, etc., in one or other or both editions.
2. Hegel, G. W. F., *Logic, Part One of the Encyclopaedia of the Philosophical Sciences* (Oxford: Clarendon, Oxford University Press, 1975), pp. 55–56, 'Zusatz'.
3. Ibid., 'Zusatz', p. 79.
4. Ibid., §§ 157–158 and 'Zusatz', pp. 219–220.
5. Marx, *Grundrisse. Foundations of the Critique of Political Economy (Rough Draft)*, translated by Martin Nicolaus (London: Penguin Books in association with New Left Review, 1973), p. 51. Foreword by Martin Nicolaus.
6. Marx, *Grundrisse*, p. 325.
7. Marx, *Capital. A Critique of Political Economy*, Vol. 1, translated by Ben Fowkes (London: Penguin Books in association with New Left Review, 1976), pp. 165–166.
8. Marx, Karl, *Capital. A Critique of Political Economy*, Vol. 3, translated by David Fernbach (London: Penguin Books in Association with New Left Review, 1981), p. 991.
9. Marx, *Grundrisse* (London: Penguin Books, 1993), p. 325.
10. Marx, *Theories of Surplus Value, Part 3*, translated by Jack Cohen and S. W. Ryazanskaya, edited by S. W. Ryazanskaya and Richard Dixon (London: Lawrence & Wishart, 1972), p. 129, Chapter XX, 'Disintegration of the Ricardian School'.
11. Marx, *Theories of Surplus Value, Part 3*, p. 296, Chapter XXI, 'Opposition to the Economists (Based on the Ricardian Theory)'.
12. '*merely internally or merely externally*': Here Marx means merely potentially or merely actually. 'Merely internally': as in private labour being only potentially general, abstract, social labour and then becoming actually (i.e. 'merely externally') stamped with this character in the process of exchange and only through exchange on the market; that is, at that moment within which the products of private concrete labour become articulated as commodities, as manifestations of abstract, general social labour.
13. Marx, *Grundrisse* (London: Penguin Books, 1993), p. 832.
14. Mészáros, István, *Marx's Theory of Alienation* (London: Merlin Press, 1975), p. 313.
15. Mészáros, *The Challenge and Burden of Historical Time: Socialism in the Twenty First Century* (New York: Monthly Review Press, 2008), p. 42, 'The Tyranny of Capital's Time Imperative'.
16. Marx, *Grundrisse*, p. 160 (see also p. 161 ff., chapter on money).
17. Marx, *Capital*, Vol. 1, p. 77, 'Section 4. The Fetishism of Commodities and the Secret Thereof' (London: Lawrence & Wishart, 1983).

18 Marx, *Capital. A Critique of Political Economy*, Vol. 1, translated by Ben Fowkes (London: Penguin Books in association with New Left Review, 1976), p. 993, Appendix: 'Results of the Immediate Process of Production'.
19 Engels, Frederick, and Karl Marx, 'The German Ideology'. In *Marx-Engels Collected Works, Volume 5, 1845–1847*, pp. 19–581, 263 (London: Lawrence & Wishart, 1976).
20 Marx, ibid., p. 262.
21 Marx, ibid., p. 378.
22 Marx, *Economic and Philosophic Manuscripts of 1844*, translated by Martin Mulligan (Moscow: Progress Publishers, 1959), 'Third Manuscript. Private Property and Communism' (Part 3) <https://www.marxists.org/archive/marx/works/1844/manuscripts/preface.htm> (Last accessed 6 November 2016).
23 Marx, *Capital. A Critique of Political Economy*, Vol. 1, translated by Ben Fowkes (London: Penguin Books in association with New Left Review, 1976), p. 618.
24 Marx, 'Critique of the Gotha Programme'. In *The First International and After. Political Writings. Volume 3*, edited by David Fernbach, p. 345 (London: Penguin Books in association with New Left Review, 1974).
25 *'Thus, even with "communal labour" in its spontaneously evolved form [...] the social character of labour is evidently not effected by the labour of the individual assuming the abstract form of universal labour or his product assuming the form of a universal equivalent. The communal system on which this mode of production is based prevents the labour of an individual from becoming private labour and his product the private product of a separate individual; it causes individual labour to appear rather as the direct function of a member of the social organization. Labour which manifests itself in exchange-value appears to be the labour of an isolated individual. It becomes social labour by assuming the form of its direct opposite, of abstract universal labour.'*

Marx, Karl, *A Contribution to the Critique of Political Economy* (Moscow: Progress Publishers, 1977), pp. 33–34.
26 Marx, *Grundrisse*, pp. 171–173.
27 Ibid., p. 708.
28 Ibid., pp. 705–706.
29 Marx, *Capital*, Vol. 3, Chapter 48, 'The Trinity Formula', op. cit., pp. 958–959 (London: Penguin Classics Edn, 1991).
30 Marx, 'Critique of the Gotha Programme', subsection I.3, op. cit., p. 347.
31 Marx, *Grundrisse*, p. 611.
32 Marx, 'Critique of the Gotha Programme', op. cit., p. 347.
33 Marx, Karl, *Theories of Surplus Value, Part 3*, translated by Jack Cohen and S. W. Ryazanskaya, edited by S. W. Ryazanskaya and Richard Dixon (London:

Lawrence & Wishart, 1972), p. 256, Chapter XXI, 'Opposition to the Economists (Based on the Ricardian Theory)'.
34 Ibid., p. 257, 'Opposition to the Economists (Based on the Ricardian Theory)'.
35 Marx, *Grundrisse*, p. 712.
36 Marx, *Economic and Philosophical Manuscripts of 1844*, op. cit., 'Third Manuscript. Private Property and Communism' (Part 4).
37 Marx, *Theories of Surplus Value, Part 1*, translated by Emile Burns, edited by S. W. Ryazanskaya (London: Lawrence & Wishart, 1969), p. 288, Chapter IV, 'Theories of Productive and Unproductive Labour'.
38 Marcuse, Herbert, 'The Realm of Freedom and the Realm of Necessity – A Reconsideration', *Praxis*, No. 1 (International Edn) (1969): p. 67 <http://www.marcuse.org/herbert/pubs/60spubs/69praxis/69praxis7pagePDF.pdf> (Last accessed 2 November 2016).
39 Engels, Frederick, and Karl Marx, 'The German Ideology'. In *Marx-Engels Collected Works, Volume 5, 1845–1847*, pp. 19–581, 78 (London: Lawrence & Wishart, 1976).
40 Marx, *Theories of Surplus Value, Part 1*, translated by Emile Burns, edited by S. W. Ryazanskaya (London: Lawrence & Wishart, 1969), p. 285, 'Theories of Productive and Unproductive Labour'.
41 Lenin, V. I., *State and Revolution* (Moscow: Progress Publishers, 1969), p. 87.
42 Marx, *Theories of Surplus Value, Part 2*, translated by Renate Simpson, edited by S. W. Ryazanskaya (London: Lawrence & Wishart, 1969), p. 118, Chapter IX, 'Notes on the History of the Discovery of the So-Called Ricardian Law of Rent' [Supplementary Notes on Rodbertus] (Digression).

APPENDIX II

The Broadcasting and Print Media: In the Ideological Service of Capital and its State Power

The print and, increasingly and more significantly, the broadcasting media both have a pivotal ideological role to play in maintaining the rule of capital and defending the established social conditions of that rule. The latter's broadcasts reach into the homes of many millions, day and evening. There are now twenty-four-hour news channels. Chomsky and Herman assert that ...

> It is our view that, among their other functions, the media serve, and propagandize on behalf of, the powerful society interests that control and finance them. The representatives of these interests have important agendas and principles that they want to advance, and they are well positioned to shape and constrain media policy. This is not normally accomplished by crude intervention, but by the selection of right-thinking personnel and by the editors' and working journalists' internalization of priorities and definitions of newsworthiness that conform to the institution's policy.[1]

What is clearly emerging – as the crisis of the whole capital system unfolds – is the unswerving loyalty and 'reflex' responses of a media which stands as an ideological pillar of a repressive order. Such a media – and especially the broadcasting news media which serves directly as the official, televised propagandist mouthpiece of the state power of capital and the social relations which it defends – is a vital, integral and indispensable part of such an order. As such, it must be subject – as an organically mediating part of this order – to the impact and influence of the broader mediations and determinations of its unfolding structural crisis.

As media of and for capital, it can do no other than articulate and defend all those state structures and social relations whose inalienable and intrinsic *modus operandi* and *modus vivendi* operate to serve to maintain the capital system. Indeed, to purvey the bizarre notions that such a system is as 'natural' as nature's creation itself and that it is unthinkable to question the endurability of its existence.

The print and broadcasting media are as much a part of the arsenal of the state power of capital as are its police, armed forces and prisons. They do not simply act as a directly politicized propagandist mouthpiece for the capital system, serving an indispensable ideological function in the apparatus of state repression. They also daily articulate and impose 'as gospel' the 'official morality' of the capitalist system and of the complex of social relations intrinsic to it. And, as Trotsky keenly observed, in the conflicts between capital and labour ...

> morality is one of the ideological functions in this struggle. The ruling class forces its ends upon society and habituates it to considering all those means which contradict its ends as immoral. That is the chief function of official morality. It pursues the idea of the 'greatest possible happiness' not for the majority but for a small and ever diminishing minority. Such a regime could not have endured for even a week through force alone. It needs the cement of morality.[2]

He adds that ...

> morality more than any other form of ideology has a class character.[3]

To listen to the broadcasting media today in 2017 – the BBC, ITN, CNN, Fox News, etc. – or to read the print media, tabloid or broadsheet, is to recognize the living truth of Trotsky's conception here. Their output constitutes the collective articulation of this 'official morality' produced and reproduced daily for the forced consumption of millions. This is the character and function of the media in the epoch of capital; to act as an ideological and political agency for the maintenance of the capital system and its state and global agencies upon which this media feeds like a dependent, bloated parasite.

In the age of capital, the morality purveyed by the media grows out the character of capital's rule. It is organically inseparable from that rule and from the need to maintain it against all forms of opposition. This is the bottom line (default) of the role of the capitalist media in its different forms which becomes an animating ideological *sine qua non* for the rule of capital and its political agencies.

Ultimately, it can only mean the justification of oppression, exploitation and the death and destruction with which the continuation of capital's rule must always be intrinsically associated. The capitalist media is the central ideological support for this moral justification of the continuing rule of capital. Even as it systematically descends into the most disturbing forms of pillage, destruction and barbarism.

It is in the interests of the capitalist class and its state power to purvey the conception that morality founded on the existence of private property is the absolute morality. That it is the eternal 'natural' morality, the morality of some eternal, nebulous 'human nature' and that anyone who contradicts it in thought and practice is immoral, arraignable, imprisonable or even worthy of hospitalization. It is the morality of subjection to capital and its state power. Always on hand are its willing and salaried ideologues, chatterers and news controllers in the media and elsewhere to reinforce all those hideous, ahistorical moral precepts which serve to 'cement' the capitalist order together. To keep it in one big ugly, grotesque piece.

Of course, for the socialist, capitalism is an inherently unethical system of social relations founded, as it is, on exploitation and inequality. It is supremely ethical to put an end to its existence by whatever means are actually necessary. For if these means be actually necessary to end the age of capital and replace it with a global socialist human life, and these means necessarily realize ends which are historically ethical in themselves, then the means through which these ends are realized are also ethical. Indeed, the means share the same degree of ethicality as the realized ends themselves. The bourgeois moralists and ideologues of capital and its state power will whinge and whine about this assertion. They will label it 'immoral', 'dangerous' or even 'Machiavellian'. They will seek to qualify it and convolute it into forms which are designed to confuse, bamboozle and present problematics of one kind or another. Unfortunately, we can do nothing about that. But leave them to their metaphysical perambulations. *The welfare of the revolution – that is the supreme law!**

The supremely ethical precept – which is predominant above all others – is an end to the global epoch of capital and the creation of a communist life by humanity for humanity; regardless of what that is going to involve in the course of an unfolding global struggle and period of transition.

Any form of morality which ideologically serves to prop up the capitalist order is, accordingly, supremely immoral. We do not agonize about the abstract, transcendental morality (based on religious doctrine and the 'fictions' of bourgeois democracy) aired by the ideologues of capital. We recognize that what we are doing is supremely ethical because it is putting an end to a barbarous social system and putting one in its place which will create social relationships far more human than the present one.

It will create a totally different type of human being and human personality to the current one. It will be one in which the oppression and exploitation of man by man has come to a final, irreversible end. Furthermore, a society where the conditions for the flowering and flourishing of the human personality will be posited and daily reproduced in continuously higher and increasingly more developed forms.

The print and broadcasting media of capital daily purveys a moral outlook to many millions which serves to defend and maintain a highly immoral social order. In that activity, they share the same degree of immorality as the very system which they are serving to protect. And, likewise, in that regard, they deserve to share the same fate. The broadcasting and print media are, taken collectively, the propagandist mouthpieces of capital and its state power. They are as much a part of the continuing rule of capital as its bureaucracy and armed forces.

References

1. Herman, Edward S., and Noam Chomsky, *Manufacturing Consent: The Political Economy of the Mass Media* (New York: Pantheon, 2002), p.xi.
2. Trotsky, Leon, *Their Morals and Ours* (New York: Pathfinder, 1979), p. 20.
3. Ibid., p. 21.
4. Ibid., p. 65.

APPENDIX III

Whatever Happened to the 'National Liberation Struggle'?

The proletariat is the universal structural antagonist of globalizing capital whose political representatives are found in the nation-states, regional and global powers across the world. The ruling elites of these nation-states and powers are in thrall to globalizing capital and identify their own interests with it in opposition to the historic interests of the proletariat. This was very clearly demonstrated in the referendum campaign in Britain (2016) to decide on the question of Britain's membership of the European Union (EU) capitalist club. The predominant position of the ruling class and its state elite was to oppose withdrawal from the EU which stands as a socio-economic medium and arrangement to facilitate the interests and exploitative activities of transnational capital over European labour.

The 'elites' of those countries which went through wars of so-called 'national liberation' – from the end of the last world war onwards – are not exempt in regard to serving the same global capitalist interests. From Vietnam to Nicaragua, from South Africa to China and now, in process, Cuba, transnational capital incorporates and dominates all areas of the globe in its singular embrace. All predations of the major powers of global capital now find their accomplices in the national ruling elites and the nation-state powers arising out of so-called 'national liberation'.

'National liberation' created the freedom of each local bourgeoisie to attempt to restructure economy in its own class interests in alliance with transnational capital. This alliance for some came later – with the opening up of Stalinist regimes to global capital (for example, Vietnam) – but it demonstrated the thesis that ...

> The very concept of a liberatory national sovereignty is ambiguous if not completely contradictory. While this nationalism seeks to liberate the multitude from **foreign** domination, it erects **domestic** structures of domination which are equally severe ... The state is the poisoned gift of national liberation. *[emphasis in the original]*[1]

The 'multitude', of course, was not 'liberated'. The 'erected structures' merely served to replace naked colonialism or imperialist domination via crony regimes with open channels for investment by the transnational corporations. This is continuing apace today. The ruling elites of the 'nationally liberated lands' have become 'pecuniary parties'. This process is now starting to unfold in 'revolutionary' Cuba.

These 'domestic structures' in the 'liberated lands' now serve as the political facilitators of the interests of the transnationals and the banks. These capitalist giants circumnavigate the globe – in the epoch of capital's structural crisis – like leviathanic vampires seeking out the highest possible rates of exploitation, sucking the lifeblood out of labour and dominating all regions of the planet.

Those nation-states which offer resistance are eliminated and 're-incorporated' by means of 'sanctions' and war. Uncannily, in this regard, the 'Pax Capitalis' resembles that of the 'Pax Romana': co-operate to serve the interests of global capital or suffer the consequences. For those facing conquest by the Roman imperium, it was a case of co-operation and integration into a system of plunder, tax and tribute or extermination and enslavement. The destruction of Carthage by the Roman Republic in the Third Punic War (149–146 BCE) and the brutal eradication of Dacian culture by Trajan between 101–106 CE illustrated this approach of 'unconditional surrender or annihilation'.

Capitalist globalization has provided an invaluable retrospective on the 'national liberation struggle' which 'liberated' areas of the globe from colonialism and its imperialist legacies only for these struggles to prepare the ground for the predations of global capital. The dialectical gods of history imposing a mocking return to the old out of its negation.

The transfer of power from colonial authorities to the indigenous national bourgeoisie or Stalinist party machines only served to replace the exploitation of imperialist national colonial capital with globally mobile capital. The new ruling elites in the 'liberated' lands are now, essentially, serving as the self-enriching agents of this globalizing capital. A perfect example of this is the regime in Vietnam. Decades of struggle against three major powers, millions dead in war, the land bombed with high-explosives and poisoned with teratogenic toxins. Vietnam, today, is one of the most attractive destinations for the transnational corporations ...

> According to data from the Department of Foreign Investment, as of 2004, there were 415 transnational corporations (TNCs) investment registration in Vietnam, including 106 of the top 500 TNCs world's largest TNCs ranked by Fortune magazine. The situation of the TNC investment in Vietnam today continued rapid growth. As of 2013, Vietnam attracted 15,932 FDI projects with total registered capital of more than U.S. dollars 234 billion and realized capital over 112 billion U.S. dollars, of which about 500 of the TNC projects with total registered investment capital up around 140 billion U.S dollars, investors focused on R&D (research and development), technology, product quality uncensored ...
>
> After conducting a survey, the U.S. Chamber of Commerce in Shanghai confirms the attractiveness of investment in Vietnam is growing and is becoming the preferred address in Asia in the choice of international investors. Evidence that Vietnam has market presence, companionship and strong development of the big names like Samsung, Intel, Nokia, Honda, Canon ...
>
> Most recently, Ariston – brand water heater industry leader has decided to invest in Vietnam plant scale second largest in Asia, is also located in the aforementioned general trend.[2] *[The poor English syntax and grammar has been left uncorrected – SM]*

Today the proletariat in these lands faces both the exploitations and oppression of global capital and those of invariably and deeply corrupt indigenous ruling elites which do everything within their power to accommodate themselves to the interests of the 'TNCs'. As always, in Vietnam for example, the intentions and the results of struggle did not coincide without real difference. The 'anti-imperialist', 'national liberation struggle' established the social conditions necessary for the exploitation of human labour power by global capital in the various 'liberated' national arenas. And, indeed, often at rates of exploitation which would have shamed the most malevolent of colonial administrators.

The question of revolutionary agency now becomes a global question in which the proletariat must build organizations which are capable of linking the different sections of the proletariat *in all regions across the world* in struggle against capital-in-crisis. The age when many socialists tied themselves, like obedient mouthpieces, to the coat-tails of the so-called 'national liberation struggle' (and blindly ignored the monstrous truth that these 'liberators' were often butchering fellow socialists whilst they were engaged in their 'anti-imperialist' struggle) is over. All struggles now, if they are to be *truly emancipatory* – wherever they are in the world – must gravitate against the capital order itself in any part of the globe. The so-called 'national liberation struggle' has created nation-states which today act as proxies of global capital in the 'liberated' lands. This is the truth (the outcome) of 'national liberation'.

The establishment of 'domestic structures of domination which are equally severe' was clearly illustrated by the Iranian Revolution from 1979. The overthrow of the Pahlavi regime was followed by theocratic dictatorship in which thousands of socialist oppositionists were arrested and executed. 'Liberation', 'Anti-Zionism' and 'Anti-Imperialism' was, generally, accompanied by arrests and executions of socialists. 'Anti-Imperialism' became the spellbinding watchword deployed by the national bourgeoisie or Stalinist party machine in order to assert 'nation-statehood'. The state power which resulted from 'liberation' was one which articulated the interests of this class or ruling 'Communist Party' stratum under the pretence of 'national liberation'.

The Janus-character of the 'national liberation struggle' (a 'double-edged sword') served to oppose both external 'imperialist' and internal socialist enemies as it unfolded. The successors of these former 'imperialist' enemies are today on 'diplomatic and business terms' with the successors of the 'liberators'. The millions of lives sacrificed in many years of struggle has served to replace the capital of colonial powers with the capital of the transnational corporations. Subordination to capital now takes on a different form involving the co-operation between these national elites and the transnationals and banks. This mutually beneficial alliance is supported by the major national state and global powers of capital such as the United States, European powers (the European Union), Japan and, increasingly, China which has become the world's banker.

The various 'anti-imperialist' struggles have created regimes which now give complete access to their regions for globalizing capital to exploit the 'liberated' peoples of these regions. If anything, 'national liberation' was the creation of the freedom for national elites to establish control over the local proletariat and peasantry. By doing this, as 'globalization' has started to unfold, these elites have prepared local labour for the exploitation of global capital. The last bastion of 'national liberation', the *faux, bella figura* 'revolutionary' regime in Havana, is now putting in place measures for the restoration of capitalism. The well-cut suit of an aspiring elite is replacing the military garb of the Castroist functionary.

Underlying and mediating this process of global domination is the momentum given to it by capital-in-crisis. Its structural crisis is driving capital globally to appropriate all spheres – extensively and intensively – as a means of *seeking to displace and attenuate* the structural character of this historic crisis of the capital relation which is itself *absolutely unresolvable*. This growing and intensifying momentum of capital-in-crisis underlies and has mediated the fall of the Soviet system, the opening up of China to the world market and the transnationals and their capture of the vast reserves of obscenely cheap labour-power of the 'liberated' peoples of the Earth. It is no overestimation to assert that 'globalization' itself is rooted in and arises out of the emergence and development of the structural crisis of capital itself since the 1970s. That 'globalization' is a historic response to this same crisis and has now posited the developing world conditions within which this crisis must play out, deepen and intensify.

The so-called 'socialist forms' of 'national liberation' have now become integrated (and are becoming increasingly so with each passing year) into the system of globalizing capital. The former 'Communist Party' ruling strata in these regions of 'liberation' have either disappeared and 're-invented' themselves or are in the process of doing so in the rush to appropriate state assets, resources and land. They have reconstituted or are in the process of reconstituting themselves as a corrupt, wealthy capital-owning class and political hierarchy to serve the newly emerged 'globalized' capitalist relations. The collapse of the Soviet system in Russia and the ensuing national 'smash and grab' by the top echelon has clearly illustrated this process of return to capitalism. As is the current process of 'restoration' under way in China.

'National Liberation' became a means whereby the 'liberated' nation-states around the globe were historically 'prepared' or 'readied' for the emerging 'globalized' stage of capital's destructive self-reproduction. Today, the slogans and 'sincerities' of these regimes ring hollow in the ears of millions. What, for example, does the slogan of 'Defend the Cuban Revolution' mean today when it is the 'revolutionaries' in Havana who are now constituting themselves as the major force for capitalist restoration within Cuba itself? The regime is encouraging the growth of capital-in-circulation (money and commodity capital) and the entry of private capital into agricultural production. The next step is private capital in industrial production. How long before the US sugar corporations are renting (or even buying) land from the Cuban state?

The continuously unfolding realization of the historic task of eliminating capital from the social metabolism as whole on a global scale means that world perspectives and strategies will have to be developed as the situation unfolds and demands their elaboration. It is the actual unfolding of capital's structural crisis-process itself which will necessitate the initiation and development of these global perspectives and strategies. This is why international solidarity and fraternalism between the peoples of the globe against the common enemy is necessary. Supporting struggles against capital in other parts of the globe is vital for our struggles 'at home' and elsewhere and vice versa. A fraternal joining up of organization globally – involving mutual support and solidarity – will be required to defeat capital and its state powers across the world. The failure and barbarities of the antisocialist Stalinist Soviet system are instructive in this regard. The failure of 'socialism in one country' is a testament to the need for this 'joining up'. This reactionary conception served the interests of the self-serving ruling strata of the now defunct Stalinist regimes. Socialism as a new way of life for humanity will only succeed if it is established and grows on a global scale, eclipsing the old, outmoded capital order.

References

1. Hardt, Michael, and Antonio Negri, 'The Poisoned Gift of National Liberation'. In *Empire* (Cambridge, MA: Harvard University Press, 2000), pp. 132–134.
2. Nguyen, Y., 'Vietnam – an attractive destination of transnational corporations', *Nhut Thanh Daily News* (22 September 2014) <http://anha.vn/en/chi-tiet-tin-tuc-43/Vietnam--an-attractive-destination-of-transnational-corporations.html>.

Bibliography

Alley, Richard B. 'Ice-core evidence of abrupt climate changes', *Proceedings of the National Academy of Sciences of the United States of America* (PNAS), Vol. 97, No. 4 (15 February 2000) <http://www.pnas.org/content/97/4/1331.full> (Last accessed 3 November 2016).

Anderson, Perry. *Passages from Antiquity to Feudalism* (London: NLB, 1974).

Arnot, Chris. 'Society Interview. Great Expectations', *The Guardian* (3 October 2007) <https://www.theguardian.com/society/2007/oct/03/guardiansocietysupplement.communities2> (Last accessed 4 November 2016).

Bauer, Otto. *Die Nationalitätenfrage und die Sozialdemokratie* (Vienna: Ignaz Brand, 1907).

BBC News. 'Call Centres "bad for India"', *BBC News* (11 December 2003) <http://news.bbc.co.uk/1/hi/world/south_asia/3292619.stm> (Last accessed 3 November 2016).

BBC News. 'Hinchingbrooke Hospital: Circle to withdraw from contract', *BBC News* (9 January 2015) <http://www.bbc.co.uk/news/uk-england-cambridgeshire-30740956> (Last accessed 3 November 2016).

Bellamy Foster, John. 'Marx and the Rift in the Universal Metabolism of Nature', *Monthly Review*, Vol. 65, No. 7 (2013): 1–19 <http://monthlyreview.org/2013/12/01/marx-rift-universal-metabolism-nature/> (Last accessed 2 November 2016).

Bellamy Foster, John. *Marx's Ecology. Materialism and Nature* (New York: Monthly Review Press, 2000).

Benjamin, Joel. 'Seven things everyone should know about the Private Finance Initiative', *Open Democracy* (17 November 2014) <https://www.opendemocracy.net/ournhs/joel-benjamin/seven-things-everyone-should-know-about-private-finance-initiative> (Last accessed 3 November 2016).

Brontë, Charlotte. *Jane Eyre* (New York: Dover Publications, 2011).

Burkett, Paul. *Marxism and Ecological Economics: Toward a Red and Green Political Economy* (Chicago: Haymarket Books, 2009).

Caixiong, Zheng. 'Robots go it alone at factory with no assembly workers', *China Daily* (5 May 2015) <http://www.chinadaily.com.cn/china/2015-05/05/content_20620184.htm> (Last accessed 3 November 2016).

Cambridgelibdems.org.uk. 'Huppert fights to bring Hinchingbrooke Hospital back to the NHS', *Cambridgelibdems.org.uk* (9 January 2015) <http://www.cambridgelibdems.org.uk/huppert_fights_to_bring_hinchingbrooke_hospital_back_to_nhs> (Last accessed 3 November 2016).

Carchedi, G. 'Behind and Beyond the Crisis', *International Socialism*, No. 132 (October 2011) <http://isj.org.uk/behind-and-beyond-the-crisis/> (Last accessed 2 November 2016).

Clausewitz, Carl von. *On War*, edited and translated by Michael Howard and Peter Paret (Princeton, NJ: Princeton University Press, 1989).

Climate Emergency Institute. 'Atmospheric Greenhouse Gases & Greenhouse Emissions', *Climate Emergency Institute*, n.d. <http://www.climateemergencyinstitute.com/greenhousegases.html> (Last accessed 3 November 2016).

Cole, Mike. *Marxism and Educational Theory: Origins and Issues* (London and New York: Routledge, 2008).

Committee on Abrupt Climate Change et al. *Abrupt Climate Change: Inevitable Surprises* (Washington, DC: The National Academies Press, 2002) <https://www.nap.edu/catalog/10136/abrupt-climate-change-inevitable-surprises> (Last accessed 2 November 2016).

Communist Party of Great Britain (CPGB). 'What we fight for', *CPGB* (2015) <http://cpgb.org.uk/pages/what-we-fight-for/> (Last Accessed 2 November 2016).

Datablog. 'University funding cuts: which institutions are worst hit?', *The Guardian* (17 March 2011) <https://www.theguardian.com/news/datablog/2011/mar/17/university-funding-cuts-institution-hefce-universities> (Last accessed 4 November 2016).

Dawkins, Richard. *The God Delusion* (New York: Bantam Books, 2006).

Degras, Jane., ed. 'Conditions of Admission to the Communist International Approved by the Second Comintern Congress, 6 August, 1920'. In *The Communist International: 1919–1943 Documents. Volume 1 1919–1922*, pp. 166–172 (Oxford: Oxford University Press, 1956).

Department for Business, Innovation & Skills. 'Trade Union Membership 2014. Statistical Bulletin', *Department for Business, Innovation & Skills* (June 2015) <https://www.gov.uk/government/uploads/system/uploads/attachment_data/file/431564/Trade_Union_Membership_Statistics_2014.pdf> (Last accessed 3 November 2016).

DePillis, Lydia. 'Auto union loses historic election at Volkswagen plant in Tennessee', *The Washington Post* (14 February 2014) <https://www.washingtonpost.com/news/wonk/wp/2014/02/14/united-auto-workers-lose-historic-election-at-chattanooga-volkswagen-plant/> (Last accessed 3 November 2016).

Elk, Mike. 'After Historic UAW Defeat at Tennessee Volkswagen Plant, Theories Abound', *In These Times* (15 February 2014) <http://inthesetimes.com/working/entry/16300/after_uaw_defeat_at_volkswagen_in_tennessee_theories_abound> (Last accessed 2 November 2016).

Engels, Frederick. Frederick Engels to Franz Mehring (14 July 1893). In *Marx-Engels Selected Works in One Volume* (London: Lawrence & Wishart, 1973).

Engels, Frederick. 'Ludwig Feuerbach and the End of Classical German Philosophy'. In *Marx-Engels Selected Works*, pp. 324–364 (London: Lawrence & Wishart, 1950).

Engels, Frederick. 'Ludwig Feuerbach and the End of Classical German Philosophy'. In *Marx-Engels Selected Works* (London: Lawrence & Wishart, 1973).

Engels, Frederick. 'The Part Played by Labor in the Transition from Ape to Man'. In *The Origin of the Family, Private Property and the State*, pp. 260–261 (New York: International Publishers, 2007).

Engels, Frederick, and Karl Marx. 'The Alleged Splits in the International'. In *The First International and After. Political Writings. Volume 3*, edited by David Fernbach, pp. 272–314 (London: Penguin Books in association with New Left Review, 1974).

Engels, Frederick, and Karl Marx. 'The German Ideology'. In *Marx-Engels Collected Works, Volume 5, 1845–1847*, pp. 19–581 (London: Lawrence & Wishart, 1976).

Engels, Frederick, and Karl Marx. 'The Holy Family, or Critique of Critical Criticism'. In *Marx-Engels Collected Works, Volume 4*, pp. 5–211 (London: Lawrence & Wishart, 1975).

Engels, Frederick, and Karl Marx. 'Manifesto of the Communist Party'. In *Marx-Engels Selected Works, Volume One*, translated by Samuel Moore in cooperation with Frederick Engels, pp. 98–137 (Moscow: Progress Publishers, 1969).

Farrell, Sean. 'Grangemouth crisis: Unite union now accepts plant rescue plan', *The Guardian* (24 October 2013) <https://www.theguardian.com/business/2013/oct/24/grangemouth-crisis-unite-accepts-survival-plan-ineos> (Last accessed 4 November 2016).

Financial Times. 'Record profits for global banking as China dominates list of top banks'. *Financial Times* (30 June 2014) <http://aboutus.ft.com/2014/06/30/record-profits-for-global-banking-as-china-dominates-list-of-top-banks/#axzz3Rw8ZKPVu> (Last accessed 2 November 2016).

Freire, Paulo. *Pedagogy of the Oppressed* (London: Penguin Books, 1996).

Gilmore, Inigo. 'Mandela applauds South Africa's rising arms trade'. *The Times* (23 November 1994).

Green Party. 'Capitalism should exist for the good of the people, not the other way round'. *Green Party* (20 January 2012) <https://www.greenparty.org.uk/news/capitalism-should-exist-for-the-good-of-the-people-not-the-other-way-around.html> (Last accessed 3 November 2016).

Hackman, Rose. 'Detroit demolishes its ruins: "The capitalists will take care of the rest"', *The Guardian* (28 September 2014) <https://www.theguardian.com/money/2014/sep/28/detroit-demolish-ruins-capitalists-abandoned-buildings-plan> (Last accessed 4 November 2016).

Hardt, Michael, and Antonio Negri. *Empire* (Cambridge, MA: Harvard University Press, 2000).

Hegel, G. W. F. *Logic. Part One of the Encyclopaedia of the Philosophical Sciences* (Oxford: Clarendon, Oxford University Press, 1975).

Hegel, G. W. F. *Science of Logic* (London: George Allen & Unwin, 1929).

Herman, Edward S., and Noam Chomsky. *Manufacturing Consent: The Political Economy of the Mass Media* (New York: Pantheon Books, 2002).

Howard, Brian Clark. 'Aral Sea's Eastern Basin is Dry for First Time in 600 Years', *National Geographic* (2 October 2014) <http://news.nationalgeographic.com/news/2014/10/141001-aral-sea-shrinking-drought-water-environment/> (Last accessed 3 November 2016).

ICEF Monitor. 'China and India to produce 40% of global graduates by 2020', *ICEF Monitor* (16 July 2012) <http://monitor.icef.com/2012/07/china-and-india-to-produce-40-of-global-graduates-by-2020/> (Last accessed 3 November 2016).

Jeffries, Stuart. 'What is TTIP and why should we be angry about it?', *The Guardian* (3 August 2015) <https://www.theguardian.com/business/2015/aug/03/ttip-what-why-angry-transatlantic-trade-investment-partnership-guide> (Last accessed 5 November 2016).

Lenin, Vladimir I. 'Draft Resolutions for the Third Congress of the R. S. D. L. P.' In *Lenin Collected Works, Volume 8*, pp. 191–196 (Moscow: Progress Publishers, 1965).

Lenin, Vladimir I. 'Imperialism, the Highest Stage of Capitalism'. In *Lenin's Selected Works, Volume 1*, pp. 667–776 (Moscow: Progress Publishers, 1963) <https://www.marxists.org/archive/lenin/works/1916/imp-hsc/index.htm#ch10> (Last accessed 2 November 2016).

Lenin, Vladimir I. *Lenin Collected Works, Volume 38. Philosophical Notebooks* (Moscow: Progress Publishers, 1972).

Lenin, Vladimir I. 'Preface to the Collection Twelve Years'. In *Lenin Collected Works, Volume 13*, pp. 94–113 (Moscow: Progress Publishers, 1972).

Lenin, Vladimir I. 'The Reorganization of the Party'. In *Lenin Collected Works, Volume 10*, pp. 29–39 (Moscow: Progress Publishers, 1965).

Lenin, Vladimir I. *State and Revolution* (Moscow: Progress Publishers, 1969).

Lenin, Vladimir I. 'What is to be Done? Burning Questions of our Movement'. In *Lenin Collected Works, Volume 5*, pp. 347–530 (Moscow: Foreign Languages Publishing House, 1961).

Leon, Abram. *The Jewish Question: A Marxist Interpretation* (New York: Pathfinder Press, 1971).

Liodakis, George. 'The New Stage of Capitalist Development and the Prospects of Globalisation', *Science & Society*, Vol. 69, No. 3 (July 2005): 341–366.

Lukács, Georg. *History and Class Consciousness: Studies in Marxist Dialectics*, translated by Rodney Livingstone (Cambridge, MA: MIT Press, 1972).

Luxemburg, Rosa. *The Junius Pamphlet: The Crisis in the German Social Democracy* (London: Merlin Press, 1967).

Luxemburg, Rosa. 'The Mass Strike, the Political Party, and the Trade Unions'. In *The Essential Rosa Luxemburg*, edited by Helen Scott, pp. 105–182 (Chicago: Haymarket Books, 2007).

McCormack, Richard A. 'America's Biggest Companies Continue to Move Factories Offshore and Eliminate Thousands of American Jobs', *Manufacturing and Technology News*, Vol. 20, No. 10 (31 July 2013) <http://www.manufacturingnews.com/news/TAA0731131.html> (Last accessed 3 November 2016).

McVeigh, Karen. 'DWP urged to publish inquiries on benefit claimant suicides', *The Guardian* (14 December 2014) <https://www.theguardian.com/society/2014/dec/14/dwp-inquiries-benefit-claimant-suicides> (Last accessed 4 November 2016).

Marcuse, Herbert. 'The Realm of Freedom and the Realm of Necessity – A Reconsideration', *Praxis*, International Edition, No. 1 (1969): 67 <http://www.marcuse.org/herbert/pubs/60spubs/69praxis/69praxis7pagePDF.pdf> (Last accessed 2 November 2016).

Martin, Kingsley. 'Trotsky in Mexico' (10 April 1937), *The New Statesman* (29 January 2007) <http://www.newstatesman.com/society/2007/01/trotsky-mexico-russia-trial> (Last accessed 3 November 2016).

Marx, Karl. *Capital*, Vol. 1 (New York: International Publishers, 1967).

Marx, Karl. *Capital. A Critique of Political Economy*, Vol. 1, translated by Ben Fowkes (London: Penguin Books in association with New Left Review, 1976).

Marx, Karl. *Capital. A Critique of Political Economy*, Vol. 3 (London: Lawrence & Wishart, 1974).

Marx, Karl. *Capital. A Critique of Political Economy*, Vol. 3, translated by David Fernbach (London: Penguin Books in Association with New Left Review, 1981).

Marx, Karl. 'The Class Struggles in France, 1848 to 1850'. In *Marx-Engels Collected Works, Volume 10. 1849–1851*, pp. 45–145 (London: Lawrence & Wishart, 1978).

Marx, Karl. *The Civil War in France* (Peking: Foreign Languages Press, 1966).

Marx, Karl. 'Contribution to the Critique of Hegel's Philosophy of Law. Introduction'. In *Marx-Engels Collected Works. Volume 3. 1843–1844*, pp. 175–187 (London: Lawrence & Wishart, 1975).

Marx, Karl. *A Contribution to the Critique of Political Economy* (Moscow: Progress Publishers, 1977).
Marx, Karl. 'Critique of the Gotha Programme'. In *The First International and After. Political Writings. Volume 3*, edited by David Fernbach, pp. 339–359 (London: Penguin Books in association with New Left Review, 1974).
Marx, Karl. *Economic and Philosophic Manuscripts of 1844*, translated by Martin Mulligan (Moscow: Progress Publishers, 1959) <https://www.marxists.org/archive/marx/works/1844/manuscripts/preface.htm> (Last accessed 6 November 2016).
Marx, Karl. 'The Eighteenth Brumaire of Louis Bonaparte'. In *Surveys From Exile*, edited by David Fernbach, pp. 143–249 (New York: Vintage Books, 1974).
Marx, Karl. *Grundrisse. Foundations of the Critique of Political Economy (Rough Draft)*, translated by Martin Nicolaus (London: Penguin Books in association with New Left Review, 1973).
Marx, Karl. 'Instructions for Delegates to the Geneva Congress'. In *The First International and After. Political Writings. Volume 3*, edited by David Fernbach, pp. 85–94 (London: Penguin Books in association with New Left Review, 1974).
Marx, Karl. Karl Marx to Frederick Engels (8 October 1858). In *Marx-Engels Collected Works, Volume 40* (London: Lawrence & Wishart, 1983).
Marx, Karl. Karl Marx to Johann Baptist von Schweitzer (13 October 1868). In *Marx-Engels Collected Works, Volume 43* (London: Lawrence & Wishart, 1988).
Marx, Karl. Karl Marx to Wilhelm Blos (10 November 1877). In *Marx-Engels Collected Works, Volume 45* (London: Lawrence & Wishart, 1991).
Marx, Karl. 'On the Hague Congress. A Correspondent's Report of a Speech Made at a Meeting in Amsterdam on September 8th, 1872'. In *Marx-Engels Collected Works, Volume 23. 1871–1874*, pp. 254–256 (London: Lawrence & Wishart, 1988).
Marx, Karl. *The Poverty of Philosophy* (London: Martin Lawrence, n.d.).
Marx, Karl. 'Provisional Rules'. In *The First International and After. Political Writings. Volume 3*, edited by David Fernbach, pp. 82–84 (London: Penguin Books in association with New Left Review, 1974).
Marx, Karl. 'Report to the Brussels Congress'. In *The First International and After. Political Writings. Volume 3*, edited by David Fernbach, pp. 94–99 (London: Penguin Books in association with New Left Review, 1974).
Marx, Karl. *Theories of Surplus Value, Part 1*, translated by Emile Burns, edited by S. W. Ryazanskaya (London: Lawrence & Wishart, 1969).
Marx, Karl. *Theories of Surplus Value, Part 2*, translated by Renate Simpson, edited by S. W. Ryazanskaya (London: Lawrence & Wishart, 1969).
Marx, Karl. *Theories of Surplus Value, Part 3*, translated by Jack Cohen and S. W. Ryazanskaya, edited by S. W. Ryazanskaya and Richard Dixon (London: Lawrence & Wishart, 1972).

Marx, Karl. 'Theses on Feuerbach'. In *Marx-Engels Collected Works, Volume 5, 1845–1847*, pp. 3–5 (London: Lawrence & Wishart, 1976).
Marx, Karl. *Value: Studies by Karl Marx* (London: New Park Publications, 1976).
May, Shaun. 'Synopsis of Hegel's "Science of Logic"', *spmay.wordpress.com* <https://spmay.wordpress.com/synopsis-of-hegels-science-of-logic/> (Last accessed 3 November 2016).
Meiksins Wood, Ellen. *Empire of Capital* (London: Verso Books, 2005).
Mészáros, István. *Beyond Capital: Towards a Theory of Transition* (London: Merlin Press, 1995).
Mészáros, István. *The Challenge and Burden of Historical Time: Socialism in the Twenty First Century* (New York: Monthly Review Press, 2008).
Mészáros, István. 'Marxism Today: An Interview with István Mészáros'. Interview with Chris Arthur and Joseph McCarney. *Monthly Review*, Vol. 44, No. 11 (April 1993).
Mészáros, István. *Marx's Theory of Alienation* (London: Merlin Press, 1975).
Mészáros, István. *The Structural Crisis of Capital* (New York: Monthly Review Press, 2009).
Michigan Urban Farming Initiative. 'All About MUFI'. Michigan Urban Farming Initiative, n.d. <http://www.miufi.org/about> (Last accessed 3 November 2016).
Milmo, Dan. 'Former Unite leader paid £500,000, sparking "golden goodbye" row', *The Guardian* (18 July 2011) <https://www.theguardian.com/politics/2011/jul/18/unite-leader-golden-goodbye-row> (Last accessed 4 November 2016).
Moody, Kim. 'Kim Moody interview: the superpower's shopfloor'. Interview with Martin Smith and Chris Harman. *International Socialism*, No. 115 (July 2007) <http://isj.org.uk/kim-moody-interview-the-superpowers-shopfloor/> (Last accessed 3 November 2016).
Moody, Kim. *Workers in a Lean World: Unions in the International Economy* (London: Verso, 1997).
Moore, Joe. *The Other Japan: Conflict, Compromise, and Resistance since 1945* (Armonk, NY: M. E. Sharpe, 1997).
Mortimer, Caroline. 'British Army "could stage mutiny under Corbyn", says senior serving general', *The Independent* (20 September 2015) <http://www.independent.co.uk/news/uk/politics/british-army-could-stage-mutiny-under-corbyn-says-senior-serving-general-10509742.html> (Last accessed 3 November 2016).
Nestlé. 'Flexible, fast and functional: Nestlé to adopt modular factories', *Nestlé.com* (4 July 2014) <http://www.nestle.com/media/newsandfeatures/modular-factories> (Last accessed 3 November 2016).
Nguyen, Y. 'Vietnam – an attractive destination of transnational corporations', *Nhut Thanh Daily News* (22 September 2014) <http://anha.vn/en/chi-tiet-tin-tuc-43/Vietnam--an-attractive-destination-of-transnational-corporations.html> (Last accessed 2 November 2016).

Nuccitelli, Dana. 'Nigel Lawson suggests he's not a sceptic, proceeds to deny global warming', *The Guardian* (28 July 2014) <https://www.theguardian.com/environment/climate consensus-97-per-cent/2014/jul/28/nigel-lawson-suggests-not-a-sceptic-denies-global-warming> (Last accessed 4 November 2016).

Onesto, Li. '"Dying Detroit": The Impacts of Globalisation. Social Decay and Destruction of an Entire Urban Area', *Global Research. Centre for Research on Globalisation* (23 June 2010) <http://www.globalresearch.ca/dying-detroit-the-impacts-of-globalisation-social-decay-and-destruction-of-an-entire-urban-area/19856> (Last accessed 3 November 2016).

Palma, Stefania. 'Top 1000 World Banks: Chinese banks go from strength to strength', *The Banker* (29 June 2016) <http://www.thebanker.com/Top-1000-World-Banks/Top-1000-World-Banks-Chinese-banks-go-from-strength-to-strength> (Last accessed 3 November 2016).

Pannekoek, Anton. 'The New Blanquism'. Published originally in *Der Kommunist* (Bremen), No. 27 (1920) <https://www.marxists.org/archive/pannekoe/1920/blanquism.htm> (Last accessed 2 November 2016).

Pearce, Brian. 'Some Past Rank-and-File Movements', *Labour Review*, Vol. 4, No. 1 (April–May 1959): 13–24 <https://www.marxists.org/history/etol/writers/pearce/1959/04/rankandfile.html> (Last accessed 2 November 2016).

Pearce, Brian. 'Some Past Rank-and-File Movements'. In Pearce, Brian, and Michael Woodhouse, *Essays on the History of Communism in Britain*, pp. 105–137 (London: New Park Publications, 1975).

Prasad, Raekha. 'English riots were "a sort of revenge" against the police', *The Guardian* (5 December 2011) <https://www.theguardian.com/uk/2011/dec/05/riots-revenge-against-police> (Last accessed 4 November 2016).

Rentoul, John. 'John McDonnell: Shadow Chancellor is the new voice of fiscal responsibility'. *The Independent* (13 March, 2016) <http://www.independent.co.uk/voices/john-mcdonnell-shadow-chancellor-is-the-new-voice-of-fiscal-responsibility-a6927926.html> (Last accessed 3 November 2016).

Reuben, Anthony. 'Who owns the UK's debt?', *BBC News* (26 February 2010) <http://news.bbc.co.uk/1/hi/business/8530150.stm> (Last accessed 3 November 2016).

Rushe, Dominic. 'United Auto Workers union drops lost vote appeal at VW Tennessee plant', *The Guardian* (21 April 2014) <https://www.theguardian.com/world/2014/apr/21/volkswagen-tennessee-auto-workers-union-drops-appeal-lost-vote> (Last accessed 4 November 2016).

Schavione, Michael. 'Moody's Account of Social Movement Unionism: An Analysis', *Critical Sociology*, Vol. 33 (2007): 279–309.

Science@NASA. 'A Chilling Possibility. By disturbing a massive ocean current, melting Arctic sea ice might trigger colder weather in Europe and North America',

Science@NASA (5 March 2004) <https://science.nasa.gov/science-news/science-at-nasa/2004/05mar_arctic/> (Last accessed 3 November 2016).

Second World Congress of the Communist International, Petrograd, 19 July to 7 August 1920, *Minutes of the Second World Congress of the Communist International, Petrograd, July 19 to August 7, 1920* (2 Vols), translated by Robert A Archer (London: New Park, 1977) <https://www.marxists.org/history/international/comintern/2nd-congress/index.htm> (Last accessed 6 November 2016).

Shah, Anup. 'Today, around 21,000 children died around the world', *Global Issues. Social, Political, Economic and Environmental Issues That Affect Us All* <http://www.globalissues.org/article/715/today-21000-children-died-around-the-world> (Last accessed 6 November 2016).

Skidmore, Chris. MP. *A New Beveridge: 70 Years on – refounding the 21st century welfare state* (Free Enterprise Group, n.d.) <https://chrisskidmoremp.files.wordpress.com/2012/11/beveridge2.pdf> (Last accessed 6 November 2016).

Slaughter, Cliff. *Bonfire of the Certainties – The Second Human Revolution* (Lulu.com, 2013).

Slaughter, Cliff. *Not Without A Storm – Towards A Communist Manifesto for the Age of Globalisation* (London: Index Books, 2006).

Smith, Cyril. *Mészáros on Lenin*. A Contribution by Cyril Smith to the International Socialist Forum Seminar on 'Beyond Capital', by István Mészáros, 28 June 1998 <https://www.marxists.org/reference/archive/smith-cyril/works/articles/meszaros.htm> (Last accessed 4 November 2016).

Standing, Guy. *The Precariat – The New Dangerous Class* (London: Bloomsbury, 2011).

Ste Croix, G. E. M. de. *The Class Struggle in the Ancient Greek World from the Archaic Age to the Arab Conquests* (Ithaca, NY: Cornell University Press, 1981).

Thomson, Rebecca. '"Prison-like" conditions for workers making IBM, Dell, HP, Microsoft and Lenovo products', *Computer Weekly* (17 February 2009) <http://www.computerweekly.com/news/2240088431/Prison-like-conditions-for-workers-making-IBM-Dell-HP-Microsoft-and-Lenovo-products> (Last accessed 3 November 2016).

Trades Union Congress. 'TUC Directory 2016', *Trades Union Congress* (2016) <https://www.tuc.org.uk/sites/default/files/TUC_Directory_2016_Digital_Version_AW.pdf> (Last accessed 3 November 2016).

Trading Economics. 'India Unemployment Rate 1983–2016', *Trading Economics* <http://www.tradingeconomics.com/india/unemployment-rate> (Last accessed 4 November 2016).

Trotsky, Leon. 'On Democratic Centralism and the Regime (1937)', from a US *Internal Bulletin* (December 1937) <https://www.marxists.org/archive/trotsky/1937/xx/democent.htm> (Last accessed 4 November 2016).

Trotsky, Leon. *Their Morals and Ours* (New York: Pathfinder, 1979).
Trotsky, Leon. *Trade Unions in the Epoch of Imperialist Decay* (1940) <https://www.marxists.org/archive/trotsky/1940/xx/tu.htm> (Last accessed 4 November 2016).
Trotsky, Leon. *Trade Unions in the Epoch of Imperialist Decay* (New York: Pathfinder Press, 1990).
Trotsky, Leon. *The Transitional Program. The Death Agony of Capitalism and the Tasks of the Fourth International* (1938) <https://www.marxists.org/archive/trotsky/1938/tp/> (Last accessed 4 November 2016).
Trotsky, Leon. *Trotsky's Notebooks, 1933–35. Writings on Lenin, Dialectics, and Evolutionism*, translated by Philip Pomper (New York: Columbia University Press, 1986).
TU Fund Managers Limited. 'Trade Union Unit Trust. Manager's Final Report. For the year ended 15 August 2015. 108', *TU Fund Managers Limited* <http://www.tufm.co.uk/tufmwordpress/wp-content/uploads/2015/10/Trade-Union-Unit-Trust-ANNUAL-15-08-15.pdf> (Last accessed 3 November 2016).
TU Fund Managers Limited. 'Trade Union Unit Trust. Monthly Factsheet as at 31 December 2014', *TU Fund Managers Limited* (January 2015) <http://www.tufm.co.uk/tufmwordpress/wp-content/uploads/2015/01/TUUT-Factsheet-31Dec-2014.pdf> (Last accessed 3 November 2016).
Unite the Union. *Unite the Union. Rule Book. Effective from Rules Conference 2011 (Updated by the Executive Council to December 2012)* (Unite the Union, n.d.) <http://www.unitenow.co.uk/index.php/documents/documents/union-procedures-rules-and-policy-documents/206-rule-book-dec-2012/file> (Last accessed 2 November 2016).
University Of Illinois At Urbana-Champaign. 'Shutdown Of Circulation Pattern Could Be Disastrous, Researchers Say', *ScienceDaily* (20 December 2004) <http://www.sciencedaily.com/releases/2004/12/041219153611.htm> (Last accessed 2 November 2016).
Warren, Des. *The Key to My Cell* (London: New Park, 1982).
Williams, Raymond. *Resources of Hope. Culture, Democracy, Socialism* (London: Verso, 1989).
Wintour, Patrick. 'Biggest crackdown on trade unions for 30 years launched by Conservatives', *The Guardian* (15 July 2015) <https://www.theguardian.com/politics/2015/jul/15/trade-unions-conservative-offensive-decades-strikes-labour> (Last accessed 4 November 2016).
Wolff, Richard. 'Detroit's decline is a distinctively capitalist failure', *The Guardian* (23 July 2013) <https://www.theguardian.com/commentisfree/2013/jul/23/detroit-decline-distinctively-capitalist-failure> (Last accessed 4 November 2016).

Index

Advisory Conciliation and Arbitration Service (ACAS, Britain) 132
Aeschylus 142
Alesia, battle of (52 BCE) 271
alienation *passim*
Amazon (rainforest) 23
American Federation of Labor – Congress of Industrial Organizations (AFL-CIO) 140, 153
anarchism 113, 315
animal welfare and rights movement 23, 73, 76, 383
Antiquity 252, 294 (note 3), 326–327 (note 16), 353
Antonine Roman Emperors (second century CE) 41
Aral Sea 82
Arctic 78
Aristophanes 142
Athens 41
Atlantic Ocean 78–79
automation 27, 36 (note 12), 58, 241, 336

Bank of England 136 (note 10), 174
'benefits culture' 57, 65, 117–118, 127–135, 155
'Big Society' 120
biotechnology 336
Blair, Tony 119, 152, 158–159, 164–165, 168, 182–183, 223, 280
Bolshevism
    approach to trade unionism 331ff
    'democratic centralism' 304–305, 352, 360
    formed and developed under specific, historical conditions 323, 364
    ideological positioning on agency 352–353
    'mass communist consciousness' and 361
    organizational flexibility 312–313
    relationship to soviets 314
    Pannekoek's criticism 317, 327 (note 18)
bourgeoisie
    'bloody history' in England 269–270
    'cannot rule alone' 171
    'democracy' contrasted with revolutionary democracy 238
    European 327 (note 18)
    historical role of Parliament in England 269
    history of political organization as a class 329–330 (note 19)
    mode of life 120, 130–131
    morality and 421
    'national liberation struggle' and 423, 424, 426
    social representation of the capital relation 386
    structural crisis and 158
Bretton Woods Agreement (1944) 163, 343
'BRICS' countries 60, 165, 188 (note 3)
British Army 270–271
British Broadcasting Corporation (BBC) 105, 420
Brown, Gordon 128, 159
Burger King ('Kings') 64

Cable News Network (CNN) 420
Caesar, Julius 271
call centre workers 126–127
Callaghan, James ('Jim') 136 (note 8)
capital *passim*
Carchedi, Guglielmo 36 (note 5)
Carthage 424
Castle, Barbara 136 (note 8)
child mortality 294 (note 1)
Chile 267, 270
China
    automation in 36 (note 12)
    capitalist restoration in 288, 290, 291–292, 427
    global capital system and 44–46, 59, 105, 423, 427
    mass of absolute surplus value 19, 59, 105
    proletarianization within 65–66, 302
    'socialist planning' and 82
    world's banker and creditor 46–47, 48, 136 (note 10), 426
Chomsky, Noam 419
Christianity 121, 328, 388
CityLink (Britain) 168–169
'clean coal technology' 86, 90 (note 15)
'climate change' 77–87
Cole, Mike 320
colonialism
    imperialism and 42, 163, 270
    'national liberation struggle' and 424–426
    'spheres of influence' 43–44
    trade unionism and 170–171, 172
colonus 246, 252
Comintern (Third International)
    conditions for admission 327 (note 17), 372 (note 8)
    'democratic centralism' 304–305, 307, 309, 316, 332, 351, 361, 365

    'from outside' to 'from above' (Mészáros) 326 (note 15)
    'general line' after Lenin (Mészáros) 306
    ideologically posited internationalized statutes 310ff, 315–318
    Lenin's 'appeal to the model character of the Russian Revolution' (Mészáros) 306, 313, 316, 317
    Pannekoek's criticism 317
    Trotsky's prognosis on (1937) 348 (note 3)
communism *passim*
'Communist Parties'
    formation of 163
    Pannekoek on 327 (note 18)
    secondary political articulations of capital 113, 141, 168, 369–370
    vanguardism and 52
'computerization' 27, 58, 106, 255, 256, 336
Corbyn, Jeremy
    Keynesianism and the structural crisis of capital 124–125, 153, 164, 165, 170, 182, 222–223, 278, 343
    operating within power structures in favour of capital 142–143, 165, 275–276
    threats of 'mutiny' against in armed forces 270–271
Craxi, Bettino 142
'credit crises' 46–48, 122–123, 125, 127, 175, 189 (note 12)
crime 65, 110, 128
Cromwell, Oliver 271
Cuba 82, 288, 423, 424, 427–428

Dacia 424
Dawkins, Richard 344, 349 (note 11)
'debt crises' *see* 'credit crises'
Delian League 41

Detroit (Michigan, United
    States) 95–96
dialectics *passim*
Die Neue Zeit (Kautsky) 319, 326
    (note 15)
dilemma 97, 131, 184–185, 306
Diocletian (Roman Emperor) 41
dogmatism
    characterization of sect existence
        (Marx) 339, 341–342
    Marx and Engels 'premises' 307
    peaceful transition to
        socialism 269–270
    post-Lenin *Comintern* and 306
    practical class consciousness and 359
    provisionality of conceptions
        and 207
    'real movement' and 10
    revolutionary agency and 210–211,
        307
    sect politics 151, 179–180, 304,
        308, 311, 337, 341, 346, 347, 357,
        360–361, 365
    statutes of the *Comintern*
        and 316–317
    theory of revolutionary agency
        and 308
    Trotsky and 333, 346
Duggan, Mark 65, 132
Dunbar, battle of (1650) 271–272

economic 'crash' of 2008 32, 47, 121–122,
    128
Engels, Frederick
    'armed bodies of men' of state power
        of capital 266–267
    'bourgeois intellectual' 321–322
    conception of 'ideology' 308–309
    Marx and in the 1840s xiv, 7–8, 275,
        361

note on Marx's theoretical
    development 347
'premises' of Marx and 307
'superstitious belief in authority' 349
    (note 9)
English Revolution (1640–1660) 132,
    269
Euripides 142
European Union (EU) 125, 143, 423, 426

'false consciousness' 308–309
fascism 32–34, 42, 50, 133, 199
fatalism 181, 183, 190 (note 19), 246–247
feminism 198–200
feudalism 71, 76, 188 (note 10), 252,
    269, 272, 294 (note 3), 326–327
    (note 16), 329 (note 19), 353,
    363–364
Feuerbach, Ludwig Andreas *see* 'Theses
    on Feuerbach'
'fictitious capital' (Marx) 48, 189
    (note 12)
First International *see* International
    Workingmen's Association
food banks 131, 134
Fourth International
    critique of xvi
    'democratic centralism' 307, 316, 325
        (note 2), 361, 365, 372 (note 8)
    Kingsley Martin interview with Trot-
        sky 336, 348 (note 3)
    regroupment strategy 337–338, 345,
        352, 356–357
    revolutionary agency and 313, 318,
        326 (note 15), 346–347, 366
    sectarian development 335–336, 337,
        370
    sectarianism within *see* 'left-wing
        sectarianism'
    trade unionism and 331ff

Fox News 420
Franco, Francisco 34, 124
Freire, Paulo 181, 190 (note 19)
French Revolution (1789-1794) 132

General Association of German
    Workers 339
'globalization' *passim*
Gonzales, Felipe 142
'Great Depression' (1930s) 33, 163, 336, 343
Greece 125, 127-128, 142, 168, 175, 276, 277
Green Party (Britain) 75, 89 (note 3)
'Greenhouse Gases' 81-82, 86-87, 90 (notes 12 and 15)
Greenland 78
Gulags (Soviet penal system) 50, 82, 262
Gulf Stream 78-79, 89 (note 6)

Healy, Gerry 352
Hegel, G. W. F.
    an sich and *gesetzt* 180-181
    classical bourgeois political economy and 386-387
    concept of alienation 386-388
    concept of 'Measure' relative to capital's structural crisis 251
    'freedom and necessity' 377-380
    Lenin's studies in 160 (note 6)
    Logic xi, 214-215 (note 10), 321, 377ff
    societies start to decline at their zenith 41
    'spurious infinite' 264
    Verstand 377
Hegelianism 320-321, 387
Herman, Edward 419
Hinchingbrooke Hospital 118, 119
Hitler, Adolf 34, 124, 134
House of Lords (second chamber of British parliament) 151, 188 (note 10)

'human nature' 390, 421
Huppert, Julian (Liberal Democrat) 118

ideology *passim*
imperialism xi
    'epoch of socialist revolutions' 41, 42, 48-49
    Lenin's analysis of xiv, 39ff
    'national liberation' and 271, 423ff
    structural crisis of capital and 40, 42, 45, 77
    trade unionism and 146, 172, 181, 334
India 19, 43-44, 45-46, 59, 60, 64, 65-66, 70 (note 10), 105, 170, 188 (note 3), 301-302
Indonesia 46
'Industrial Revolution' 81
'In Place of Strife' (Labour government white paper, 1969) 136 (note 8)
In These Times (American journal) 103
Independent Television News (ITN, British news broadcaster) 420
'intelligentsia' 58, 158, 319ff, 326 (note 15)
International Business Machines (IBM) 105
International Labour Organization (ILO, UN) 96
International Monetary Fund (IMF) 44, 46
International Workingmen's Association (IWMA) (First International)
    Lenin's conception of agency and 311
    Marx's conception of the proletariat within 311, 314, 326 (note 15), 364
    role of according to Marx 311, 340-341
    sectarianism within 339-341
Internationals, failure of 369
Iran 265-266, 426
Iraq 280

Irish Republicanism 271
Islam 124, 266

Japan
    post-war (1945) workers' councils within 210
Jews 326–327 (note 16), 353, 371 (note 1)
Jones, Richard (English Political Economist, 1790–1855) 69 (note 3), 295 (note 10)

Kautsky, Karl
    Die Neue Zeit and 319, 326 (note 15)
    'modern socialism' and 319–323
Keynesianism
    capital's structural crisis and 21, 117, 124–125, 153, 164, 165, 170, 223, 278
    economic policy in post-war (1939–1945) inflationary expansion of the capital system 93, 157–158, 343
    labour hierarchy and 124, 153, 164–165, 170, 223, 278–279
    post-war (1939–1945) 'left-wing sectarianism' and 345–346, 351–352
King, Bob (President, United Automobile Workers of America) 100
Kinnock, Neil 159, 163–164, 182–183

labour *passim*
Labour Party (Britain) *passim*
Lassalle, Ferdinand 339–340, 349 (note 9)
Lawson, Nigel 80
left-wing sectarianism *passim*
Lenin, Vladimir *passim*
Liodakis, George 31
London Metropolitan Police ('The Met') 65, 132

Lukács, György 208–210, 305
Luxemburg, Rosa 3, 228

McCluskey, Len (General Secretary, UNITE, British trade union) 94
MacDonald, Ramsay 142
MacDonalds ('Macs') 64
McDonnell, John 143, 165
Machiavellianism 421
Major, John 119
Malthusianism 27, 79
Mandela, Nelson 142, 143
Maoism 344, 370
Marcuse, Herbert 408–409
Maritime Climate 78–79, 89 (note 6)
Martin, Kingsley (editor of *The New Statesman*) 336, 348 (note 3)
Marx, Karl *passim*
mass media
    anti-Corbyn position 164, 271
    dehumanizing role relative to proletariat 65, 134
    'feminism' and 198–199
    pro-capital role 20, 46, 79, 115 (note 11), 248, 419ff
    trade unions and 98, 102, 106, 169, 173, 220, 230–231, 356
materialist conception of history 2, 307, 319, 336, 361
Mészáros, István *passim*
Microsoft (computer corporation) 105
'middle class' 57, 205
Miliband, Edward ('Ed') 159
miners strike (Britain, 1984–85) 7, 96, 152–154, 169, 352
Ministry of Defence (MOD, Britain) 271
Mitterrand, François 142
'Momentum' (British Labour Party movement) 164, 370
Moody, Kim 179

Morris, Bill 188 (note 10)
Mussolini, Benito 124

nanotechnology 336
'nation state' 43–46, 194, 207, 268, 286, 423–424, 426, 427
National Front (France) 133
National Health Service (NHS, Britain) 21, 135 (note 4), 157
National Institute for Health and Care Excellence (Britain) 118, 135 (note 4)
'national liberation struggle' xvi, 343, 423ff
National Union of Mineworkers (NUM, Britain) 152
'Natural Necessity', ('Realm of') (Marx) 263, 375ff, 396ff
Negri, Antonio 424
Nestlé (transnational corporation) 104
'New Deal' (Franklin D. Roosevelt, United States) 34, 331
New Era Estate (Hackney, London) 229
'New Labour' *see* Blair, Tony
New Statesman (British politics journal) 336, 348 (note 3)
Nicaragua 423
Nicolaus, Martin 378–379

objectification *see* alienation
'objectivism' 8, 173, 246–247, 274, 324 (note 1)
'occupation and appropriation' tactic 107–108, 233, 279–282
see also 'social unions'
Ochrana 338, 353
'organic composition of capital' 18, 20, 24–26, 36 (note 5), 61–62
'origin myth' (of socialism) 321
Owen, Robert 295 (note 9)

Pahlavi autocracy (Iran) 426
Pannekoek, Anton 317, 327 (note 18)
Paris Commune (of 1871) 272, 311, 314
parliamentarism
  dissolution of under socialism 268–269
  draconian legislation by the 'parliamentary back door' 124, 270
  history as bourgeois institution in England 269
  institution of state power of capital 267–268, 270
  means for social reforms 157, 267
'Party-form' 67, 213, 304–316, 330 (note 19), 332, 351ff
pauperization *passim*
Pax Americana 48
Pax Capitalis 424
Pax Romana 48, 424
Peloponnesian War 41
platonism 320–321, 338–339
Podemos (Spain) 276
positivism xii, 207, 222
Postone, Moishe 320
'prescription' (concept of in theory of agency) 9, 176–177, 339, 342
Private Finance Initiative (PFI, Britain) 119, 126, 135 (note 5), 157–158
'private individual' (of bourgeois society) 378–379, 382, 387, 395, 408
'privatization' 20, 107, 117, 119–120, 124–126, 158
Privy Council 136 (note 8)
production *passim*
proletariat *passim*
Proudhon, Pierre Joseph 176–177, 339
psychology
  epoch of global capital and 45–46, 72–74, 121, 125, 129, 134, 392ff, 411

global commune and 185, 378–379,
    384, 401, 406–407, 413
realm of 'natural necessity' and 403
socialist technological development
    and 85
state power of capital and 155–156
Punic Wars 424

Rail Maritime and Transport Union
    (RMT, Britain) 168–169
'reformism' 129, 164–165, 171–173, 175,
    181–182, 222–223, 228–229, 370
religion 257, 344, 348 (note 3), 349
    (note 11), 386, 388, 391, 412, 422
Republican Party (United States)102
'restructuring' (of 'social
    metabolism') *passim*
revolutionary agency *passim*
revolutionary agency (theory of) *passim*
Romanticism 320–321
Rome (ancient) 41, 48, 231, 246, 251–252,
    294 (note 3), 424
Roosevelt, Franklin D. 34
Russian Revolution *passim*

sadism 73–74
Scargill, Arthur 152
Schweitzer, Johann Baptist von
    (Marx's letter to, 13 October
    1868) 339–340
Shakespeare, William v
Shelley, Percy Bysshe v
Simpson, Derek 155
Slaughter, Cliff 48–49, 52
Smith, Adam (Classical Political Econo-
    mist, 1723–90) 56, 69 (note 3)
Smith, Cyril (socialist academic) 361
Smith, John (Labour Party leader) 159
social democracy 42, 50, 113, 124–125,
    141, 157, 163–165, 168, 172, 328,
    369

'social individual' (of classless soci-
    ety) 64, 378–379, 386–387, 390,
    395, 399–408
'social media' 173
'social movement unionism' 179
    see also Moody, Kim
'social movements' 6, 109, 177–180, 223,
    266
social provision *passim*
social unions *passim*
'social unions movement' (SUM) 231ff
socialism (origins as theory of
    development) 319ff
'socialism in one country' 306, 348
    (note 3), 370, 428
'socialist accountancy' 255–256, 258,
    383–385
Socialist Labour Party (SLP, Britain) 152
socialist planning 81–87, 234, 240–241,
    250, 384–385, 398
'socialist pluralism' (Mészáros) xv, 193ff
'socialist sectarianism' (Marx) 338ff
'sovereign debt' 175, 189 (note 12)
'soviet system'
    decline and fall of 50, 427
    ecological destruction within 82
    faux socialism 82, 254, 272, 426–427,
        428
    'planning' from 'above' 82
    political organization over and
        against proletariat 82, 238,
        253–254, 272, 288–292
    'post capitalist capital system'
        (Mészáros) 254
Stalin, Joseph 82, 262, 305, 314–315, 318,
    330 (note 20), 331, 348 (note 3)
stalinism *passim*
state power (of capital) *passim*
stoicism 246
structural crisis of capital *passim*
surplus value *passim*

Syriza (Greece) 125, 127–128, 142, 168, 176–177

'technological fetishism' 83–86
Thatcher, Margaret 80, 115 (note 10), 126, 140, 154, 158–159, 164, 167, 184
Theses on Feuerbach (Marx) xiv, 1–5, 324 (note 1), 352, 361, 393
Third International *see* Comintern
Tolpuddle Martyrs 167, 171
trade unionism *passim*
Trades Union Congress (TUC, Britain) 96, 124, 140, 152–153, 161, 166–167, 181, 184, 188 (note 5), 239
Trajan (Roman Emperor) 424
Transatlantic Trade and Investment Partnership (TTIP) 125
'Troika' 142
Trotsky, Leon *passim*
'True Realm of Freedom' (Marx) 75, 260, 261, 263, 265, 273, 293, 375ff
Tsipras, Alexis 143

Ulster 271
'underclass' 65, 134
unemployment *passim*
  see also 'benefits culture'
Union of Construction Allied Trades and Technicians (UCATT, Britain) 174
UNITE (trade union, Britain)
  'community sections' initiative 224ff, 231–232
  Petroineos dispute, Grangemouth 93–95, 99, 104, 155

Simpson, Derek (former General Secretary) 155
United Automobile Workers of America (UAW) 99–104
United Kingdom government debt 136 (note 10)
United Kingdom Independence Party (UKIP, Britain) 133
United Nations (UN) 96, 294 (note 1)
United States Federal Reserve ('The Fed') 46
United States National Research Council 79
untermensch 65, 134

value *passim*
'vanguardism' *passim*
Vietnam 423, 424–425
Volkswagen (Chattanooga, Tennessee, United States) 99–104
Von Clausewitz, Carl 272

Warren, Des 174
Westbrook ('property developers') 229–230
What is to be Done? (Lenin) 309–313
Williams, Raymond 111
Wilson, Harold 136 (note 8)
Women's Institute (WI, Britain) 225
workers' councils 67–68, 204–213, 237
Workers Revolutionary Party (WRP, left-wing sect, Britain) 352
World Bank 44, 46
World Trade Organization (WTO) 44, 46

www.ingramcontent.com/pod-product-compliance
Lightning Source LLC
Chambersburg PA
CBHW070006010526
44117CB00011B/1441